**SAGE** was founded in 1965 by Sara Miller McCune to support the dissemination of usable knowledge by publishing innovative and high-quality research and teaching content. Today, we publish over 900 journals, including those of more than 400 learned societies, more than 800 new books per year, and a growing range of library products including archives, data, case studies, reports, and video. SAGE remains majority-owned by our founder, and after Sara's lifetime will become owned by a charitable trust that secures our continued independence.

Los Angeles | London | New Delhi | Singapore | Washington DC | Melbourne

# Advance Praise

This book traces the remarkable ascendency of the Indian middle class over time, particularly following liberalization since the early 1990s. It establishes the intersection of the middle class, media and Modi phenomenon in India and highlights the reasons for their sanguine overlap. While being appreciative of the shift in Indian politics with the entry of Modi, it scrupulously avoids adulation which a section of the Indian media has indulged in recent years.

—Valerian Rodrigues, Former Professor,
Centre for Political Studies, Jawaharlal Nehru University, New Delhi

Nagesh Prabhu has tackled a timely and understudied topic in this book. Modi's successful campaigns have used effective aspirational strategies to draw support from both India's middle classes and social groups aspiring to gain the middle-class status. This book provides an extremely valuable study of these dynamics. It provides a critical resource for anyone interested in understanding India's middle classes and contemporary politics in India.

—Leela Fernandes, Director, Center for South Asian Studies,
University of Michigan, USA

Understanding and explaining the rise of the BJP from the prism of the emerging new middle class is the focus of this book. While a lot of the analysis on the rise and growth of the BJP and its current leadership has been from the perspectives of caste, identity politics, leadership and the multiple contours of Hindutva, this book weaves an analysis that is refreshingly new, privileging a focus on the role of the middle class in India. The author persuasively draws a linkage between Modi's rise to power, the role of the media in this regard and the increasing space that the middle class has come to occupy in electoral politics.

—Sandeep Shastri, Pro Vice-Chancellor,
Jain University, Bengaluru

# MIDDLE CLASS, MEDIA AND MODI

# MIDDLE CLASS, MEDIA
## AND
# MODI

## THE MAKING OF A
## NEW ELECTORAL POLITICS

**NAGESH PRABHU**

Los Angeles | London | New Delhi
Singapore | Washington DC | Melbourne

*First published in 2020 by*

**SAGE Publications India Pvt Ltd**
B1/I-1 Mohan Cooperative Industrial Area
Mathura Road, New Delhi 110 044, India
*www.sagepub.in*

**SAGE Publications Inc**
2455 Teller Road
Thousand Oaks, California 91320, USA

**SAGE Publications Ltd**
1 Oliver's Yard, 55 City Road
London EC1Y 1SP, United Kingdom

**SAGE Publications Asia-Pacific Pte Ltd**
18 Cross Street #10-10/11/12
China Square Central
Singapore 048423

Published by Vivek Mehra for SAGE Publications India Pvt Ltd. Typeset in 10.5/13 pt Adobe Caslon Pro by Zaza Eunice, Hosur, Tamil Nadu, India.

**Library of Congress Control Number: 2020930732**

**ISBN:** 978-93-5388-259-4 (HB)

**SAGE Team:** Amrita Dutta, Shruti Gupta and Anupama Krishnan

*To*
*my parents, my family*
*for their*
*silent sacrifices*

Thank you for choosing a SAGE product!
If you have any comment, observation or feedback,
I would like to personally hear from you.

*Please write to me at* **contactceo@sagepub.in**

**Vivek Mehra,** Managing Director and CEO, SAGE India.

## Bulk Sales

SAGE India offers special discounts
for purchase of books in bulk.
We also make available special imprints
and excerpts from our books on demand.

*For orders and enquiries, write to us at*

Marketing Department
SAGE Publications India Pvt Ltd
B1/I-1, Mohan Cooperative Industrial Area
Mathura Road, Post Bag 7
New Delhi 110044, India

*E-mail us at* **marketing@sagepub.in**

## Subscribe to our mailing list
*Write to* **marketing@sagepub.in**

This book is also available as an e-book.

# Contents

# List of Abbreviations

| | |
|---|---|
| AAP | Aam Aadmi Party |
| ABVP | Akhil Bharatiya Vidyarthi Parishad |
| ADB | Asian Development Bank |
| AICC | All India Congress Committee |
| AIMO | All-India Manufacturers' Organization |
| AIR | All India Radio |
| AJSU | All Jharkhand Student's Union |
| BBB | Banks Board Bureau |
| BHIM | Bharat Interface for Money |
| BJP | Bharatiya Janata Party |
| BMS | Bare metal stents |
| BSP | Bahujan Samaj Party |
| BWIs | Bretton Woods Institutions |
| CAD | Current account deficit |
| CAG | Comptroller and Auditor General |
| CBI | Central Bureau of Investigation |
| CFD | Congress for Democracy |
| CGST | Central GST |
| CIRP | Corporate Insolvency Resolution Process |
| CMIE | Centre for Monitoring Indian Economy |
| CPGRAMS | Centralized Public Grievance Redress and Monitoring System |
| CPI(M) | Communist Party of India (Marxist) |
| CPI | Communist Party of India |
| CSDS | Centre for the Study of Developing Societies |
| CVD | Cardiovascular diseases |
| DBT | Direct Benefit Transfer |
| DES | Drug-eluting stents |
| DTAA | Double taxation avoidance agreements |
| ECI | Election Commission of India |
| ED | Enforcement Directorate |

| | |
|---|---|
| E-NAM | National Agriculture Market |
| EVM | Electronic Voting Machine |
| FDI | Foreign direct investment |
| FMCG | Fast-moving consumer goods |
| GoI | Government of India |
| GSDMA | Gujarat State Disaster Management Authority |
| GST | Goods and Services Tax |
| GSTN | Goods and Services Tax Network |
| HJV | Hindu Jagarana Vedike |
| IAC | India Against Corruption |
| IAS | Indian Administrative Service |
| IBBI | Insolvency and Bankruptcy Board of India |
| IBC | Insolvency and Bankruptcy Code |
| ICS | Indian Civil Service |
| IGST | Integrated GST |
| IIM | Indian Institute of Management |
| IIT | Indian Institute of Technology |
| IL&FS | Infrastructure Leasing and Financial Services Ltd |
| IMF | International Monetary Fund |
| INC | Indian National Congress |
| I-PAC | Indian Political Action Committee |
| IT | Information technology |
| JAS | Jan Aushadi Scheme |
| KBC | Kaun Banega Crorepati |
| LoC | Line of Control |
| MISA | Maintenance of Internal Security Act |
| MGNREGA | Mahatma Gandhi National Rural Employment Guarantee Act |
| MPs | Members of Parliament |
| MRP | Maximum retail price |
| MSMEs | Micro, Small and Medium Enterprises |
| MSP | Minimum support price |
| NCAER | National Council of Applied Economic Research |
| NCC | National Cadet Corps |
| NCD | Non-communicable disease |
| NCLAT | National Company Law Appellate Tribunal |
| NDA | National Democratic Alliance |

| | |
|---|---|
| NGOs | Non-Governmental Organizations |
| NLEMs | National List of Essential Medicines |
| NPAs | Non-Performing Assets |
| NRC | National Register of Citizens |
| NRI | Non-resident Indian |
| NYAY | Nyuntam Aay Yojana |
| OBCs | Other Backward Castes |
| ODF | Open defecation free |
| PAN | Permanent Account Number |
| PIB | Press Information Bureau |
| PLFS | Periodic Labour Force Survey |
| PMC | Professional-managerial class |
| PMJAY | Pradhan Mantri Jan Aarogya Yojana |
| PMLA | Prevention of Money Laundering Act |
| PMO | Prime Minister's Office |
| PNB | Punjab National Bank |
| PPP | Purchasing Power Parity |
| PRAGATI | Pro-Active Governance and Timely Implementation |
| PSBs | Public sector banks |
| RBI | Reserve Bank of India |
| RSS | Rashtriya Swayamsevak Sangh |
| SBM | Swachh Bharat Mission |
| SCs | Scheduled Castes |
| SFIO | Serious Fraud Investigation Office |
| SGST | State GST |
| SIT | Special Investigation Team |
| SP | Samajwadi Party |
| STPs | Software technology parks |
| TDS | Tax deducted at source |
| TRAI | Telecom Regulatory Authority of India |
| TRPs | Television rating points |
| UDAN | Ude Desh ka Aam Naagrik |
| UJALA | Unnat Jyoti by Affordable LEDs for All |
| UNDP | United Nations Development Programme |
| UP | United Provinces |
| UPA | United Progressive Alliance |
| VRS | Voluntary Retirement Scheme |

# Foreword

Most of the analyses that emerged after the baffling results of the 2014 and 2019 Parliament elections illustrated how ill-equipped we are in grappling with the winds of change blowing in the political landscape of the country. Articles that emerged based on worn-out theories and traditional explanation hinging on caste, religion, region and other such factors did not help understand what appeared to be an inexplicable phenomenon. When the usual theories did not explain the results, there were rather facile attempts at blaming it on the tampering of Electronic Voting Machines (EVMs). It is in this context that Nagesh Prabhu has come out with an interesting analytical pointer that foregrounds a concoction of the emerging middle class and media that led to the 2014 and 2019 results.

He traces its genesis to a phenomenon that began on 5 April 2011 with Anna Hazare sitting on a fast at Jantar Mantar against increasing corruption. The anticorruption movement to pass a Jan Lokpal Bill reached its crescendo, and surprisingly the Bharatiya Janata Party (BJP) as well as the Communist Party of India (Marxist) supported Hazare's movement along with many young new-generation professionals. The young middle class rising against corruption was historic. A new force in the form of a professional new or middle class was born, emphatically recording their protests against the corrupt regimes and trying to search for a clean alternative. Some of the prudent political pundits noted that this emergence of a new force was going to be the decision-maker in the political scenario.

The new middle class, as a political force, was noted by Nagesh Prabhu in some of his writings 2012 onwards, and he continuously pursued the hypothesis that this new class was going to be crucial in the coming decade. His futuristic thinking came true during the 2014 Parliament election. The middle class was expecting an alternative, and a slot was created for that in the minds of people by the visual, print and also social media. There were not many alternatives available in the field, and exactly at that time, the BJP took an important decision of projecting Narendra Damodardas Modi as the chairman of the 2014 Lok Sabha Election Campaign Committee of the BJP on 9 June 2013. Modi was the chief minister of Gujarat and was heralded by the media as a non-corrupt, no-nonsense leader with Hindutva agenda at his heart. He was perpetually present in the media positively due to his development initiatives in Gujarat (Gujarat Model) and negatively for his perceived role in the 2002 Gujarat riots. His critics and admirers kept him at the forefront in the media. Either way, Modi stayed in media glare and attracted unprecedented crowds with his oratory. He presented an image of a tough taskmaster and a committed national-ist. Thus, the role of the media in creating an image of a future prime minister was very clear, which Nagesh Prabhu brings out well. Many analysts extolled the role of Prashant Kishor, political strategist of the BJP, as the main factor, but his presence was just incidental and the stage was perfectly set for Modi to ride on both negative and positive images. The middle class and the media were thus the main sculptors of the image.

The neo-middle-class emerged as an important gift of liberaliza-tion and globalization. New industries, new vocations and the new generation began with a zest for deciding the voting pattern. There are even instances of people taking off from their work and going to campaign for Modi in Varanasi and for Arvind Kejriwal of Aam Aadmi Party (AAP) in Delhi. The social media also emerged as an important and effective tool in order to pass the messages across the new middle class, and this was handled by technically competent persons appointed by both the parties. Possibly, the BJP had put forth an effective campaign, but, more than that, it was the image of their leader that mattered a lot along with the punchlines that he used during his rallies. The crescendo of the 2014 elections was so powerful that every household and every individual was charged with the fever of the election. Nagesh Prabhu catches the very pulse of the Indian electorate which operated through the media and middle class.

This book does not recognize the old and worn-out political theories but breaks a new ground and a new hypothesis based on middle-class moorings and media provocations. Prabhu has painstakingly sketched an unbiased picture of a very complex story. The book challenges political analysts and those interested in understanding the Indian political mind and voting behaviour. It forces one to rethink the idea of Indian masses. The book demands political theorists to look for new hypotheses beyond the typified relationship between the voters and the leaders. I am sure it would shake the usual beliefs in political analytics and incite one to search for new grounds and new theories.

I am not formally trained in political science, but I constantly hone my skills with the help of my students, my colleagues and my friends working in political science and psephology. I am sure this book will attract a lot of admirers as well as a good number of sceptics. I would however suggest that it be read as a treatise on political analytics than as a book on the political situation as such.

—R. S. Deshpande
Former Director, Institute for Social and
Economic Change, Bengaluru

# Acknowledgements

There are many wonderful people who have helped, guided and supported me in my research and writing that took well over a decade and finally in editing and fine-tuning, and I wish to thank them most sincerely.

First, my teacher, guru and economist Professor R. S. Deshpande, former ISEC Director, who encouraged me into undertaking this challenging project—a decision I made without fully understanding how much work it would involve—and guided the manuscript to take shape, in the form which it is now before you.

Despite his busy schedule and onerous responsibilities, Professor Deshpande always had time for me to discuss, give detailed pointers and painstakingly revise my drafts in addition to sharing his insights on the middle class and Indian politics. It is largely due to his affection, tutelage, valuable suggestions, patience and encouragement that I undertook the task of writing this book. I am grateful to him and his family members for their constant kindness and generosity in warmly welcoming me during all my frequent visits at odd hours. Without him, this book would not have been possible.

It all started with a small research work, 'Middle Class in India and its Constitution and Politics' (1993) in Mangalore University, Karnataka, under the guidance of Political Science professor Valerian Rodrigues. Professor Rodrigues has rekindled my interest in the study of middle-class society and its politics. I thank him for initially constructing and shaping my ideas with the fundamental lessons in my research. I owe a great deal to him for honing my unrefined ideas.

I am very fortunate in receiving insightful comments, articulation of ideas and fitting analogies from faculty members of Gauhati University,

Assam, and the Centre for Culture and Development, Vadodara, Gujarat.

I am grateful to the Editor of *The Hindu* for granting me permission for publication of the research work. I wish to acknowledge the support offered by Bageshree S., Chief of Bureau, *The Hindu*, Karnataka, and my colleagues Anil Kumar Sastry and Sandeep Phukan. I would also like to personally acknowledge the valuable support, assistance and guidance offered to me by all colleagues in *The Hindu*, Bengaluru.

A handful of close journalist friends read the manuscript at different stages and offered useful comments. They are: Gabriel Vaz, Ramnath Shenoy and Hemanth Kumar. Friends like K. S. Prasanna Kumar, chartered accountant, and Ashutosh Kumar, professor of political science, Punjab University, Punjab, provided valuable inputs, critical suggestions and guidance, which have been of immense help. K. Srinivasa of the ISEC library was involved in providing research materials on time, for which I am grateful. To all my friends who provided invaluable personal support, distractions and even fun, I am grateful.

On a lighter note, the Bangalore Metro Rail Corporation Ltd., has also been of great help in providing metro rail connectivity between areas of my residence and office, which saved a lot of my travelling time and enabled me to devote more time for reading and writing this book, and wish to express my gratitude.

Interactions with leaders of several political parties, mainly with those of the Congress and the BJP, increased my understanding of middle-class politics. Interviews and conversations with leaders helped me in drawing broader insights into the role of the media and the middle class and their contributions to the rise of the BJP and Prime Minister Narendra Modi. My debt is owed to them.

I am grateful to Amrita Dutta, Assistant Commissioner Editor, SAGE, for cross-checking facts, references and citations and offering ideas, and the entire team of SAGE, for their support in the publication process.

I have no words to express my gratitude to my parents, whose boundless love and guidance sustained me through the years, and their many sacrifices have taught me to respect and learn from people. Their firm beliefs, principles and commitment to family remain an inspiration to this day. I know that my late parents, who were the source of inspiration in all aspects of my life, would have been very proud and the happiest of all at this point, and I am happy to dedicate this book to them.

Above all, I want to thank my dear wife Vidya and son Gaurav for bearing with me with patience and understanding, and for their unstinted support, giving me the freedom to complete this task. My in-laws, brothers-in-law and relatives have always stood by me, and I am grateful to them. Finally, I wish to acknowledge the support, guidance and assistance and express my heartfelt gratitude to everybody who have been helpful to me all through my life and in this project either directly or indirectly. To every one of you, a big thank you!

# Introduction
## *Middle Class, Media and Modi—Ascending the Power Steps*

There has not been any serious academic discussion on the role of the Indian middle class in the Bharatiya Janata Party's (BJP) electoral successes both at the national and sub-national levels. Hitherto, we have come across mostly pre-poll and exit poll survey findings capturing the preference of the middle class towards a political party during the elections. The findings of these surveys are largely published in mainstream media and occasionally in academic journals. Of course, some analytical articles are also published in mainstream media. Generally, pre-poll and exit poll surveys are largely caste and religion based and not class based. The old political school of thinkers still believes that caste and religious identities supposedly decide political preferences and voting patterns while education, income, occupation and class have been taken as insignificant influences in shaping election results in India. The ideological preferences influencing Indian voter behaviour are poorly studied, given that the traditional wisdom among the political thinkers holds that identity, not ideology, shapes the voting pattern to a large extent. These erroneous beliefs have resulted in a negligible amount of academic literature on the middle class, and its role in the BJP's electoral success can be attributed to a few factors. We intend here to focus on the nuances of this hypothesis.

First, it is cumbersome to establish the boundaries of the middle class from other classes and arrive at what constitutes this class. Moreover, ambiguity in the notion of the middle class or the new middle class gets confounded due to the different approaches that are prevalent in social analysis. Economically, it is argued that the rise of the middle class has gone hand in hand with the tremendous growth of productivity of capital as a whole. Politically, the rise of the middle class has made class relations (that of the bourgeoisie and the proletariat) fuzzy. In academic discussions, reference to class generally comes under Marxian perspective. But, during the last decade, the extreme ends in class structure have thinned whereas the middle-class belly has bloated.

Second, it is difficult to define the middle class owing to its complex character. The class was usually seen from the perspective of its apathy towards politics in a crowded democracy. These factors dissuade academicians and political commentators to focus much on the middle class as a voting group and the social group supporting the saffron party. It is often assumed that the middle class constitutes mostly the working class whose interests are more on work and day-to-day life challenges rather than politics.

Third and probably the most important, India's middle class is not a homogenous group. It is difficult to estimate the size of the middle class. The middle class in our country is now epitomized by the young, educated, tech-savvy and professionally diversified with a stable income. This class comes from both urban and rural areas and is an ever-expanding constituency of the population. However, the estimates of the size of the middle class have always been at the centre of the narrative around India's economic growth. But the notion of the middle class remains arbitrarily defined with estimates of its size and features varying significantly, based on subjective notions and proclivities of researchers. Depending on the criteria used, the estimated size of this middle class in India ranges from 78 million (*The Economist* 2018) to 604 million (Krishnan and Hatekar 2017).

In the 19th and early 20th centuries, a wide range of public discourses was addressed in the literature on the middle class and its association and leanings with British India. Such debates unfolded in the areas of civic associations, social reform movements, literature, cinema and the Indian national movement. An analysis of the historical roots of the middle class and its role and functions in the post-Independence era allows us to identify the particular characteristics of the middle class associated with the growth of the state under Jawaharlal Nehru and his successors until the end of the 1970s. The discussion on this connects to the political participation of the middle class.

The middle class is now a social mainstay of the country that affected the turn towards economic liberalization. The BJP's laissez-faire policy was a welcome reprieve for the newly rising urban middle class. The BJP clearly rejected the Nehruvian model of economic development. Narendra Modi's idea of a 'new' India is ideologically and culturally different from the Nehruvian one. Modi's idea is based on the thoughts of Mahatma Gandhi, Sardar Vallabhbhai Patel and of course that of Deendayal Upadhyaya, who have clear Hindu cultural credentials, in contrast to Nehru's Western value system. The decisions to disband the Planning Commission and abrogation of Article 370 of the Constitution have to be seen in this context. The BJP, which has sensed the advantages of liberalization offered to the aspirational middle class, established itself as the pro-liberalization party and aligned itself with the interests of the middle class (Fernandes 2006). By striking a balance between development/governance and ideological issues, the BJP made inroads into every demographic profile such as caste/tribal, gender and age, by mainly focusing on the aspirational youth and the middle-class voters for whom jobs, higher income, choice in consumption and governance mattered more significantly. Moreover, the middle-class support to the BJP is not based strictly on economic issues but also has the strong nationalist moorings experienced inherently. The urban middle class, also, sought social security and stability. It was fuelled by Hindu nationalism propagated by the BJP and its leader Narendra Modi.

Here is our attempt to answer several questions about the role of the middle class in Indian politics. Did this class form the backbone of the Indian freedom movement? How did this middle class contribute to the evolution of India's stable democracy? What are the political implications of the ever-expanding class on Indian politics? Is it interested only in the economic well-being of its own and shuns participation in electoral politics? What are the factors that made this middle and new middle-class support the BJP in the late 1980s and onwards? Why did the middle class firmly rally behind Narendra Modi in the 2014 and 2019 parliamentary elections?

On the question of politics, the opinions are highly diverse. While some argue that this class has distanced itself from mainstream politics, the educated professional middle-class people saw politics as a major cause of distraction for the growth of their careers. It craved for its own economic well-being. Others argue that this class is demonstrating its proclivity towards a Hindu majoritarian politics by supporting the BJP and its policies.

Indeed, it is argued that the presence of a sizeable number of the middle class and its active engagement in the electoral process, state bureaucracy, law-making bodies, judiciary and media has ensured the stability of the Indian democratic polity, especially after economic liberalization. Fuelled by the economic liberalization and encouraged by its enormous growth in recent years, the middle class, or classes, are now negotiating the political frame and penalizing those who are seen as halting their growth and prosperity in the globalized economy. The class which bore the brunt of taxation, multiple rules, doling out of subsidies and the 'pampering of the poor' is no longer being ignored by the political class, irrespective of ideologies, hoping to do well in the electoral arena.

With significant rise in the size of the middle class, many politicians have started to proudly proclaim their middle-class moorings. For instance, taking a jibe at the then Congress President Rahul Gandhi, the present Finance Minister Nirmala Sitharaman, when she was the defence minister, during the debate on the Rafale-deal controversy in the Lok Sabha on 4 January 2019, said, 'I come from a middle-class family and not a *khandan*'. Prime Minister Narendra Modi too always speaks of his humble middle-class background going to the extent of recalling his role as a *chaiwala*. The Congress, despite claiming to be the 'manufacturer' of this class by introducing a series of economic reforms during the Rajiv Gandhi regime in the 1980s and later in the 1990s, is certainly not in sync with aspirations of the class.

Both economic liberalization and Hindu nationalism, with their sometimes 'contradictory but often surprisingly complementary' agenda for 'new India', can be described as 'vehicles' for meeting the material and cultural interests as well as aspirations of the consumerist middle class. In its uncritical support of a 'strong' and 'decisive' leader such as Modi, who would not brook any nonsense when it came to national interest, the middle class is very much in sync with the global trend, argues Ashutosh Kumar, a political science professor of Punjab University, India. In this context, Modi is clearly seen by many as holding forth the promise of such a cultural nationalism. The Indian middle class has rallied round, in a big way, to dream of its future on this promissory note.

The middle class walked into mainstream political activism with the famous anticorruption movement led by Anna Hazare in the national capital. This was a morphed blueprint of Jayaprakash Narayan's Nav Nirman Andolan. The Anna Hazare movement began on 5 April 2011 and ended on 28 December 2011, but it enabled the gathering of young full-time and part-time activists from across the country subconsciously realizing their innate potential to achieve results! The focus was anticorruption and the demand was the establishment of Lokpal. Anna Hazare's fast ended by creating a mass of young political force in the form of a huge middle class. This remained dormant for the next couple of years and erupted with full force in the 2014 election, and Modi was there at the right time to play the role of being the right kind of person to lead the nation. Modi transformed a parliamentary election into a presidential style referendum in an age of coalition politics that India had witnessed since 1989.

Gujarat chief minister and the BJP's prime-ministerial nominee Modi had a better understanding of the middle-class constituency. Born in a middle-class family, he began to sell the dream of *achhe din* (good times) to the people of India in 2014. By drawing public attention to his self as the *vikas purush* (the development man) during his rule as the Gujarat chief minister, he promised to bring alive the middle-class dreams of prosperity, opportunities and a better standard of living, all delivered by a strong leader, who does not squirm in the face of opposition. Modi developed his appeal by focusing on what the people urgently needed—more development, better governance, more socio-economic opportunities—as the United Progressive Alliance

(UPA II) led by the Congress was unable to address the aspirations of the class that high growth heralded during its rule in the early 1990s and during a few initial years of the UPA I (2004–2009).

India's political landscape has undergone a major change owing to globalization, Hindutva and the Mandal agitation in the late 1980s and 1990s, and those issues are still casting their shadows on the political alliances. Anna Hazare's campaign against corruption and 'policy paralysis' in the economy under UPA II, and perhaps the immature and uninspiring leadership of Congress leader Rahul Gandhi led to the emergence of Modi on the national stage and new narratives of religious nationalism. All these have changed the Indian political dynamics in the second decade of this century. The BJP, which was on the brink of irrelevance after its two successive defeats in 2004 and 2009, has undergone a massive metamorphosis and has become India's most formidable political force under the leadership of Modi. The BJP's rise can be attributed to a combination of many factors, including the party's Hindutva agenda, RSS support, organizational skills, a well-oiled electoral machinery and, more than all these, the massive support of the middle class and the contribution—both positive and negative—of the visual, print and social media.

The sensational sweep and scale of BJP's victory in the 2014 general elections surprised many scholars the world over. The Gujarat chief minister was the star campaigner with his mesmerizing oratory, hurricane tours and technology-backed rallies, and a massive favourable wave flared the imagination of large sections of the Indian electorate aided by the scams and unimpressive UPA II rule. Modi rode to power not only on the chariot of Hindutva but by promising to energize the economy which had been stalled because of the 'policy paralysis' of the UPA II. The BJP winning a majority on its own was a remarkable paradigm shift that has taken place in the trajectory of India's parliamentary politics. Prior to 2014, India witnessed seven consecutive general elections (1989–2009) with no single party getting a clear majority in the Lok Sabha, resulting in minority governments, unwieldy minority coalitions that were always hooked precariously on outside support. The media, too, contributed significantly provoking the middle-class young voters on the basis of these factors.

The decisiveness of the mandate in 2014 could not be brushed as a reflection of the enormity of anti-incumbency feelings among the Indian voters. The mandate ended the trend of no party getting a majority on its own since 1989. As in the 1980s, there was diminishing appeal of the poverty-removal paradigm of the Congress in the second decade of this century owing to the increased social mobility among the new middle classes. A large number of people, who were once poor, graduated to the middle class or new middle class with an improved economic situation and an expanding private sector. The middle class widely believed that policies driven by subsidies could be economically harmful and a burden to the state exchequer. The rising middle-class anger as a result of the UPA's stalled economic growth and worst of all, endless corruption scandals, created a hunger for change, especially among the young middle-class Indians who pinned their hopes on the arrival of long awaited 'good times' under the leadership of Modi. This suggested that the Indian middle class was gradually becoming a player of importance as it embraced the ethos of 'change', which was commensurate with its size and societal role.

The prowess of middle-class influence in the context of contemporary Indian democratic politics comes here for analysis. Tracing the historical emergence of the middle classes, from the British Raj to contemporary times, we map how the middle class changed with the change in economic policies. After discussing the divergent positions on size and growth of the middle class and its relevance to the prosperity and stability of the democracy, the impact of this resurgent class on Indian politics and, conversely, on the impact that the state policy had on the making of the middle class is deliberated upon.

It can be visualized that the middle class made its fundamental political shifts and embraced the ideology of the Hindutva propagated by the BJP and the strategies the saffron party adopted to address aspirations of the class in global economy. It is essential to unravel the factors that caused middle-class disillusionment towards the Congress and how it got enamoured of espousing the ideology propagated by Modi and the BJP.

Here is the analysis of the rationale behind the rise of Modi, the BJP's spectacular victories posted in the 2014 and 2019 parliamentary elections. It examines the strategy Modi adopted—from social engineering to communication with the Indian electorate. Unfolding of these events slowly constructed the image of Modi as a charismatic leader who rose to the post of prime minister, not once but twice. The making of this is looked at in great detail.

The size and attributes of the Indian middle class deserves special attention. The liberal economic policies unleashed with unprecedented dynamism in the Indian industry. The discussions on the Indian middle class itself has been fuelled by reasons more to do with economic policy than interest in scholarly political analysis. The larger the density of the middle class, the higher will be the number of consumers, and the size of the market would depend on them. Therefore, there has been a speculation about the construction of the size of this constituency to attract capital into the market as well as to direct the consumer flock to different sectors depending upon the projected fancies of this class. All these issues opened a new vista for their political participation, and the narrative gets drafted by them.

The English-educated urban middle class propelled the core of the new middle class. This new middle class, which is the most powerful and dominant subgroup of the Indian middle class, is becoming more and more homogeneous. Its influence goes beyond mere numbers, not just due to the use of modern technology such as social media. This dominant group is largely comprised of prosperous white-collar young professionals, mostly upper and middle-caste Hindus in the urban areas. Unlike the old middle class that largely depended on the public sector and government jobs, today's post-liberalization middle class is wedded to the private sector, having a stronger entrepreneurial spirit and greater economic freedom. This class is growing fast and is keen on owning the Western style of consumer durables and even attitudes. Unlike in the past, this new middle class is beginning to act as a class that engages in collective action, widely interactive within the country and even abroad, besides making new political demands and holding potentially aggressive views on civic issues, policies, corruption, government accountability and inequality in sync with their contemporaries abroad.

Reviewing contemporary middle-class politics in India, one cannot miss the importance of the new Indian middle class emerging on the political scenario during the great win of the BJP in the 2014 elections. It was the middle class which supported the right-wing party for various reasons as also due to the relative neglect of this class by the Congress. Many factors encouraged the middle class to extend support to the BJP in the 1980s and 1990s and some of them are the Ram Janmabhoomi movement, the Bofors scam, the Mandal–Mandir agitation, the demolition of the Babri Masjid, failed governance during coalition rule with the external support of the Congress. Above all, the daily doses of new scams and the angst over increasing corruption created uneasiness and gave rise to agitating mood among them. This gave rise to the middle-class revolution which was hidden but most effective in terms of outcome.

After losing power in 2004, the right-wing party returned to power after a gap of a decade in 2014. The BJP's prime-ministerial nominee Modi emerged as a leader bigger than the party. Modi single-handedly pulverized the opposition, questioning the dynastic rule of the Congress. The war of words over Modi's humble background as a *chaiwala* only added to the agony of the Congress. Modi won the hearts and minds of the middle class by catchy slogans and lofty promises of providing jobs and ensuring their safety. The election campaign and media strategy aided by experts and meticulous planning contributed to the electoral success. The 2014 election campaign and reasons for the middle-class rallying behind Modi for securing the historic mandate after a gap of three decades are discussed.

Why Indian people have chosen Modi for a second term is the question that has bothered many political analysts. Riding on the 2014 mandate, the first term of Modi's tenure saw a flurry of activities with schemes and reforms launched to address many social and economic issues. Several policy initiatives were launched to crack down on corruption and eliminate middlemen in the delivery of services. The intellectuals associated with the Congress and the Left questioned his fulfilment of promised two crore jobs a year for unemployed youth. The government made an attempt to provide for an enabling environment to set up start-up ventures and promoted entrepreneurial spirit through several programmes such as the Digital India, the Make in India and the Mudra scheme. All these had a deeper but silent influence on the voters, and the hatred campaign against him helped to boost his image rather than dent it.

Despite a historic low inflation since 1999, questions were raised about the Modi government's commitment towards containing prices of basic goods/necessities. In fact, the middle class, particularly on the lower rung that was struggling to meet daily ends owing to high inflation during the UPA regime, had voted out the Congress in 2014. Scholars from diverse fields questioned the policies of demonetization, Goods and Service Tax and improving rankings in the 'Ease of Doing Business' index. Did these policies benefit the middle class? Did this class endorse these policies? What are the reasons contributed to the BJP's spectacular show in the 2019 general elections? The challenge was to ride on the programmes during 2014–2019, and possibly Modi fulfilled that in great measure.

Modi's dominance and management of mainstream media and social media and its role in contributing to his emphatic victories in 2014 and 2019 general elections have been acknowledged. The middle class followed Modi's unflagging visual images beamed into all TV news channels and social media on a daily basis. The complexities of relationship between mainstream media comprising newspaper and TV channels and Modi, previously as the chief minister of Gujarat and later as the prime minister of India, played a big role. The coverage of issues by the media during 2014 and 2019 elections were really the centrifugal force that pushed him towards an enormous victory. In fact, instead of interacting with the media on a regular basis or even occasionally, and much less opening himself to searching questions through media interviews, Modi sought to reach out to the masses directly through his *Mann Ki Baat* programme on All India Radio.

With huge spread of smartphones, it is interesting to know the role of social media in India's 16th and 17th general elections. These results posed many questions. The answers lead to media and middle-class chemistry striking in favour of Modi. What were the topics Modi raised on social media during elections? Was social media successful in mobilizing the voters for his party in the 2014 and 2019 elections? How did Modi expand his support base on social media? To what extent did the prime minister use e-governance in the delivery of administrative services and implementation of flagship campaigns? All the answers to these questions provide the explanations sought.

This book is a product of research that began in the early 1990s when the growth of the middle class was at the nascent stage. For writing on the middle class/new middle class and its politics, I have been searching for a leader representing this class. Although Rajiv Gandhi emerged as the 'romantic liaison of Indian middle class with politics' (Palshikar 2001, 171), his tenure was short-lived and the middle-class played a vital role in voting him out in the 1989 general elections with the taint of the Bofors scam. Rajiv Gandhi's successors did announce several policy initiatives, particularly on the economic front, to expand the growth of the middle class/new middle class. But they spoke more about uplifting the poor rather than about the emergence of the middle class in the wake of new economic liberal policies. It is only Narendra Modi who spoke more about the middle class and launched several policy initiatives for fulfilling the aspirations of the class not only as the Gujarat chief minister for 12 long years but also as the prime minister of the country. He is the hero of the middle class (Mustafi 2013). The victory in the 2019 elections is nothing but endorsement of his policies by the middle class. While it is clear that Modi has brought a new style of leadership to Indian politics, he is the 56-inch-chest macho man, who works 24 × 7 without a break for his people. In fact, by winning two consecutive general elections with a vast majority, he has succeeded in transforming India's polity into being unipolar again.

There are a few books on Modi, most of which have been written either by Modi loyalists or critics, and hence, biased one way or the other from the ideological point of view. There are a few biographies of Modi which largely focus on his childhood days, his life in the early days in the RSS and later in the BJP. This book seeks to make a clear departure from such already existing books and unravels the rise of the BJP and Modi from the middle-class perspective.

The media is the primary source for this study. It is the media that provided national political information to the middle class and forced attention on certain issues and built up the public images of the political party, the BJP, and its leader. Modi's social-media platforms such as Twitter provided valuable information on diverse issues. Conversations with a number of neighbourhood associations and gated communities, political leaders cutting across parties, journalists, business people and various categories of professionals have widened my understanding of the class as well as the perspectives on Modi's administration.

Modi's emergence as a mass leader with absolute majority for the BJP and NDA in the 2014 and 2019 elections baffled many political analysts. The trends started becoming clear with the results of exit polls, and the most childish reaction was the hacking of EVMs.

A deeper investigation leads us to two very important but certainly dependable hypotheses: First, the process of liberalization and globalization has brought forth a swarm of middle class who are earning substantially and have lived through the years of bad and good phases of Indian economy. This new middle class is equidistant from the capitalist class on one side and the working blue-collared class on the other. They form a huge mass of new consumer voters leading not only to consumerism but to a big influence on the market and opinion. With the spark released by the anticorruption movement of Anna Hazare creating a new fire all over, and the Delhi assembly elections giving 67 out of 70 seats to the AAP, the middle class became the powerful decision makers in the political field too. Second, with the IT revolution, the social media also became the main opinion maker and directed the society towards what the media felt was right. Increasing corruption and scams in the administration gave good fodder to media and fired the middle class towards an unspoken revolt. Modi had to be just there standing and throwing his hands towards the sky with promises of good governance on every facet. There was, therefore, no political alternative in front of the middle and the new middle classes but to back him strongly against the worn-out election techniques of the opposition parties. He placed himself comfortably in the mould of a promising prime minister, carefully sculpted by the media and the middle class.

# CHAPTER 1

# The Nebulous Domain of the Middle Class

## Introduction

The process of the formation of the middle class is specific to the history and development of the country. Many historians and social scientists have recognized contributions of the middle class or middle classes in the country's freedom movement. In post-Independence India, this class is behind just about everything in India's development—its democracy, the growth of the economy, English education, technology, urban development, to name just a few. The middle class is driving the economy and its growth. A strong middle class provides a stable market for consumers that drives productive investment in the emerging economy of a country such as India. These sections of the society are a prerequisite for robust entrepreneurship and innovation. Interestingly, the Indian middle class is rising at a time when the middle classes in the USA, Europe and other advanced capitalist countries seem to be shrinking in their influence! Not surprisingly, the expansion of the middle class is a strong debatable topic in the media and survey/research reports of the major global consultancy agencies and multilateral development aid agencies.

In the West, prior to the French Revolution and the Industrial Revolution, social inequality had a customary sanction. These events changed not only the face of Europe but the network of the entire world. Henceforth, one's position in society—higher or lower—was to be determined not by birth into a particular caste or religion but by one's efforts. In this way, static society came to be replaced by the concept of a dynamic society, within which an individual was to be guaranteed freedom of mobility through equality of opportunity and liberal education. With the freedom of mobility, mercantile classes, bankers, merchants, shop owners, wholesale dealers and numerous brokers have emerged in Europe through the pursuits of commerce and industry (Wade 1966). The change in social relationships that the Industrial Revolution produced has been described as a movement from 'customs' to 'contract' (Polanyi 1957). Perhaps the most significant change in this context was the emergence of the market as an institution for ordering economic transactions. This also indicates that the emergence of the 'middle class' as an economic hierarchy is detached from inherited wealth and status, and is based more on location in business, education and similar professions.

The size of the middle class was small until the end of the Second World War. In the second half of the 20th century, the middle class started to expand in many modern societies. With the end of the Cold War between the USA and the erstwhile USSR in the late 1980s, the middle classes began to emerge as a critical factor for understanding the implications of globalization, particularly the rise and spread of neoliberal policies and movement of white-collar jobs from the West to India, China and other emerging Asian economies. Today, the middle class is a worldwide phenomenon, although the size, composition, characteristics and relationship of the middles classes with other social classes and categories differ from one country to another.

Specifically, September 2018 marks a global tipping point, because over 50 per cent of the world's population or some 3.8 billion people come under the middle-class category. 'For the first time since agriculture-based civilization began 10,000 years ago, the majority of humankind is no longer poor or vulnerable to falling into poverty' (Kharas and Hamel 2018). Therefore, the middle classes have become the most important drivers of social and economic change, not just in the West—where it will remain as significant despite the West's relative decline—but in a majority of countries around the world. This represents a tectonic shift (Burrows 2015, 7).

There was a huge growth in the middle classes in the last couple of decades, but the increase in prosperity was largely concentrated only in certain regions—China and Eastern Europe—after the fall of the Berlin Wall. The changing composition of the middle class and its cultural, political and economic implications have attracted the attention of public intellectuals, policymakers and academics from a variety of disciplines, and this has resulted in the emergence of an insightful scholarship which made attempts to understand implications of these shifts for the global economy and for people's daily lives.

The deliberations focused on explaining the ambiguities surrounding the term 'middle class'. More attention is given to understanding the significance of the middle class for sustaining liberal democracy and economic growth. An overview is taken further of existing criteria for measurements of the middle class and the size of the global middle class. A literature review on the middle class, new middle class, both from the Marxian and Weberian perspectives, and limitations of both the approaches is examined for an in-depth understanding. Our study not only adds to the existing body of literature on the nature of the middle class but also provides critical insights about the role of this class in India's path of development in recent years. In this study, 'middle class' and 'middle classes' are used synonymously, according to the context.

## Who Constitutes the Middle Class?

Before proceeding to analyse the political and economic significance of the rise of the middle classes globally, it is necessary to step back and ask ourselves who constitute the middle class. The category 'middle class' is a problematic one, especially in the Indian context. Generally, the middle class is understood as a class of people in the middle of a social hierarchy. It includes both the old and the new middle classes. While the old middle class consists of small industrialists, business-men and traders, the new middle class comprises employees in the corporate sector, and the middle ranks of the professions and the civil service. Now, the middle class also includes a large number of rich peasants or farmers.

The middle class has expanded with the development of advanced capitalism, and it is difficult to locate this class in social relations and their analysis, familiar now for over 150 years. It is difficult to establish the boundaries of this class from other classes—capitalists and working classes. This reconciliation of strata and the factions has to be included within this class. Such conceptual ambiguity, however, does not affect the economic and political spheres. Economically, it is argued that the middle class has grown with the advancement of modern industrial growth as a whole. Politically, the rise of the middle class has blurred class relations and has acted as a social base of support for capital.

There is a difference in the way sociologists/political scientists and economists think about this class. The very definition of the term 'middle class' is highly contested by various schools of political science and economics. Modern social theorists, especially economists, tend to define the middle class in terms of income or consumption/expenditure. While some economists defined the middle class as all those living in households with daily per capita income between $10 and $100, others define the class members as those with daily per capita expenditure between $2 and $10. In India, the middle-class households are identified as those earning an annual income between ₹2 lakh and ₹10 lakh, which we shall discuss in detail in the later section of this chapter. There is no one criterion for defining the middle class owing to its diversity. Therefore, Adam Smith noted in *The Wealth of Nations* that a pauper in 18th-century England might have lived like a king in Africa (quoted in Fukuyama 2014, 440).

Following the traditions of Karl Marx and Max Weber, sociologists and most political scientists tend to focus on occupational status, level of education, societal status and ownership of assets such as house/apartment/consumer durables while defining the middle class. For the purpose of understanding the political significance of the growing size of the middle class, the sociological approach is more preferable.

Simple yardsticks of income or consumption, whether relative or absolute, may only tell us about the consumption behaviour of the person in question but little about his/her political inclinations (Fukuyama 2014, 440). A vast number of studies, which we discuss in the next section, have shown that middle-class people support democracy, individual freedom, right to property and liberal economy. Members of the middle class give preference to education, health, stability and positive outcomes. People build their career based on merit, efficiency, leadership qualities and not on birth into a particular caste or religion.

## Why Does This Class Matter?

Before studying the size of the global middle class and theories of the middle class, it is relevant to examine whether and why the middle class is currently significant for democracy and economic growth/ development. In the literature on social sciences, the relevance of the middle class has been seen in distinct ways. While economists largely link the growth of the middle class to economic growth and development, social/political scientists highlight political aspects of the middle class and its contributions to democracy, the stability of institutions and good governance.

A strong middle class, as thinkers from Aristotle to James Madison to modern political scientists have noted, fosters better governance by ensuring that the government is well-run, increasing citizen participation, minimizing factional fighting and promoting policies for the benefit of all sections of the society rather than special interests (Madland 2011). Societies with extremes of wealth and poverty are susceptible to oligarchic domination or populist revolution (Fukuyama 2014, 439). Many thinkers (Birdsall 2010; Kenny 2011; Lipset 1959; van de Walle 2012) suggested that the middle class constitutes the backbone of democracy and ensures economic and political stability by promoting social cohesion and mitigating tensions between the poor and the rich. The Asian Development Bank (Amoranto, Chun, and Deolalikar 2010) finds that 'political activism is to a greater degree driven by the middle class rather than the upper class or the lower class', and this was realized during the anti-corruption movement led by Anna Hazare in 2011. Many empirical analysts have demonstrated that lower inequality and a larger 'class in the middle' lead to better institutional outcomes and good institutions (Barro 1999; Easterly 2001). A few even went to conclude that the growth of the middle class will also put an end to clientelism.[1]

The literature on the middle class seems to be divided by its social, political and economic impact. One group of scholars argue that the middle class can be a dynamic force for change (Kochhar 2016; Lash and Urry 1987) and contributor for economic growth (Easterly 2001). Another set of scholars have pointed out that middle classes can often be a powerful supporter of the status quo and traditional social and economic structures (Erikson and Goldthorpe 1992), for example, the middle class in China and Thailand, which we will discuss later in this chapter.

From an economic viewpoint, the middle class is a major source of economic growth. A strong middle class provides a stable consumer base that drives productive investment. It is a prerequisite for robust entrepreneurship and innovation, a source of trust that facilitates social interactions and reduces transaction costs (Madland 2011). In his 1936 book, *The General Theory of Employment, Interest and Money*, John Maynard Keynes described one of the core links between the middle class and economic growth that stable middle class consumption is vital to spur investment. A large and stable middle class has ramifications for boosting purchasing power and demand-driven growth in developing countries.

The growth of the middle class in emerging markets is termed as 'hitting sweet spot' (Ernst & Young 2013) given the strong influence of this group on political economy. Easterly (2001) suggests that the middle class helps to produce economic benefits and foster economic development through its emphasis on human capital investment, consumption and savings, which, in turn, incentivizes a virtual circle

---

[1] Clientelism is an early form of democracy in which masses of poor or uneducated voters are mobilized for electoral purpose by promising or offering public-sector jobs, handouts or political favours. Clientelism will start to decline as voters become educated and wealthier (Fukuyama 2014, 444).

contributing to further expansion of this social group. A stable middle class is claimed to induce entrepreneurial development and long-term investments (Rosling 2017) and a 'just and sustainable economy' (Wiemann 2015). Economic growth and the middle class complement each other. Economic growth led to the emergence of the middle class in recent years in countries such as China, Brazil, India, Indonesia, South Africa and Turkey. But the research on the middle class globally is quite divided on its social and political origins.

## Middle Class Strengthens Democracy

The discussion that makes an attempt to link social stratification with different forms of governance can be traced back to ancient Greece and to Aristotle in particular. Aristotle was the first author to stress the importance of middle classes in his *Politics*. The community of people 'in the middle' is considered instrumental in keeping balance within society. According to Aristotle, the middle class consists of people who neither own a lot of property and wealth nor are totally deprived of them. He defines the middle class as those people who neither want the property of others (like the lower classes) nor someone else takes away or acquires their properties. This is why the middle class can maintain a political system that is neither a tyranny of the rich nor the all-too-enthusiastic democracy of the poor. In fact, Aristotle has a separate word for the democracy of the middle class—polity (Aristotle 1999).

In political narratives, it is traditionally assumed that a high level of upper mobility facilitates democratic stability. The strength of America's democracy too is derived from the middle-class prosperity and the possibility of upward mobility. French political scientist Alexis de Tocqueville (1805–1859), visiting America in the 19th century, relates the emergence of a stable democratic system to an economic structure with relatively high rates of social mobility. For Tocqueville (1835), the middle classes were the mainstay of American democracy.

Many commentators have continued to view social mobility as a vital factor for the health of American democracy. Blau and Duncan (1967, 439) concluded that 'the stability of American democracy is undoubtedly related to the superior chances of the upward mobility'. In the political sphere, some theorists have traditionally assumed that a high level of upper mobility facilitates democratic stability. Interestingly, two nations that have stable and noisy democracies and have preceded capitalism are the USA and India. The USA is the oldest modern nation, and India is one of the oldest civilizations. The USA established democracy in 1776 but did not embrace full-blooded capitalism until the early 19th century with the Industrial Revolution. India established its democracy in 1950 and ventured into capitalism only in 1991 with the reforms. For the rest of the world, it has been the other way around (Das 2002, 313).

There is a long tradition of linking poverty reduction and middle-class growth to political transitions and democratization processes. Starting with the modernization theory, analysts of political transitions have suggested that falling poverty numbers and middle-class growth are conducive to the emergence of stable democracies (Wietzke and Sumner 2014, 6).[2] According to the modernization theory, the expansion and strengthening of the middle class tilt the balance of power towards pro-democracy forces. Economic development can promote political democracy because it transforms a traditional society into a modern society that constitutes a necessary and sufficient condition for new democratic politics (Huntington 1991; Lipset 1960). Such societal transformations include the spread of education, urbanization and increase of social mobilization. Accompanied by economic growth, the transformed modern society becomes more diversified and complicated and thus more difficult for the authoritarian regime to rein. Many (e.g., Dahl 1971; Fukuyama 1993; Glassman 1995; Huntington 1991; Lipset 1959; Moore 1966) argued that economic development destabilizes an authoritarian regime by nurturing a politically autonomous and empowered middle class.

[2] This argument is based on historical observations about the role of bourgeois middle classes in the development process of advanced European democracies as well as on more recent cross-national statistical associations between the size of middle-income groups and political development/stability and social cohesion (see Barro 1999; Easterly 2001).

Primarily, there are three major approaches for understanding the role of the middle class in a democracy. First, Lipset's modernization theory; second, Samuel Huntington's study of democratization from 1974 to 1990; and third, Barrington Moore's structural theory.

The modernization theory establishes a correlation between socioeconomic development, the rise of a liberal middle class and democratic government. Based on studies of democratic and non-democratic states in Europe and Latin America, Lipset established requisites for democratization via modernization (Lipset 1960, 52). He believed that a middle class created both a more engaged citizenry and greater moderation. Lipset first established the theoretical link between the level of development of a given country and its probability of being democratic. His general argument was simply that 'democracy is related to the state of economic development. The more well-to-do a nation, the greater the chances it will sustain democracy' (Lipset 1959, 75). He states that the strongest democratic states have strong economies, efficient agriculture, advance industrialization and a large middle class with increased purchasing power. Weaker democracies and authoritarian states have weaker economies, labour-intensive agriculture, limited industrialization and a small middle class with less purchasing power.

Samuel Huntington's work shows the result of modernization on democratization, particularly in Asia. He provides three explanations in *The Third Wave* (Huntington 1991, 59) on how economic development provides the basis for democratization from 1974 to 1989. First, rising oil prices worldwide weakens states that had adopted Marxist/Leninist economic policies. Second, sufficient economic development has reached in other states that facilitate democratization. Finally, rapid economic development destabilizes authoritarian regimes and compels the ruling elites to either liberalize or repress reformers. The third wave of global democratization, which culminated in the fall of communism in Eastern Europe in 1989, increased the number of electoral democracies around the world from around 45 in 1970 to more than 120 by the late 1990s (Fukuyama 2012, 56). Huntington identifies the predominant economic conditions that effect regime change in the late 20th century where Asian states experience economic growth and an expansion of the middle class. Huntington (1991) noted that rapid economic growth before the transition to democracy increased the size of the middle class and at the same time empowered them with newly founded independence, coupled with rising expectations.

However, what Huntington mentions and was missed by Lipset (1960) is the fact that, in certain countries, the middle class was supportive of authoritarian regimes and not pro-democratic at all; examples of this are countries of South America and Brazil in particular during the 1960s and the 1970s. But Fukuyama (2012, 56) argues that middle-class people do not necessarily support democracy in principle: Like everyone else, they are self-interested actors who want to protect their property and position. In countries such as China and Thailand, many middle-class people feel threatened by the redistributive demands of the poor and hence have lined up in support of authoritarian governments that protect their class interests. Despite the vast size of the middle class in China, owing to enormous economic growth and development over the past four decades, democracy has not yet happened and authoritarianism remains consolidated in the communist country (Gallagher 2002; Tang 2011). Possibly, due to the acceptance of the political philosophy by the Chinese middle class.

The middle class in China is depended on the support of the Chinese Communist Party. Unger (2006) pessimistically predicts, 'Don't expect regime change or democratization any time soon. The rise of China's middle class blocks the way [to democratization]' (17–31). Despite its serious challenge to liberal democracy, Fukuyama (2012, 56–57) says, many people currently admire the Chinese system not just for its economic record but also because it can make large, complex decisions quickly compared with the agonizing policy paralysis that has struck both the USA and Europe, and even India during the second term of the Manmohan Singh government (2009–2014). Similarly, despite recording high development, nations such as Iran and Saudi Arabia rejected liberal democracy in favour of a form of Islamic theocracy.

The structural theory emphasizes changing structures of power favourable to democratization. In his classic comparative study of the *Social Origins of Dictatorship and Democracy* in the modern world, Barrington Moore (1966) views the middle class as the key actor in the processes that ultimately lead to democracy. He, for example, emphasized the importance of the bourgeoisie but broadly construed this to include what we refer to as the middle classes. Writing in comparative historical mode, Moore has emphasized the importance of the bourgeoisie (the middle class and the owners of the property) for democracy. He explains that an active and independent urban middle class is an indispensable element for the creation of parliamentary democracy. For Moore, if there is no bourgeoisie, there will be no democracy!

Moore (1966, 314) argues that Indian political democracy at the time of Independence was weak because India established political democracy without witnessing any form of the Industrial Revolution. Therefore, democracy has not done a great deal toward modernizing India's social structure (Moore 1966, 316). India achieved political democracy but was not able to establish social and economic democracy owing to the weakness of the bourgeoisie and the persistence of the peasantry during the Independence. True, democratic institutions were set up before the country had the opportunity to become industrialized. Two-thirds of the people still live in rural areas and organized labour constitutes less than 10 per cent of total labour, and, until 1980, the middle class was less than 10 per cent of the population. We began to think in terms of 'welfare' before there were welfare-generating jobs. The result, as we have seen, was a suffocating economic environment, slow growth, missed opportunities. It is the price we have paid for having a democracy before capitalism, or not enough capitalism (Das 2002, 315).

Besides these, a number of theorists suggested that a growing middle class strengthens democracy. Moreover, the middle classes in the South are commonly identified as 'supporters of democracy and progressive political platforms'. They can influence economic development through more active participation in the political processes, expressing support for more 'inclusive growth' (Pezzini 2012). The middle class has also contributed to the emergence of new social movements such as socio-political movements by socialist Jayaprakash

Narayan's Total Revolution' in the 1970s, India Against Corruption movement led by a Gandhian social activist Anna Hazare in 2011, and environmentalism in India and developing nations. Andre Beteille (2001) suggests that the Indian middle class 'has played a leading part in the modernization of Indian society; without it, there would be no modernization'.

It has been argued that stable democracy rests on a broad middle class and societies. Fukuyama views that when the middle class is small in size, constituting less than 30 per cent of the population, it may side with anti-democratic forces because of the fears of the intentions of the large mass of poor people below it and the populist and distributive policies they may pursue (Fukuyama 2014, 442–446). But when the middle class becomes the larger group in the society, the danger is reduced and it may support democracy. Therefore, the ability to consolidate a stable liberal democracy is greater in countries that have large and broad middle classes in contrast to one in which a small middle class is sandwiched between a rich elite and a vast mass of poor people. Just the existence of a broad middle class is neither sufficient nor as necessary a condition to bring about liberal democracy. Although it is extremely helpful in sustaining it. Noting the trend of declines in the size of the middle class in advanced countries such as the USA,[3] Fukuyama (2014) asks, what happens to liberal democracy if the middle class reverses and starts to shrink?

## Middle Class: Drivers of Economic Growth

The middle class is considered as the real motor of economic growth. Bhalla (2007) calls the middle class 'development's secret weapon'. This class not only has more resources to spend on non-basic goods but has the desire for higher quality branded goods that require a more complex productive structure which, if developed internally,

---

[3] Income inequality has increased in some of the advanced countries since the 1980s. In the USA, the top 1 per cent of families took home 9 per cent of GDP in 1970 and 23.5 per cent in 2007. The economic growth in this period went to a relatively small number of people. The flipside of the phenomena is the stagnation of middle income since the 1970s (Fukuyama 2014, 445–446).

may induce development. To fulfil its aspirations, the middle class is investing in education and other sources of human capital, which are vital to prosperity. The 2019 Nobel Prize winner economists, Banerjee and Duflo (2008), say that the middle class favours economic development by savings. A larger middle class can increase savings, so necessary for financing domestic investment without any balance of payments problems. The 'African Rising' narrative too found the African middle-class as the 'driver of development' (Fletcher 2013). All of this implies that the existence of a large middle class makes economic growth more sustainable, something that has been crucial to all developing countries, especially Latin America and Asia that have gone through waves of growth and recession.

A 'middle-class' consensus 'facilitates economic growth by allowing society to agree on the provision of public goods critical to economic growth. These include goods such as public education, public health services, physical infrastructure' (Easterly and Levine 2001). The larger the middle class, the more progressive are the social policies on health and education and the quality of governance (Loayza, Rigolini, and Llorente 2012). The middle class is crucial to hasten economic growth, to transit from a low- to a high-income economy and to avoid the middle-income trap. Several Asian countries escaped from this middle-income trap (Ozturk 2016, 727). Many Latin American countries have been stuck in this middle-income trap at least in the last two decades. In India too, the middle class is driving the economy and accelerating its development. Middle-class people promote human capital accumulation and generate entrepreneurs who create jobs and foster productivity. Entrepreneurs such as N. R. Narayana Murthy of Infosys, who was born in a middle-class family, contributed immensely to IT growth in the country. Because of the passion for entrepreneurship in the IT industry, largely dominated by the middle class, India seems to be all set to become a genuine boom country for new enterprises (Rosling 2017). Companies such as Infosys and Wipro as well as non-resident Indian (NRI) tech entrepreneurs such as Vinod Khosla, Kanwal Rekhi, Sundar Pichai, Satya Nadella, Ajay Banga have become role models for aspiring software engineers, symbolizing what Indians can achieve as entrepreneurs if the economy is freed by liberalization. Gurcharan Das (2002), a key preacher of liberalization, in his writings, continually lauds the software industry for its entrepreneurial spirit, ability to accumulate wealth and the numerous rags-to-riches stories of Indian start-up companies that made it big. The new millionaires did not inherit wealth. They have risen with the help of their education, talent, hard work and professional skills. Overall, we find that when the size of the middle-class increases, generally, the quality of governance improves which in turn provides equal opportunities for all.

## Global Middle Class

The global middle class expanded due to the increase in average incomes and the fall in the levels of poverty, in particular, during the last decade. We acknowledged that the middle class does not have a precise definition that can be globally applied. Different agencies, institutions and economists have used different measures to define the middle class. The size of the class also varies depending on the criteria used for its measurement.

### Criteria for Identifying the Middle Class

Nowadays, we need class categories for economic policy purposes, for marketing strategies and for analysing political developments. Owing to its diversity, different criteria such as income, occupation, education and consumption are used to define the middle class. Generally, surveys conceived the category middle class in terms of subjective variables. The subjective variable pertained to the respondent's own identification as 'middle class' and an explicit rejection of 'working class' identity for themselves.[4]

Kapur and Vaishnav (2014) used the subjective criteria by conducting face-to-face interviews of 69,920 randomly selected Indians across 25 Indian states between January and March 2014. Subjective measures rely on personal statements such as 'I am in the middle class'.

---

[4] This approach is more common for media outlets rather than for academic scholarship, and it relies on information collected through polls and questionnaire. Put it simply, it asks respondents to place themselves in a certain socio-economic category according to their personal perceptions.

This form of self-identification is a distinctive way to define an amorphous group where there is little agreement on objective measures. As India is a diverse country, there was a significant degree of variation across states. Nearly 49 per cent of all survey respondents believed that their family was a middle-class family. There were great variations in responses across states. Whereas 68 per cent of respondents in the south Indian state of Karnataka believed they belonged to the middle class, only 29 per cent of respondents in the Hindi heartland state of Madhya Pradesh did so. In addition to Karnataka, the urban city-state of Delhi and Gujarat are placed at the upper end of the spectrum. At the opposite end are Madhya Pradesh, Odisha and Maharashtra.

Overwhelmingly, economists have identified the middle class according to the income and/or consumption. There are two different approaches. One identifies the middle class relative to their specific countries and societies, that is, they are in the middle strata in terms of income in each country (relative terms). The other defines the middle class by reference to socio-economic data such as poverty, income or expenditure levels, either globally or continentally (absolute terms). Unsurprisingly, the resulting definitions vary widely (Neubert 2014, 23), whereas some scholars prefer a relative, rather than an absolute, definition of well-being that is built around income distribution. A cross-national analysis by Easterly (2001) defined the middle class as those individuals who were living between the 20th and 80th percentiles on the consumption distribution. The problem with this approach stems from the variation in relative income and income inequality across countries (Wietzke and Sumner 2014).

The middle class of developing countries is compared with the global middle class. Kharas (2010) and Meyer and Birdsall (2012), and Bhalla (2007) follow this approach. Kharas (2010) defines a global middle class as all those living in households with daily per capita incomes between $10 and $100 in purchasing power parity (PPP) terms. By combining household survey data with growth projections for 145 countries, Kharas shows that Asia accounts for less than one-quarter of the middle class in 2010. By 2020, that share could be double. More than half the world's middle class could be in Asia, and Asian consumers could account for over 40 per cent of global middle-class consumption. The lower boundary is chosen with reference to the average poverty line in Portugal and Italy, while the upper boundary is chosen as twice the median income of Luxembourg, the richest advanced country. Bhalla (2007) also takes an absolute approach by defining the middle class as those with an annual income of over $3,900 in PPP terms by considering the country's growth since the 1980s.

Based on estimated income distributions, Meyer and Birdsall (2012) calculate the size of the middle class using minimum threshold of $10 per capita per day (2005 PPP) and a maximum threshold of $50 a day. They argue that the lower limit of $10 is the global minimum to be classified as the new middle class. The upper limit is set at $50 because most of Latin American households earning beyond this limit consider themselves rich, not middle class.

Defining the middle class in India just like anywhere else is tricky. India's National Council of Applied Economic Research (NCAER) definition identifies middle-class households in India as those earning an annual income somewhere between ₹2 lakh and ₹10 lakh at 2001–2002 prices (Shukla 2010, 100). Assuming an average household size of five, this approximately equals $11 and $55, respectively, per capita per day, in 2005 PPP terms, close to the bounds defined by Meyer and Birdsall (2012). Chancel and Piketty (2017) found that one in 10 adults had an annual income of more than $3,150 in 2014. That leaves only 78 million Indians making close to $10 a day. However, Krishnan and Hatekar (2017) argued that these income limits of the new middle class put forth by Kharas (2010), Meyer and Birdsall (2012) and NCAER are quite high, making them unsuitable to be applied to a developing country such as India.

The new middle class is also defined by developing country standards alone. The definitions proposed by Ravallion (2009), ADB (Amoranto, Chun, and Deolalikar 2010), and Banerjee and Duflo (2008) are consumption-based, set at a lower limit of $2. Ravallion (2009) defines the 'developing world middle class' as having those who are not poor when judged by the median poverty line of developing countries but are still poor by the USA standards. He defines the new middle class as the median of poverty lines of 70 developing countries, which is $2 per person per day (PPPD), measured in 2005 PPP. The upper limit is defined as the poverty line of the USA in 2005, which is $13. Using household surveys of 13 developing countries including India, Banerjee and Duflo (2008) used two alternative absolute measures: those with daily per capita expenditures between $2 and $4 (the lower middle class) and those with daily per capita expenditures between $6 and $10 (the upper middle class), valued at 1993 PPP. Similarly, ADB (Amoranto, Chun and Deolalikar 2010) identifies the new middle class in Asia using the lower bound of $2, but a higher upper bound of $20 PPPD, measured at 2005 PPP. Two dollars a day is a commonly accepted definition of the poverty line in developing countries; people above this line are middle class in the sense that they have moved out of poverty.

In recent years, an income of $10 PPPD to attain middle-income status is gaining acceptance among economists. In 2018, this $10 PPPD works out around a monthly income of ₹20,000 in India. Several people (Birdsall 2010; Birdsall, Lustig and Meyer 2013; Ernst & Young 2013; Kharas 2010; World Bank 2007) defined the middle class as comprising households with per capita income between $10 and $100 PPPD in 2005 PPP terms. There is a growing consensus that the $10 threshold is associated with economic security and 'insulates' people from falling back into poverty (Kochhar 2016).[5]

The affluent 'global middle class' consuming more than $10 per day has expanded significantly over the past decades. Although such better-off groups still account for a small size of the population in their countries, their actual numbers are beginning to exceed in advanced economies: In Asia alone, over 525 million people were living on incomes between $10 and $100 a day—more than the entire population of the European Union (Ernst & Young 2013, 2). Around the world, this 'affluent' population is expected to grow by up to another

---

[5] Lopez-Calva, Rigolini and Torche (2011) and Birdsall et al. (2013) note in Latin America that households below the income of $10 per day have higher probabilities of sliding back into poverty.

three billion in the next two decades, making it the largest income group in the global income distribution (Ernst & Young 2013; Kharas and Gertz 2010).

## Estimating the Size of the Global Middle Class

There are a few good studies in the last decade or so, attempting to estimate the size of the middle class in India and other 'emerging economies'; some even venture to project its growth over the next few decades. Using different methodologies and data sources, different studies estimate the size of the global middle class in the range of 3–4 billion in the next few years. As noted earlier, the latest study of Brooking's Kharas and Hamel (2018) pegs the size of the global middle at 3.8 billion in 2018. This means a majority of the world's population, for the first time ever, is living in middle-class or rich households.

According to the United Nations Development Programme (UNDP 2013, 14), between 1990 and 2010, the South's share of the global middle-class population expanded from 26 per cent to 58 per cent. By 2030, more than 80 per cent of the world middle class is projected to be residing in the South and to account for 70 per cent of total consumption expenditure. The World Bank in 2007 witnessed the global middle class increasing from 456 million in 2000 to somewhere between 1.4 billion, which is estimated to be 1.6 billion in 2030. Goldman Sachs in 2008 predicted the global middle class rising from 1.9 billion in 2008 to 4.25 billion, or approximately 50 per cent of the global population in 2030 (Kharas and Gertz 2010).

Among all countries, China emerged as the principal contributor to an expanding global middle class. China's middle-income population jumped from 32 million in 2001 to 235 million in 2011, an increase of 203 million. In 2011, China's middle-income population accounted for 30 per cent of the global middle-income population (Kochhar 2016). The growth of the middle-income people has been low in India compared to that of China. The difference in the timing of economic reforms, which began in 1978 in China and in 1991 in India, is considered as one of the reasons for the difference in outcomes.

However, scholars and global agencies agree that the most rapid growth will occur in Asia in the coming years. Kharas (2017) found that an overwhelming majority of new entrants into the middle class—88 per cent of the next billion—will live in Asia. Big geographic distributional shifts in markets are happening, with China and India accounting for an ever-greater market share, while the European and North American middle class basically stagnates. India became the world's sixth largest economy in 2018. By the year 2022, India, after China and the USA, could become the third-largest middle-class market in the world, thanks to India's population growth and liberal economic policies implemented during the last 25 years.

Emerging economies are having two middle classes. One consists of those who are middle class by any standard/criteria and this group has the makings of a global middle class whose members have common features. However, the size of this middle class is very small. The other group consists of those who are middle class by standards of the developing world but not of the rich one (*The Economist* 2009a, 2009b). This category of the intermediate class is expanding rapidly since the 1990s. In short, the rise of the middle class can be an economic and political game changer in dialogues on trade-related matters between developed and developing nations. Despite its critical role in driving the growth at the national level and at the global level, there is no consensus about the size of the global middle class because of its diversity and different criteria used for its measurement.

Do size and income alone determine the nature of a particular class? By referring to various approaches on class and the middle class, sociologists and political scientists have critiqued these income and size-based definitions of class to suggest that qualitative attributes such as occupation, status or even ideology need to be taken into account while defining a class. Political scientist Achin Vanaik (2002) and the sociologist Satish Deshpande (2003) have been critical of income- and size-based assessments of the middle class. They have analysed the middle class from the Marxist perspective and examined it with respect to ideology and power. While Vanaik contends that the middle class is a part of the ruling elite, Deshpande argues that the Indian middle class is hegemonic. Most importantly, they look at class through the lens of power and contend that the middle class derives power from ideological representations. We will discuss different approaches to the study of the middle class in the next section.

## Approaches to Study the Middle Class

The ambiguity in the notion of the middle class gets confounded because of the different approaches that are prevalent in the social analysis. Occupational function and employment status are the two most significant criteria for approaching the middle classes. Goldthorpe (1987) focused on differentiating class positions in terms of employment relations. It is based on employment relations and employment status that workers grouped into different social groups. The class schema that Goldthorpe identified grouped 11 classes into three main clusters: employers, the self-employed and employees. Goldthorpe argued that it was the position of individuals within his class schema, rather than simply their income that determined what was in their interests and, thus, shaped their political behaviour. Andre Beteille's (2001) position is that occupational function and employment status are the two significant criteria for defining the middle classes, although education and income are also widely used. The important occupational division is between manual and non-manual work, with typical middle-class occupations being non-manual ones. In fact, the stability of employment appears to be the one issue that distinguishes the middle classes from the manual working classes (Banerjee and Duflo 2011, 414).

It is argued that Goldthorpe's scheme has relevance in the European society of the 1970s and not today's world, particularly in the Indian context. Goldthorpe does not acknowledge some of the fundamental changes in the labour market such as the rise of the service sector and proliferation of people working in these service industries such as in India, and the increased number of women workforce who are now part of the labour but were not 40 years ago (Oesch 2003). The women labour force has been gradually increasing while the labour force comprising men has been declining with economic development and growth of the service sector. The presence of 'service workers' and 'low-level salaried employees' has created 'a twilight zone between the working and the middle classes' (Sainsbury 1987).

French sociologist Pierre Bourdieu has pointed out that the middle class should not be defined by just one criterion but by a variety of other parameters such as gender, age and ethnicity, education and cultural habits. He provided significance to the cultural, economic and social capital of the middle class. The middle class is a social class consisting of 'grey areas, ambiguously located in the social structure, inhabited by individuals whose trajectories are extremely scattered' (Bourdieu 1996, 111–112). Others followed him later on and asserted that both material and cultural practices are constitutive for the modern middle classes (Heiman, Freeman and Liechty 2012).

## Classical Views

Basically, there are two classical approaches to the middle class. The Marxian approach locates the middle class in a set of definitive social relations to mark out the trajectory of politics. The Weberian view conceives class as individuals with common economic life chances which determine their opportunities for income in the market and identifies the middle class as those equipped with skills and education.

The rich tradition of Marxist political economy has offered a critical lens through which struggles between a ruling class and a subordinate class, bourgeoisie and proletariat, have constituted the central drama of capitalism. Karl Marx and Friedrich Engels have been therefore criticized for neglecting the growing importance with developed capitalist societies of the middle class in their early works. Marx provided little insight into the position of middle classes, envisioning their eventual dissolution into either capitalist or labouring groups. Marx did not anticipate the emergence of a welfare state within a capitalist society and consequent growth of an employee class providing the many welfare services and the growth of bureaucracy overseeing them. Marx also did not anticipate the emergence of the managerial class which forms an important element in modern capitalist development (Dandekar 1998, 39–69). As famously remarked by

Marx and Engels (1968 [1848], 18) in *The Communist Manifesto*, the Marxist analysis suggests that 'the middle class is expected to sink gradually into the proletariat'.

Almost two decades later, in *Theories of Surplus Value* (1863), Marx acknowledged the importance of the growing middle class for the development of capitalism. Marx was referring this class as the petty bourgeoisie, which included small produce, artisans and farmers (Bottomore 1965). For Marx, this middle class was 'unproductive labour', necessary for capitalism to function (Urry 1973). In the theories of surplus value, for example, Marx argues that the displacement of workers by machinery not only opened new areas of productive employment in other branches of industry but also enabled capitalists to hire increased numbers of unproductive employees, which Marx referred to as the 'middle class' (Burris 1986, 321). But it is also clear that Marx paid insufficient attention to the consequences that this development would have.

The middle class does not form a major part of Marx's analytic scheme of the three great classes of modern society. It has grown steadily in size and complexity not only in the industrially advanced countries of West Europe and North America but also in the post-colonial societies of Africa and Asia, including India (Beteille 2001, 2007). In advanced countries, the working classes through unionization and political struggle won greater privileges for themselves and became middle class in political outlook (Fukuyama 2014, 439).

Marx believed that the middle classes would remain a small and privileged minority in modern societies. Yet by the second half of the 20th century, the middle class constituted the vast majority of the population of most advanced societies, thereby undercutting the appeal to Marxism (Fukuyama 2014, 439). The failure to account for the 'empirical evidence' of a large middle class in advanced capitalist societies ultimately led to what E. O. Wright (1989, 3) describes as the 'embarrassment of the middle class' for Marxists. So, the Marxists didn't get their communist utopia because the mature capitalism generated middle-class societies, not working-class ones (Fukuyama 2012, 58). Later Marxists, including Nicos Poulantzas, have rejected some of the orthodox Marxist ideas.

Max Weber speaks of 'the middle classes' as those groups who have all sorts of property or marketable abilities through training and who are in a position to draw their support from these sources. Later, he adds that 'independent peasants and craftsmen are (also) to be treated as belonging to the "middle classes"'. This category often includes in addition officials, 'the liberal professions and workers with exceptional monopolistic assets or positions' (Weber 1947, 425–427). Weber distinguishes the two main groups within the middle class. One consists of the petty bourgeoisie, comprising people who earn incomes for their livelihood through ownership of property. The petty bourgeoisie, lacking high-level managerial/professional training and qualifications, were those who owned and ran small businesses—the owner of small factory or workshop employing a handful of people, the self-employed plumber or builder, the small family farmer and so on (Saunders 1980, 92).

The other section of the middle class identified by Weber was the acquisition class or the service class. The class situation of this class member is primarily determined by their opportunity for the exploitation of service in the market. For Weber, this class comprised people such as civil servants, technicians and various professional groups who could combine high income by virtue of their training and qualification. It is this part of the middle class which has grown enormously over the years.

Both Marx and Weber differ in their understanding of the middle class, but they tend to agree that 'middle class' as a modern category emerges with the development of industrial capitalism and market economy. Unlike Marx, Weber sees a vast expansion of white-collar middle-class employees with the development of capitalism.

Wages in the labour market, of course, depend on the supply as well as the demand of labour. Weber recognized that a section of the middle class often attempts to maintain or bolster its market value by restricting entry to others, thereby ensuring its own continued scarcity. In pursuing such strategies of 'social closure' (Weber 1978), it has often sought to enlist the help of the state, for example, through state licensing of the right to practise as in the case of medicine and law. The closure has been suggested as a cause of intergroup inequality across professional, ethnic, religious and national boundaries, among others (Saunders 1980).

In India too, the middle class tended to produce an exclusionary closure for those who have historically been on the margins of society such as the Dalits, the Adivasis and the religious and linguistic minorities. It is this closure tendency of the upwardly mobile middle-class Indians that keeps identities of caste and community alive. Varma (2007, 64) argues that the English language had become an instrument for social exclusion in India: The upper middle class presided over this linguistic apartheid; the rest of India consisted of victims and aspirants. The ability to speak English with the right accent, fluency and pronunciation was the touchstone for entry into many professions in modern liberal India, particularly after 1991.

Later, British sociologist and novelist Frank Parkin developed the concept of social closure. Social closure is the process by which groups seeks to maximize rewards by restricting access to resources and opportunities to a limited circle of eligible individuals (Parkin 1979, 45). He goes on to elaborate this concept, by identifying two main types, exclusionary and usurpationary closures. 'The distinguishing feature of exclusionary closure is the attempt by one group to secure for itself a privileged position at the expense of some other group through processes of subordination' (Parkin 1979). He refers to this metaphorically as the use of power downwards. Usurpationary closure refers to the collective use of power by the excluded group (proletariat) in order to prevent exclusionary closure taking place and thereby secure access to resources for the negatively privileged group.

The idea of an objective determinant of class, outlined by Weber and adopted by Parkin, is open to criticism. The major criticism of Weber's approach is his narrowing of class to the market situation, which seriously limits the understanding of the relationship in capitalist society by concentrating on distributional rewards rather than relationships with the production process (Carter 1985, 41–42). There are a number of difficulties in Parkin's closure theory too. The main problem is that the property and monopolization of professional services through credentials are not a form of closure at all. There is no formal legal ban in the contemporary capitalist society on certain categories of individuals owning or acquiring a property. Managerial positions and positions in media and schools (as primary and secondary school teachers), for instance, are not subject to the kinds of control by professional associations that are typical in medicine and law. It is quite misleading, therefore, for Parkin to speak of the legal monopolization of professional services as a fundamental strategy which promotes inequality (Carter 1985, 44–45).

British sociologist David Lockwood's influential book *The Blackcoated Worker* (1958) can be seen as an attempt to overcome the limitations of the orthodox Marxist position that clerical workers or blackcoated workers share a common situation of 'propertylessness' and are therefore an integral part of the working class, as well as to take into account the absence within the Weberian framework of an examination of relations inside the productive process. Lockwood synthesizes the analysis of Marx and Weber and argues that clerical workers in Britain identified with the middle class by not joining the trade union movement.

Lockwood, following the Marxian frame of reference, argued that instead of identifying themselves with manual workers, blackcoated workers have identified with the middle classes. This phenomenon is not in accord with the Marxian theory. Marxists have explained their refusal to join the trade union movement on the grounds that clerical workers are deluded by 'false consciousness'. Lockwood explores this theme and demonstrates that British clerical workers do have class consciousness. It is not 'false' and it is not the working class. The blackcoated worker is middle-class in his social values (Hollingshead 1959). Just as the market determines differential rewards, so does the work situation determine different experiences (Carter 1985, 43).

Both Marxian and Weberian approaches lose much of their relevance in India. In contrast to both theories discussed here, we argue that caste and class cannot be considered separately but need to be studied together. They do not coincide but closely interact in the social life of India and exert a strong influence over the identity of the middle class (Jaffrelot and van der Veer 2008, 17). Although a number of non-traditional, non-caste occupations have emerged, traditional identities such as caste and kinship have not been fully replaced in India. Instead, they still occupy centre stage in Indian politics after the implementation of the Mandal Commission Report providing 27 per cent reservation for Other Backward Castes (OBCs). Moreover, networking and marriage or funeral rituals are conducted on caste lines. Many of these caste conscious urban middle-class members are framing socio-economic and political narratives around caste and class status. We have discussed issues related to caste and class politics in India in Chapters 4 and 5.

## The New Middle Class

The last two or three decades saw the emergence of the 'new middle class' with dramatic changes in the income levels of populations in many developing economies, particularly India. This class gained momentum along with the growth of the third sector, the services, which developed at the expense of industry and agriculture. The more it developed, the more it got fragmented in a number of distinguishable strata. It is essentially a collection of individuals enjoying more or less similar privileges and lifestyles. These salaried employees are incorporated in various big corporations, organizations and administrative machinery of the state. These employees are social groups with considerable income, influence and prestige. They also share in authority and fringe benefits, which distinguishes them from the traditional middle class. They start a career within a bureaucratic hierarchy, of subordination and defence, and competition for promotion. Fernandes (2006), Fuller and Narasimhan (2007) and Upadhya (2016) claim that the newness in the new middle class lies in its employment in new service activities brought about by economic reforms through liberalization and globalization. We will discuss in detail the significance of the new middle class in the Indian context in Chapter 3 of this book.

Contrary to the traditional middle class, this new middle class has no independent existence, acquisition of property, ownership and control, and, if any, these are incidental. Therefore, there is no unanimity among the academic scholars about the definition of the new middle class.

The essential features which distinguish the old middle class from the new middle class are discussed here briefly.

First, the old middle class was located externally to capitalist relations of production as independent artisans, small landholders or small family-based productive units. They were neither part of the capitalist class nor of the working class. The new middle class did not enjoy such independence. They were part of the big organizations. Their intermediate position came from their place inside the industrial or capitalist economy. The new middle class expanded because of the new demands of modern industry that required services of a large number of specialists and skilled personnel, at both technical and administration fronts.

Second, the old middle class is the owner of the means of production. The new middle class is not the real owner of the means of production. One of the characteristics of the new middle class is that it performs the global function of capital even without owning the means of production, and it performs this function in conjunction with the function of the collective worker.

While the old/traditional middle class emerged from the populist, modernist and bureaucratic, state-driven economic policies of the mid-20th century in capitalist, quasi-capitalist countries such as India and Egypt, the new middle class is a product of the post-1980 global liberal turn (Harvey 2005). In fact, old and new middle classes coexist, often uneasily.

Members of the new middle class are white-collar people on salary. C. Wright Mills (1956, 63), who coined the term 'white-collar', notes that labour market, not control of a property, determines their chances to receive income, exercise power, enjoy prestige, and learn and use skills. For Mills, these classes are diversified in social form, contradictory in material interest, dissimilar in ideological illusion; there is no homogeneity of base among them for a common political movement (Mills 1956, 351). Like Marx, Mills does not regard the middle class as a separate class but considers it more akin to the working class. His contention is that both the white-collar worker and working classes do not own the means of production and that while working classes sell their labour power, the white-collar workers sell their services, and therefore, they belonged to the same category.

Examining the two groups that constitute the middle class—the traditional middle class (old petty bourgeoisie) and the new middle class (new petty bourgeoisie)—Marxist scholar Poulantzas (1975) argues that both the groups have different economic relations but there's one thing in common: They belong neither to the bourgeoisie nor to the proletariat. He distinguishes these two classes and argues that, with the development of capitalism, the old petty bourgeoisie is threatened with extinction. The new petty bourgeoisie is not faced with the threat of extinction as capitalism grows (Poulantzas 1975, 209). The new petty bourgeoisie is distinguished on the economic, political and ideological criteria. The working class is not only exploited and politically dominated but is also dominated ideologically (Poulantzas 1975, 230–270).

The sociological literature, particularly in the West, abounds with various versions of the class character of the middle class and the new middle class. With the growth of the capitalist society, a protracted debate has taken place and generated two conflicting theories in the literature: 'proletarianization' and 'non-proletarianization' of the middle class. One strand of scholars argues about the decline in the standard of living of the middle class members, particularly lower professionals in the West, largely on account of the changes in the capitalist structures and technology and therefore proletarianization of the middle class (Braverman 1974; Carchedi 1977; Corey 1935; Kelly 1980; Klingender 1935; Speier 1939; Westergaard and Resler 1975). Another set of scholars point out that the middle class maintained its distance from the manual workers in all spheres of life and ruled out proletarianization of the class (Ehrenreich and Ehrenreich 1979; Johnson 1982; Nicolaus 1970; Poulantzas 1975; Wright 1980). It is beyond the scope of this study to examine in detail the relevance of these theories. Moreover, these theories are largely relevant in the context of European countries.

The middle class in India is better positioned in terms of monetary benefits. The recent economic slowdown and the volatile economic climate made several professionals feel insecure about their jobs. However, their job profile and living style put them above the manual working classes. Even if they resort to union activity seeking hike in salary and other allowances, their bargaining power with authorities make them distinct from trade unionism of manual workers. The consumption identity of the middle class makes it distinct from the lower classes. In fact, the explosive growth of the middle class in developing nations, including India and China, has brought sweeping changes in consumption behaviour. As income levels rise, consumer spending patterns change, as more cash is left at the end of the month to pay for the finer things in life.

Like a change in the consumption behaviour of the middle class, the role of the state too has changed in the new economy. While the middle class was a product of India's state-managed model of development, by the mid-1980s, the political identity inherent in organized middle-class activities was shaped by a sense of state failure in delivering on its promises of the benefits of modernity to the middle class. It is this middle-class frustration stemming from the over-extended politics of state-management that has led to an increasingly assertive and visible middle-class role—one that has specifically been manifested through the rise of a new middle-class identity in liberalizing India.

Here is an attempt to not just analyse the middle class of India in a colonial and post-colonial context but comprehend its political behaviour after India embarked on a process of economic reform. Perceiving it as a class with aspiration, we have tried to study the reasons for the shift in the loyalty of this class from the Congress party to the BJP. The middle class increasingly began to turn to the BJP believing that it would safeguard its interests in the globalized economy through its well-known capitalistic and market-friendly traits. Our endeavour is to study the role of the Indian middle class contributing to the BJP's electoral victories both at the national and state levels, particularly under the leadership of Narendra Modi, and electoral and media strategies adopted by Modi to secure the support of the middle class for the BJP.

# CHAPTER 2

# Indian Middle Class
## British Raj to Post Emergency

## Introduction

The middle class in India did not evolve overnight; it has a history. The evolution of the middle class in India and the different social fragments that were co-opted into it are part of the history and development of modern India, following the colonial impact. The British educational and legal system greatly contributed to the process.

During the freedom movement, the middle class with its fractions has been able to throw up a galaxy of leaders, who played a leading role in pulling the Indian people out of the colonial bondage. After Independence, it served as the decisive factor in generating ideas, aspirations and in moulding public opinion among the masses for a fundamental socio-economic transformation through the development of modern trade and industry. Sure enough, the Indian middle class has its own story to tell although certain elements of this category are common the world over as far as the making of this class is concerned.

Like in the West, the Indian middle class is too diverse in terms of education, experience, occupation, income, wealth and status of living. High inequality exists within the class. The middle class is often sub-categorized into the 'upper', the 'lower' and 'those in-between' segments, depending upon education, occupation, income, wealth and so on. The Indian middle class is largely drawn from a salaried and professional class, and their services are hired by institutions in the public and private sectors. The members of this class were not drawing high salaries in comparison to global standards. However, their influence was significant as 'they were short on money but long on institutional perks' (Mazzarella 2004, 1). In post-Independent India, the middle class is a product of both capitalist development and the welfare state. The growth of the middle class and the economic growth of India are in a virtuous cycle.

The middle class in India is not a monolithic entity. There are significant regional differences owing to variations in the levels of socio-economic development in each region/state. For instance, there is the 'Bengali middle class', the 'Muslim middle class', the 'Dalit middle class' and so on. The religious diversity of Delhi or Lucknow, with a larger Muslim middle class, shaped a different sort of public religiosity as compared to the largely Hindu Chennai. Even within regions, there seems to be an absence of perfect unanimity characterizing the middle class (Joshi 2017). The growth of the middle class has followed different patterns in different regions and sometimes within a state from one region to another. For instance, among the people of the plains, who were closely linked with the rest of India, the middle class grew more rapidly than in the hilly areas which were on the periphery of the greater Indian civilizational process. This is also because of the absence of a single uniform development policy among states in India. Different states followed different economic growth strategies according to their socio-economic and geographic characteristics.

Further, those who identify themselves as the 'middle class' do not abandon their group identities of caste, community, religion, ethnicity, region and so on. These identities tend to be sources of privilege for the class and are often used to enhance the individual's capacity to compete through a group for jobs, political power and so on. There were intense debates within the middle class that highlight the different access to material resources that shaped lifestyle and behavioural pattern. Yet, the Indian middle class generally stood for certain liberal democratic values and traditions. Stability of political democratization and social mobility are identified with the middle class. It has contributed to the political modernization, nation-building and economic development of our country in the post-Independence period. Therefore, we need to understand the middle class and their importance in the Indian context.

An understanding of the middle class is the key for comprehension of the modern Indian society and culture. Dhurjati Prasad Mukerji (1894–1961), fondly called 'DP', one of the founding fathers of Indian sociology, identified the Indian middle class as a product of the colonial socio-economic and educational policies. According to Mukerji, this class played a significant role in Indian history: (a) contributed to the consolidation of the British rule, (b) led a successful nationalist struggle against that very regime, (c) launched a socialist struggle, (d) brought about Partition of the country and (e) became the main force behind planned social change in post-Independent India. The exposure of this class to Western education and values made its members conscious individuals. However, its distance from Indian tradition, essentially, social nature, not only made this class poor in terms of collectivistic orientation but also set it apart from the majority of the Indian population, who lived by traditions. The English-educated middle class acted as a medium, a sort of transmission belt of Western culture (Chakrabarti 2010, 236; Mukerji 1958, 1979).

Many argued that the indigenous middle class was distinct from its 'authentic' counterpart in the advanced industrialized countries of the West.[1] The colonial middle class did not get much opportunity to turn into an industrial middle class like its counterpart in the capitalist countries. This was due to various constraints, including the cultural, imposed on India's economy by colonial state policies and practices. The 'native' middle class, instead of being a 'manufacturing' class, was itself culturally 'manufactured/invented' by the imperial masters (Kumar 2015, 137–138).

---

[1] Beteille (2007), Chatterjee (1993), Deshpande (2003), Joshi (2001) and Kumar (2015) draw this distinction.

Linkages between the state and the middle class that were created through colonial educational policies and state employment were expanded. Historically, a large section of the middle class depended on the state for jobs during the British rule, and the state employees were commonly referred to as the *babu* class (native clerk who writes English). Hindutva ideologues denounced these English-speaking Indians as *Macaulayputra*.

After Independence, the development role of the state has invested heavily in public-sector enterprises. The Indian middle class with all its contradictions expanded in size and, in its influence, has changed much over a period owing to the expansion of education, public sector and increasing reservation in government jobs. Today, the middle class is differentiated not only by caste but also by income, education, occupation and consumption. Change from hierarchal inequality based on birth and patronage to competitive inequality based on the difference at the level of achievement in education, occupation and income makes the middle class more precisely a variegated category (Beteille 2002, 6, 24, 252).

## Middle Class under British Rule

In the West, the middle class grew because of expansion in trade, commerce, industry, education, administrative machinery and different welfare schemes. In India, it has grown because of the British system of education and the employment sector in which the English language played a vital role (Frankel 1988; Sharma 1988). Why the advent of the middle class in India has to wait for the British rule? This section stiches together important issues that throw light on the making and ascendancy of the middle class during the British rule in India.

We can consider two explanations that have assumed prominence in sociological literature that of Marx and Weber. Marx focuses on the peculiar, unique and distinctive character of the Indian society responsible for the late development of modern capitalism in India. What strikes Marx in Indian society is its stagnancy, its unchangeable character. Whatever is changing in India is originally caused not by any inner dynamics of the society but by the impact of European trade, war and colonial rule (Wielenga 1976). The reasons for the slow growth of the middle class were stationary, autonomous and self-centred village communities and the absence of private property. The private property was a powerful force of change in the West, where it helped to dissolve primitive formations of society. Marx argues that real changes have taken place in India due to the British intrusion. External forces, it can be concluded, imposed the process of exchange and eventually the form of private property. Although Marx denounced British rule in India, calling it 'swinish', he approved of its modernizing influence (Jani 2002, 83).

Weber's work, *The Religion of India: The Sociology of Hinduism and Buddhism* (1958), contains his views mainly on Indian religion. Weber argues that all three religions—Hinduism, Buddhism and Jainism—are 'otherworldly' and do not lay emphasis on a rational outlook in life. In Hinduism, the Brahmans headed and perpetuated the caste system, an institution rigid and hereditary (Madan 1991). For Weber, the caste was a closed group, and the stability of caste order blocked technological change and occupational mobility. Weber observed that the Hindu caste order was profoundly shaken by the railway system, the taverns, the changing occupational stratification, the concentration of labour through the imported industry, Western education, colleges/universities and so on. With a few differences, both Marx and Weber agree that it was the colonial impact that opened the avenues for the rise of the middle class in India.

Swedish economist Gunnar Myrdal in his work, *Asian Drama: An Inquiry into the Poverty of Nations* (1968), found that India's social system and attitudes were major causes of its primitive production techniques and low levels of living. According to him, poor work discipline, contempt for manual work, lack of punctuality, low aptitude for cooperation and superstition were the result of inhibiting attitudes. Existence of land tenure system, low standards of efficiency and weak public administration, low level of participation of the people in local affairs as well as a rigid and unequal social structure created unfavourable conditions for the adoption of technology and high productivity. Myrdal believed that the only Indian state had to attack these pre-modern attitudes, institutions and economic stagnation. But the Indian government would not be able to do it, because it was a 'soft state'.

Indian scholars have attempted to fuse elements of Marx's and Weber's propositions to explain the retarded growth of the middle class in the country. Despotic regimes, agricultural economy, low levels of technological development, self-sufficiency of the village economy, static and stagnant society embedded in caste, religion and joint family led to the stunted growth of the middle class in India. One of the earliest contributions to the Indian middle class is by B. B. Misra (1961), who argued that traditional segregation of occupational groups, the supremacy of literary and bureaucratic classes and the hegemony of commercial monopolists were some of the factors which prejudiced the growth of the middle class.

Countering both Marx and Weber as well as Indian scholars' views, Mukerji (1948, 2, 216) argued that each culture had its own mechanism of change. Indian tradition was not a static reality. It continuously assimilated diverse elements within its fold. The initial conflict was culminated in the accommodation of old and new. Synthesis had been the dominant organizing principle, and the Hindu, the Buddhist and the Muslim had together shaped a world view. He felt that Westernization led to the emergence of class consciousness, which would mark India's emancipation from primordial loyalties of religion and caste.

The impact of British rule on the Indian economy and Indian business is hotly debated by historians and scholars even now. Indian authors have argued that British rule led to the de-industrialization of India. R. C. Dutt (1950) points out that the British destroyed indigenous merchant capital, trade and commerce, self-sufficient rural economy and traditional panchayat. India in the 18th century was a manufacturing hub as well as an agricultural country, but the colonial regime clearly discouraged modern industry and engendered an anti-business bias among the educated groups. The colonial policy was to make India subservient to the industries of Britain and make the Indian people grow only raw product in order to supply material for the looms and manufacturers of Great Britain. India's manufacturing economy had to contend with the Lancashire lobby in England. Interestingly, Europeans began to wear underwear in the 17th century when they discovered soft and affordable Indian cloth brought by the East India Company (Das 2002). In turn, the import of cheap goods from Britain was cited as the major reason for the decline of vibrant artisanal industries and the old middle class in India. Will Durant (1930), J. T. Sunderland (1929) and Shashi Tharoor (2016, 3) argue that the India that the British East India Company conquered was no primitive or barren land, but the glittering jewel of the medieval world. Its accomplishments and prosperity and 'the wealth were created by vast and varied industries' in India.

British control blunted the kind of full-fledged industrialization that would have led to the expansion of an industrial middle class. In his 'economic drain' theory and *Poverty and Un-British Rule in India*, Dadabhai Naoroji, who in 1892 became the first Indian elected to the British Parliament, was among the first to accuse the British of damaging the Indian economy. Many scholars have followed him by pointing to low or static economic growth under the East India Company and the Raj. The 'drain of wealth' theory was a mainstay of the nationalist movement until 1947. It had the great virtue of tapping a chord and holding together a diverse political constituency. The drain theory appealed equally to Indian capitalists and socialists, and even to some Gandhians (Corbridge and Harriss 2000, 14). Shashi Tharoor has updated this argument in his hard-hitting book, *An Era of Darkness* (2016), in which he paints an unforgivingly negative picture of the record of the British in India in economic, political and moral terms. However, a section of the middle class, such as the Bengali middle class (bhadralok), and intellectuals such as Nirad C. Chaudhuri, who in a series of books put forward pro-English views, praised the virtues of the British Empire and lamented its passing. But 'the biggest loss of the 200 years (of colonial rule) wasn't the Kohinoor, it was self-confidence' of Indians (Rosling 2017, 12).

The structural characteristics of the political economy of colonialism shaped the rise of the middle class. According to Misra (1961), the middle class is 'a product of British benevolence'. With the advent of Western systems, new forces were let loose in the society requiring new types of services, professions and skills. New social classes emerged with the mechanization of industries and transport. The establishment of the railways during the middle of the 19th century and the Swadeshi movement of the national leadership during the early decades of the 20th century gave a boost to the native industry. Apart from giving employment to the labour force, the native industry employed white-collared skilled workers. The employees of the colonial rulers and the growing white-collar employees of the native industrial sector added to the size of the middle classes during the colonial period. These classes were unknown in the past in the Indian society, since they were primarily the offspring of the new capitalist structure which developed in India as a result of the British conquest and trade ties with the world economy (Desai 1981).

The middle class emerged in India as a consequence of the introduction of English education by the British. The intention was stated without the slightest ambivalence by Lord Macaulay as far back as 1835. In his *Minute on Education*, Macaulay spoke uncompromisingly, and many would say arrogantly, of an ethnocentric stand on the issue (Tharoor 2016, 220). In the words of Macaulay, the 'pope' of British schooling India, 'We must at present do our best to form a class who may be interpreters between us and the millions we govern; a class of persons, Indians in blood and color, but English in taste, in opinions, in morals and in intellect'. As argued by Mukerji, Anil Seal's *The Emergence of Indian Nationalism* (1968) showed that by the late 19th century, the fruits of Macaulay's policy of educating Indians in English language and civilization were not only civil servants who served the Raj but also nationalists who challenged it.

In a country whose culture and civilization was thousands of years old, this was an audacious enunciation of policy. Why has the English education policy succeeded beyond the wildest hopes of Macaulay? The British rulers successfully imposed on Indians an 'educational system' with English as the medium of instruction because (a) the British were convinced about the superiority of their own language, race, religion and culture,[2] (b) the Hindu revivalist movement of the 19th century, led by English-educated Hindus from the middle and upper classes, was exposed to the new learning of the West and was genuinely appreciative of its emphasis on humanism and science,[3] (c) the Christian missionaries were instrumental in opening the floodgates of English education to the 'natives' and (d) unlike other colonial powers such as the French and the Dutch, the British followed a liberal policy of giving English-educated Indians access to jobs in the administration.

The Western education set in motion an unprecedented degree of occupational mobility which helped to increase social mobility. In fact, ideas and institutions of a middle-class social order were imported into India. They were implanted in the country without comparable development in its economy and social institutions. Through the Indian middle class, the British aimed at creating a class of imitators, not the originators of new values and methods (Misra 1961, 11). These assumptions were followed by scholar Harjot Oberoi (1994) in his work on culture, identity and diversity in the Sikh tradition and by Joya Chatterji (2002) in her work on Bengal's partition.

## Strengthening of Middle Class during British Rule

In the second half of the 19th century, the dominant theme for the English-educated Indian middle class was the opportunities of jobs and service in the colonial setting. The English educational policy and spread of educational institutions in presidency towns (Calcutta, Bombay and Madras, now Kolkata, Mumbai and Chennai,

---

[2] English education was imparted to groom a native elite class and impose Victorian values—Macaulay believed that a shelf of British literature was far better than entire Oriental works (Tharoor 2016).

[3] The important revivalist movements were the Brahmo Samaj and the Arya Samaj. Raja Ram Mohan Roy founded the Brahmo Samaj in 1828. He viewed that Western education alone would eliminate evils from Indian society. Roy founded the first English school (Hindu School in Calcutta in 1817) and, he, more than Macaulay, was responsible for the decision to impart Western education. Leaders such as Motilal Nehru, who did his early education in Persian and Arabic, looked to the West and felt greatly attracted by Western progress.

respectively) increased the number of the middle class and intelligentsia employed in professional occupations such as law and government service in these towns (Dobbin 1972). While the English education contributed to the emergence of the Bengali middle class in east India (Chatterjee 1992; Sangari 2001), it became a critical marketable skill for middle class and means of access to colonial modernity in the north (Joshi 2001, 7). Establishment of English-medium schools, trade and commerce and British settlements in Madras and Bangalore contributed to the rise of the middle class in the south.

After being educated in colonial institutions, members of the middle class initiated a new kind of civic activism in the public sphere. They started publishing newspapers, magazines and journals. Members of the newly emergent middle class did not do it to serve universal interests but to establish their own position as the new leaders of a changing India (Jodhka and Prakash 2016, 43). Joshi (2001, 7) describes this civic activism of the middle class as 'cultural entrepreneurship' in the public sphere. It is argued that no real public sphere existed in colonial India. The only 'public sphere' that existed in colonial India consisted of 'European residents of the country' (Chatterjee 1993). English education gave birth to a class that would support the colonial masters, and this class was psychologically and socially distant from the general Indian public who did not know English. Moreover, this class had an uneasy relationship both with traditional elites and with other less-privileged segments of the middle classes, particularly the vernacular, lower-middle classes, owing to their English language skills. This exposed the contradictory political character of the middle class. It is argued that, on the one hand, the middle class invoked modern language and represented as a harbinger of modernity; on the other hand, it pursued a sectarian agenda by pushing Muslims, women and Dalits to margins. In the cultural and political spheres, members of the middle class distanced themselves from the common class.

In the colonial political economy, English education provided major access for upper-caste middle-class individuals to consolidate their socio-economic position. Joining the Indian Civil Service (ICS) was a dream for many English-educated middle-class-people. The administrative elite was overwhelmingly British in composition.

Initially, the entrants were drawn from the presidency towns, then from other provinces.

Nehru often ridiculed the ICS for its support of British policies. He noted that someone had once defined the ICS, as 'neither Indian, nor civil, nor a service' (Rao 2013). As the prime minister, he retained the structure and its top people, albeit with a change of title to the 'Indian Administrative Service' (IAS). Nehru was highly critical of the middle class for its alienation from the masses and even the lower middle class during the national movement. But the state apparatus under his administration in the post-Independence era led to a vast expansion of this class which we will discuss in the latter part of this chapter.

## Religion and Caste Identities

In addition to English education and occupation, the boundaries of the colonial middle class were subject to the reworking of social identities around religion and caste. In a deliberate strategy, the British used religion as a tool to divide and rule, putting Hindus against Muslims. A large number of Muslims were excluded from the middle class because they were lagging behind Hindu elites in receiving education in English and therefore a fewer Muslims were absorbed in the ICS. In 1933, for example, 16 per cent of the ICS staff were Muslims and by 1941, only 20 per cent (Potter 1996, 117; Sangari 2001, 140).

As said earlier, the growth of the middle class varied from region to region. If in Bengal, the Muslim middle class were backward, they were not so in the United Provinces (UP) or in Bombay. In Punjab, the Hindu middle class were more advanced but no less communal. In fact, almost until 1947, Muslim communalism was stronger in UP than any other province (Nagesha 1994). In contrast to Bengal, the upper tier of Muslims in the UP were trained in institutions such as Aligarh Muslim College and had access to urban centres and government jobs (Sangari 2001). Partition of India contributed to substantial depletion of the Muslim middle class in northern India (Hasan 1997, 182). The movement of the educated upper-caste Hindus to

Lucknow reduced Muslim influence in government, business, trade and professions (Hasan 1997).

The problem of communalism appeared as a major obstacle for unity after the Minto–Morley Reforms (1909) introduced the system of separate electorate for Muslims and landed interests. In UP, conflicts over government jobs with the 1916 Municipalities Act's reservations for Muslims in municipal bodies provoked strong opposition from the Hindu middle classes. The Hindu Mahasabha strongly opposed the extension of a separate electorate in favour of Muslims at the municipal level. There were large-scale communal conflicts between groups of Hindus and Muslims over cow protection at the end of the 19th century; causes for this can be traced to policies of the colonial state and the politics of an Indian middle-class leadership (Freitag 1989). In fact, the first major mobilization of the Indian National Congress (INC) had been to demand a ban on cow slaughter in the 1880s; the issue had enabled the party to gather support beyond urban professionals for the first time and helped to create a broad base in the Hindi heartland (McLane 1977, 271).

Tracing the history of Hindu and Muslim movements in the late 19th and early 20th centuries, Gyanendra Pandey (1990) suggests that religious communalism was in larger parts a colonial construction. The divide and rule project reached its culmination in the horrors of Partition that eventually accompanied the collapse of British authority in 1947. The Hindu organizations such as Rashtriya Swayamsevak Sangh (RSS) were very critical of Muslims.

Post-Independence India abolished a separate electorate, and it is argued that a separate electorate was the main stumbling block to the development. In the Constituent Assembly debates, only Dr B. R. Ambedkar held on to the political reservation for Scheduled Castes (SCs) and other constitutional guarantees for them.

Inherited caste identity is an important part of the Indian society and has continued to provide segments to the middle class with an important source of a kind social capital, which has shaped the upper-caste character of the emergence of the new middle class. In the east, west, north and south of India, middle-class membership came from upper-caste Hindus or high-born (Ashraf) Muslims or from service communities that had served in the courts of indigenous rulers and big landlords (Dobbin 1972). Some, belonging to the upper spectrum of the class, had their higher education in England. But almost all its members spoke and wrote English. This class praised Britain for its scientific, technical, legal and social achievements.

The caste and community-based associations played a vital role in opening educational institutions to members of their caste and communities. In theory, the caste system was rejected as a relic of the past and against equality. In practice, however, the middle class largely remained upper caste in character, allowed considerations of caste to govern important decisions relative to rituals and marriages. To this day, there has been uneasy, troubled coexistence of liberalism and caste endogamous practices in virtually all parts of the country.

## Politicization during the Colonial Rule

Members of the middle class did not just confine themselves in securing jobs in the British administration. To safeguard their interests in the public and the private spheres, they actively pursued politics in urban municipalities[4] and a number of civic associations in the presidency towns. Many of the leaders of the national movement were schooled and had their first exposure to administration in municipal-level politics. Leaders such as C. Rajagopalachari, Jawaharlal Nehru, Chittaranjan Das, Subhash Chandra Bose, Rajendra Prasad and Vallabhbhai Patel served actively in municipal bodies before plunging themselves into a national movement.

[4] The first Municipal Corporation was introduced in Madras (now renamed as Chennai) in 1688, which was followed by municipal corporations in Bombay (now renamed as Mumbai) and Calcutta (now renamed as Kolkata) by 1762. The current form and structure of municipal bodies is based on a resolution of local self-government passed during then the Viceroy of India, Lord Ripon, who is known as the Father of Local Self Government. Ripon laid the democratic forms of municipal governance in India in 1882.

Before the formation of the INC in 1885, there had emerged in different parts of India, particularly in presidency towns, several political associations, caste and community-based associations, voluntary associations, educational societies and cooperative unions. These associations were formed to spread political education and to initiate political work in the country (Haynes 1992; Watt 2005). Caste associations founded caste-specific schools and cooperative movements. Many movements emerged across India and of them the Brahmo Samaj, founded in 1828, and the Arya Samaj, founded in 1875, were most prominent. Both these movements were founded by the educated upper-caste and middle-class Hindus, Raja Ram Mohan Roy and Swami Dayananda Saraswati, respectively.

Middle-class professionals, shopkeepers and traders formed associations such as the Indian Association of Calcutta (1876) and the Poona Sarvajanik Sabha (1870) and backed the local ratepayers' movement in Bombay (1870) during the British rule. Unlike caste associations, these associations worked at promoting the political, intellectual and material advancement of the people. These associations not only worked upholding civic rights of the people but also created forums for the emergence of future political leaders. The English-educated middle class involved in managing these civic bodies and associations and made the middle class' claims to represent the public's civic interests. Douglas Haynes (1992) traced the history of Surat from the 17th century to the late 19th century and demonstrated the ways in which English-educated professionals used the local electoral politics of municipal councils to gradually displace the notables, the traditional elites that had dominated local politics and used the language of civic politics to develop relations with the colonial state. By the end of the First World War, the English-educated middle class had captured significant positions in the municipality and as advisors to the British.

After all, the middle class by the late 19th century did not seek to challenge British rule but created forums which could facilitate dialogues with the British on matters related to increasing participation by members of this class in the legislative councils set up by the colonial government and the progressive recruitment of locals in the civil services and the army. The method to achieve these goals was to be within the framework of the law, through constitutional agitation and the presentation of petitions and appeals. Newspapers and journals were used and civic and political associations were established to represent the public interests.

## The Middle Class and Movement of Independence

It is hardly an exaggeration to say that Indian politics, until the time of Independence, was an exercise in accommodation of the middle classes, accepting the term in a more inclusive sense. The leadership of nationalist organizations of the INC and the Muslim League drew in large part on the literary and professional classes. The INC had been founded as a pressure group for safeguarding their interests by the middle class, professional men, most of them from the high castes. Initially, pro-British in its attitude, the middle class felt cheated by the British when it found that industry, trade and commerce, and even government employment, went out of their hands. The English-educated middle class expanded in size, and its political aspirations also grew. They aspired for more share in the state power. It is in this context that the middle class supported the cause of national movement against the colonial power and began to articulate the idea of India as an independent nation state. Hence, Indian nationalism was a by-product of the frustration of the middle class (Mukerji 1958). The representative of the middle class had led the freedom movement and mobilized the people behind the demand for freedom from colonial rule.

Although the Congress received support in its early years from some of the landed gentry and in later years from the big capitalists, it was essentially a movement led by educated middle-class professionals— lawyers, mainly practising advocates, medical doctors, journalists/ writers, traders and teachers. The social milieu that largely dominated the Congress was unfortunately enough to be described as the 'middle class' (Misra 1961). The Congress and the middle class used the very condition of unemployment, economic stagnation, underdevelopment and the atmosphere of frustration and unrest to arouse anti-imperialist sentiments among the people, including other sections of the middle and lower-middle classes. Frustrated young men embraced socialist ideas to fight against oppression and inequality. In fact, sections of the middle and lower-middle classes formed the backbone of both militant national movements from 1905 and the left-wing movements, parties and groups after the 1920s (Chandra 1984, 36).

The leadership that hailed from the middle class was motivated by the highest ideals of patriotism and national sentiment and not by narrow material class considerations. They fought the war of Independence on the platform of desire to improve the standard of living of the poor and the rural population, to spread education and remove illiteracy, and to bring the average Indian the dignity, the freedom and the human rights that the citizens of the free nation states supposedly enjoyed the world over. The middle class played a vital role in the awakening of national consciousness by drawing the attention of the common people to the evils of foreign rule. It organized meetings and spread awareness of the plundering of resources by colonial rulers through newspaper and journal writings.

The middle class gave the nation outstanding leaders such as Lala Lajpat Rai, Bal Gangadhar Tilak, Bipin Chandra Pal, Gopal Krishna Gokhale, Subhas Chandra Bose, Mahatma Gandhi, Sardar Vallabhbhai Patel and Jawaharlal Nehru. Among these, Lala Lajpat Rai, Bal Gangadhar Tilak, Bipin Chandra Pal (Lal, Bal, Pal), a triumvirate of assertive nationalists, advocated the Swadeshi movement, involving the boycott of British goods in the early 20th century. All these leaders integrated to a great extent the Indian people into a modern nation and organized progressive social/religious reform movements across the country. They brought ideas of nationalism and freedom to wider sections of Indian people through education publicity and agitation which involved great self-sacrifice and suffering. They created rich provincial literature and cultures, trying to infuse them with the spirit of nationalism through its different nuances (Desai 1981, 184).

In several ways, the first half of the 20th century is when the Indian middle-class 'came of age' (Kosambi 1946). Although the political emergence of Gandhi in 1920 gave, for the first time, a mass character to the national movement, Gandhi did not succeed in dislodging the middle- and upper-class leadership of the Congress. The drawing-room politics of the English-speaking leadership of the Congress continued to preserve the interests of the middle class, and Aurobindo simply called the Congress a 'middle-class machine' (Joshi 2017). The lower classes, urban and rural, participated in nationalist agitations only under the hegemony of the properties classes (Kumar 1987). Whatever the shortcomings of the middle class during the freedom movement was, both Gandhi and Nehru became heroes for the Indian middle class during the fight against the British rule and post-Independence because of their charismatic personalities. Their legacy helped motivate the middle class to play a major role in nation-building with both the optimism and the idealism.

Not surprisingly, the Constituent Assembly dominated by middle-class Indians set out to write the Constitution for independent India. When Rajendra Prasad was elected the Chairman of the Constituent Assembly, the first seven speakers who rose to felicitate him spoke, in tribute to that prophetic strategist Macaulay, in English and looked up to the British model as the best. The upper-caste men dominated the 20-member drafting committee of the Constitution: eleven were Brahmins, two Amil, one Kayasth, one Bania, one Rajput, one SC, (B. R. Ambedkar), two Muslim and one Christian (Austin 1966, Appendix III). Sunil Khilnani has described the Constitution of India as 'a baroque legal promissory note' (1997, 35).

It was a written Constitution that included, among others, statements on Fundamental Rights, Parliamentary form of government and an independent judiciary. Through such a statement, attempts were made to realize the intent of the national movement— establishing a welfare state. It was the genuine expression of the desire of the Western-educated liberal middle class which had suffered politically under the British rule. It was desired to safeguard the people from authoritarian rule (Sharma 1988, 34). The Constitution has exercised a far-reaching influence over India's history since 1950 and especially gave a concrete shape to the aspirations of the liberal middle class. It provided everything that these middle classes of all cultural hues needed in the new country.

The analysis of the historical emergence of the middle class allows us to identify its few characteristics in the British colonial period. First, the distinctiveness of this social group is access to English education and jobs in the administrative apparatus. These two resources distinguished this class from other traditional elites and social groups. Second, the political assertiveness of the middle class rested on its claim to represent the general interests of the public, often against colonial state power. Third, its main adherents came from those in government services, qualified professionals such as doctors, engineers and lawyers, journalists, partially or fully educated among the middle-level peasantry, and the white-collar employees in the private sector. Finally, the middle class in the West were universal and part of the process of secularization; members of the Indian middle class did not serve universal interests but sought to establish their own position as the new leaders of a changing India. In short, it has been argued that the Indian middle class was the most porous repository of the Western values of democracy and liberalism.

## The Middle Class in Independent India

The Indian middle class across religious and cultural groups participated wholeheartedly in the freedom movement led by the Gandhi–Nehru Congress. Some of the extremely right-oriented groups did prefer revolutionaries, but the peaceful co-existence and the Swaraj movement under Gandhiji's ideological leadership held sway. The middle class heralded Independence as their singular win over the British Raj and against the militant solutions. A peaceful nationalism emerged among them and that led to the construction of independent India.

### The Middle Class under Nehru

If one looks back immediately after Independence, it's clear that the direction of state policy was subject to the middle-class interests. This was not the result of a conscious or pre-planned strategy, but a consequence of the predominant position of the middle class during the colonial rule influencing and making of state policy. The middle class found its place in various democratic institutions of the Indian state and society. The middle-class leadership of the freedom movement ensured that the institutions built up during the colonial era remained largely intact. There was an Indianization of the institutions of governance, but the institutions adopted a few changes. The ICS, the zenith of middle-class aspiration, was retained in spirit and letters in spite of the trenchant criticism by Nehru about a decade earlier. Only a nomenclature was changed from ICS to IAS. Sardar Vallabhbhai Patel, the first home minister of the country and the 'Iron Man of India', was credited for establishing the modern all-India services. The judicial structure, armed forces hierarchies and education system evolved under British rule continued without substantial modifications. It was just the emerging middle class that occupied the vacant chairs of the British administrators, named as 'Brown Sahibs'.

The historical relationship between the state and class politics played a major role in shaping the direction of economic development during the Nehru period. The state contributed directly and indirectly to the expansion and consolidation of middle-class interests in many ways. The expansion of the state resulted in the bewildering expansion of 'collectivist' institutions, organizations, corporations, departments and a plethora of autonomous and semi-autonomous associations. The state interventionist model of planned development under Nehru consolidated the relationship between the development role of the state and the middle class.

For building a self-reliant Indian economy, Nehru, the country's first prime minister, laid emphasis on industrialization. Despite criticism from the established industrialists and businessmen, who were not too happy with the mixed economy, Nehru's government espoused the cause of the public sector, and the middle class supported it. During Nehru's regime, the large factories, power stations and dams were seen as the new 'temples' of modern India. These 'temples' of modern India were run by middle-class professionals. Industrialization was seen as not only an instrument to spearhead economic growth but was also an institution that could positively influence the socio-economic fabric. The process of industrialization, viewed as a capable instrument for denting the regressive social and economic structures and something that could help equalize wealth and income in rural areas, loosen traditional caste ties, and which may in turn also promote inter-religious and inter-caste marriages (Bayly 2012). In short, the economic framework of development, coupled with representative democracy, was expected to usher in social, cultural and economic modernization of India.

Although Nehru was not consciously anti-rural, the state was mainly making investments for the development of the industry. What can, however, be said is that the most articulate and influential members of the middle class had a lesser interest in rural development and agriculture. Balakrishnan (2007) points out that Nehru emphasized agriculture no less than industry. Nehru pointed out that the development of industry was necessary for the expansion of agriculture. To grow the economy, agricultural growth was equally needed for supplying raw materials to industries such as textiles, sugar and so on. Moreover, agricultural production was relatively free from controls in the Nehruvian era while private industry was subject to stringent controls, notably licensing.

Under Nehru, India embarked on a strategy of limited autarky based on investment in heavy and basic industry and import substitution. It was a democratic regime with command politics. Nehru and his planners did not trust private entrepreneurs and underestimated the potential of private-sector enterprise by imposing several restrictions on its operations. With no global competition owing to import substitution policy, industrialists manufactured poor-quality, high-cost goods without any reference to comparative advantage. All these reasons explain why India did not produce innovation and failed to create an industrial revolution after Independence (Das 2002, 86). This is probably the reason why the current NDA-led BJP's Prime Minister Narendra Modi believes that had Sardar Patel become our first prime minister, our future could have been different. Patel was not only less ideological but also was pro-business.

After the Second World War, India had seen many plan documents. There was the 'Bombay Plan', the Gandhian Plan, Jayaprakash Narayan's Sarvodaya Plan, radical humanist M. N. Roy's

People's Plan and Sir M. Visvesvaraya's *Planned Economy for India* (1936). Each of these presented a perspective on the kind of economic and social policies that independent India ought to pursue. Nehru was largely influenced by planned economy ideas envisaged by Visvesvaraya (1936, 146) and the Bombay Plan (Chibber 2003, 94–104). However, by striking a 'middle path', neither socialist nor capitalist development, Nehru was able to meet the aspirations of the middle class, who were equally divided between left and right ideologies.

Following the 'middle path', Nehru was able to exploit the rivalry of the USA and the erstwhile USSR to secure aid funds from the Bretton Woods Institttuions (BWIs) and the Western powers for the country's developmental projects. The decade of the 1950s was notable for many major landmarks, including resolving the Indus River dispute between India and Pakistan, and the establishment of the Aid India Consortium for providing aid for India. Noting all these developments that took place in the first decade of Independence, Sudipta Kaviraj (1991, 85) has described Nehru as a rationalist 'philosopher king'.

In the 1950s, the Planning Commission enjoyed unprecedented powers. The five years plans were formulated primarily by the middle-class professionals with the backing of the state. With one-party dominance in Lok Sabha, Nehru constituted the Planning Commission through a Cabinet decision without discussing it in the Parliament. The economy was to be run through technical expertise rather than the democratic process of decision-making. Partha Chatterjee (1994) sees this step as a conscious drive to marginalize the democratic element and consolidate a version of passive revolution. As a result, plans did not encourage the common people to participate in the developmental process. Deen Dayal Upadhyaya too echoed the similar view. The sectional interest of the middle class was found crystallized in these plans. Therefore, the Zamindari Abolition Act, 1955, the Community Development Programme, agricultural cooperatives, the Panchayati Raj, mainly fell under the control of upper-caste landlords and the middle class, served their interests and failed to realize significant improvements in agricultural performance (Thorner 1964).

## The Middle Class and Higher Education

While the Nehru regime spoke volumes about the poor and social justice, the middle class continued to focus on promoting higher education instead of primary education. In the first two decades of Independence, growth rates in enrolment in higher education consistently outpaced primary education. In 1955–1956, the increase in enrolment in higher education was 74 per cent, compared to 31 per cent in primary education and 42 per cent in secondary education. In 1970–1971, the increase in higher education was 67 per cent, compared to 12 per cent in primary education and 46 per cent in secondary education (Rudolph and Rudolph 1987, 298). Atul Kohli (2004, 266) notes that 'Nehru's government spent little on health and primary education, underlining the superficial quality of Indian socialism'. As a result, nearly 70 per cent of Indians remained illiterate during the Nehruvian era.

The state-sponsored higher education institutions continued to play a major role in shaping the middle class in India. During the Nehruvian era—the 1950s and the early 1960s—Indian Institutes of Technology (IITs) and Indian Institutes of Management (IIMs) were set up for promoting innovation, industrialization and supply of human resources for the management of industries. However, the decline of standards in teaching and learning had become visible in the first two decades after Independence. The lopsided development of education was enormously linked to the structure of Indian society. There existed social and economic inequalities among different groups in India, but connecting these directly with the levels of learning may be too long a logic. The educational inequalities both reflect and help to maintain social and economic disparities. None of the higher educational institutions of India is in the top 50 global rankings.

## English versus Hindi

Under Nehru, another serious charge against the English-speaking middle class in the higher echelons of the Indian administration and in the federal units was that they had no intention of seriously implementing the stipulations of the Constitution. Article 351 laid out the policy guidelines framework through which English was to be progressively phased out to make way for Hindi as the national language. A little progress was made in this direction. Although nationalist leaders such as Bankim Chandra Chatterjee, Dayananda Saraswati, Rabindranath Tagore and Mahatma Gandhi endorsed Hindi as the future national language of India, Nehru's administration was not effective in the implementation of the language.

Nehru, who was critical of the English-speaking middle class during the colonial rule, surprised everyone preferring the colonial language over the native. Nehru's speech in English, on the eve of Independence, towards midnight of 14 August 1947, famously called 'Tryst with Destiny', to the Indian Constituent Assembly in the Parliament, was clearly addressed to the fellow political elite and the English-speaking middle class of India. The question in everybody's mind is that why he chose to speak to people on such a momentous occasion in a language they did not comprehend or love (Varma 2007, 62). Due to excessive usage of English, the *Angrezi Hatao* agitation was launched countrywide in 1963 under the leadership of Ram Manohar Lohia.

The imposition of Hindi led to the Hindi–English controversy and agitations against Hindi in parts of southern India, particularly in Tamil Nadu. In India, we have no single national language, and Article 343 of the Constitution makes it very clear that Hindi is an official language. Therefore, the formative years after Independence witnessed the growth of 'English-medium' schools in the country, particularly in urban centres, and the trend continued in the later decades.

Now, English is the mother tongue of a few Anglo-Indians in the country and the official language of two north-eastern states— Meghalaya and Nagaland. The fact of the matter is that English is rarely a mother tongue of Indians but is often taught as a first language. Speaking on the occasion of Hindi Divas on 14 September 2018, India's Vice President M. Venkaiah Naidu castigated English as a 'disease' left behind by the British, and he was misrepresented by many. But if English is a 'disease' left behind by the British, then it is an advantageous disease: It has enabled the educated Indian middle class to be internationally competitive without much efforts by the Indian government (Khair 2018). Indian IT companies have an edge over other nations largely owing to proficiency in English, which is the global language.

Until now, we have highlighted the role played by Nehru and the Congress party in the construction of modern India. We have paid attention to the limitations of Nehru's rhetoric of socio-economic transformation. The Nehru regime embraced ideals of democracy, federalism, socialism, secularism and world peace. Nehru always gave priority to the unity and integrity of India. He also gave importance to the unity of the Congress as the instrument of nationalism—expressed directly in the first election slogan of 1952: 'The Congress is the country and the country is the Congress'. Democracy was captured by the educated middle class and dominant classes. The growth of the economy was slow. Under Nehru, the state was not only the principal organ to make the policy but also the chief implementing agency. As the state's development role expanded, so did the size, influence, power and geographical spread of the middle class. The middle class, which was serving the nation in all fields, became the backbone of the social and economic structure of the country.

## Middle Class and Crisis of the 1960s

The 1960s—the third decade after freedom—was considered the watershed decade in the life of independent India which was just then entering the teens and was prone to all the negative and positive symptoms of growing adolescence. The decade witnessed many ups and downs in politics and economy and saw the emergence of new political leaders. It was a decade when India slowly and gradually started embracing socialist democracy with many leaders from lower castes and middle castes making their voices heard in the political sphere. It was the decade that sowed the seeds of the Green Revolution and many other developments, some good and some bad, but has far-reaching implications on the future polity for generations.

## Period of Despair

The decade began promisingly with the liberation of Goa from the Portuguese and the launch of two of India's leading financial dailies, *The Economic Times* and *The Financial Express*, in 1961. But, for the middle class, this illusion would not last long.

India's defeat by China in 1962 and death of Nehru in 1964 signalled a new phase in the evolution of the Indian state. Nehru's high-minded idealism in terms of his expectations from China had taken a severe beating. Nehru's faith in morality and idealism in international affairs cost the country dearly. In as early as 1959, the Working Committee of the Jana Sangh reacted to the growing influence of China in Tibet. It demanded from Nehru's government to accord top priority to the country's security along the Indo-Tibetan border and that the territories that had been occupied be liberated. When Chinese invasion appeared in May 1962 with the capture of two Indian frontier posts and the defeat of India in the war, the Jana Sangh could pride itself on having always given warning of a Chinese threat to Nehru whose idealism had led him to underestimate it (Gopal 2014, 212–224).

A defeat by the Chinese was the first serious blow to the easy confidence and sense of well-being of the middle class. The impact was psychological, not physical. Its invasion of India and India's inability to repulse the attack seriously corroded some of the assumptions on which the middle class had structured its hopes and expectations. It was the beginning of the end of the age of innocence and a severe blow to some of the assumptions underlying the Nehruvian consensus (Varma 2007, 68–73).

The impact of India's defeat in the hands of China was such that to get the country better prepared militarily, the National Cadet Corps (NCC) training was made compulsory in higher secondary schools and colleges in 1963. Students were told that they would not be allowed to appear for their graduation examinations unless they underwent three-year mandatory training in NCC. In 1968, NCC was again made voluntary by the Indira Gandhi government.

The years of the mid-1960s were considered the worst years for India. The war with Pakistan in 1965, two successive droughts of 1965–1967, food crisis and high inflation, and the shortage of foreign exchange adversely affected the segments of the middle class that came to the streets to voice their protest against the economic hardships. The shortfall in the balance of payments in the mid-1960s created a situation where India became dependent on shipments of US PL-480 wheat.

Food price inflation is a major setback for any Indian political party. India's strained resources drove the country to two years of a planned holiday (1967 and 1968). The World Bank and the USA had imposed a condition that no substantial aid would be available to India for its Fourth Five Year Plan without accepting the basic changes recommended by the Bank Mission on economic policy: devaluation of the Indian rupee and introduction of liberal reforms. India was holding negotiations with the powerful aid givers from a weak position, owing to its economic and political crisis of 1965–1967. The failure to tackle the agrarian issues and unrealistic targets of Indian planning during the Nehruvian period was considered the prime cause for economic despair in the 1960s and sufferings of the middle class.

After Nehru's death on 27 May 1964, transfer of power was highly dignified, matured and peaceful. Lal Bahadur Shastri, who succeeded Nehru as the prime minister, inherited an economic crisis. Shortage of food and high inflation increased misery all round. Agriculture has been stagnant. It was not the best time for the new leader. It was the scarcity of food that changed the food habit of Indians, particularly the middle class. Adding to the woes, the USA threatened to cut supplies of wheat if India refused to halt war with Pakistan in 1965. Undeterred by the USA's warning, Lal Bahadur Shastri, a pragmatic leader, appealed to the countrymen on All India Radio to skip a meal at least once a week. Even all eateries abided by his words for the next few weeks. As Bose (1999) writes,

> All at our dining tables we were told that we should eat less rice and have more wheat: so cut out the plate of rice for dinner, have chapattis instead. All have been told to follow the 'Guest Control

Order' which prohibited meals for more than 50 people. This led to the most curious wedding receptions.

Shastri then gave a famous slogan 'Jai Jawan, Jai Kisan' and left a memorable imprint on the nation's heart.

For obtaining $900 million aid from the World Bank, India devalued 36 per cent of its rupee in June 1966. India's vulnerability was fully exploited by the aid givers and concessions were extracted for imports from the Western capitalist countries. The premise of these policy changes was that once irritants were removed, India would receive more foreign aid from donors. The devaluation has been criticized as a failure in several ways due to poor harvest and other external factors. There was an instant political uproar in the country against devaluation, which was regarded as surrender to American dictation (Krueger 2002, 14; Nayar 2003, 10). But Indira Gandhi declined to introduce liberal economic reforms, and India missed an opportunity of introducing liberal economic reforms in 1966. It was exactly after 25 years, in 1991, that India introduced economic reforms with the aid of the World Bank and International Monetary Fund (IMF). Like Nehru, Indira Gandhi too undermined the private enterprises and curbed the growth of the middle class in the private sector, which subsequently expanded after the opening of the economy in 1991.

The only positive development in the 1960s was the launch of the Green Revolution, which was realized at the end of the decade. When the new technologies were made available, middle-level farmers were the first to adopt them, which heralded positive changes in the farming sector. India emerged as a major exporter of food grains in recent years. It also contributed to the emergence of a sizeable middle class in rural India. By the 1970s, the Indian countryside in the Green Revolution pockets began to change socially, economically and politically. A new class of surplus-producing farmers emerged on the scene. This class was to increasingly become integrated with the urban market and social life and eventually aspired for urban middle-class life (Jodhka and Prakash 2016). With the assurance of the minimum support price (MSP) for commercial crops, the children of farmers in Punjab, western Uttar Pradesh and other prosper pockets, such as the sugar belt in Maharashtra, seamlessly entered the middle class.

## The Middle Class under Indira Gandhi

Indira Gandhi became a Congress leader in the background of a difficult situation prevailing in the country. The two successive droughts and the long-drawn war with Pakistan had crippled the Indian economy. Food insecurity and poverty threatened as the worst problems. Industrial production was slowed down, and there was continued pressure from the educated Left lobby representing the middle class. The young Turks in Gandhi's cabinet turned the focus of polity towards a socialist state, followed by the 42nd Constitutional Amendment. This provided new power to the middle-class democratic socialists.

### Fighting Crises

A few days after the death of Lal Bahadur Shastri in Tashkent (then in the USSR, now in Uzbekistan), Indira Gandhi was sworn in as the prime minister of India in January 1966. Indira Gandhi was not the automatic choice of the Congress party leadership, which was dominated by a group, unofficially called the Syndicate. This time, the wise old men of the Congress party plumped for a much younger and less experienced Indira Gandhi, the daughter of Jawaharlal Nehru, famously dubbed as a 'Goongi Gudiya'[5] (the Dumb Doll) through whom they thought to rule by proxy, as a consensus candidate. They were only to be proved totally and terribly wrong in their assessment. She was the first prime minister who moved away from the idealist policy framework and built her politics around populist schemes. Today, Indira Gandhi is best remembered for historical events such as the creation of Bangladesh and the imposition of national emergency

---

[5] Much before Indira Gandhi became the authoritarian and popular leader, socialist stalwart Ram Manohar Lohia dubbed her the 'Goongi Gudiya'.

in the country which were the biggest turning points in the annals of Indian political history and were to have a lasting impact on the Indian polity for decades to come. After she became the prime minister, the concept of dynastic rule was introduced in the world of Indian politics for the first time. She ended up being the second longest-serving prime minister of the country after Nehru.

Indira Gandhi, who assumed office in the midst of economic crisis, took a Left turn and nationalized private-sector assets in the areas of insurance, banks, coal and significant parts of the steel industry in 1969 to express displeasure when the USA and the World Bank were not forthcoming with the amount of aid for which they had given assurances. She not only rejected the remainder of the liberalization programme but also the set-up of government-controlled financial institutions for the mobilization of financial resources. These financial institutions played a significant role in the expansion of the small-scale sector and the emergence of new entrants to the middle class.

Indira Gandhi, knowing well that a group of Syndicate within the Congress party was more sympathetic towards the large corporations, took all measures to control the private capital to consolidate her position as the prime minister. After the political uproar against the devaluation of the currency, Indira Gandhi learnt bitter lessons. The decision caused a rift in the Congress and contributed to the Congress party's heavy losses in the 1967 elections (Bjorkman 1980). After suffering political embarrassment, Indira Gandhi took drastic measures for the nationalization of banks. Thus, the 'License Raj' system prevailed during the Indira Gandhi regime.

Two decades after Independence, the Congress system began to exhibit serious signs of strain. In 1967, the party suffered a series of electoral losses at the state level, which marked the beginning of the unravelling of its political hegemony. After 1967, the Congress maintained power in Delhi but a much competitive multi-party system took root in the states, thanks to the rise of a motley group of regional, caste-based parties (Vaishnav 2017, 32–33). The Congress lost power in eight states for the first time after Independence. The support of middle castes such as the Jats, Yadavs, Kurmis and others for regional parties in North India contributed to the downfall of the Congress

(Brass 1980). Eventually, the grand old party was split vertically in 1969. The Congress for the first time was depended on the support of other parties such as the Communist Party of India.

In a tactical move, Indira Gandhi decided to delink national and state assembly elections in 1971. She called for fresh general elections early in 1971. The first mid-term election was held after the abolition of privy purses and the nationalization of several major banks. The party's slogan for the election was *Garibi Hatao* (remove poverty). The opposition parties, including the Congress (Organization), routed in the elections. Indira Gandhi's Congress made a strong comeback in the elections, securing 352 seats in the Lok Sabha.

Towards the end of 1971, India witnessed a war with Pakistan. In the war, Pakistan abjectly surrendered and a separate nation, Bangladesh, was born. Indira Gandhi emerged as an icon for the middle class for leading the Indo-Pak war in 1971. For war victory, Indira Gandhi was hailed by A. B. Vajpayee as goddess Durga. She once again established her dominance in states by winning the state legislative assembly elections in 1972. Indira Gandhi sought to establish control by centralizing power into her own hands in what Stanley Kochanek described as 'Mrs Gandhi's Pyramid'. The elections of 1971 and 1972 marked the restoration of Congress dominance at the Centre as well in the states, a return to strong central leadership and the apparent emergence of a more broad-based, ideologically coherent party (Kochanek 1976, 93).

After the electoral victories, she could not contain the travails of transition for long. In fact, there were massive agitations against the government across India from the second half of 1973 onwards which were brought together into a precarious block by veteran socialist leader Jayaprakash Narayan, popularly known as JP. His demands included accountability of public power, the right to recall elected representatives and civic autonomy.

The country was facing problems on many fronts—droughts that lingered in some parts of the country almost until 1975, food shortage, rise in prices and refugees from Bangladesh. The slogan of eliminating poverty sounded terribly hollow when even a basic need such as food was in short supply and prices were skyrocketing, pinching pockets of middle-class families (Rudolph and Rudolph 1987). In Kerala, Bihar and Gujarat, students were restless and staged protests owing to food scarcity and price rise that led to soaring mess bills. Indira Gandhi's attempt to roll back social unrest through slogans as *Garibi Hatao* could not stem the tide.

Anti-corruption crusader JP provided a platform for the middle-class ambitions and successfully channelized their resentments against Indira Gandhi. JP's concept of 'total revolution' was endorsed by the RSS and its student wing, Akhil Bharatiya Vidyarthi Parishad (ABVP). At a rally in Delhi, then RSS head Balasaheb Deoras called JP 'a saint' who had come to rescue society 'in dark and critical times'. JP reciprocated the compliment in ample measure. He attended the 20th All India Session of the Jana Sangh where he declared, 'If the Sangh is fascist, then I too am a fascist' (Kamath and Randeri 2009, 28). Throughout the Emergency, Narendra Modi, current prime minister, played an important role within the Sangh Parivar and was a vital component in the anti-Emergency machinery that the RSS was able to run efficiently despite a major crackdown from the government. He was an important cog in the wheel of all anti-Emergency forces throughout India, arranging shelter for many in Gujarat.

JP is remembered for leading the opposition against Indira Gandhi whose overthrow he called a 'Total Revolution' (Sampoorna Kranti), popularly known as the JP Movement. The Left did not participate in the anti-Congress agitations in the early 1970s. For many younger Indian generations, the popular Sampoorna Kranti Express running between Patna and New Delhi remains the only visible imprint of the most storied political clarion call this country had heard on a hot summer's day in 1974 in Patna.

By 1973–1974, the Nehruvian model of state-led economic development had run its course, and the 'Congress System',[6] as described

---

[6] Rajni Kothari advanced the argument that there was a single-party dominance in the country, which he denoted as 'the Congress system'. Such a position did not deny the democratic character of the Indian polity as the Congress itself, according to Kothari, was made of many factions, some of which networked with factions outside the party.

by Rajni Kothari (1964), was beginning to crumble. In the 1970s, Congress dominance whittled down and the centralized polity was challenged. Indira Gandhi was faced with a political and economic situation that went beyond her control after 1974. The economic growth rate slipped, and there was social unrest against both the personalization of politics and economic hardships.

In fact, two developments on 12 June 1975 changed the direction of politics in the country. First, the results of the elections to the Gujarat Legislative Assembly were declared and the Congress dealt with a severe blow. The Janata Morcha under the leadership of Morarji Desai trounced the Congress. Babubhai Patel, a veteran leader of Congress (O) was elected the new chief minister. Second, the Allahabad High Court delivered its judgement convicting Prime Minister Gandhi of electoral malpractices and debarring her from holding any elected office for six years.[7] The verdict, it is widely believed, led to the imposition of Emergency on 25 June 1975.

Of these two significant developments, the second one had sent shock waves through the Congress party while simultaneously producing unity among non-Congress leaders. For those who cherish democracy, 25 June 1975 will remain one of the darkest days in the history of independent India. Overnight, the world's largest democracy was sunk into a dictatorship. The Parliament became merely a rubber stamp as were the other organs of the government. The Judiciary came to be filled with pliant judges,[8] and the term of the Parliament was extended. Some of the most draconian laws, including Maintenance of Internal Security Act (MISA), were passed. Within a month of the proclamation of Emergency, the 'Twenty-Point Programme' was announced with virtually no discussion, as most of the articulate members of the opposition were in jail. The government-controlled

[7] Indira Gandhi had won the 1971 Lok Sabha election from Rae Bareli seat in Uttar Pradesh, convincingly defeating socialist leader Raj Narain, who later challenged her election alleging electoral malpractices and violation of Representation of the People Act, 1951.

[8] Indira Gandhi government appointed A. N. Ray as the Chief Justice of the Supreme Court in 1973, superseding three senior judges: J. M. Shelat, K. S. Hegde and A. N. Grover.

media carried out relentless propaganda about the success of the 'Twenty-Point Programme'.

Democratic rights were suspended. Censorship was imposed all over the country and journalists were detained under MISA in July 1975. Many dailies, weeklies and monthly magazines had ceased publication. Tens of thousands of political activists belonging to the Opposition, including L. K. Advani, A. B. Vajpayee, Jayaprakash Narayan, Morarji Desai, Chandra Shekhar, Madhu Dandavate and many members of the RSS, were arrested and put into prison.

The Shah Commission,[9] appointed later by the Morarji Desai's government to investigate the excesses and atrocities committed during the Emergency, made a scathing attack on Indira Gandhi, her Cabinet colleagues and her son Sanjay Gandhi for prison conditions, torture and forced mass-sterilization atrocities. Seeing this authoritarian rule, Jana Sangh leaders compared Indira Gandhi to Adolf Hitler, what Hitler had done to Germany to what the Congress government was doing to India. In its three-volume report totalling 525 pages, the Shah Commission brought out illegal events during the Emergency and called the Emergency a 'fraud on the President, a fraud on the council of ministers and a fraud on the people' (Guha 2000).

As a result of a glorious struggle launched by the people of India against the Congress party's authoritarianism, the Emergency finally ended. If the Emergency was the darkest period in independent India's history, the righteous struggle for the restoration of democracy was undoubtedly the brightest (Advani 2008, 202).

## The Middle Class and Emergency

Indira Gandhi tried to justify Emergency by arguing that selfish, anti-social and politically destabilizing activity had to be checked and replaced by state-imposed 'discipline'.[10] Authoritarian, repressive rule

---

[9] The commission was headed by J. C. Shah, the former Chief Justice of India.

[10] Reported incidents of student indiscipline declined dramatically in 1976 (from 11,540 in 1974 to 1,190 in 1976) as did the number of workdays lost due to strikes (from 40 million to 13 million) (Rudolph and Rudolph 1987, 240).

won tacit approval abroad, particularly in banking and financial circles. The Emergency regime also proved to be business-oriented because it allowed private enterprises to import more freely and to expand their share of the market. The World Bank and the IMF praised the economic performance of the Emergency regime (Prabhu 2017b). The World Bank's assessment supported Gunnar Myrdal's earlier diagnosis: India's inability to develop rapidly was attributable to its *soft state*.

Apparently, the middle class, largely government employees, supported the Emergency. The Indira Gandhi government's decision to hike pay for central government employees in 1973 seems to be one of the reasons for middle-class support of the Emergency. Hardly any officials resigned in protest against the Emergency.

Back in the days of British rule, Mahatma Gandhi's call for 'noncooperation' with the rulers led to thousands of resignations of teachers, lawyers, judges and even ICS officers. Now, the abrogation of democracy was protested by only a handful of people in state employment. These included Fali Nariman, who resigned as additional solicitor general, M. L. Dantwala, who declined to continue as an adviser to the Reserve Bank of India, and Bagaram Tulpule, who left his high position in a public-sector undertaking (Guha 2007, 504). Nobody spoke of the Emergency on the university campuses; it was as if nothing had happened. Students and teachers in Miranda House, a women's college in Delhi, avoided touching on anything that was committed to politics and government (Subrahmaniam 2015). This is because by the end of the 1960s, the Congress, which was an all-inclusive party, came to be increasingly identified with upper castes, big industry, a section of the urban middle class and the rich rural peasantry (Brass 1984). The bureaucracy and the government employees largely belonged to the upper castes who supported the Emergency to ensure that their positions were safe.

One of the most respected and senior journalists, Inder Malhotra, after 40 years of the Emergency, recalled how the middle class supported it. He says,

I was surprised to see that there was no protest anywhere in the city (Mumbai). During the first few days of emergency, the same middle class that was protesting with the JP against her was now in support of the Emergency! This was because after three years of chaos, the public was seeing order. I was shocked. (Ranka 2015)

When the Emergency was declared, Sanjay Gandhi, Indira Gandhi's elder son, had a significant influence on the functioning of the government. Members of the middle class supported Sanjay Gandhi's attempt to enforce the small family norm (Varma 2007, 111–112). In the name of 'beautificaion' of Delhi, the middle class also extended support to the slum clearance drive, although most government employees' homes required domestic help to clean the houses, toilets, wash clothes and utensils. Sanjay Gandhi believed that people lived in slums not because of poverty but because they were lazy; perhaps they even enjoyed living there (Mehta 2012, 116). Many of the domestic servants, who worked for a pittance, lived in these slums. This exposes the middle-class' conviction and double standards with regard to the slum-dwellers, who are poor and illiterate. Both these programmes of Sanjay Gandhi earned the wrath of the poor and common masses.

Another significant feature of the late 1960s and 1970s is that the country witnessed the emergence of a new generation of political leaders such as Mulayam Singh Yadav, Lalu Prasad Yadav, Sushma Swaraj, and many of them were imbued with a vision of reinvigorating Indian democracy. Unfortunately, the authoritarian rule of Indira Gandhi, the Emergency and other political developments of this period stifled the flowering of this leadership. The period also witnessed systematic undercutting of social base of either major or emerging leaders of the Congress in the provinces that questioned Indira Gandhi's leadership.

## Janata Experiment

In January 1977, Indira Gandhi unexpectedly called for the general elections. The country's electoral mood was against Congress. To defeat Indira Gandhi, five constituent parties—Jana Sangh, Congress (O), Socialist Party, Lok Dal and Congress for Democracy (CFD)—merged to give birth to the Janata Party under the leadership of JP. The combined opposition, coming together under the Janata marquee, coined the slogan, *Indira Hatao, Desh Bachao* (get rid of Indira, save the country). The Janata Party that came to be formed was primarily an attempt by the rich and middle agrarian classes and backward classes to assert their claim to political power at the national level. The party adopted the 'plough-bearing kisan' as its election symbol.

The rout surpassed the wildest expectations. Indira Gandhi, her son Sanjay and their coterie in government and party were decimated. For the first time, a non-Congress government came to power at the centre. The Janata Party won a clear majority by securing 298 seats in the House of 542 seats.[11] The Congress registered a huge slump securing only 154 seats. More humiliating to the Congress was the defeat of Indira Gandhi in Rae Bareli, and the fact that her son Sanjay Gandhi was trounced in Amethi, both being their own constituencies. The defeat of Indira Gandhi's Congress (I) was one such event that brought about a decisive shift in the form and content of democracy. The authoritarian rule by Indira Gandhi during the Emergency, bureaucratic excesses, in north India, of the urban resettlement programme, and of family planning—associated especially with Sanjay Gandhi—were largely seen as factors for the massive upset of the Congress in the elections. Rise of the Janata party was hailed by most Indians, especially those who had suffered greatly during the Emergency, as a 'revolution by the ballot box'.

JP was perceived by many in the country as the 'Second Mahatma' leading India's 'Second Freedom Struggle' (Advani 2008, 286). He was the principal architect of the Janata Party's victory, and, like Mahatma Gandhi, he had renounced power politics. Commentators at that time observed the development that India had at last established a competitive two-party system. After much deliberation on the issue, Morarji Desai, at the age of 81, sworn-in as the fourth Prime Minister of India on 24 March 1977.

The opposition's unity was a decisive factor for Congress' defeat. However, due to its disparate composition, the ruling party could not put its act together. Two factors were responsible for the collapse of the Janata Party government and disintegration of the party. The first was

[11] The largest number of newly elected Members of Parliament (MPs) belonged to the erstwhile Jana Sangh (93), followed by Lok Dal (71) and Congress (O) (44). The Socialists and CFD accounted for equal number of MPs (28 each).

self-centred and undisciplined conduct of certain ambitious leaders, who put their self-interest above the interest of the nation and the party. The Janata government collapsed owing to diverse ideological positions and political divisions in the coalition. Ambition, greed and competition wrecked the alliance. The second was that the socialists in the Janata Party wanted the Jana Sangh to sever ties with its spiritual guru, the Hindu nationalist RSS.[12] The RSS wanted the erstwhile Jana Sangh members to stay on in the government because elected office conferred legitimacy, which had always eluded the Sangh and facilitated the expansion of the Hindutva project. But a separation, despite several rounds of talks, was inconceivable, and, in the end, the Morarji Desai government collapsed due to its own internal contradictions before it could complete even half its term (Subrahmaniam 2015). The socialists in the Janata Party feared that RSS would become the extra-constitutional authority. Therefore, it is argued that Sangh Parivar outfits were careful in concealing their links with the BJP to avoid the controversy of dual membership.

Morarji Desai resigned as prime minister on 15 July 1979. Charan Singh, his deputy, was sworn in as the new prime minister with the support of Indira Gandhi. Charan Singh fulfilled his life's ambition of becoming the prime minister. Indira Gandhi, who was defeated by Raj Narain at Rae Bareli in the 1977 elections, returned to Lok Sabha by winning a by-election from the Chikmagalur constituency in Karnataka in 1978. However, Indira Gandhi withdrew the support to the Charan Singh government in less than six months. During his six-month tenure as prime minister, Charan Singh never faced Lok Sabha even once! Singh remained only as a caretaker prime minister before the general elections of January 1980.

---

[12] Socialist Madhu Limaye and some other leaders raised the bogey of 'dual membership' where members of the Janata Party who had earlier been part of the Jana Sangh continued to be associated with the RSS. Limaye and others saw this as a threat and they argue that the Janata Party would not get Muslim voters support if the former Jana Sangh members were allowed to keep their association with the RSS. Advani (2008, 303) argues that the 'dual membership' controversy, more than anything else, destroyed the unity of the Janata Party and led to its disintegration.

The electorate disillusioned by the power struggle and the split of the Janata Party blessed Indira Gandhi with power. The ordinary voters preferred the Congress with its dark history to the daily *tamasha* (farce) of the Janata Party. In the 1980 elections, the Congress won 351 parliamentary seats with almost 43 per cent of the popular vote, as compared to 352 seats and nearly 44 per cent of the popular vote in 1971.

Indira Gandhi's winning slogan in the 1980 elections was 'vote for a government that works'. The slogan had influenced the voters since they were disgusted with the constant infighting in the Janata Party and Indira Gandhi's derogatory description of the Janata Government as *khichadi sarkar* (mixed government). The angry electorate punished the Janata Party for its betrayal of the mandate of 1977. The party secured just 31 seats compared to the 298 that it had won in 1977.

We believe that the end of the Janata Party government marked the conclusion of the second phase in India's political history after Independence. The first phase was that of the Nehruvian regime marked by a near absence of the opposition. The Janata Party period marked the arrival of the Hindu nationalist Right—the formation of the BJP in 1980.

During 1950–1980, the middle class largely coming from upper and middle castes grew in size and was influenced owing to the expansion of the public sector during Nehru and Indira Gandhi. The source of middle class power was largely through its mediating role in executing state initiatives. The middle class played a decisive role in drafting policies/planning documents and managing every state-run institutions. Overall, it suggests that the middle class of the Nehruvian and Indira Gandhi regimes was more loyal towards the state, and this was exemplified during the Emergency. With the limited growth of the private-sector enterprises, the state was looked upon as the major agency for seeking jobs. The middle class owned the notions of Gandhian austerity and Nehruvian socialism. The middle class was very much focused on saving for the future. It was not after consumerism as the present new middle class.

It is largely believed that the Indian middle class that existed heterogeneously in the form of caste and religion got consolidated into English-educated *babus* during and after the British rule. This class supported the British rulers by providing administrative structures and obedient official staff. The freedom movement brought them to the fore divided into two groups, namely, those who supported the revolutionary path and the others majority who backed Gandhian peaceful cooperation movement. Therefore, even though the middle class had a strong role in the freedom movement, it was at varied levels. A big share of the middle class supported the British administration and even worked against the freedom seekers. After the achievement of Independence, these splinter groups merged into a seemingly monolithic middle-class.

In the post-Independence period, the Nehruvian era witnessed the middle class largely backing the Congress. There were splinter groups spread from the rightist ideological set-up (RSS, Jana Sangh) to the leftist groups (Communist Party of India [CPI], Communist Party of India (Marxist) (CPI[M]), Forward Bloc and CPI-ML). All these had their ideological stands vis-à-vis political parties and the state. After Nehru, the Indira Gandhi regime had a mixed experience of the middle class and their political inclinations. The middle class showed three swings. First, completely backing Indira Gandhi's policies of the nationalization of banks and abolition of privy purses; second, totally opposing Indira Gandhi under the leadership of JP owing to inflation, food crisis and slow economic growth during her regime. After the 1977 debacle of Indira Gandhi, the Janata Party government did not sustain and again, as a third swing, the middle class favoured the Congress until V. P. Singh took over in 1989. The decade of the 1990s witnessed the biggest change due to both the new economic policy and change in industrial structure. The liberal economic reforms of the 1990s changed the face of the Indian economy and its people. We will discuss the emergence of the new middle class and the changing composition of the middle class and its consumerism in the next chapter.

# CHAPTER 3

# Birth of the New Middle Class during Liberal Raj

## Introduction

A lively discourse has been constructed on the rise of the new middle class in India with the implementation of the economic liberalization process in the early 1990s. The growing discourse of the new middle class embodies the emergence of a wider national political culture, the shift from older ideologies of a state-managed economy to a new economy dominated by the private enterprise. By incentivizing private capital and promoting foreign investments, the 'neoliberal' turn helped India to accelerate the pace of its economic growth by leaps and bounds. Liberalization unleashed market forces into areas of the economy controlled by the state. It freed the business firms from the license-permit raj, promoted entrepreneurship and eased banking regulations to increase consumer credit and encourage spending.

The liberalization of the economy expedited its growth. The high growth of the Indian economy during the last 25 years has been alternatively described as 'India Rising', 'India Shining', 'Emerging India', 'New India', 'Reinventing India' and 'India Unbound'. This led to a growing body of insightful scholarship not only among the Indian middle class (Baviskar and Ray 2016; Brosius 2010; Das 2002;

Fernandes 2006; Gupta 2000; Lobo and Shah 2015; Saavala 2010; Varma 2007) but also on drawing comparison of the Indian economy with China's expanding market economy, the new 'Asian tigers' (Basu 2004; Gill 2005; Jaffrelot and Van der Veer 2008; Jha 2002).

In 1991, India had embarked on economic reforms in response to the balance of payment crisis of the early 1990s. Noticing the Hindu growth rate during the state-managed economy, *The Economist* magazine noted wryly that India was like a tiger that had been caged for so many years in a crouched position that it would be unable to leap even if it were uncaged.[1] The economic reform in India in the 1990s took the form of urban middle-class protest against the state's interference in the economy. Reforms have fundamentally altered the development paradigm of the country and ended four decades of planning and have initiated a quiet economic revolution. There has been a tide of support for the World Bank- and IMF-dictated path of adjustment among the media, academics and other people, which has seldom been witnessed before (Nayak 1991). Expanded economy offered plenty of job opportunities and brought cheers in the lives of the majority of educated Indians in the 21st century than their parents' and grandparents' lives.

The liberalization process caused a sea of change in the composition of the Indian social structure, from a society featured by a vast divergence between a small elite and a huge impoverished mass to a society of being one with a substantial intermediate class. There is a close linkage between economic growth and the rise of a new middle class. The new middle class identified with a free-market approach for development has resulted in the structural changes in the economy and occupation/employment. The service sector of the economy expanded many folds, and it resulted in increased hiring of professionals and white-collar employees. Of course, the new middle class, particularly urban, equipped with higher education and skills, has benefited immensely from the new employment opportunities provided by the new economy sector.

---

[1] https://www.firstpost.com/business/economy/poor-will-pay-as-india-goes-from-miracle-to-mirage-336762.html (accessed on 10 March 2015).

The IT boom at the turn of the millennium offered jobs for the thousands of engineering graduates produced by the expanding network of higher educational institutions. Existing studies on the new middle class confirm that liberalization and globalization have changed the nature of jobs that the Indian middle class is engaged in. Fluency in English locates the individual within the new middle class and determines their socio-economic status in the society. In fact, English language skills are mandatory for new economy jobs (Fuller and Narasimhan 2007). A number of non-traditional, unbound-to-caste occupations and new types of social relations among occupational groups have emerged. However, there are substantial differences in the occupational distribution within the new middle class.

The middle class became increasingly supportive of the new economic policies as these policies brought tangible economic benefits to them in the form of more job opportunities, tax breaks, raising the personal income tax ceiling and choice in consumer goods. More foreign investment and expansion of industries, particularly in the service sector, provided an opportunity for job changes and higher salaries for this class (Prabhu 2017b). A new breed of entrepreneurs, particularly in the IT sector, showed interest in the reform which promises to make their business free from bureaucratic regulations that existed during the Nehru–Indira regime. They aggressively advocated the 'need to reduce the role of the state and turn to the market as a catalyst of development' (Kothari 1993, 555).

The chapter provides insights into the significance of the new middle class in the transformation of the Indian political economy, particularly after the wave of economic reforms. Several factors triggered the emergence of the new middle class, its diversity and special features that distinguish the middle class emerged from the colonial period and in the immediate years of post-Independence. We have seen an increasing number of women joining the workforce and becoming members of the new middle class. In a new regime of consumption among the new middle class, the media and social media have been influencing and shaping middle-class identities and aspirations.

Does the new middle class rescind its family, caste and religious identities? Will this class distinguish its identity from other classes by indulging in a consumption spree? What is the role the state has been playing in the changed economic scenario? Attempts have been made to address these questions for an adequate understanding of the new middle class.

## Who Constitutes the New Middle Class?

The new middle class in India, as many argued, emerged only after the introduction of new economic policies in the 1990s. This new middle class, comprising a large number of urban youth, is bilingual or trilingual when compared to their older family members. The unprecedented popularity of Hindi and Hindi movies in the South is proof of this. Some of the features associated with new middle class culture are valourization of education and professional education and training in particular, support of knowledge-based occupations/professions, career-oriented work culture in cosmopolitan cities, transnational connections, stress on material success, family of one or two children, own house and a vehicle/car, acquisition of consumer goods, technological gadgets, and planning for the future.

Even though we locate this class around these common features, there are baffling diversities within the new middle class, which are based on caste, religion, profession, education, family and residence. The new middle class does not have to struggle for daily survival as they have regular means of income. Some families depend on a number of other sources of income besides a base salary, such as renting out property, offering tuition, arranging chit funds or engaging in some side businesses such as direct marketing. Upper sections of this class lead a comfortable lifestyle: weekends to resorts, dinners at star hotels and access to elite private schools. But the same class members also face professional competition, tension at work, more responsibilities and desire for independence.

The old middle class, grown during the first three decades of independent India, was to articulate the hegemony of the ruling class, which it did through the legitimizing ideology of state-managed model of economic planning and development. With the demise of state-dominant ideology, and as the middle class shifts its allegiance from the state to the market, it has to re-orient itself ideologically and start advocating the rhetoric of globalization (Deshpande 2003, 139, 150). In the market-driven economy, the new middle class reinvented, and has come to define and represent, the nation as a whole. The consumption style has become a marker of the difference between the old and new middle classes. The most visible cultural coding of the new middle class is the emergence of the consumption pattern and lifestyles associated with the newly available brand commodities. Opponents of liberal economic policies have condemned the emergence of a Westernized consumerist culture that is visibly associated with this class. Advocates of liberalization have argued that the new middle class sets an idealized standard that other social groups can aspire to.

The 'new' middle class located itself with the rapidly expanding private sector and the globally integrated economy. The difference between the 'old' and the 'new' middle class was more of economic orientation, consumption and culture. All contemporary literature on the Indian middle class or new middle class has some commonalities (Brosius 2010; Deshpande 2003; Fernandes 2006; Fuller and Narasimhan 2007; Jodhka and Prakash 2016; Saavala 2010; Varma 2007). Studies of many scholars on the new middle class analyse the influence of liberalization, globalization and privatization on the 'new middle class' lifestyle. The popularity of Sony's *Kaun Banega Crorepati* (KBC, an adaptation of *Who Wants to Be a Millionaire?*) sums up the aspirations and values of the new middle class.

What is 'new' about this middle class? 'The newness' of this middle class is in its attitudes, drive to earn more money, desire to have a comfortable life and consumption behaviour. This is in contrast with Nehruvian state socialism and Gandhian ideals of austerity (Khilnani 1997). The 'newness' is explained as,

> More cosmopolitan in outlook and lifestyle, global in aspirations, time-investing and risk-taking in jobs, demanding in leisure-time services (tourism and hospitality in hotels) and at the same time watchful of values and lifestyle laid down by age-old tradition emphasizing austerity, frugality, and voluntary poverty. (Mathur 2010, 227)

This new middle class has been alternatively described as the 'new rich', 'metropolitan' and 'global citizens' on account of its association with the transnational corporates that are based in the mega/fast-growing cities. This class was epitomized by the young, tech-savvy, professional with a stable income who largely hailed from urban areas. The parents of most software professionals belong to the 'old' middle class: They are college-educated salaried professionals, teachers, managers, technical and clerical workers employed primarily in government and public sector enterprises.

Unlike the old middle class which opposed the introduction of computers in public sector banking, insurance and government departments, this new middle class is in a constant process of adapting and acquiring various strategies and resources for obtaining skills leading to employment. The cultural capital of higher education and social capital acquired through professional careers continue to dominate the new middle class (Udupa 2013). The heterogeneous middle class of globalizing India is marked by self-definitions of belonging to the world-class. It's a strong, confident and growing middle class on its way to lift the country's reputation at the global level by shaking off the burden of the colonial past and economic backwardness attached to the 'Third World' countries (Brosius 2010, 4–5).

The new middle class is strongly committed to neoliberalism which associates 'efficiency' with the private sector (Bourdieu, Accardo, and Emanuel 1999). The performance of private enterprises is assessed on profit, products/services, dynamism and initiative. Here, employees are extolled for their virtues of punctuality, diligence, dedication and enthusiasm. The new middle class does not seek an endorsement from the West for its work. It is result-oriented and pragmatic, pushing the politicians to liberalize and globalize, but tends to be apolitical. Its primary preoccupation is with improving its standard of living and social mobility and enthusiastically embracing consumerist values and lifestyles. The residential spaces of these young middle class men and women comprise at least two- or three-bedroom apartments in upscale areas. Some of them even espouse ethnicity and religious revival, and a few even endorse fundamentalism (Das 2002, 285). There are instances wherein new middle-class members are actively involved in religious activities, social campaigns against corruption and clean environment drives to demonstrate their care for the society.

This heterogeneous, dynamic and metropolitan segment of the Indian society is yet to come to terms with the idea of its own identity in the national and globalized economy and public culture. Traditional identities such as caste, kinship and religion have not been fully replaced. Instead, they still occupy centre stage in certain contexts, for instance, networking and marriage or funeral rituals or house-warming ceremonies (Brosius 2010, 17). Among the educated middle-class Indians, 70 per cent marry (broadly) within caste (Munshi 2014, 2016). Caste, as Liechty (2003) has argued, is still an important means of framing narratives around class status in particular, and social mobility in general. Minna Saavala (2010) too highlighted the dominant relationship of caste and class among the urban middle class in her study in Hyderabad. Many of these caste-conscious urban middle-class members are also obsessed with the considerations of Vaastu. Vaastu experts are consulted for setting up the modern kitchen with a refrigerator and gadgets, study room, bathroom and bedroom with even air-conditioning in houses. Vaastu experts are hired to get rid of social, economic and health problems by reorganizing the location of entrance doors of house/flat and windows to secure a harmless flow of light, air and energy through the house. Many of my informants highlighted that urban middle-class families are more Vaastu compliant than their counterparts in rural parts. In fact, urban, educated Indians are more religious than their rural and illiterate counterparts,[2] and this is judged by the fact that crores of people visited the Ardh Kumbh Mela held in Uttar Pradesh in 2019.

## Drivers of the New Middle Class

IT, biotechnology, telecom, banking/financial, consultancy, realty, infrastructure, entertainment sectors and start-ups are the most significant drivers of new middle-class formation in India. At the

---

[2] https://www.outlookindia.com/magazine/story/the-rush-to-rediscover-religion/209899 (accessed on 2 March 2019)

structural level, these sectors enhanced the economic and social power of the middle classes by providing new employment opportunities and thereby contribute to the expansion of the new middle class.

The country's $155 billion flagship IT industry has played a vital role in expanding the new middle class in urban and rural India. Significantly, women are well represented in the software industry. Upadhya (2016, 169) argues that the software industry has come to represent the 'new India' that is striving to become a global economic and political player, and the founders/leaders of this industry have assumed intellectual, economic and ideological leadership of the new middle class and indeed of the nation as a whole. The IT professionals constitute the most visible section of the new middle class. IT firms recruit employees on the basis of merit, and hard work and not on caste or language reservation. In the words of Infosys Foundation Chairperson Sudha Murthy,

> The IT industry requires skills and merit. We have to compete globally with other companies. So, the IT industry recruits employees on the basis of skills and merit. (Prabhu 2018b)

Merit-based recruitment is one of the factors responsible for the IT industry's success.

Start-ups are other business ventures attracted by the growing opportunities offered by liberalization-provided jobs, although not in a big way like IT, which helped in expanding the new middle class. In 2018 alone, more than 1,200 start-ups emerged in India, taking the total number to around 7,700.[3] Start-ups from Tier 2 and Tier 3 are also seeing the growth, with the NASSCOM report showing that 40 per cent of the start-ups operate outside Bengaluru, Delhi NCR and Mumbai (Chitra 2018).

In rural India, advances in the IT sector have been critical in opening up new potential and lowering barriers to entry. Small IT firms

[3] Start-ups generated more than 40,000 direct jobs in 2018 in India, taking the total employment in the segment to around 1.7 lakh. Another 4–5 lakh people are estimated to be employed indirectly.

and the entertainment industry provided jobs for some young people from the lower middle class, semi-urban and rural backgrounds, who have obtained necessary education and training skills from engineering colleges, and are thereby creating a new entry point into the middle class (Upadhya 2016, 172). Owing to many advantages,[4] young entrepreneurs set up start-ups in rural India and hired educated rural unemployed youth, that is, who are at least graduates and do not want to be engaged in farming (Kumar 2015). Based on the 55th, 61st and 68th rounds of NSSO data on household expenditure, Krishnan and Hatekar (2017) argue that rural India contributed to the bulk of expansion of the new middle class, which constituted three-fourths of the total new middle-class population.

The growing entertainment industry such as television channels comprising news and entertainment, multiplexes, malls and retail industries such Metro Cash and Carry, Food World, Spencer's, gas bunks such as Total Gas and Shell established by MNCs, food restaurants have provided jobs to lakhs of youth graduated from Tier 2 and Tier 3 towns of India. The construction sector, infrastructure projects and cab services (Ola, Uber India), e-commerce firms, and security agencies appear to have lifted several households out of poverty by providing jobs to skilled personnel and have enabled them to enter the lower middle class, which in turn helped in expanding the size of the middle class.

## Understanding the New Middle Class

The definition of a new middle class and its size vary greatly in terms of income and occupation.[5] Our aim here is to highlight some of the interesting criteria adopted by scholars to define this new middle class.

---

[4] Many young people in the hinterlands chose to work closer to home/village in small towns operating IT business, stockbroking, agro-marketing and FMCG, industries located in special economic zones. Although the salaries and perks are much less than those of their urban counterparts, low expenditure on account of being closer to the village attracts them to these white-collar jobs.

[5] In a survey of urban consumers—'India Retail Report 2005'—KSA Technopark, Gurgaon, the global management consulting firm, has differentiated

Like in other parts of the world, the middle class in India is ambiguous and highly contested and known for its 'elasticity' (Ganguly-Scrase and Scrase 2016). The new middle class is highly heterogeneous, made up of 'professional, administrative, managerial, clerical, and other white-collar occupations' (Beteille 2001, 77). Generally, the Indian new middle class is understood as people with a relatively high level of education, engaged in professional service activities and largely belonging to the upper castes. The ambiguity of the middle class/new middle class as a category provided scope for multiple interpretations.

The new middle class is defined through occupation-based definitions corresponding to white-collar, professional-managerial workers. Fernandes (2006), Fuller and Narasimhan (2007) and Upadhya (2007, 2016) opine that the newness in the new middle class rests in its employment in the service sector expanded with the introduction of economic reforms. Recent studies on the new middle class of India discuss the emergence of this class in India, associated with a certain level of income and consumption expenditure (Baviskar and Ray 2016; Krishna and Bajpai 2015; Lahiri 2014). The new middle class is distinct from the other middle classes in socio-economic and cultural characteristics. The new middle class calls for practices of consumption that mark one's social identity as distinct from the middle class of the past and lower classes of the present (Bourdieu 1996). Various studies (Donner 2008; Jaffrelot and Van der Veer 2008; Mankekar 1999; Mazzarella 2004; Rajagopal 1999; Srivastava 2007) have mainly focused on patterns of consumption and related them to the formation of cultural identities and orientation towards modernity.

The new Indian middle class, according to Deshpande (2003), occupies a hegemonic position in so far as they represent India's modern aspirations: educated, upwardly mobile, with Westernized consumption patterns (but not necessarily Westernized values). Referring to Gramsci, Deshpande (2003) argues that the main

---

the new middle classes into 32 million 'technological babies' (8–19 years), 16 million 'impatient aspirers' (20–25 years), 41 million 'balance seekers' (25–50 years) and 9 million 'arrived veterans' (51–60 years) (see, Brosius 2010, 3). Using NCAER data of 1994, Varma (2007, 179) defines the new middle class and names 275 million 'aspirants', 275 million 'climbers' and 150 million 'consumers'.

function of the middle classes is to build hegemony; further, the elite fraction of the middle classes (new middle class) specializes in the production of ideologies, while its mass fraction 'engages in the exemplary consumption of ideologies thus investing them with social legitimacy' (Deshpande 2003, 141). These ideas are potentially useful in analysing the growing legitimacy of economic liberalization as a policy paradigm and also, perhaps, of the Hindutva ideology and of the BJP as a political party (Hasan 2001; Palshikar 2001), which we will discuss in Chapter 4.

In developing economies such as India, the new middle class is still working with traditional segments of the middle class that are largely dependent on the state for jobs. The new middle class is not vastly different from that of the old middle class, and most new middle-class members come from the pre-existing middle class, belonging to the upper castes. The new middle class is yet to cement its role in nation-building activities, and it has not yet transcended traditional and caste barriers.

In spite of several studies, we are still left with considerable theoretical and conceptual ambiguity about the new middle classes. Definitional clarity becomes blurred owing to quantitatively and qualitatively distinct subgroups on account of different levels of education, income and occupational groups.

## Why Size of New Middle Class Matters?

The size of the new middle class assumes significance since it determines the market for consumer goods and the growth potential of the Indian economy. It also dominated the discussions of business analysts and corporate media, who are keen to repackage their newspapers or television channels as delivering a guaranteed audience to advertisers. Under the pressure of liberalization, the rich found new opportunities for investments in malls, entertainment, infrastructure and trade. This created a large volume of the new middle class and, as a result, inequality increased. The Fast-Moving Consumer Goods (FMCG) industry has been constantly assessing the strength of this class and its consumption habits to tap the market for its products. However, there has been very little systematic data on the new Indian middle class despite the general feeling that the new middle classes have increased over the years as strata. Estimates of the size, distribution and impact of this new middle class vary, depending on definitions and categories of variable markers such as income, education and social identity.

Many scholars agree that the new middle class has grown enormously since the 1990s owing to the expansion of the economy in general and the service sector in particular. Traditionally, both the Indian and foreign media have pegged this figure as ranging from 200 million to 600 million. According to NCAER,[6] between 1995–1996 and 2001–2002, total middle-class homes grew twice in size: from 4.5 million households to 10.7 million and expected to rise to 28.4 million by 2009–2010. About two-thirds of the Indian middle class is to be found in urban India, and there is not much change in this trend. More importantly, while the middle class formed just 11.4 per cent of the total Indian households in 2007–2008, its share of total income is nearly one-fourth and saves more than 55 per cent of its income (Shukla 2010, 10). Presenting it in relative terms, Raveendran and Kannan (2011) estimated the number of middle-income Indians at around 19 per cent of the total population in 2011. By Brookings Institution calculations, the middle-class market in India in 2030 will be $12.3 trillion, comparable to China's $14.1 trillion and USA's $15.9 trillion (Kharas and Hamel 2018). To be sure, much of the middle-class market will be in the south and west of India and not in economically lagging states such as Uttar Pradesh, Bihar, Odisha and the north-eastern states.

The McKinsey Global Institute (2007) estimated the expansion of the Indian middle class to 583 million by 2025. Television channel CNN-IBN, in its middle-class survey in 2007, utilized consumption-based household criteria such as a car, a motorcycle, a colour television or a telephone, and estimated the size of the middle class at 200 million or approximately 20 per cent of the population (Salve 2015).

---

[6] The NCAER defines the middle-class households as those whose annual incomes lie between ₹200,000 to ₹1,000,000 (at 2001–2002 prices).

The Global Wealth Report (2015)[7] said India added 6.7 million adults to the middle class during 2000–2015, and middle-class wealth rose by $1.2 trillion. It said India has 23.6 million adults who qualified as middle class in 2015 (Salve 2015).

Using three rounds of NSSO data on household consumption expenditure (55th, 61st and 68th rounds), Krishnan and Hatekar (2017) found an astonishing change in the class composition in India during 2004–2005 and 2011–2012. They have argued that the poor declined from over 70 per cent to less than 50 per cent of the population. The new middle class, which accounted for less than 30 per cent of the population earlier rose to over 50 per cent. In absolute size, the new middle class almost doubled, from 304 million in 2004–2005 to 604 million in 2011–2012. The middle-middle and upper middle classes also expanded, from a mere 5 per cent of the population in 2004–2005 to 13 per cent in 2011–2012. Also, unlike the earlier period, both rural and urban areas recorded an increase in the share of the new middle class and the reduction of the poor. The author's analysis suggests that eight years between 2004–2005 and 2011–2012 have been significant for India in both rural and urban areas. The new middle class has swelled, mainly in the $2–$4 category. India's GDP growth was over 7 per cent during the period and also witnessed political stability, high growth of the service and construction sectors. Although economic slowdown started in 2008–2009, India had not been affected by it much like the Western countries. Among all the factors, it is the entry of educated office-going women into a new middle class that significantly expanded the middle-class composition in India.

## Women in Context of the New Middle Class

Sustained high economic growth since the last two decades has brought significant changes in Indian society. One visible change is that women are increasingly engaged in paid employment in public

---

[7] https://scroll.in/article/765677/indias-middle-class-is-24-million-not-264-million-report (accessed on 20 June 2018).

and private sectors of the globalized economy. About one or two generations ago, restraining the women's education to either secondary schooling or college education was basically related to the reason for acquiring a good husband. Now, acquiring not just education but higher education is indispensable for socio-economic freedom. The middle-class women perceive their individual career independent of their husband and family. An increasing number of women are working outside of the home, in spite of a minimal change in women's roles or societal expectations of them (Lau 2010). However, significant changes occurring in the Indian urban society are opening avenues for acceptance of numerous identities of women. More women in various professions see themselves and their lives beyond relationships and marriage. More than financial independence, it is the freedom to be who you are that is the attraction of singlehood (Purie 2019b). This led to a growing body of insightful scholarship on gender studies in India.

In the earlier economic order, women were largely recruited for the posts of teachers and nurses. Many women were expected to do unpaid household work. The new economy provided plenty of job opportunities for women, and almost all sectors are absorbing women on account of their education, merit, efficiency and leadership qualities. IT/BT, banking, entertainment, media, fashion design, consultancy, hospitality, retail, education, healthcare and communication sectors provided jobs to women in large numbers. Women even entered professions hitherto largely dominated by men such as engineering, business, law and medicine. In the world of economics too, women have shattered the glass ceiling. The IMF has Indian-born American Gita Gopinath as its chief economist. Women's cricket has become more popular as more and more young girls are seeking admission in cricket academies across the country. Similar is the trend in badminton. Historically, the medical profession was open only to members of higher-status communities. Now, ambitions for social mobility have led initiatives among lower-status communities as well, including Muslims, for accessing the training that leads to a respected profession like medicine. The new middle-class women studied abroad or with work experience in global companies have not shied away from assuming leadership roles such as directors, editors, managers, supervisors in the emerging sectors of the new economy.

In the 1990s, the first decade of the reform period alone, the number of women employed in the public sector increased from 22.50 lakh in 1990 to 28.11 lakh in 1999. There was a significant increase in the participation of women in the private sector as well, an increase from 13.94 lakh in 1990 to 20.18 lakh in 1999 (Chowdhury 2016). The overall representation of women in the 100 best companies for female employees was 30.5 per cent in 2017, up from 25.25 per cent in 2016.[8] A number of women are aspiring to get jobs as not only for negotiating the increasing household expenditure but also catering to meet the needs of new lifestyle standards in metropolitan cities. Greater participation of women in the workforce is a double win-win situation as this would significantly boost the country's growth prospects and also improve socio-economic conditions, which, in turn, would expand the basket of the powerful new middle class in India.

In the post-liberalization period, advertisements in both print and electronic media highlighted a remarkable increase in 'consumption'-oriented spending and significant change towards targeting women as consumers to a large extent. A contemporary media focus on the new middle-class women suggests that professional women, especially in high-profile industries, such as IT, banking fashion design, have come to signify broad progress for India, indicating advancement in a country long thought to be of patriarchal traditions (Oza 2006). Before the 1990s, women were seen in advertisements as daughters/housewives/mothers (Bhattacharya 2005, 104). In the 1990s and onwards, women were seen in advertisements from body cream products to cars, soaps to the realty sector and cell phones to banking. In social and electronic media, there were ads telling stories with humour and tenderness, and tugging at heartstrings like children influencing the parents.

In recent times, based on the Sexual Harassment of Women at Workplace (Prevention, Prohibition and Redressal) Act, 2013,

[8] Tata Consultancy, Accenture Solutions, Deloitte India, Procter & Gamble, and IMB India are some of the corporates which figure among the top 10 best companies for women in India. The study also found 11 per cent surge in women workforce at entry levels in 2017, from that of 2016. https://m.economictimes.com/news/company/corporate-trends/women-representation-in-india-inc-up-5-this-year-study/articleshow/61105083.cms?from=desktop (accessed on 20 October 2017).

corporates have established internal mechanisms for addressing griev-ances of sexual harassment in workplaces. The recent Supreme Court's landmark judgements on privacy, triple *talaq*, entry of women into the Sabarimala temple in Kerala, decriminalizing homosexuality and adultery, all augurs well for ensuring safeguarding women's rights and ensuring equality society.

Presently, for the urban middle class, mythological *pativratas* such as Sita and Savitri are no more role models. Although arranged mar-riages are the prevalent norm, inter-caste and inter-religious marriages and 'love-cum-arranged' marriages are growing among middle-class families in India. But there are instances wherein inter-religion mar-riages and love affairs come under sharp attack and condemnation from some of the Hindu outfits such as Bajrang Dal, Hindu Jagarana Vedike (HJV, the Hindu Awareness Forum) and Sri Ram Sene in coastal parts of Karnataka and some parts of other states.

Women registered remarkable gains in terms of education, mon-etary freedom and changes in society in recent decades. But the idea was not to change their roles in society. The Women's Reservation Bill for 30 per cent reservation in Indian Parliament and state legislatures was pushed aside by subsequent governments for two decades. With families becoming nuclear, women employees continue to juggle with daily household chores, dedicate their life for husband and children and act as 'guardians of tradition'. Women rights and education were considered important because they allowed women to become respect-able wives and mothers who could serve the nation by raising proud daughters and powerful sons.

## Tools of the New Middle Class

The swift advancement of technology in recent years has significantly improved the access and use of mass media. There was a frenzy of new launches of television news channels and news dailies, not to speak of the innumerable small tabloids, gaudy magazines and online news portals. Millions of households added cable services, and the media's far-reaching influence on the Indian populace is evident from the recent modernization of the country as well as people's emulation of what they perceive to be desirable behaviours and attitudes.

Electronic and print media and Internet-driven social media platforms have grown exponentially enticing readers, particularly targeting the new urban middle class into impulse buying. Impact of the new media (e.g., TV) is such that the people are apparently becoming more unsocial and are restricting themselves to the four walls of their homes. Social media has not only changed the patterns of communication but has also dramatically altered the lifestyle of people and particularly the youth, who are the most active users of new media.

The post-liberalization media is vastly different from media at the dawn of Independence. The media during the Nehru and Indira Gandhi regimes was dedicated more to the objective of public welfare. Nehru was hesitant of introducing television in India as he was apprehensive that it would be monopolized by the middle class rather than be of use for the welfare and development of the masses.

Nehru believed that a poor country like India could ill afford the extravagance of television. Prior to reforms, the media was largely focused on nation-building and social reformation and used to convey messages of the government to the public. After 1990, satellite television in India has become transnational in nature. It coincided with the entry of MNCs in the markets. The agenda of the media was largely governed by commercial considerations, and advertisements have become the principal arbiter in deciding coverage of news. The concept of television as an intimate and family medium is being utilized to its fullest to influence the rapidly expanding middle class.

All types of media—print, electronic and social media—positioned themselves as representatives of 'urban' India by giving voice to middle-class residents to vanguard their rights against corruption and sexual harassment. It provided platforms for expressing middle-class voices against the rise in fuel or commodity prices, road-widening and flyover projects and basic service issues. The media projected new lifestyle, economic and leisure activities; anxieties and aspirations of the new middle class evolved in the aftermath of economic liberalization.

Media personnel, particularly in English media, themselves drawn from the more privileged sections of society and overwhelmingly upper castes, especially targeted a middle-class audience and addressed a range of issues.

The ideological edifice of 'the new urban middle class' constituted new definitions of news, and new audiences and editorial teams of English dailies consciously focused on urban readers since they constituted the most profitable readership market for newspapers (Udupa 2015). In Bengaluru, news related to IT professionals and IT business is prominently covered by the English media because they carry significant social and symbolic weight in the middle-class public sphere. Moreover, IT professionals are considered as a lucrative readership market as well as a source of advertisements which brings revenue. Images and narratives about this new category of upwardly mobile and global professionals circulate continuously in the media. For instance, the weekly magazine, *India Today*, regularly come out with special issues consisting of 'Indians who made it to the top', be it in the industry, spirituality or sports. Such people build their career based on merit, not on birth into a particular caste or religion, and their 'market value' depends on their success.

In the last couple of decades, the cities have registered tremendous growth in population owing to the influx of people from rural areas in search of jobs. This has caused haphazard growth of the city, traffic congestion, encroachments, illegal constructions, pressure on basic services such as housing, drinking water, power, environmental pollution, garbage, maintenance of law and order. All these issues have been denying the quality of life for the upwardly moving middle class in cities. As brand-building exercise as well as for addressing the problems faced by the urban middle class, newspapers and TV news channels have been providing prominence to news related to bottlenecks in physical infrastructure. TV channels keep separate slots in the evenings for telecasting news developments of the city. For instance, at 10:00 pm every day, TV9 Kannada telecasts 'Just Bengaluru' and highlights city-related civic issues affecting the urban middle class.

The proliferation of satellite television significantly reduced viewership of state programming on the DD channel. Shows such as Indian

Idol, KBC, Big Boss, India's Got Talent, Koffee with Karan, CID, Crime Patrol and so on are keeping people hooked to the small screen. The Indian version of American shows such as game shows, talk shows, dance shows, adventure shows also notch the highest viewership. News channels revolutionized the concept of news on Indian television and changed the news formats.

With the growth of the middle class, almost all news channels conduct shows related to health, fitness and beauty for creating aware-ness about sex and other health-related topics and address a range of issues such as the cultural effects of consumerism, changing food habits, changing youth attitudes and gender roles. The media, thus, positioned itself as representatives of 'urban' India by giving voice to the middle-class residents to express voice against the rise in fuel or commodity prices and thereby put pressure on the government to contain inflation.

Following the expansion of the new economy, the print media has been consciously focusing on new middle-class lifestyle issues, fashion and entertainment, and publishing 'soft' news stories related to celebrities, entertainment, beauty pageants, youth icons and sportspersons with large photographs on Page 3, for generating the 'feel good' factor among the readers. Events such as beauty pageants and film award functions were routinely covered and well displayed. National English dailies such as *The Hindu, The Times of India* and *Hindustan Times* have not only added new supplements for specifically catering to lifestyle concerns of the new middle class but also bring out glossy colour pages. The traditionalists complained that Fashion TV and beauty pageants were an affront to Indian modesty and culture. But the expansion of the soft news should be understood within the larger context of India's embrace of consumer modernity and the spread of multiplex culture (Udupa 2015).

As brand-building exercise as well as to bring more revenue from sponsors and advertisements, media houses conduct/sponsor music festivals, theatre festivals, education fairs, property exhibition, auto exhibition and talk shows. For fulfilling 'dream house' aspirations of 'hi-tech' migrant population, investment interest of NRIs as well new middle-class professionals, newspapers as well as TV channels find innovative marketing practices and conduct property shows. Newspapers such as *The Hindu* (Property Plus) and *The Times of India* (Times Property) bring out weekly supplements to sell editorial and advertisement space to private property builders and developers, with several new features. The media houses are also reaching out to the flood- and cyclone-affected families by raising funds by appealing to the public for fund donation. The English dailies have been providing advice to middle-class individuals investing in the stock market, newly available financial products, and new commodities, which marks the new standard of liberalizing the middle class. Media provides positive coverage for events such as the cycle rally, walkathon, marathon, urging middle-class residents to participate to support the social cause as well to maintain their fitness. In recent years, it was noticed that social movement activists, environmentalists and NGOs prefer to use their privileged access to media to achieve their ends (Baviskar 2016, 404).

FM radio channels such as Radio City, Radio Indigo, Red FM, Radio Mirchi, Big 92.7 FM also provide platforms for the new middle class to address grievances related to civic issues. With the arrival of online education portals and expansion of education, education-related supplements and advertisements too gained prominence since they cater to the readership market dominated by the new middle class that is aspiring to study in prestigious institutes abroad.

The advertisement industry is a classic avenue for representational practices of middle class-consumption. Advertisers employ words and images that appeal to the dreams and aspirations of the new middle class. Advertisements portray images of models and celebrities for consumer products such as automobiles, cellular phones, jewellery, etc., and create a standard of progress to which the urban middle class can and should aspire. In India's 'emotional economy', advertisements are connecting to consumers through long messages or stories through YouTube and WhatsApp (Sengupta 2018).

With data becoming cheaper by the day, the popularity of subscription-based services such as Amazon Prime, Netflix and Hotstar are also becoming popular, and more people are bidding goodbye to cable television. Added to these are hundreds of dotcoms delivering customized services from jobs (Naukri.com) to event management to weddings (Shaadi.com). The intense price war between retail e-commerce firms during festival days is encouraging middle-class families to indulge in undue consumption. For attracting consumer, e-commerce firms provide jacket ads to English dailies during flagship 'big shopping days'.

India's shift to a consumer society has accelerated as more people become 'connected' via mobile phones, the Internet and TVs, and as advertising becomes a more prominent part of people's lives. Advertising is catering to the needs of consumers. As children are exposed to TV advertisements and the Internet, they are absorbed to the general mood of consumerist buoyancy. Parents often found complaining about the pressure their children exerted on them to purchase high-end cell phones, motorcycles, clothing/shoes and so on. This leads to the talk of a 'generation gap' among parents and adolescents around the issues of consumption goods, particularly at the dining tables. In case both the parents are earning in families in urban areas, children increasingly engage in talks with mothers, and even demand money, to purchase goods such as clothes, cell phones, and this has been acknowledged by many parents during informal talks.

## Consumer Identity and the New Middle Class

India's middle class has been driving consumption growth and has brought a sweeping change in consumption behaviour. Prior to global economic integration, the dividing line between the rich and the middle was based on income standards within individual societies. With the substantial surge in income after economic liberalization and globalization and movement of goods across boundaries, consumption is not simply an act of economic activity but also a source of identity for the middle class (Brandi and Buge 2014). There is a perpetual need to spend money to participate in the consumption of leisure and 'upscaling' of lifestyle norms.

Historians, anthropologists and sociologists have repeatedly linked middle-class formation with the emergence of consumer cultures. In India, consumption is shaping middle-class culture and identity. In fact, our standing and influence in society are judged by where we live, what we wear, how we travel, how we spend time, where we dine and shop, and what media we consume. John P. Dorschner (2015) says the Indian middle class has adopted a consumerist lifestyle and adopted conspicuous consumption which is outstripped by legitimate income.

When people climb up the income ladder, their patterns of consumption also change—move from basic necessities in life to luxurious items. Experiences of different cities in India and other countries show that as their incomes rise, consumers tend to spend proportionately less on basic necessities of life such as food and clothing and more on discretionary and high-end luxury goods such as cars, air conditioners, electronic gadgets, interior decoration and so on. Under these conditions, the noticing of one's consumption and lifestyle by neighbours have become a matter of (de)valuation in society. There is a desire to prove one's worth to class fellows through conspicuous consumption (Wessel 2004). This type of consumption behaviour is more visible in gated communities in India.

In general, it is agreed that the characteristic feature of the new middle class is its high level of consumption expenditure relative to the earlier understanding of the middle class and its changing consumption habits. New technologies, new ventures and new jobs are being introduced as salaries soar. The new economy, as mentioned earlier, provided a variety of career options, even reversing the brain drain of earlier emigrants. Increased salary and wealth and availability of a wide range of goods have made a new standard in consumptive aspirations. Availability of personal loans from financial institutions promises to make the dreams a reality in equal monthly instalments.

The 'feel-good' factor seemed to be catching up fast among the youth and professionals who constitute a majority of the Indian population below the age of 30. With 'world-class' imagery,[9] branded clothes are becoming a fashion for the new middle class, which in

---

[9] Brosius (2010) discusses the concept of 'world class' and transnational networks of the Indian middle class.

turn signifies upward mobility. The Bollywood film industry has been influencing the consumption pattern of this class. With upward mobility in incomes, the desire to own the most expensive goodies, such as BMWs, Mercedes-Benz cars, home-theatre television sets, iPhones, double-door refrigerators, Italian suiting, 'imported' brand-name shirts, Mont Blanc pens, etc., has increased among the middle classes. With a breathtaking increase in salary in some professions, professionals are spending their leisure time playing golf, tennis and doing physical exercises in high-end fitness clubs. Indeed, many of them adopt dogs. Some have Labradors! This class that dresses in Western casuals speaks English better than any of the vernacular languages. However, the process of cultural identification is full of ambiguities (Mooji 2005, 43).

As consumers are becoming more and more quality conscious, domestic companies have to move their focus from price competition to quality and branding to challenge the dominance of global brands. Consumer products manufactured by the Baba Ramdev-led Patanjali group have virtually challenged the market dominance of MNC brands in consumer products, thanks to price positioning. Marketing of goods by e-commerce firms, such as Amazon, Flipkart, Snapdeal and Myntra, and mobile-banking offer tremendous experience, and consumers in this category have emerged as smart or aware consumers. But the benefits of all these recent waves of technological innovation and marketing have accrued disproportionately to the talented and well-educated members of new middle-class society. In a report prepared by French economists, Chancel and Piketty (2017) debunk cynical distortion in stories about the rising middle class of India and show that economic liberalism has benefited 10 per cent of the population, especially the top 1 per cent of the income earners. 'Shining India' corresponds to the top 10 per cent of the population (approximately 80 million adult individuals in 2014) rather than the middle 40 per cent. 'It is also important to stress that, since the early 1980s, growth has been highly unevenly distributed within the top 10 per cent group' (Chancel and Piketty 2017, 29–30). This phenomenon has caused massive growth of inequality in India which has led to the emergence of the Bharat versus India narrative.

For generations, Indians did their daily shopping at fresh-food markets and regarded packaged foods as 'stale'. With families becoming nuclear and both husband and wife become salary earners, just like their Western counterparts, a new generation of the busy urban middle class is starting to appreciate the convenience and choices offered by packaged foods (Farrell and Beinhocker 2007). Food delivery apps such as Swiggy, Zomato, Uber Eats, Foodpanda, Domino's, Pizza Hut, JustEat, Faaso's, TastyKhana and FoodMingo have made ordering easier and have changed the way food chains think about their business. The number of food delivery app downloads is up many folds in the last few years, and this may reduce the number of people visiting restaurants in the future. Still in India, one can find food courts of shopping malls full on a weekend. Availing oneself of restaurant food and fast food is becoming more common in metropolitan cities. With their transnational network, new middle-class Indians meet and appropriate the West, in the form of birthday cakes and McDonald's fast food. They eat food either watching TV or keeping a tab on cell phones. As a result, the routine media story is about the rapid rise of obesity and diabetes as the urban middle classes get richer.

Market research firms have been preoccupied with assessments of the size of the middle class and its potential as an untapped consumer market from Tier 1 to Tier 3 cities. Amazon has committed $5 billion to establish a presence in India. Alibaba has backed Paytm, a local e-commerce venture, to the tune of $500 million. SoftBank, a Japanese investor, has funded a slew of start-ups on the grounds of buying potential of the middle class. Uber, the world's largest ride-hailing firm, has hit the roads. Google, Facebook, Instagram and Netflix are vying for online eyeballs. IKEA has opened its first shop in Hyderabad and laid foundation stones for establishing shops in other cities. Therefore, there have been speculations about the construction of the size of this constituency in India to attract capital into the market as well as to direct it to different sectors depending upon the projected fancies of this English-speaking class.

Consumerism, therefore, is no longer a dirty word for the present new middle class. A generation ago, Indian middle-class families viewed spending on gold jewellery as an asset for future emergencies, but young Indians today are likely to see jewellery as a fashion statement, not a savings plan. They are also increasingly comfortable using credit/debit cards and mobile wallets such as Paytm, PhonePe and Google Pay. New forms of leisure consumption such as visiting shopping malls, multiplex cinema theatres, theme parks and bars and restaurants have become a common phenomenon in urban centres. Membership of prestigious clubs, professional bodies, and dining out with friends and relatives on weekends have become a source of identity for the new middle class. All these created what Robert Frank and Philip Cook (1995) call a 'winner-take-all' society, in which a disproportionate and growing share of income is taken home by the very top members of any field, whether CEOs, doctors, academics, musicians, entertainers or sportspersons.

The desire for wealth and consumerism among the new middle-class Indians is changing very fast. The Bharatiya Jana Sangh leader Pandit Deendayal Upadhyaya saw modern materialism as a major social flaw.

Instead of character, quality, and merit, wealth has become the measuring rod of individual prestige. This is a morbid situation.... It must be our general approach to look upon money as a means towards the satisfaction of our everyday needs: not an end in itself. (Bhishkar 2014, 4)

Pavan Varma (2007) launched a sharp attack on the declining social responsibility of the middle class and its gradual abdication of a broader ethical and moral responsibility to the poor and to the nation as a whole. Rajni Kothari (1993) has termed middle-class consumption behaviour a 'growing amnesia' towards poverty. Wessel (2004) terms the present-day consumer culture as 'debased materialism'.

While many public critics of liberalization have tended to focus on middle-class consumerism, proponents of liberalization have projected this new middle class as an idealized standard for an Indian state that is finally competing in a global economy with its changing role. The question is whether the increase in consumption expenditure is the result of increased incomes and expansion of the new middle class or is this growth driven by credit is going to be exposed in the event of an economic slowdown like in the West. Only time will provide an answer!

## The New Middle Class and the State

While the traditional middle class emerged from the populist, modernist, bureaucratic, state-driven economic policies of Nehru's India, the new middle class is a product of the post-1990 neoliberal turn. By the mid-1980s, the political identity inherent in organized middle-class activity was shaped by a sense of state failure in delivering on its promises of the benefits of modernity to the middle class. Owing to the middle class' frustration stemming from the over-extended politics of the state, the Rajiv Gandhi government initiated liberal economic policies to meet middle-class aspirations and consumption practices. Rajiv Gandhi, who initiated the reforms in the mid-1980s, provided opportunities for the rise of a new middle-class identity.

The 'triumph' of liberalism within the state is one of the crucial conditions of possibility for new middle-class formation. The state has been facilitating the growth of the IT industry by providing support, direct and indirect. The state has provided 10-year tax holidays, duty-free import of equipment, provision of free or subsidized water, power, road and land for promoting the growth of the industry. In some cases, the state land acquisition agencies acquired lands from private people at subsidized prices for setting up software technology parks (STPs).

While middle-class employees in the public sector are highly organized and protected, employees in the new economic private sector adopt highly individualized strategies of upward mobility. Their upward mobility and job security depend on their annual appraisals and their contribution to the organization rather than the overall performance of the organization. In contrast to the public sector employees who are historically dependent on the state, the new middle class has increasingly resorted to privatized strategies designed to gain individual benefits, rather than through organized political pressure on the state. However, in recent years, private airlines have been seeking the government's bailout packages to continue their operations. In fact, Jet Airway employees sought the government's intervention to address issues related to delayed payment of salary by the management.[10] The private sector continues to be dependent on the state either to solve its problems or to obtain benefits.

One of the most striking features of the globalization process has been a marked change in the role of the state, with a dramatic scaling back of state involvement in the productive sectors in India. Under the new liberal policies, the role of government remains limited and subordinate to that of the market. India has witnessed a fundamental shift in the role of the state from being a welfare state in the pre-1990s to a minimal state in the post-liberal era. The beneficiaries of such a strategy are the capitalist class, with private profits enhanced through the state's limited but 'enabling' role (Crawford 2006, 109–134) through privatization, deregulation and letting the market work its magic (Mosley, Harrigan and Toye 1991). The state's role was reduced by cutting down government expenditures, withdrawal of subsidies, giving up ownership of the productive enterprises and greater reliance on market mechanisms in the areas of exchange rate adjustment and trade.

The most visible effect for middle-income households has come in the form of reductions in traditional middle-class jobs. In India, the public sector has trimmed jobs in order to achieve fiscally sustainable growth and remain competitive. Nowadays, with increasing automation and computerization, job opportunities for the middle class are shrinking across all public and private sectors of the economy. People are being given golden handshakes by the introduction of the voluntary retirement scheme (VRS) and lay-offs under restructuring and privatization of state-owned enterprises resulted in the elimination of thousands of secure jobs. The unemployment rate is higher, and it has become a major public debate since the right-wing BJP came to power in 2014. We will discuss this issue in Chapters 5 and 6. In addition, a developing country such as India has been increasingly outsourcing white-collar jobs that have no protection and in which workers have no written contract and/or social benefits. In India, the decline in

---

[10] https://www.thehindu.com/news/cities/mumbai/jet-employees-march-over-salary-delay/article26824718.ece (accessed on 13 April 2019).

'protected' jobs has certainly affected middle-class families the most. Therefore, Fukuyama (2012, 53) says, 'Serious intellectual debate is urgently needed, since the current form of globalized capitalism is eroding the middle-class base on which liberal democracy rests'.

New technologies are proved to be economically disruptive, displacing if not destroying job categories in banking and manufacturing and making it harder for the rising middle classes to find their footing on the ladder to professional success. Today, we are living in 'the age of the smart machines' in which technology is increasingly able to substitute for more and more human functions (Zuboff 1988). Installation of tea- and coffee-vending machines not only displaced support staff in many corporate offices in India but also led to the closure of welfare measures such as the provision of subsidized meals and snacks in canteens thereby pinching pockets of middle-class employees.

In the private sector, reductions in the workforce have been happening all over India. HR personnel used instruments such as exit, layoffs, VRS, lockouts and coercive measures, dismissals through annual employees' appraisals, and post-merger restructuring is used for the reduction of workforce. There are no official figures to sum up the extent of downsizing that happened, but the rough estimates vary from 1 million organized sector workers to 3 million over the decade. This has generated a lot of debate and VRS has been ridiculed as 'voluntary retirement scandal' (Ghosh 2002). Very often, restructuring of staff happens when a new CEO takes charge and s/he wants to produce immediate results on the bottom line.

Implementation of VRS or downsizing staff has its own social and economic consequences. There are reports of the increase in urban crime rates as one of the consequences of large-scale VRS and unemployment. Many employees squandered VRS money on social evils such as drinking alcohol and gambling. The VRS introduced by the Karnataka government in India in some of its public sector industries had a negative impact. Nearly 70 per cent of the employees who opted for VRS did not get new jobs, and only a few opted for self-employment to sustain the family income. The fall in the income of employees forced their families to cut down daily expenses (Prabhu 2003).

Aggressive implementation of the liberalization programme and withdrawal of subsidy schemes were considered as some of the major reasons for the defeat of the NDA government led by A. B. Vajpayee in the 2004 parliamentary elections. Sensing the marginalization of the poor under the Vajpayee government, the United Progressive Alliance (UPA) government (2004–2014) employed an inclusive growth policy and announced several programmes, promoting the empowerment of weaker sections, ensuring entitlements to employment and the like, and stepping up public investment, particularly in the farm sector, to speed up growth, although it was a different matter that the UPA was defeated in the 2014 general elections.

The middle-income group has been affected by reduced trends in public expenditures, as the focus of public expenditure shifted from universally available public services to targeted families in low-income groups. In India, where the shift has occurred and provided benefits for the poor, it has come much at the expense of middle-class households. The increased expenditures on anti-poverty schemes have been financed largely by the tax paid by the middle-class families. Many Indian states have written off farm loans for the benefit of 'distress' farmers by raising revenues by imposing higher excise and taxes on petroleum and diesel products which largely affected the middle-income groups.[11]

The withdrawal of the state and privatization of basic public services such as water supply, electricity, healthcare, schooling and roads on the grounds of resource mobilization resulted in limited access to services and at a higher cost. Introduction of user fee charges in water, health, education and road sectors adversely affected middle-class families. This caused social unrest and protests in several parts of India. Similarly, the poor too have been impacted by city beautification projects in various cities in India. Mumbai, Delhi, Bengaluru and Chennai have undergone large-scale social

---

[11] For example, Chief Minister H. D. Kumaraswamy waived crop loans of ₹34,000 crore in Karnataka State budget for 2018–2019. To fund the loan waiver scheme, the budget increased tax on petrol, from 30 per cent to 32 per cent, and on diesel, from 19 per cent to 21 per cent. Tax on liquor and electricity was increased from 4 per cent and 3 per cent, respectively.

and spatial structuring that resulted in working-class citizens losing jobs and homes (Baviskar 2009). This displacement of the poor was a consequence of the closure of manufacturing firms and the removal of squatter settlements—state actions prompted by middle-class initiatives in the 'public interest' to cleanse the city's air and water. Footpath beautification project under TenderSure in Bengaluru has thrown several street vendors out of petty business and source of their livelihood.

The middle class wanted to control the public spaces through demands for beautification projects and at the same time attempted to control the movement of lower-class people in residential areas, although they are needed as domestic servants in their houses. Similarly, in June 2006, the Delhi High Court banned cycle rickshaws from Chandni Chowk in Delhi arguing that cycle rickshaws caused congestion and inconvenience to the City's commuters, although they are the only non-polluting mode of public transport. Such a decision in the 'public interest' for bringing order to Delhi's streets would deprive a substantial section of the city's working class of its basic source of livelihood. People from 'all walks of life' use cycle rickshaws, and yet the upper classes, which propagate 'India Shining', look down on this mode of transport. Therefore, both Sudipta Kaviraj (1997) and Partha Chatterjee (2003) argue that a public sphere/space in India has never been open to all alike. The public sphere of Indian cities is reserved for selected few 'publics', whether they are defined through caste, education or religion.

Despite the expansion of the private sector in India, liberalization does not lead to a decline in the significance of state intervention as assumed by economists. The state remains strong in the crucial functions of governance still, and state sovereignty has been strengthened rather than weakened. The state has been providing *bijli, sadak, paani* (power, roads and water supply) to all residents, institutions and industries. It has held free and fair elections without interruptions. It has been engaged with the functions of maintaining law and order, providing education and employment.

While the future of the new Indian middle class remains highly unpredictable, it has made its stamp on contemporary India in many ways. This class establishes a relationship between liberalization and Hindu nationalism and religion. Following the decline of the Congress in the late 1980s onwards, this class seems to have supported the BJP which has played a vital role in the formation of the second non-Congress government in 1989. In the next chapter, we will discuss the role of this middle class and reasons for its support to the rise of the right-wing BJP and its coming to power in the 1990s and in the 2014 and 2019 general elections.

# CHAPTER 4

# Middle Class, Media and the BJP

## Introduction

The rise of the new middle-class identity has begun to shape contemporary political discourse in India in distinctive ways. The growing size of the new middle class, its visibility and its influence in moulding public opinion, assertiveness and spread of media has profoundly changed India's political culture. Identified with the liberalized culture of consumption, the new middle class first began to surface in a unique form through the policies and discourses associated with Rajiv Gandhi's regime in the 1980s. The introduction of economic reforms in the early 1990s marked a significant shift in the country's economic policy, and the new middle class has spread its wings in an unprecedented manner, which in turn has transformed Indian polity in a big way. This has intensified scholarly and public interest in the political behaviour and preference of the middle class.

The new middle class, which started expanding along with the spectacular growth of the electronic and print media since the last decade of the 20th century, is pushing the politicians to embrace economic liberalization and globalization. The BJP, which has sensed the benefits and privileges of liberalization offered to the middle class, attempts to position itself as a party for India's growing middle class (Mehta 2019). In a broader sense, the BJP is the party of the urban middle class largely comprising small traders, civil servants and professionals (Kim 2006). The 'democratic upsurge' of the OBCs in the electoral process, which occurred alongside with reforms and the rise of the BJP, marked the reinvention of India's politics dominated by the politics of Hindutva. This 'second democratic upsurge' is closely identified with three 'Ms'—'Mandal' (B. P. Mandal Commission's report), 'Mandir' (Ram Temple–Babri Masjid dispute) and 'Market' (a new economic order) (Kapila 2016, 47).

The mass media played a major role in shaping the BJP's identity and projecting it as a pan-Indian Hindu national entity. Mass media did so by allowing the BJP to project a single image that reaches its wider constituency, which allows disparate groups to overlook their differences and unite under the Hindutva ideology (Hardgrave 1993). Indeed, these issues essentially constituted watersheds in the life of the nation.

In this context, the chapter becomes necessary to uncover the major changes in the topography of Indian politics since the establishment of the BJP. Although existing studies have tended to focus primarily on the politics of the elite, the peasants and the OBCs at the national and local levels, it is an approach that has led to the neglect of impact of the new middle class on the Indian polity. The question explored in this chapter is how the rise of the new middle class along with the media changed the dynamics of Indian democratic politics during the last few decades. The most perplexing question is what persuaded the Hindu electorate, particularly the Hindu new middle class, to increasingly vote for the BJP. One wonders whether it is one single Ram Janmabhoomi movement or multiple developments that enable the BJP to garner the support of the middle class. It is essential therefore to analyse circumstances under which the new middle class supported the rise of the BJP. The BJP, which has emerged as one of the two principal poles in India's polity today, contributed to the transformation of Indian electoral politics from a Congress's single-party-dominated system to a multi-party system where coalition-building has become a necessity for forming a government.

Undoubtedly, the new middle class created niches for the BJP right from its inception. It not only contributed to the BJP's rise to power in 1998 but also the re-election of its coalition, the NDA, in 1999. The middle class sets the terms of reference of Indian society and polity not only because of its development but also because it is the darling of the official discourse and policymakers (Jaffrelot and Van der Veer 2008, 20). As the BJP and the new middle class have grown parallel to each other since the mid-1980s, the chapter primarily focuses on the role of the new middle class and media influencing and shaping the democratic polity of India since the 1980s. The influence of the new middle class and media in Indian politics and reasons for their support for the BJP, which challenged the dominance of the Congress, are examined. Here, the terms 'middle class' and the 'new middle class' used to refer to the essentiality of the same economic and political philosophy. In reality, the middle class includes the new middle class.

## From Jana Sangh to the BJP

The BJP has its roots in the Bharatiya Jana Sangh (Indian People's Party), popularly known as Jana Sangh. The Jana Sangh was formed in 1951, on the eve of the first national elections, by Shyama Prasad Mukherjee in collaboration with the RSS as a 'nationalistic alternative' to the INC. Mukherjee was appointed the President of the Hindu Mahasabha in 1944 and was Union Minister for Industry for three years (1947–1950). In line with its ideology, the Jana Sangh strongly supported a stringent policy against the hereditary foe, Pakistan and arch enemy, China. It is also averse to the communism of erstwhile USSR. The Jana Sangh demanded a ban on cow slaughter since the early 1960s and revocation of Article 370 of the Constitution that gave special status to Jammu and Kashmir, a state in India.

Soon after Independence, the RSS leaders realized they could not remain out of politics. The formation of Jana Sangh was precipitated by the ban of the RSS after Mahatma Gandhi's assassination in January 1948 by Nathuram Godse, a member of RSS from Maharashtra. The RSS made it clear that it was vulnerable to politically organized groups and had no political representation at the national level. Those who had gone underground then discovered that no major political party was prepared to support the cause of the RSS in parliament or elsewhere. K. R. Malkani, one of the RSS leaders, supported the formation of the party. The second 'Sarsanghchalak' (supreme chief) of the RSS, M. S. Golwalkar, approved the opinion of Malkani and others regarding the formation of a new party in 1950, after the demise of Deputy Prime Minister Sardar Vallabhbhai Patel who, in his opinion, could have transformed the Congress by emphasizing its affinities with Hindu nationalism. Sardar Patel, whom the BJP claimed was a conservative leader for his tolerance of Hindu orthodoxy, was interpreted as a Hindu nationalist. In the 1950s, Patel successfully got a resolution passed in the Congress Working Committee which opened doors to the RSS *swayamsevaks*. However, Jawaharlal Nehru, who was abroad at that time, after his return, reversed the decision (Jaffrelot 2007, 176, 188). Patel's sudden death in 1950 is believed to have allowed Pandit Nehru's 'pseudo-secular' suppression of Hindu culture in favour of Muslims and other minorities to flourish unchecked (Rajagopal 2001, 57). On 5 January 1952, Nehru said that the Jana Sangh was the 'illegitimate child of the RSS' (Noorani 2009). Knowing well Nehru's secular credentials, the RSS lent its support to the formation of the Jana Sangh. It has been recognized that the RSS never shed its sociocultural focus while supporting the Jana Sangh.

The Jana Sangh could not compete with the well-organized electoral machinery of Nehru's Congress which had a network from rural to the national capital. Moreover, in the 1950s, Nehru succeeded in isolating and marginalizing the Hindu nationalists, contesting their legitimacy, repressing their activities and establishing secularism as the norm of the Indian political system. The Jana Sangh's support for a Hindu state did not materialize with the electorate as the Congress party dominated the Indian politics until 1977. The Jana Sangh had more or less stayed close to its North Indian petty bourgeois constituents, mainly the upper castes, and had never made efforts to cast itself as a national party (Graham 1990). Its upper-caste bias made it electorally weak. Although it contested all general elections before the merger with the Janata Party in 1977, its best performance was in 1967 with 35 Lok Sabha seats.

In 1977, the Janata Party established the first non-Congress national government and erstwhile Jana Sangh leaders Atal Bihari Vajpayee and Lal Krishna Advani served as cabinet ministers in the Morarji Desai government. But the Janata Party government did not last long as a full-blown controversy erupted over the dual membership of the Jana Sangh members to the Janata Party and the RSS. With the dual-membership issue turning into a major cause of friction amongst a section of party leaders, the Janata Party national executive expelled former members of the Jana Sangh from the organization on 4 April 1980. It is in this context that, on 6 April 1980, over hundreds of delegates assembled at the Feroz Shah Kotla Ground (now Arun Jaitley Stadium) in the national capital and endorsed Atalji's proposal that the new party be named 'Bharatiya Janata Party', which, emphatically affirmed the leaders' link with both the Bharatiya Jana Sangh and the Janata Party. Vajpayee was elected the first President of the BJP.

There was significant ideological re-projection of the new party. Although Pandit Deendayal Upadhyaya's[1] 'Integral Humanism' continued to be the guiding philosophy of the BJP, the party also reaffirmed its commitment to 'Gandhian socialism'. Advani argues that the BJP adopted Gandhian socialism as a positive alternative to communism. The BJP also adopted 'five basic commitments'; these were (a) nationalism and national integration, (b) democracy, (c) Gandhian philosophy (d) positive secularism and (e) value-based politics.

The formation of the BJP had a definite political context. From the early 1980s, separatist movements became increasingly more vocal, which had the effect of encouraging Hindu nationalism. The Sikh separatist Khalistan movement, the Assamese students' protest against Bangladeshi illegal immigrants and Tamil separatism in neighbouring Sri Lanka helped the BJP to carve out a distinctive space for itself as a defender of Hindu interests (Tharoor 2018a, 179–180). The BJP officially adopted Hindutva, the concept coined by a former anti-British revolutionary, V. D. Savarkar, as its defining credo in June

---

[1] Pandit Deendayal Upadhyaya was the President of the Jana Sangha after the sudden death of S. P. Mukherjee in 1953. He was, first and foremost, an ideologue, probably the last major Hindu nationalist ideologue.

1989 at its convention at Palampur in Himachal Pradesh. Savarkar wrote *Hindutva: Who Is a Hindu?* in 1921 while he was in a prison of the British at Ratnagiri, Maharashtra. His book was the first attempt at endowing what he called the Hindu Rashtra (the Hindu nation) with a clear-cut identity, namely, Hindutva.[2] It is the doctrine industriously promoted by the RSS, and its affiliated family of organizations in the 'Sangh Parivar', mainly the Vishva Hindu Parishad (VHP), established in 1964.

## Rajiv Gandhi's Rise with Middle-Class Support

The 1980s fundamentally altered India's political landscape, and the decade witnessed two major political developments that stood out for their significance in the long run: the end of Congress hegemony in politics and the emergence of the nationalist party, BJP. The decade began with Indira Gandhi's triumphant return to power in January 1980, just three and a half years after her stunning electoral defeat, caused largely by her Emergency excesses. The formation of the BJP did not result in immediate electoral gains for it.

Prime Minister Indira Gandhi was assassinated on 31 October 1984. In no time, two developments took place. First, in a hurried decision, President Giani Zail Singh administered an oath of the Prime Minister's Office (PMO) to Rajiv Gandhi, which was considered constitutional. But it legitimized dynastic succession. Second, the assassination was followed by the orgy of retaliatory violence against Sikhs, who were unjustifiably held to be responsible for the assassination, merely because Indira Gandhi's killers were her Sikh bodyguards

---

[2] According to V. D. Savarkar, the term 'Hindutva' describes the 'quality of being Hindu' in ethnic, cultural and political terms. He argued that a Hindu is one who considers India to be his motherland (*matrbhumi*), the land of his ancestors (*pitrbhumi*) and his holy land (*punya bhumi*). The three essentials of Hindutva were said to be the common nation (*rastra*), common race and common culture/civilization (*sanskriti*). India is the land of the Hindus since their ethnicity is Indian and since the Hindu faith originated in India. The notion of Hindutva formed the foundation for Savarkar's Hindu nationalism, which included in its fold the followers of all Indian religions including Buddhism, Jainism and Sikhism, but excluded followers of 'foreign religions' such as Islam and Christianity.

(Subrahmaniam 2015). Unfortunately for Sikhs, the Congress was voted to power. Instead of controlling the shameful anti-Sikh riots in Delhi and some surrounding areas that had begun immediately after Indira Gandhi's assassination, Congress leaders joined in engineering the programme. To make matters worse, Rajiv insensitively told a public meeting that 'when a big tree falls, the earth is bound to shake'. He played heavily on the anti-Sikh sentiments, appeased Hindu chauvinism much like Indira had tried to do during the early 1980s (Malhotra 2003). Therefore, the anti-Sikh riots of 1984 still stand as an indictment of Nehruvian secularism (Meghnad Desai 2016, 20). After 35 years, in 2019, the former Prime Minister Manmohan Singh blamed the then Home Minister P. V. Narasimha Rao for the anti-Sikh riots and said the massacre could had been avoided if Rao had heeded the advice of the former Prime Minister I. K. Gujral in deploying the army at the earliest.[3]

Within hours of the assassination of Indira Gandhi, the ruling Congress made the most brazen use of government-owned Doordarshan (DD), the only TV channel at that time in the country, for its narrow political gains. The DD cameras were focused almost exclusively on Rajiv Gandhi sitting beside his mother's bullet-ridden body. Homage and condolence offered by the Opposition leaders were completely blacked out.[4] The media played an important role in political campaigns during Rajiv Gandhi's 1984-bid for the position of prime minister (Chopra 2006; Gould 1986).

Riding on the sympathy wave of Gandhi's assassination, the Congress secured an unparalleled victory (404 seats) in the 1984 parliamentary elections. The Lok Sabha elections in the two states of Punjab and Assam were not held in 1984 due to the ongoing terrorist activities in the states. Elections were held in these two states

---

[3] https://www.indiatoday.in/india/story/1984-sikh-riots-could-have-been-avoided-if-narasimha-rao-listened-to-ik-gujaral-manmohan-singh-1625242-2019-12-04 (accessed on 6 December 2019).

[4] On funeral day (2 November 1984), DD deliberately chose not to show the presence of Opposition leaders such as A. B. Vajpayee, L. K. Advani, Chandra Shekhar and Madhu Dandavate. The DD's coverage had given impression to the public that the Opposition boycotted Gandhi's funeral (see Advani 2008, 434).

in 1985. The Congress won six and four seats in Punjab and Assam, respectively, taking the party's total tally to 414 in the Lok Sabha. In spite of the middle-class hatred towards the Nehru–Gandhi family, it had elected Rajiv Gandhi for the PMO (1984–1989) when he was just 40. The BJP became the worst victim of the 'sympathy wave' in the elections and managed to win just two seats. Disillusioned with this unsuccessful attempt at seeking political respectability by tempering its core beliefs, the BJP transformed itself into an explicitly Hindu party, stirring up Hindu sentiment.

The Rajiv Gandhi period what political scientist Suhas Palshikar (2001, 171) says was an era that 'witnessed the romantic liaison of Indian middle class with politics'. The 'middle-classes were keen supporters of Rajiv Gandhi' (Hasan 2001, 159). Before he became the prime minister, the middle classes were generally believed to hold a cynical attitude towards politics. In a crowded democracy, politics was largely seen as a field where the illiterate and uneducated masses mattered more than the educated middle class. Rajiv Gandhi changed, at least momentarily, some of these images of politics and politicians. He promised a form of modernity epitomized by his motto 'to prepare India's entry into the 21st century' (Weiner 1989). His good manners, contrasting with Sanjay Gandhi's brashness combined with his 'Mr Clean' image, added to his popularity (Malhotra 2014).

Rajiv Gandhi brought in new faces—many of them were professionals and experts—into politics. Development for Rajiv Gandhi meant technological development, a gateway to the '21st century'. The middle class appreciated his style of politics since he was free from all ideological hues and was practical with an open mind. In his taste and style of dress, familiarity with computers and technology, he was a visionary man. He had encouraged Texas Instruments to set up a satellite facility in Bengaluru, India's Silicon Valley, way back in 1985. Political scientist Varshney (1999b) says Rajiv Gandhi was the first prime minister who knew what modern technology, market competition and private entrepreneurism could do to the country's economic upliftment. Nehru understood the power of modern technology, not that of market competition; Indira understood neither; Rajiv understood both.

Moreover, a new Indian middle class began to emerge with gradual liberalization of the economy by Rajiv Gandhi. The middle-class desire for consumption began first in a unique way through the liberal policies pursued by Rajiv Gandhi in the 1980s. Certain policy decisions were taken during the period, for example, domestic production of 'white' goods (e.g., refrigerator, television, video, washing machine and so on), catered to the needs of the new middle class, with credit from private banks. An alternative to the Ambassador car, a new brand of car, Maruti, was rolled out, and it became middle-class families' dream car, even till now.

Besides giving a boost to the software industry, the Rajiv Gandhi government deliberately lowered taxes to middle classes so as to boost demand, especially for consumer durables. Rajiv quickly won the support of the media and of urban middle classes with his promise of consumption-led growth and his criticism of the public sector. All these new policy initiatives enabled India to make a breakthrough, moving beyond the 'Hindu growth rate' to a more rapidly growing economy, an increase in GDP of around 3.5 per cent during 1950s–1970s to 5.5 per cent in 1980s. Unlike his mother, Rajiv Gandhi dropped the pretence of socialism altogether and openly committed his government to a new 'liberal' beginning (Kohli 2004).

## Causes for the Rise of the BJP and the Middle Class

Rajiv Gandhi was caught up in a whirlpool of difficulties in the late 1980s. Major developments such as the Bofors scandal, the Shah Bano case, the Salman Rushdie affair and the launch of the Jan Morcha (people's platform) movement by V. P. Singh against the government not only sullied the image and credibility of the ruling Congress and its prime minister but also created the political space for the BJP to emerge as the national party in the 1989 national election.

Rajiv Gandhi's 'Mr Clean' image received a major dent when the Bofors corruption scandal broke out in public. The man who lit the fuse of the major scandal was a political insider and Rajiv Gandhi's Finance Minister, V. P. Singh. As the finance minister, Singh won public acclaim for launching an offensive against tax evaders, gold smugglers and black-money holders. A number of high-profile income tax raids were conducted on suspected tax evaders and well-known industrialists who had supported the Congress financially in the past. This had caused some sorts of political embarrassment for the Congress, although it posed no threat to the government which commanded a historic majority in the lower house of the parliament.

In an act of spectacular political misreading in 1987, Rajiv Gandhi shifted V. P. Singh from the Ministry of Finance to the Ministry of Defence amid speculation that he was unhappy with this crusade against certain corporate wrongdoers. Singh immediately busied himself to enquire into the opaque system of defence procurement and ordered an investigation into the alleged scandal involving the acquisition of German submarines (Ram 2017, xxiii). This did not go well with the prime minister, who said he had not been consulted. Singh further ordered an investigation into the suspected payoffs in the government's procurement of 155 mm Howitzer field guns from the biggest Swedish arms manufacturer, Bofors. The deal was signed between the two countries on 24 March 1986.

Singh, who was defence minister for just four months, resigned from the government, alleging a cover-up and walked with the honour of an anti-corruption crusader. Shortly thereafter, he was expelled from the Congress party. A few days later, the Swedish State Radio had broadcast a startling report alleging that Bofors paid kickbacks to Indian politicians and key defence officials for signing the deal. The Swedish radio report hit the Indian political establishment badly. The campaign against the cover-up in the deal caught the nation's attention which led to the ouster of the Rajiv Gandhi's government in the 1989 general election. Now, over three decades after the deal, the Bofors saga continues to echo in the Indian parliament, and, has persisted even in the Modi government.

One of the blatant cases of government intolerance of the media exposure of its misdeeds, particularly Bofors, was the massive country-wide raids conducted by officials of Central Intelligence and Directorate of Revenue Intelligence in the offices of the English-language daily *The Indian Express* on 1 September 1987. Rajiv Gandhi's efforts to pass the Defamation Bill, 1988 through Parliament, which threatened the freedom of the press, has not gone well with the English-educated middle class. The Bill aimed at curtailing press freedom rekindled the dark memories of the Emergency. Apart from media organizations all over the country, groups of advocates, students, teachers and trade unions joined in the protest opposing the Bill. The BJP and non-Congress parties too opposed the Bill by giving a call for a week-long agitation. They, in fact, used the Bill to bolster their argument that the ruling Congress was corrupt and that it was trying to muzzle the press to pre-empt publicizing of further scandals. Finally, the Bill was withdrawn. More crucial than the victory for the media was the defeat for the ruling party (Chawla 1988). Undoubtedly a vital factor influencing the decision was the kind of across-the-board support that the anti-Bill agitation had acquired.

The urban middle class grew alienated from Rajiv Gandhi's regime as he became mired in corruption scandals and cover-up attempts as he turned away from earlier promises of economic reforms in favour of more populist electoral strategies. Rajiv Gandhi failed to live up to his promise as a new urban middle-class-oriented prime minister and was unable to meet the rising expectations of an increasingly vocal middle class that had begun to identify itself as a distinctive group with specific interests that needed political representation. Middle-class frustration was constructed through a political perception of a democracy that was decaying because it had abandoned middle-class interests and been muddied by the demands of subordinated social groups (Hansen 1999, 58). That state power that was used as far as possible to suppress dissent was an attempt of the failure of Rajiv's initiatives in the face of familiar political pressures.

If the Bofors controversy seriously damaged Rajiv Gandhi's integrity, the Shah Bano case once again placed a question mark on the secular credentials of the leader and the government. In 1987, the Congress felt obliged to court its traditional support base among India's Muslims. Rajiv Gandhi ensured the passage of the Muslim Women (Protection of Rights on Divorce) Bill, 1986 through the Parliament. This bill emerged in the wake of the Shah Bano case and was a sop to conservative Muslim thinking on the family and divorce. As per the Act, the 'liability' of a husband to pay maintenance was thus restricted to the period of the *iddah* (period of waiting) only. The Act nullified the decision of the Supreme Court in the Shah Bano case.

Shah Bano Begum, a 62-year-old Muslim mother of five from Indore in Madhya Pradesh, was divorced by her wealthy husband in 1978. She filed a criminal suit in the Supreme Court of India. The Supreme Court delivered a judgement favouring maintenance given to an aggrieved divorced Muslim woman. The BJP opposed the Bill and saw it as another attempt at appeasement of the Muslim vote bank against genuine demands of gender justice. With nullification of the Apex Court order, Rajiv Gandhi greatly weakened the secular foundations of the state that had been fought for by his grandfather, Nehru. Whatever the reasons for Congress volte-face, one of its major effects was to further encourage the rise of Hindu nationalism.

The parliamentary means to overturn a Supreme Court ruling in the Shah Bano case and the ban of Salman Rushdie's book *The Satanic Verses*[5] in October 1988 from the Rajiv Gandhi government enabled the BJP to effectively portray the Congress as a party that pandered to conservative Muslim leaders. The Hindu middle class, prone to appeals of cultural and religious nationalism, interpreted the ban of *The Satanic Verses* as an indication of the appeasement of the Muslims. The well-established Shan Bano case and ban of *The Satanic Verses* attracted scholarly and public attention as a defining event that helped the BJP to gain public support and delegitimize Congress rule.

Media and academic analysts have widely discussed the political implications such events had for debates on secularism as the BJP was effectively able to portray the Congress as a 'pseudo-secular' party because of its protection of Muslim personal law and its rejection of a uniform civil code. Hindu nationalists denounced the Congress as 'pseudo-secular' because of its bias in favour of religious minorities. The government's visible pro-minority appeasement politics brought to the surface underlying political frustrations of the upper-caste Hindu middle class, which wanted to rescue democracy

---

[5] The publication of *The Satanic Verses* in 1988 was followed by a fatwa by Iran's religious leader Ayatollah Khomeini, leader of the 1979 Iranian Revolution, calling for Rushdie to be killed, forcing the author to go into hiding.

from corruption, patronage and 'special interests' of rising politically assertive subaltern groups that diverged from middle-class models of citizenship and civic and political life (Fernandes 2006, 178–179). The 'secular arrogance' to co-opt minority religious voices proved costly to the Congress and helped sow the seeds for the division between Hindus and Muslims (Vaishnav 2019, 15).

## Ayodhya Movement and the Middle Class

In the last two decades of the 20th century, the BJP promoted Hindutva by rallying around issues such as the construction of the Ram temple at Ayodhya, taking out *rath yatras*, taking out Ganesha idols in procession in neighbourhoods and raking up land issues, for instance, Idgah Maidan in Hubballi, Karnataka. Among all issues, Ayodhya movement has brought the most decisive transformational shift in Indian politics and was responsible for a spectacular expansion of the popular base of Hindu nationalist politics in the 1980s and onwards.

Why did the Ayodhya movement give rise to the biggest mass movement, with a pan-national appeal, in post-independence India? How did the BJP get involved in the movement for the construction of a temple in Ayodhya has gained unprecedented support from the Hindu society? All these questions need to be answered.

VHP, which had become the preferred offshoot of the RSS, aggressively revived the Ayodhya dispute over Ram Janmabhoomi in March 1984 after getting encouraged by the strong response it had received from *Ekatmata Yatra* (journey of unity) it organized across the country in 1983 in which millions of people participated. The *yatra* was aimed at Hindu unity and self-protection against Islam and Christianity.[6] The effort was declared to have 'changed the mood of the entire

---

[6] VHP launched a massive campaign for the 'protection of Hinduism' after nearly 150 Dalit families of Meenakshipuram in Tirunelveli district in Tamil Nadu converted en masse to Islam in 1981 owing to caste oppression. After this incident, it shifted its focus and turned against Muslims. And for VHP, Muslims and Christians were not part of the Hindu nation.

Hindu society' (Rajagopal 2001, 62). Perceiving the *Ekatmata Yatra* as a success, VHP entered direct political activism through mass-based programmes such as *yatras* and the use of cultural symbols, of which Lord Rama was the most important, to bring about a Hindu militant flavour to Indian politics. VHP wanted to 'liberate' Ram, prisoner of the Babri Masjid in Ayodhya (Van der Veer 1987). It also started making contact with opinion leaders in society, professionals, business-men and thus served as extremely useful sites of publicity (Rajagopal 2001). It was responsible for the widespread acceptance of Hindu nationalist politics in the country.

The Ram Janmabhoomi movement's declared aim was to reclaim the 'birthplace of Lord Ram' and to build a Ram temple in its place. VHP demanded that the lock on Lord Ram's birthplace be opened. The movement came to be the most effective mobilizational means of extending the ideas of Hindu nationalism, and it was mainly because of this that VHP 'grew spectacularly in power and strength in the 1980s and developed an authority of its own, separate from the RSS' (Vanaik 1997, 312). Importantly, the appeal of Hindutva, an important dimension of upper-caste, middle-class identity, is transnational. Many diasporic Hindus supported the Ayodhya movement by giving donations for the construction of the temple in Ayodhya (Davis 1996, 40–41).

Until 1986, when the gates of the disputed structure were unlocked under the Congress regime in New Delhi, the Ayodhya issue had remained a purely local issue. The Allahabad High Court's verdict in 1986, on unlocking the gates of the disputed structure, led to a dramatic change in the profile of the dispute. The VHP's campaign involved a series of national mobilizations including *rath yatras* during the second half of the 1980s. For the *shilanyas* (laying a foundation stone) ceremony on 9 November 1989, millions of supporters of VHP brought bricks from far-off villages and towns to Ayodhya to build a Ram temple. This clearly symbolizes a growing inclination towards cultural chauvinism among the contemporary Indian middle class. In large part, this unites new rich, upper-caste Hindus with some ele-ments in the wider Hindu middle class, but marginalizes the Muslims. With this, a substantial section of the middle class is increasingly characterized by religious nationalism (Lakha 1999, 267–268).

Until the late 1980s, the politics of Hindutva saw VHP grow in importance to the BJP, whose later success owed much to the former. Manjari Katju (2003) argues that between the mid-1980s and early 1990s, the leadership of VHP gradually passed from the political elite and religious leaders into the hands of traders, small industrialists and service professionals. In the 1980s, VHP actually made significant inroads into the middle-class constituency to the advantage of the BJP. The 1980s are remarkable for the rise of the BJP, and it positioned itself as the leading opposition party in the early 1990s. Certainly, it would have been difficult to predict in the 1980s that the BJP would come to power in the 1990s and secure absolute majority in the 2014 and 2019 parliamentary elections. Most of the non-BJP parties opposed the construction of the Ram temple.

One cannot ignore the role of media in building up the Ram Janmabhoomi movement and rise of the BJP. Rajagopal (2001) noted that both English and Hindi press provided wide coverage not only to the Ram Janmabhoomi movement, its legal and political issues but also to the social and cultural hues of the movement. A large section of the Hindi print media turned into 'Hindu' media and quite blatantly fabricated facts and data, while sections of the so-called 'national' English press were equally prone to reportage that was provocative, relied on rumour and was sympathetic to the goals and the vision of the leaders of the Ayodhya movement. As part of this phenomenon linking Hindu organizations, ideology, imagery and the media, 'the "Hinduisation" of the press thus led to the portrayal of the upper-caste Hindu's view as the only and true reality' (Jeffrey 2002 quoted in Ogden 2012, 32). The 1990s witnessed the emergence of right-wing electronic media entrepreneurs such as Subhash Chandra (Zee TV) and Rajat Sharma (India TV); over the two decades, both have grown into multi-core empires. It is argued that the Sangh Parivar used the right-wing media to gain wide publicity for its events and views.

It is argued that the Ayodhya movement was largely aided by DD which broadcast a Hindu epic in serial form, the *Ramayana*, to nationwide audiences, in 1987–1988. To control the damage done in the handling of the Shah Bano case, which was widely perceived as surrender under the Muslim leaders' pressure, the Congress government sponsored the serial in the hope that its flagging electoral fortunes might be revived with an infusion of 'Hindu vote'. It was the BJP, not a significant electoral force when the serial began, that seized the opportunity afforded by the serial and thereafter established itself as a major national party, one that no future ruling party or coalition could afford to ignore (Rajagopal 2001, 72–73). The opening of gates of the disputed structure by the Rajiv Gandhi government has largely worked in favour of the BJP, which had successfully mobilized the Hindu nationalist middle class from small towns as well as an educated class for building its base.

In 1989, the BJP officially declared that 'a grand temple to Lord Ram' would be built at the site of the mosque. VHP General Secretary Ashok Singhal declared that the land belonged to Ram Lalla and therefore building a Ram temple there could not be illegal. Singhal said, 'Our law says this is the land of Lord Ram and that is all that matters' (Awasthi 1992). Why the BJP supported the Ram Janmabhoomi movement? BJP's veteran leader L. K. Advani who led the movement argued that the Ayodhya is no longer limited to the construction of the Ram Janmabhoomi temple. It became the symbol of a struggle between genuine secularism and pseudo-secularism. It became the source of India's nationhood and national identity: The unifying concept of cultural nationalism and dividing the concept of anti-Hindu nationalism (Advani 2008, 367).

There was an effort on the part of the BJP to jumpstart a new movement to reinvigorate the nation and revitalize the party. Earlier, the Jana Sangh invoked Bal Gangadhar Tilak, who used the Ganapati festival in Maharashtra to galvanize the Hindu sentiments. The underpinning of the Hindutva or Hindu nationalist politics is that it did not only challenge the dominance of the Congress party, but also its principles of pluralism and secularism that form the institutional bedrock of the Indian state.

On 11 December 1995, a three-judge bench of the Supreme Court, headed by a justice J. S. Verma, declared that Hindutva was a 'way of life and not a religion'. Surprisingly, this Supreme Court judgement found its way into the campaign manifesto of the BJP in the general elections of the following year, 1996.

Gradually, in the 1990s, the BJP made its attempt to expand its base not only among the ordinary middle class but also among the intelligentsia. The left thinkers, Sudheendra Kulkarni and Chandan Mitra, and liberals, Arun Shourie and Yashwant Sinha, among others, joined the BJP. They were absorbed in important administrative or organizational positions. These leaders were 'outsiders' to the RSS and the BJP. They were admitted for the sake of gaining political acceptance from the middle classes and forging alliances with secular parties. But very soon, their rise in the party created internal tensions, partly because most of them were earlier severe critics of Hindutva. Leftist historian K. N. Panikkar (2009) argues that despite their visible presence and influence in the party, they were looked upon by the RSS with reservation. As a result, over the years, the former left and liberal intellectuals became critical of the party's subjugation to the RSS, not only in ideological terms but more so in practical politics. Now, they are openly criticizing the Modi government's policies and even challenging some of the decisions (Rafale deal) in the Supreme Court.

Coming back to the 1980s, the Congress party by its actions and its inactions has effectively connived in the 'communalization' of Indian politics. Unlike the BJP, the ruling Congress in the 1980s was totally confused as to what position it should take in relation to the politics of communalism or religious nationalism. The Congress failed to effectively put up a non-communal alternative and narrative. With both Muslim and Hindu communalism becoming more prominent and aggressive, Congress leaders bent over backwards more and more to accommodate them. The Rajiv Gandhi government opted for a policy of 'competitive' communalism: On the one hand, it initiated legislative measures to dilute the apex court's Shah Bano judgement, and, on the other, it considered making a concession to the VHP by opening the Ayodhya shrine.

Finally, a legal dispute dating back to the late 19th century and a political issue that has shaped Indian politics for over three decades were all addressed by the Supreme Court on 9 November 2019, when a five-judge Constitution bench led by Chief Justice Ranjan Gogoi ruled in favour of a temple in Ayodhya. In allowing a temple to come up through a government-appointed trust at the disputed site in Ayodhya, the Supreme Court has apparently chosen a path most conducive to social harmony. To compensate the Muslim litigants, who were deprived of the centuries-old Babri Masjid through an illegal act of demolition, the court has asked for the allotment of a five-acre land elsewhere in Ayodhya that may be used for building a new mosque. In the spirit of the 'new India' put forward by Prime Minister Narendra Modi, whose BJP has had the building of a Ram temple at Ayodhya as one of the commitments in its manifesto, described the verdict as neither a victory nor a defeat, eschewing triumphalism.[7]

Mohan Bhagwat, the chief of the BJP's ideological parent, the RSS, which has been, directly and through its affiliates, at the forefront of the Ram Janmabhoomi movement, echoed Modi's sentiment. The fact that the case is over at last must come as a great relief to all peace-loving people. The opposition parties, including the Congress, have signalled their acceptance of the verdict. There are signs of ferment among Muslim groups, with the Muslim Law Board expressing dissatisfaction. At the political level, the resolution of the temple issue indicates that 2019 has seen the end of both Mandal and mandir issues.

## Middle-Class Upsurge: The Congress Lost Roots

Events took off at breakneck speed after the November parliamentary election of 1989. This was India's first election without a clear winner, an election that was more about voting out the Rajiv Gandhi government than about a mandate for any one political formation. After securing 404 seats in the 1984 elections, Rajiv Gandhi was ousted from power five years later largely due to the Bofors scam, his surrendering in the Shah Bano case and his irresolute position on the Ram temple issue.

With the Ram temple issue, the BJP increased its parliamentary seat total from two in 1984 to 86 in 1989. Big business and the professional

---

[7] https://www.businesstoday.in/current/economy-politics/ayodhya-case-pm-modi-urges-indians-to-not-see-sc-judgement-as-victory-or-defeat/story/389463. html (accessed on 10 November 2019).

middle classes began to see the party as a possible replacement and successor to the moribund ruling Congress (Rajagopal 2001, 14). The election ushered an era of coalition politics at the national level. Although Congress (I) won over 40 per cent of the popular vote, and 37 per cent of the seats (197 in total) in the Lok Sabha, the Janata Dal (141 seats) formed a minority government with the outside support of the BJP (86 seats) and of the communist parties (52 seats). V. P. Singh, who headed the National Front, was appointed as the prime minister and formed the second non-Congress national government. The 1989 elections also ended the dynasty member becoming the prime minister of the country. With Rajiv Gandhi, his mother and his grandfather, Jawaharlal Nehru, the Nehru family had led India for all but four of the 42 years since Independence (until 1989). India entered into a new phase of parliamentary politics at the cusp of the 1990s.

The verdict was a clear expression of non-confidence motion in the Rajiv Gandhi government. Despite relatively better performance on the economic front, the succession of scandals in which it came to be engulfed after 1987, particularly the Bofors deal, and the brazen attempts of cover-up by conducting raids on media houses had clearly been seen as insult administered by the Rajiv Gandhi regime to an electorate, particularly the middle class, which had placed an enormous amount of trust in him. Accords, signed during his regime for buying peace with honour and national interest with Sri Lanka, and Indian states such as Punjab, Mizoram, Assam, and Jammu and Kashmir, all followed in dizzying succession, stood as signposts to failure and lack of foresight. In handling the problem of communalism, he swung between appeasing fundamentalists of one group at one place and another group at another place. If the approach to the Ram Janmabhoomi episode was a blatant attempt to play the Hindu card, it ended up in exposing Rajiv Gandhi's lack of sincerity in the matter of enunciating or implementing policy.

## Mandal and Mandir Politics

V. P. Singh made the most desperate move of his career on 7 August 1990. He dug up a nearly forgotten decade-old report of the Second

Backward Classes Commission, popularly known as the Mandal Commission.[8] It was Lalu Prasad Yadav who persuaded V. P. Singh to implement the Mandal report to strengthen his political position against Devi Lal.[9] The government accepted the report of the Mandal Commission alienating his friends on both the Right and Left.

The decision to implement the recommendations of the report without any consultation with parties supporting it from outside seemed like an attempt to cultivate a political constituency over the long term even at the risk of losing power in the short term. V. P. Singh, who justified the populist affirmative action for the OBCs, promised 27 per cent reservation in the government jobs. Although it was in fulfilment of a campaign promise, the announcement took the wind out of his opponent's sails and simultaneously revealed deep fissures in the ranks of the 'Hindu' support base.

The announcement of the implementation of the report precipitated a major social turmoil. It was an invitation to a caste war. The decision was strongly opposed by sections of the upper and the intermediate castes who by then were largely ensconced in the middle class. They saw the newly politicized lower castes forcing their way into the middle class (particularly into white-collar jobs), that too not through open competition but on 'caste-based' reservations. This created a confrontation of interest between the upper and intermediate castes on the one hand and the lower castes on the other (Sheth 1999). While the Supreme Court upheld the OBC reservation, it asked the government to exclude their 'creamy layer' from the benefits of reservation. The creamy layer issue was to become a major debating point in the Parliament in the 1990s.

[8] The Mandal Commission was established on 1 January 1979 by the Janata Government under Prime Minister Morarji Desai with a mandate to 'identify the socially and educationally backward classes' of India. It was headed by B. P. Mandal, former chief minister of Bihar and parliamentarian, to consider the question of reservation for people to redress caste discrimination and used 11 social, economic and educational indicators to determine backwardness.

[9] https://timesofindia.indiatimes.com/india/i-single-handedly-persuaded-vp-singh-to-implement-27-obc-quota-lalu-prasad-yadav/articleshow/68747791.cms (accessed on 10 May 2019).

The movement against the policy of affirmative action spread like wildfire across the country. Students belonging to upper-caste middle class staged violent demonstrations in urban centres and universities throughout the country. The national capital, New Delhi, had become the epicentre of the protest. The most sensational of such protests involved the self-immolation of upper-caste middle-class students. Given the urban-centric nature of the media, the protests captured news headlines for days on end. Photographs in the newspapers and on television of the flame-engulfed body of the first student, who immolated himself in Delhi, fuelled angry denunciations of the report.[10] The media, particularly the English press, generally on the Left in social issues, united in opposing the quota to uphold the 'meritocracy'. In a way, the mainstream media, comprising print and television, championed the cause of the upper-caste middle class. However, the agitation did not gain as much attention in southern India as it did in the North because upper-caste people constituted less than 10 per cent of the population, the figure in North India was in excess of 20 per cent. It was also because the South had a thriving industrial sector, the educated youth were not as depended on the state for jobs as those in the North (Guha 2007, 602–604).

Unfortunately, even two decades after the implementation of the Mandal Commission Report, less than 12 per cent of employees in central government ministries, departments and statutory bodies were from OBCs as on 1 January 2015. Under A, B, C and D categories of employees, out of 79,483 posts, there are only 9,040 OBC staff.[11] In this background, it is argued that the affirmative action on caste lines served only to enhance the significance of caste categories and conflicts, and the policy was discriminatory and incompatible with that efficiency and equal opportunity in public services. It is argued that preferential treatment on the basis of caste rather than qualifications was under-

[10] On 19 September 1990, Rajiv Goswami, a student at Delhi University, set fire to himself in protest against the implementation of the Mandal Commission recommendations.

[11] https://timesofindia.indiatimes.com/india/20-years-after-Mandal-less-than-12-OBCs-in-central-govt-jobs/articleshow/50328073.cms (accessed on 10 May 2019).

mining the principle of merit which in turn lowered the standard of administration and thus diminished the country's development prospects. Such claims were common among upper-caste, middle-class people opposed to the reservation policy. Significantly, these issues were not just debated among Indians in India but among diasporic Indians at different forums, including on the Internet (Lakha 1999, 266–267). Moreover, caste-based reservation seemed to be benefiting the 'creamy layer' among the OBCs and not the truly disadvantaged, whether from higher or lower castes. The RSS, which was largely dominated by a Brahmanical middle class, was opposed to reservations because they were caste based, which meant that poor people belonging to upper castes could benefit from these measures. Moreover, caste divided people and posed a challenge to Hindu nation-building.

Acknowledging the RSS stance on the issue, the BJP reacted differently to the decision. The BJP, which had the support of upper-caste white-collar professionals, middle class and merchants, had been in favour of reservation for the socially and educationally backward classes. However, the party viewed that the manner in which the government announced its decision on the implementation of the Mandal Commission Report without any consultation with the supporting parties and without qualifying it with any economic criteria was utterly wrong. The party considered that the decision was prompted not for any concern for the backward classes but considerations of political expediency. In the face of Congress confusion on the reservations issue, many high-caste middle-class people, particularly in urban North India, turned to the BJP to safeguard their interests, although the party refused to set its stall against 'reservations' owing to electoral calculus.

Since the announcement of quota for OBCs in 1990, the BJP in all its election manifestos has been advocating reservation for members of the other castes on the basis of their economic condition. In its 1998 election manifesto, the BJP promised that if voted to power, it would 'continue with the current reservations policy for the OBCs until they are socially and educationally integrated with the rest of society', but it also announced a 10 per cent quota to all economically weaker sections of society, apart from the SCs and STs and OBCs. The BJP had accepted the necessity of quotas for OBCs, but it tried to combine the criterion of caste with socio-economic criteria. In 1999, the BJP, which led the NDA, did not present its manifesto. All allies of the BJP presented the NDA manifesto. After nearly two decades now, the NDA government led by the Prime Minister Narendra Modi in its Cabinet decision on 7 January 2019 decided to provide 10 per cent quota for poor, irrespective of caste, which we will discuss in Chapter 6.

If the Mandal movement divided the Hindus into caste lines, the Mandir movement united them towards Hindutva and Hindu Rashtra by invoking their cultural identity.[12] The Palampur resolution of the BJP endorsed the VHP's position that the Ram Mandir would be built in the place where the Babri Masjid stood. Prior to the Palampur resolution, the temple had been the VHP's solo show. The Palampur resolution enabled to push VHP into frenetic activity and it took out several yatras. All this resulted in a major victory for the BJP-VHP-RSS combine: On 9 November 1989, virtually on the eve of the general elections, Rajiv Gandhi permitted the laying of the first stone for a temple in a grand *shilanyas* ceremony (Subrahmaniam 2015).

The post-Mandal period saw a rapid souring of ties between the BJP and the National Front, with the Ayodhya controversy becoming the flashpoint. On the Ram Janmabhoomi issue, both had locked themselves into irreconcilable and rigid stances. It was in this context that the then BJP President L. K. Advani launched his Ram Rath Yatra (chariot procession), a rally that was organized by the BJP and its Hindu nationalist affiliates, which covered eight states before reaching the city of Ayodhya. The purpose of the *yatra* was to support the agitation of VHP and the Sangh Parivar affiliates for the construction of the Ram temple in the site of the Babri Masjid. The *rath yatra* began on 25 September 1990, the day of Deendayal Jayanti, seeking to capitalize on the massive protests across North India against the reservation. The *yatra* began at the Hindu holy city of Somnath, after offering prayers at the temple which was reconstructed in the early

---

[12] The communities such as Rajputs, Patels, Bumihars, Jats, who opposed 27 per cent quota, rallied behind the BJP.

1950s.[13] Advani was accompanied by Pramod Mahajan and Narendra Modi (the current prime minister) and other senior functionaries. Both Somnath and Ayodhya had political significance to the Hindu nationalist movement because of their association with the legacy of Muslim invaders and rulers.

The imagery of the *yatra* was 'religious, allusive, militant, masculine, and anti-Muslim' (Guha 2007, 582–598). The media reported a huge response from the people to the *rath yatra* in Gujarat, Maharashtra and Karnataka. In the two-volume *The Saffron Swastika: The Notion of Hindu Fascism*, Koenraad Elst (2001) discusses fascism, Nazism, communism and the Hindutva movement and claims that there was no violence along the *rath yatra* of Advani. Elst argues against the idea that the BJP or RSS are fascist in ideology.

A large section of the middle class acknowledged Advani's coinages such as 'pseudo-secularism' and 'minority appeasement politics'. The *yatra* was planned to reach Ayodhya on 30 October 1990 to inaugurate the Kar Seva (the building of the Ram Mandir). The *yatra* caused growing unrest in its wake, resulting in the government being forced to take action against it (Banerjee 1991). In fact, there was a contest of sorts between the two Yadav chief ministers of Janata Dal of Uttar Pradesh and Bihar—Mulayam Singh Yadav and Lalu Prasad Yadav—each trying to project himself as more 'secular' than the other by arresting Advani. Ultimately, Lalu Prasad Yadav stopped the *yatra* by detaining Advani at Samastipur on 23 October 1990. The *rath yatra* ended with the arrest of Advani. Immediately after Advani's arrest, the BJP withdrew its support to the V. P. Singh government. The 11-month-old National Front government collapsed under the weight of its own contradictions. Later, the Chandra Shekhar government formed with the external support of the Congress lasted only 117 days.

The National Front and the BJP fought 1989 elections on two separate poll manifestos. The Janata Dal, the main constituent of the National Front, had been consciously trying to convey the public

[13] Dr Rajendra Prasad, the first President of India, inaugurated the newly constructed Somnath by ceremonially installing the Jyotirlingam. Jawaharlal Nehru vehemently protested the President's decision.

an impression that it regarded the BJP as a communal party, which thwarted the building up any abiding relationship of trust and friendship between two parties. 'The Congress, unlike the BJP which was consistent in its outside support to V. P. Singh until it broke away because of the Ayodhya issue, at no time provided unhesitant support to the Chandra Shekhar government' (*The Hindu* 1991). Both governments collapsed largely owing to the unsustainability of the concept of 'outside support'.

## Ecstasy and Agony

In the 1991 general elections, the Ram Janmabhoomi issue allowed the BJP to gain significant support in rural areas, where it had previously been restricted to support from the urban middle class (Engineer 1991). The BJP further improved its strength in the Parliament from 86 to 120 seats and established itself as the second party nationally, after Congress. It could have done even better than this had it not been for the sympathy vote for the Congress in the second phase of the election, following Rajiv Gandhi's assassination. Once again, the Congress attempted to capitalize on the sympathy factor over what it termed as the 'martyrdom' of the former prime minister. However, the 'sympathy factor' had not helped the Congress to secure a clear majority. It won 232 seats, well below the half-way mark of 273. With its increased number of seats, the BJP became more of a 'mega-regional party' than a truly national party, restricted to the Hindi belt (Corbridge and Harriss 2000, 129–130). A major milestone in the history of the Ayodhya movement was the victory of the BJP in the state assembly elections held in July 1991 in Uttar Pradesh. The BJP improved its tally from 57 seats in 1989 to 221 in 1991 in the 421-seats Assembly of Uttar Pradesh. In the battle between Mandal and Mandir, the latter seems to have won. The first BJP government headed by Kalyan Singh was formed. The BJP had secured a majority of seats in the state legislatures of Rajasthan, Madhya Pradesh and Himachal Pradesh.

The Congress government headed by P. V. Narasimha Rao returned to power in July 1991 after elections, although without a majority. It was the third minority government within a span of less than two years.[14] In a strategic move, Rao appointed Manmohan Singh, an outsider to the ruling Congress (I) and the long-time critic of India's policy of export pessimism, as the finance minister. Interestingly, both Rao and Singh were not MPs when they were sworn in. Manmohan Singh's first budget was a landmark event setting on the road to economic liberalization and structural reforms of the Indian economy. The reforms have slowly but steadily begun demolishing the socialist edifice erected by the previous Congress governments since Nehru. Interestingly, in the decade of 1990s, India's politics had become triangular (Varshney 1999a, 247). Between 1950 and 1990, the principal battle lines of politics were bipolar. The Congress was the party of government, and all other parties were opposed to it. In the 1990s, a triangular contest developed between the Left, the BJP, and the Congress. Coalitions were increasingly formed against the Hindu nationalists BJP, not against the Congress.

When the BJP felt that the Rao government stood against the construction of the Ram temple in Ayodhya, the then BJP President Murli Manohar Joshi and Advani took out a *yatra* again, and this time, the former from Mathura and the latter from Varanasi. A large number of *kar sevaks* had mounted on domes of the disputed structure and demolished the Babri Masjid on 6 December 1992. The groups of young people leaving the venue at dusk chanting *Ram Lalla phir ayenge, bhavya mandir banayenge* (Infant Ram will come again; we will build a grand temple). The news of the demolition of the mosque spread like a wildfire, and the Hindu middle-class homes erupted in joy. Some compared the demolition of the mosque to the fall of the Berlin Wall and the storming of the Bastille (Dasgupta 2012). Madhav Godbole (1996), who was the Union Home Secretary at the time of the Babri Masjid demolition, recounts that the incident caused widespread riots in cities of North India, claiming lives of 2,026 persons and injuring 6,957 persons in various incidents throughout the country, besides large-scale arson and looting.

---

[14] First one was V. P. Singh government and second was the Chandra Shekhar government.

Many observers described the events of 6 December as a turning point in the history of India, which changed the country's political discourse. Left-wing scholars such as Achin Vanaik (1992, 62) sees the demolition of the Masjid as the most serious crisis in independent India's history and termed it a calculated assault on the Indian state and its Constitution. India is now closer than ever before to having a Hindu state. On the other hand, the then BJP MP, Vajpayee saw the incident as a nationalist outburst and compared it with such expressions elsewhere: 'When Russia occupied Warsaw, a church was there. When Poland became independent the first thing it did was the demolition of the church. History bears testimony to this' (Shankar and Rodrigues 2014, 149).

The Rao government dismissed the BJP government in Uttar Pradesh headed by Kalyan Singh since it had forfeited its right to rule in the state by the brazen and shameless abdication of its constitutional responsibility. President's rule was imposed for 363 days until Mulayam Singh Yadav of the Samajwadi Party formed the government after fresh elections in 1993. The Congress government arrested BJP leaders, including L. K. Advani and Murli Manohar Joshi, banned the RSS, VHP and Bajrang Dal,[15] and dismissed the BJP-led state governments in Madhya Pradesh, Rajasthan and Himachal Pradesh. The Justice Liberhan Commission was set up to probe the demolition of the mosque and the related incidents. After 17 long years and 48 extensions from various central governments, the commission submitted its report to the government. The central conclusion of the four-volume report running over 1,000 pages is that the RSS and its affiliates and the BJP were responsible for the demolition. The commission has held that the Kalyan Singh government in Uttar Pradesh, and some of its officers, colluded with the Sangh Parivar in the demolition of the Babri Masjid. It has given a clean chit to the P. V. Narasimha Rao-led Congress government.

Like caste, religion is an important dimension of middle-class identity. The religious hostility between some Hindus and Muslims

---

[15] Ban was lifted in June 1993 by the Unlawful Activities (Prevention) Tribunal as the Congress government has failed to prove evidences to ban the RSS, VHP and Bajrang Dal.

complicated the situation in the aftermath of the demolition of the mosque. The religious and sectarian tensions and violence spread especially in Bombay in January 1993, and terrorist attacks by the 'Indian Mujahideen' took place in Delhi, Jaipur and Ahmedabad. Cities of Surat, Gujarat and Bhopal, Madhya Pradesh, too witness unprecedented communal riots. The deadly Bombay blasts of 1993, just three months after the demolition of Babri Masjid, which left 272 dead, saw the collaboration of a Mumbai mafia don with the ISI of Pakistan. These events changed the relationships between Muslims and Hindus throughout India. Actions of both Hindu and Muslim fundamentalists are against communal harmony, and both aimed at allegedly dividing the country by polarizing people along with their religious identities and focus to profit politically from such polarization. All political parties had dipped into this well of controversy for its self-serving interests (Purie 2019a).

The BJP suffered a major electoral setback in 1993 when assembly elections in Madhya Pradesh, Himachal Pradesh, Uttar Pradesh and Rajasthan were conducted. These were the four states in which incumbent BJP governments had been dismissed and President's rule was imposed by the centre after the demolition of the Babri Masjid. In Rajasthan, however, Bhairon Singh Shekhawat formed the government on the strength of 95 seats that the party had won in a house of 200. Although the BJP emerged as the largest single party in Uttar Pradesh, it was kept out of office by a coalition of hostile parties headed by Mulayam Singh Yadav. The party won a majority and formed a government for the first time in Delhi, bringing Madan Lal Khurana to the post of the chief minister.

Overall, during the first half of the 1990s, the BJP made remarkable strides mainly in the north Indian states, while it emerged as an alternative to the Congress at the centre in the second half of the 1990s. It has garnered the support from upper-caste, middle-class Hindus both in rural and urban areas in the Hindi belt. This was primarily because the party originated in the North and largely challenged the corruption and politics of appeasement of the Congress. The party's economic nationalism in the form of swadeshi, focusing on small-scale industries and internal economic liberalization, was supported by businesses and industries that felt threatened by the onslaught of globalization and flooding of foreign goods in the local markets which posed a challenge to their business.

The Congress government under Rao, which was engulfed in corruption scandals, performed poorly in the 1996 parliamentary elections. For the first time since Independence, the Congress was dethroned from its number one position and the BJP became the single largest party in the Lok Sabha by winning 161 seats against the Congress Party's 136 seats. The Janata Dal secured 46 while the CPI(M) bagged 32 seats. Several factors contributed to the loss of pre-eminent position of the Congress. The Congress' prime minister's image was sullied when the stock market scam, involving Harshad Mehta, broke out in 1992, and media revelations about Rao's sons suddenly turning into business tycoons and handling projects. Although there was no evidence of sons directly misusing his position, the blood ties with the man in the most powerful seat in the country itself opened many doors of suspicion.[16] Rao's credibility in the office also came under the scanner owing to his proximity with the controversial godman Chandraswami.

## Three Elections and Three Prime Ministers: Merrymaking

The 1990s was a period of alliances and political instability, particularly the second half of the decade. With no single party being able to attain a simple majority in the Lok Sabha elections from the early 1990s, the regional parties became crucial in the formation of a government. This dependence on the regional parties led to what Rudolph called a 'federalized coalition' (quoted in Kim 2006).

The country had seen three prime ministers within a span of two years, between May 1996 and March 1998. In three parliamentary elections held in 1996, 1998 and 1999, the BJP emerged as the largest single party. The BJP made a steady rise to power, largely owing to

---

[16] https://www.indiatoday.in/magazine/special-report/story/19920930-prime-minister-raos-relatives-range-from-petrol-pump-owners-to-industrial-ists-766888-2012-12-31 (accessed on 10 May 2018).

its spirited espousal of the Ayodhya movement for the construction of the Ram temple. The construction of the Ram temple was a major commitment of the party.

In 1996, the party won 161 seats but did not command a majority, and A. B. Vajpayee formed a government which did not survive. It lasted barely 13 days, to be replaced by a 13-party 'United Front' government. This kept going under two prime ministers—first, H. D. Deve Gowda, and later I. K. Gujral—with the outside support of the Congress. The United Front experiment did not last long. The Congress played spoilsport to two prime ministers in 18 months. The attempts to isolate the BJP did not meet with any success because of an artificial arrangement of forces and failure of the Congress to make a correct assessment of the country's future political map (Palshikar 2004).

In the 1998 elections, the BJP managed to forge alliances of convenience with many small and state-level parties and won 182 seats as against 161 seats in 1996. Gains came from East and South India where support for the BJP previously had been almost non-existent. The second BJP government led by Vajpayee fell in April 1999, after 13 months in office, following the withdrawal of support by Jayalalitha's AIADMK and elections were held again.

The BJP-led omnibus alliance secured a comfortable working majority in the 1999 national elections (13th Lok Sabha) and the verdict was more decisive than 1998 elections. The combined forces, which had 24 partners, including the BJP, was succeeded in winning enough numbers to form a government, thanks to the strategic alliances it had struck with regional parties having a dominant presence in various states, for instance, the Telugu Desam Party in Andhra Pradesh and the Dravida Munnetra Kazhagam (DMK) in Tamil Nadu. Most of the gains made by the BJP-led front came from the erstwhile United Front and the allies of the Congress (I) (Yadav et al, 1999). It is, therefore, argued that the elections produced not a national verdict, but an aggregation of local verdicts (Jenkins 2000).

In the 1999 general elections, the Congress (I) secured 114 seats, 27 lesser seats than the previous election. Yet, the party increased its share of the popular vote (to 28.5%), while, despite Vajpayee's popularity with the electorate, the vote share of the BJP fell by almost 2 per cent (from 25.59% in 1998 to 23.75% in 1999). This is also because the party had contested on 49 seats less than in the 1998 elections.[17] The BJP's alliance with regional parties in states such as Tamil Nadu and West Bengal served only its electoral gains. The BJP was better than the Congress in forming coalitions (Echeverri-Gent 2002, 26). But by entering an alliance, it largely undermined its ideological coherence as well open itself to political contestation.[18]

The BJP, after the defeat in assembly elections in Uttar Pradesh, Madhya Pradesh and Himachal Pradesh in 1993, adopted a moderate line and put on the back burner contentious issues in favour of touting legitimate issues such as national security and economic independence.[19] Further, Vajpayee, who was less marked by Hindu nationalist activism, succeeded Advani as the party's president. This moderate line helped the BJP to strike alliances and return to power after the 1999 elections.

# Turning of the Tide: The Vajpayee Government

The important milestone in middle-class assertion was that the BJP's rise had been dramatic from a mere two seats in the 1984 Lok Sabha to 86 in 1989, to 120 in 1991, to 161 in 1996, to 182 each in 1998 and 1999. What is more significant, however, is that the BJP's own tally has remained just about the same (182 seats) as in the 12th Lok Sabha, and the fresh additional MPs have come from its allies, old

---

[17] The BJP contested 339 seats in 1999 against 388 in 1998. It had given seats to allies in the 1999 general elections.

[18] For example, the BJP entered into an alliance with DMK in Tamil Nadu in 1999. The DMK was founded as an anti-Brahmin party, and, in the public, it preaches secular ideals. In Maharashtra too, the BJP had an alliance with the Hindu chauvinist Shiv Sena, and both publicly expressed differences on many occasions. The differences between the BJP and the Shiv Sena continued even during the Narendra Modi government during 2014–2019.

[19] The BJP put on back burner issues such as the construction of a temple in Ayodhya, abolition of Article 370 of the constitution and promulgation of a uniform civil code.

and new. NDA secured 306 seats. The Kargil War with Pakistan and Vajpayee's 'war hero' image apparently had an impact on the electorate, particularly in Delhi and Haryana. The Kargil war was India's first war with television accessible to Indian middle-class homes, which enabled people to watch developments on the battlefield. The outcome of the Kargil war was considered both a military and a diplomatic triumph for India.

The NDA's campaign which virtually reduced elections to a 'Vajpayee versus Sonia Gandhi' contest, with a *swadeshi versus videshi* underpinnings linked to the Congress (I) president's foreign origin; the general voter seemed to have been less impressed with Sonia Gandhi's leadership qualities especially when juxtaposed with that of Vajpayee's. The political parties opposing the BJP and representing the democratic, secular forces, particularly the Congress, have failed to bring into sharp focus and in a credible manner the emerging threat to the country's secularist fabric from the Sangh Parivar which has continued to pursue its sectarian ideology despite disavowal by the Vajpayee regime (The *Hindu* 2017). It is fair to conclude that the BJP has clearly established itself as a national party, although it was still not supported by the majority of voters, who were, however, divided in their affection for other parties. Prime Minister Vajpayee successfully ran the government, despite pulls and pressures from different constituents of the coalition.

A nuclear test was conducted on 11 May 1998 under the able leadership of A. P. J. Abdul Kalam, head of the Defence Research and Development Organization, who later became the President of India during the Vajpayee government. Surprisingly, the 1998 nuclear test was criticized by the Congress and Communist leaders.[20] The N-test and bus *yatra* to Lahore in Pakistan on 20 February 1999 raised the

---

[20] Congress leaders such as Manmohan Singh, Salman Khurshid and Mani Shankar Aiyar denounced the N-tests as being the harbinger of an arm race in the region. Prakash Karat of CPI(M), who remained silent on the nuclear policy pursued by China and erstwhile Soviet Union, hit out at the BJP government calling 'the bomb was the mascot of the RSS long before the Ram temple acquired religious-political overtones for it in the 1980s' (*Frontline* 1999, 21 May). India's traditional rival Pakistan responded with its own series of tests.

stature of Prime Minister Vajpayee as well as the popularity of the NDA government. The prime minister captured the imagination of the Indian middle class. On 27 February 1999, Finance Minister Yashwant Sinha presented his first full budget, and it offered a comprehensive package of fiscal incentives focused at middle-class investors wishing to purchase dwelling units, the promoters of middle-income housing projects. However, on 14 April 1999, the Vajpayee government was defeated in a trust vote by a margin of one vote in the Lok Sabha, following the withdrawal of support by AIADMK. Consequently, the Lok Sabha was dissolved and elections were held.

The NDA comprised of two dozen parties led by the BJP returned to power in the 1999 parliamentary elections. In the elections, the middle-class voters emerged as the 'BJP's new social bloc' (Yadav et al. 1999). This 'new social bloc' was a new coalition of various social groups that lay claims to political power. The 'new social bloc' was formed by the convergence of traditional caste-community differences and class distinctions. The decline of the Congress (I) and the rise of the BJP to power created the possibility of a new kind of cleavage-based politics: one that draws on the overlap of cleavages based on caste and class. It was not caste based or class based in any simple sense: It was woven around the ideology of nationalism and involves a reworking of *jati* (caste) and sectional divisions. Its end product was a new social bloc, one with soft edges and blurred boundaries (Yadav et al. 1999). The middle castes largely benefited from the Green Revolution in northern India and other pockets of prosperity, such as the sugar belt in Maharashtra, Gujarat and Andhra Pradesh, and seamlessly entered the middle class and supported the BJP. It reflected the growing political awareness of the subalterns. For attracting OBC votes, the BJP fielded candidates wherever possible, which paid rich electoral dividends. So, caste and class categories were closely connected (Beteille 2001, 74).

This new social block support to the BJP and the BJP-led NDA coalition government's economic liberalization programme for reasons other than purely economic, in fact, might have supported the programme because they supported the BJP and/or its coalition for essentially social reasons (Yadav et al. 1999). Therefore, the NDA was able to take a strong pro-reform line, as it did in the 2004 election campaign, because it could rely on this 'new social block' for social, that is, caste-cum-class, reasons. In fact, the middle classes, the professionals and the managerial elites had identified themselves with the BJP because of its unflinching commitment to the values and concepts of economic realism, pragmatic efficiency and organizational discipline and rejection of the strategy of class struggle.

Although the construction of the Ram temple was a major commitment of the party, the diverse nature of the NDA coalition constrained the BJP's activities while in government. Owing to the compulsions of coalition politics, the party was bound by the NDA's common minimum programme. The coalition that enabled the BJP to come to power also forced it to dilute its agenda in order to maintain its stability and continuance. Overall, the BJP was 'pulled back to the Indian centre by the logic of coalition politics and the need to meet the test of elections' (Cohen 2002, 122).

During this period, there were media reports of attacks on Christians and their places of worship. No right-thinking person would justify any act of violence in the name of caste, religion or ethnicity. On 22 January 1999, in Manoharpur village, Odisha, Graham Staines, an Australian evangelist missionary, and his two young sons were burned alive. The barbarity of the crime shook the whole nation, making every Indian hang his head in shame. The BJP claimed that all these incidents of violence against Christians were projected as proof of the 'anti-minority' character of the Vajpayee government. A sustained and systematic propaganda campaign was launched to tarnish the BJP and the NDA government, both within and outside the country.[21]

Overall, the 1990s witnessed the emergence of identity politics, and the democratic polity is seemed to mark the beginning of a third

---

[21] Home Minister L. K. Advani appointed a commission of inquiry headed by Justice D. P. Wadhwa, a sitting judge of the Supreme Court. The probe report held that one Dara Singh guilty of crime and the court ordered a life-term in prison. The Central Bureau of Investigation (CBI) too conducted the probe. Neither the Wadhwa Commission nor the CBI found any links between the RSS and those convicted by the court.

phase in the history of India's party system.[22] The decline of the 'catch-all' Congress umbrella opened up the possibility of the political consolidation of the underprivileged as it did for the privileged. We have witnessed a participatory upsurge of the socially backward castes, Dalits, women and Adivasis. India is perhaps the only contemporary democracy where the poor and the socially underprivileged participate in electoral politics more than the elite, and Yogendra Yadav (2000) called this shift the 'second democratic upsurge'.[23] While political parties such as Bahujan Samaj Party (BSP) and Samajwadi Party (SP) succeeded in drawing the attention of OBCs, SCs and STs, the Congress, however, continued to retain its traditional support base among marginal communities such as the Dalits, Adivasis and Muslims. The BJP succeeded in evolving a new block of the upper castes and middle classes.

## 'India Shining' Campaign, Defeat in Polls

Why and when does an incumbent government enjoying a full majority in the Parliament decide to seek re-election by recommending early dissolution of the Lok Sabha? In 1971, the Congress government led by Indira Gandhi advanced polls by a year, and she returned to power on her main poll plank *Garibi Hatao* (remove poverty) slogan. Sensing victory, Rajiv Gandhi advanced the Lok Sabha election by a couple of months, in a move to benefit from the sympathy wave generated in the aftermath of his mother's assassination on 31 October 1984. The Vajpayee government decided to go for early elections in April 2004, although its term was supposed to end in October 2004. Analysts felt that the decision to go for the early polls was made in view of the

---

[22] The first was that of Congress dominance; the second, from the 1970s, 'saw the emergence of genuine competition to the Congress, both at the state and at the national level, often aided by electoral waves'.

[23] The participation in a democratic process does not by itself lead to participatory democracy. Unfortunately, most of the regional political parties, especially the BSP led by Mayawati, which had given voice to subaltern groups, are themselves completely undemocratic in their organizational set-up as well as style of functioning (Yadav 2000).

booming Indian economy[24] with BJP's victory in the Hindi heartland of Madhya Pradesh, Rajasthan and Chhattisgarh in December 2003. Moreover, many media reports and opinion polls predicted a comfortable win for the BJP-led NDA.[25]

High in confidence after victory in three states, BJP leaders felt that the popularity of the NDA was at its peak, and the BJP decided to leverage its popularity and initiated a major poll campaign with the slogan 'India Shining'. The much-publicized 'India Shining' media campaign was launched during the run-up to the 2004 national election—a campaign that surrounded new middle-class visions of a prosperous liberalizing India becoming. The 'India Shining' campaign, initiated by the Government of India (GoI), was geared towards projecting India's successful economic performance, linked to BJP's election campaign. The advertising campaign is said to be one of the biggest in Indian television history, being frequently broadcast brand on television between December 2003 and January 2004. The ad appeared in the print media as well, particularly in the top national dailies. The campaign marked the beginning of a new age of political advertising in India. Political scientist Niraja Gopal Jayal (2004) characterized the 2004 elections as the first elections in which political communication came to be conducted in the corporate vocabulary of image-making, branding and marketing. The campaign was supported by the catchphrase 'feel-good factor'. The print media extensively received urban-oriented advertisements to show the lifestyle of the new middle-class families as well as the images of India's new-found success in the global economy.

The electoral plank based on the consumption of a nationalist model of 'India Shining' produced various forms of political contestation. Congress President Sonia Gandhi vehemently opposed the claims made in the 'India Shining' campaign terming it as 'India cheated'.

---

[24] India's GDP growth in the second quarter of 2004 was recorded at 8.4 per cent. The BJP leaders believed that visibility of the construction of the nationwide network of world-class highways, the telecom revolution that had taken off in a big way and the country emerging as a 'software superpower' would be advantageous for the party.

[25] An opinion poll conducted in January 2004 by *India Today-Org Marg* predicted 330–340 seats for the BJP-led NDA in the Parliament.

Congress leaders said that, in reality, the Indian economy was not booming, and there was no convincing reason for the country to feel good. It also ridiculed Advani's catchphrase by terming it as 'fail good'. Sonia Gandhi and the Congress leaders condemned the campaign for ignoring groups such as farmers, the poor and unemployed that were not benefited from the high economic growth rate.

The Congress on its part in its 2004 manifesto stated that 'the middle class of India is the proud creation of Congress' and that the policies of the party if voted to power were to be 'in sync with their aspirations'. The rural poor took the 'India Shining' as a personal affront and decided to teach the NDA a lesson by warming up to the Congress and its slogan *Congress ka haath, aam aadmi ke saath* (the hand of the Congress is with the common man). In a major setback to the BJP and NDA, the DMK, the National Conference and Lok Janashakti Party left the alliance and sided with the Congress. On the other hand, the Congress forged an alliance with regional parties such as the Nationalist Congress Party, Telangana Rashtra Samithi and the Jharkhand Mukti Morcha.

People voted for a hung Parliament. However, the Congress emerged as the single largest party with 145 seats, 31 seats more than what they won in 1999 while the BJP secured 138 seats against 182 won in 1999. The NDA's strength fell from 304 in 1999 to 186 in 2004. The UPA led by the Congress with the support of India's Left front parties formed the government. Congress President Sonia Gandhi backed out from the prime-ministerial race.

The elections results stunned the BJP leaders who were confident of winning nearly 300 Lok Sabha seats under the leadership of party President M. Venkaiah Naidu. The Congress party's electoral success was mainly on account of its electoral strategy. The BJP won just 11 out of 80 seats in Uttar Pradesh. Although a combination of factors caused the defeat of the BJP,[26] the phraseology of 'feel-good factor' and 'India Shining' hurt the party the most. The 'India Shining' cam-

---

[26] Arrogance, inaccessibility, insensitivity, rude conduct on the part of the elected MPs, neglect of *karyakartas*, shortcomings in party-government coordination, neglect of ideological constituency, inadequate attention to the views and

paign allowed the Congress and other parties to focus on other aspects of India's contemporary problems such as poverty, unemployment, farmers' suicides.

Both academic scholars and national and international media analysed the impact of the BJP's miscalculated 'India Shining' campaign. They focused on the ways in which the campaign's glorification of India's strong economic growth associated with liberalization was not in sync with the vast socio-economic inequalities, particularly in rural poverty. Satirical newspaper headlines such as 'India Shrinking' and 'Sonia Shining' reflected the ways in which the 'India Shining' campaign had come to symbolize a deep discrepancy between new middle-class perception of a prosperous, booming economy, and prevailing socio-economic disparities, unemployment and poverty in rural and urban India (Fernandes 2006, 190).

While former Deputy Prime Minister Advani has blamed the error of the 'India Shining' slogan for its debacle, pro-economic reform commentators and media pundits have unanimously blamed the Gujarat riots for the BJP's reverses. Many former MPs of the BJP and its allies, have admitted the defeat in the election that can be attributed to the communal excesses and the violence in Gujarat in 2002 during the tenure of Chief Minister Narendra Modi. On his arrival in Kullu, Himachal Pradesh, on 12 June 2004, for a week-long sojourn, Vajpayee too admitted that Godhra riots were one of the reasons for the BJP's defeat. But the then RSS Chief K. Sudarshan and Spokesperson Ram Madhav rejected the idea that the Gujarat riots were to be blamed for the BJP's defeat (Kamath and Randeri 2009, 189).

Many BJP insiders, and those from the RSS and VHP, have come up with the argument that the BJP lost because it chose to sideline the Hindutva platform while in power.[27] For the VHP leaders, the BJP-led government had betrayed the Hindus by not building the

concerns of ideological allies in the Sangh Parivar led to the defeat of nearly 50 per cent incumbent MPs in the 2004 general elections (see Advani 2008, 774–775).

[27] The moderate stand is in line with the aim of expansion of the party beyond the Hindi belt and beyond the fold of the 'upper caste'. To be a centrist party,

Ram temple they had been aggressively campaigning for the last two decades in Ayodhya. It argued that the compulsions of coalition politics had thwarted the Hindutva agenda. The fact of the matter is that the BJP did not focus on the communal issue in the election campaign. Yet, it is difficult to be persuaded by the argument that the BJP had altered its ideological position fundamentally, or that it had abandoned core issues of Hindutva for the 2004 elections. This was a continuation of the strategy adopted in 1998 and 1999. Therefore, Palshikar (2004) argues that the 2004 elections were not at least mainly about secularism.

The popular resentment against the government was not picked up by the news media. The media's failure was far more predictable than the poll results. The disconnect between the mass and the media was the major cause for the media's inability to judge the ground reality and the ordinary people's mood against the BJP (Sainath 2004). There are two reasons why the media missed the Big Story. Since the news media was made up of people comprising 'India Shining', it did not submit the dubious slogan to the scrutiny and scepticism it deserved, and they were swayed by the NDA government's propaganda about its economic record simply because the media believed that issues that really matter to it matter to the people as well. The second reason was that journalists were swept up by the propaganda about India becoming a 'superpower' under the BJP (Hasan 2004). Advani (2008, 75) says that the temptation to use the media by leaders to voice inter-party differences to settle scores was another factor that severely weakened the BJP as a 'party with difference' and the media started to describe it as a 'party with differences'.

## Congress Triumphant: Has the Middle Class Lost at Assertion?

With changing times, the 2009 national elections witnessed both parties' campaigners targeting the middle classes through the Internet marketing campaign and their manifestos making promises to

the BJP had to accommodate people from all kinds of social background, particularly from the 'lower castes'.

broaden and deepen economic reforms. The Congress won 206 seats, the best performance since 1991, while the BJP won 116 seats, its lowest tally since 1991. The BJP lost ground in a majority of states as did the 82-year-old L. K. Advani, whom the BJP had projected as its prime-ministerial candidate. In alliance with regional parties, the Congress-led UPA II formed the government and Manmohan Singh was re-appointed as the prime minister, making him the first prime minister to achieve this distinction at the end of a five-year term since India's first, Jawaharlal Nehru. The success of the Congress in Uttar Pradesh has been attributed to Rahul Gandhi, who was in charge of rebuilding the party in this former stronghold. This achievement—his first major success in fact—made him a strong contender for the post of prime minister after Manmohan Singh. The success of the Congress is also attributed to the popularity of certain social welfare policies enacted by it during the UPA I tenure. The UPA's efforts to implement job security scheme through the National Rural Employment Guarantee Act and waiver a massive amount of farm debt were identified as in large part contributed to the Congress' victory in 2009.

Based on the National Election Study data conducted by the Centre for Study of Developing Societies, New Delhi, Jaffrelot and Verniers (2009) argue that the urban middle class supported the Congress in 2009 since it appreciated the 2008 nuclear deal with the USA. The upper-class support for the Congress has increased from 25.4 per cent in 2004 to 30.3 per cent in 2009 while the support of the same class for the BJP declined from 30.3 per cent to 24.5 per cent during the same period. The middle-class support to Congress declined marginally from 29.9 per cent in 2004 to 29.3 per cent. The middle-class support to the BJP declined by more than 10 per cent from 28.9 per cent in 2004 to 18.5 per cent in 2009. The lower-middle-class support for Congress went up from 26 per cent in 2004 to 28.8 per cent in 2009 while the same class support for the BJP declined from 22.1 per cent in 2004 to 19.75 per cent in 2009. The urban middle class that had deserted the Congress and voted for the BJP in 1999 and 2004 returned to its fold in 2009 (Baru 2014, 273). Therefore, the party suffered electoral reversals consecutively following the shift of the middle-class voters away from the BJP.

The Congress was not behind in wooing the middle class. A year ahead of the 2014 elections, the Jaipur declaration of the All India Congress Committee (AICC) session (2013) acknowledged the need to take on board the concerns of the aspiring middle class and youth, even as it made a slew of suggestion both for the empowerment and security of women. In the section on 'Political Challenges', the Congress (Jaipur in Rajasthan) Declaration says,

> The Congress recognizes there is a new aspiration for advancement among the people, especially among the youth and the middle class … The Congress pledges to speak for both the young middle-class India and the young deprived India.… [It goes on to say that the party] will be responsive to the new aspirations of the youth and will offer credible policies and programs, especially job creating programs. (Prabhu 2015)

Similarly in the section on 'Emerging Socio-Economic Challenges', the document acknowledges 'that there is a rising educated and aspirational middle class, especially in urban areas, and adds that a climate conducive to their advancement must be created … by creating' 10 million jobs every year (Prabhu 2015).

With the growth of urbanization, there have been subtle changes in the political discourse in recent years. Narendra Modi, when he was the Gujarat chief minister, first spoke about the importance of an aspirational neo-middle class—recent beneficiaries of economic growth who are moving into urban life and rising the income ladder. In the run-up to the 2014 elections, leaders of the Congress and the BJP, particularly the BJP prime-ministerial candidate Narendra Modi, were active on social media to address the tech-savvy middle classes. Even the 'homegrown' leaders from the state-level parties such as Nitish Kumar and Lalu Prasad Yadav were not behind in their attempt to woo the mobile phone-holding aspiring lower middle class from semi-urban locales. Modi's victory is being considered as yet another confirmation of the growing importance of the middle class in Indian politics which we discuss in the next chapter.

## Does Middle Class Support the BJP?

The politics of India's new middle class, which emerged on the national level in the mid-1980s onwards with the decline of Nehruvian consensus and some of the liberalization policies initiated by Rajiv Gandhi, needs closer scrutiny. Although it is highly diverse and complex in its composition, this increasingly vocal urban middle class had begun to identify itself as a distinctive group with specific interests in politics. The new middle class has occupied a position of strength 1980s onwards largely because of its numerical growth. The new middle class has been instrumental in installing the BJP governments in states and at the centre 1990s onwards. No political party was able to ignore the demands and aspirations of this growing class since its support has become a decisive factor in elections. Besides, the structural changes in the Indian economy have given a fillip to the significance and role of the new middle class in the arena of public policymaking and political discourse. Hence, this section aims at capturing the complexities of new middle-class politics in contemporary India.

The political map of India had been decisively reworked since the late 1980s, in ideological as well as in party political terms, owing to the decline of the Congress's popularity. With the opening of the doors to the alleged communalization of Indian politics, the organizational ability of the Congress party has declined, and the BJP on its Hindutva plank, supported by the Sangh Parivar, reaped the rewards. The Congress opportunism and vacillation on issues such as the Shah Bano case, the Mandal and Mandir, and demolition of the Babri masjid have weakened the secular credentials of the party as well of the country. The vacuum created by the progressive self-destruction of the Congress Party has been filled by the BJP in the 1990s.

Moreover, the BJP began to advocate for members of the middle class, particularly those of the upper castes, along cultural lines. After the decision on 27 per cent quota for OBCs under the Mandal Commission, middle-class sentiments began to think of the Janata Dal and the Congress Party as the political playground of the lower-castes and religious minorities. Due to feelings of marginalization and the increased enfranchisement of lower-caste communities, the middle class needed a party able to represent its desire for economic liberalization paired with social conservatism (Bhatt and Mukta 2000). The 'democratic resurgence' of lower castes deepened the regionalism, and the growth of regional parties enabled them to wield power not only in states but increasingly at the national level by joining the alliance at the national governments.

The transformation of the liberal middle class into a new middle-class identity marked a distinctive shift in contemporary Indian politics. There was a diminishing appeal of the poverty-removal paradigm of the Congress in the 1980s and 1990s owing to the increased social mobility among the new middle classes. A large number of people, who were once poor, graduated to the middle class or new middle-class category with an improved economic situation in the aftermath of the Green Revolution and expansion of the private sector.

The rise of the new middle class brought class transformation in the country, and this class was looking forward to hearing more progressive development policies from parties which would enable its members to fulfil their aspirations either in terms of jobs or consumption of goods. Interestingly, the BJP has not invoked the poverty-removal narrative like the Congress in the elections. Instead, the BJP blamed the Congress for the sustenance of poverty. Moreover, this educated class, which travels around the globe and loves the motherland, celebrates nationalism envisioned by the BJP. Therefore, the new middle-class rise has led to the growth of the BJP, and members of this class backed its polity.

Another reason for the new middle-class disenchantment with the Congress was corruption and limited deregulation of the economy. The new middle class was supporting Rajiv Gandhi in the mid-1980s, but, by the 1990s, many of them switched their allegiances to the BJP. The new middle class shifted its loyalty from the Congress because Rajiv Gandhi undertook half-hearted liberalization measures during his reign and the government was indulged in both petty and grand corruption, particularly Bofors. During UPA I and UPA II, several scams, including coal, 2G spectrum allocation, broke out and caused resentment among the middle class.

The urban middle class increasingly began to turn to the BJP, as it represents itself as a strong middle class-oriented nationalist party—one that could provide an alternative to the Congress party that the middle class viewed as corrupt and captured by subordinated social groups (Hansen 1999, 58). Moreover, in the 1980s, the urban middle class switched its loyalty from Rajiv Gandhi's regime because it turned away from earlier promises of economic reforms in favour of populist electoral strategies. Rajiv Gandhi failed to live up to the expectations of a new urban middle-class-oriented prime minister and was unable to tackle the rise in prices of commodities which hurt the comfort level of the middle class. One of the reasons for Rajiv Gandhi's electoral debacle in 1989 was his inability to contain inflation.

One more reason for the new middle-class disenchantment with the Congress was its appeasement of minorities. The new middle-class support to the Congress was dampened by domestic religious and ethnic violence in the 1980s. The new Hindu middle-class political frustration took the form of growing alienation from the Congress party, which was increasingly perceived by the urban middle class as a party that depended on the politics of vote bank and that pandered excessively to Muslims and to the lower classes and castes. The critique of secularism that was sustained through the 1970s by the Jana Sangh—a critique that complained about special treatment for Muslims—was taken forward by the BJP in the 1980s under the leadership of Advani. The leadership of the BJP in the 1980s aimed to recover an ideology of Hindutva from the works of Jana Sangh leaders and to present these ideas forcefully to the Indian public. The BJP was pressing the argument that the Congress pursued a doctrine of 'pseudo-secularism' since the days of Nehru for electoral gains. The politics of Hindutva advocated by the BJP had filled the political vacuum created by the Congress' decline through sustained campaigns of the Sangh Parivar since the mid-1980s. The BJP found more green pasture and expanded mass base support because of changes in Indian society. These include the end of the Nehruvian consensus and the intensification of market relations.

The implementation of the Mandal Commission recommendations and the politics of Mandir symbolized in the destruction of the Babri

Masjid equally contributed to the emergence of a constituency among the new middle class in the countryside and urban areas for political Hinduism. The RSS and VHP and its affiliates, which supported the BJP, were said to be widely associated with these events. In fact, some of the young men who participated in the Ram Janmabhoomi movement belonged to the lower-middle class from the upper castes, and their participation has to be seen in the context of protests against 27 per cent reservations to the OBCs.

Did religious factor play any significant role in the new middle class while drawn into open support of the BJP? It is argued that the Ayodhya movement established the legitimacy of Hindutva among the Hindu middle class as well as confirming the party's political threat to the Congress (Hansen 1999). A survey conducted in Delhi and western Uttar Pradesh shortly after the demolition of the Babri Masjid revealed that 60 per cent of white-collar professionals and 62 per cent of traders approved of the demolition of the mosque, while support fell to 28 per cent among workers. And among a significant number of middle-class people who 'have acquired economic status but not corresponding social status', there was anxiety 'to bring the two into consonance' partly through religious observance and congregational activities (Dubey 1992, 157).

As argued by Moore (1966), India achieved political democracy but was unable to establish social and economic democracy to the extent desired. Intensive political competition, caste and communal conflicts in the 1970s and 1980s have increased a struggle to control the scarce resources of the state. The democratic upsurge concentrated in the northern heartland challenged the domination of the upper castes and upper classes in the bureaucracy, as well as parliamentary institutions. Such trends have led to the emergence of two complementary narratives that cast middle-class politics as a story of alienation and resurgence. On the one hand, the middle class alienated by the political assertion of lower caste and class groups retreated from the Congress party and from the conventional terrain of formal electoral politics. On the other hand, this alienation has led to a resurgence of middle-class politics or what Corbridge and Harriss (2000) have termed 'elite revolts', as the middle classes sought to reassert themselves through their support for both Hindu nationalism and economic liberalization in the 1990s. They saw political Hinduism as the most important apparatus for safeguarding their privileges. And the BJP wants to transform India into a sovereign, disciplined, powerful nation by invoking its greatness of Hindu India in the past and favouring globalization and integration of Indian economy into the global economy (Basu and Kohli 1998, 10). The political Hinduism and liberalization and globalization complement each other. The new middle class likened these positions taken by the BJP since they suit its interests, both ideologically and economically.

Being a pro-capitalist, liberal economic reform had always been a central tenet of BJP policy. It has sidelined the much-publicized motto during the Emergency, 'Be Indian, Buy Indian'. BJP's economic policies,[28] which were largely reshaped under the NDA, provided a big push for the second generation of reforms, opening new sectors to foreign investment. Although this new approach of liberalization caused some concern within the Sangh Parivar such as Swadeshi Jagaran Manch and Bharatiya Mazdoor Sangh, being a party of the middle class, these reforms received further push.

The BJP's newfound opposition to the state-regulated economy won the interest of business classes and brought the party a degree of support it had never previously achieved. New economic policies of the 1990s have served interests of the elite and upper and middle classes who have been in revolt against the model of state-led economic development, which at one time served their interests very well. In the modern India, the middle class made up of a variety of entrepreneurs, information technology (IT) businesspeople, traders and small and medium manufacturers benefited most from the economic liberalization. All these features firmly located the BJP within the important domestic trends present within India in 1998 as the NDA entered government. Protecting the interests and the Hindu identity of the middle class would, therefore, further allow the mainstream promotion of Hindutva and its core normative principles (Ogden 2012). The

---

[28] The BJP initially laid emphasis upon swadeshi economics, arguing that India's independence and sovereignty need to be protected from outside influence.

support for the BJP and Hindutva is by no means unanimous among the middle-class Hindus. Indeed, the allegiance of the middle class is being contested by both the religious nationalists and secular-minded organizations. Secular-minded middle-class Hindus and Muslims in India, and elsewhere, have actively attempted to promote secular views and heal the sectarian rift (Lakha 1999, 268).

For the Hindu middle class, 'BJP support of economic liberalization policies addressed their rising economic ambition' (Pandey 2007, 541). The middle classes, a major constituency of the BJP, set the party's agenda from chauvinistic nationalism to economic reform without necessarily harbouring the communalism of subordinate caste Hindus. By being in tune with the mainstream developments within Indian society, the BJP itself became part of that mainstream, legitimizing Hindutva through a consolidation of its middle-class support base (Ogden 2012). This has been seen as a shift of 'the centre of gravity of Indian politics to the right', particularly concerning capitalism and positive secularism, which questioned the legitimacy of the Congress' main poll plank secularism (Vanaik 2002, 322). The BJP came out with a range of appeals from the Ram Mandir to national security to pro-business policies combined with strong nationalist discipline in an attempt to garner the support of large sections of the 'non-committed voters' in the middle class.

The BJP's media strategy too worked well and contributed to establishing its base among the middle class. Unlike other parties, BJP media division cultivates and develops a good rapport with journalists and caters to prevailing news values with sensational quotes and eye-catching pictures. Reporters from the national and state capitals were given airfare to cover quarterly party conclaves. Sympathetic reporters were cultivated and 'rewarded' with 'exclusive' inside stories to further BJP's publicity. The BJP's website too constructs, perpetuates and maintains a political image that caters to the hegemony of the upper caste and the middle class (Atterberry 2012, 20).

Besides election results, the voting behaviour too indicates that the BJP has developed a strong electoral base among the middle class in the 1990s and onwards. The BJP has consistently received a greater share of upper-caste middle-class support, a pattern repeated in the 2014 elections. The success of the BJP in gaining middle-class support has been achieved through the conscious construction of a particular form of an upper-caste Hindu middle-class identity for what Yogendra Yadav et al. (1999) termed the BJP's 'new social bloc'. Between 1996 and 1999, while middle-class electoral support for the Congress declined by about 4 per cent from 32.1 per cent to 28.2 per cent, the middle-class support for the BJP increased from 23.9 per cent to 28.2 per cent (Palshikar 2001, 173). The N-test in May 1998, which the middle class believed enhanced the country's self-respect among the comity of nations, was said to be the major reason for the signifi- cant rise in middle-class support for the BJP in the 1999 elections. In the BJP, writes Suhas Palshikar (2001, 172), the middle classes could find almost everything they dreamt of—a frankly market-oriented economic policy, a foreign policy striving to befriend the Americans, a suave middle-of-the-road Prime Minister A. B. Vajpayee along with a strong Home Minister L. K. Advani—all coupled with an appropriate dosage of a chauvinistic cultural-nationalist assertion.

Although the BJP was defeated, the new middle class in urban constituencies supported the BJP in the 2004 general elections. Voters were also concerned with their immediate needs of water, road, elec- tricity and job rather than with the BJP's emphasis on India's economic growth that mainly benefited the middle classes (Varshney 2007). A close look at the 2004 survey data reveals that the BJP-led NDA was defeated mainly due to a loss of support among the plebeian classes (Dalits, Adivasis and the lower OBCs), who felt that they did not belong to the BJP's newly formed exclusive 'feel-good club of India' (Sheth 2005, 38).

In urban constituencies, among the urban middle class, the NDA parties enjoyed a 14 per cent lead in 2004 elections. This was largely because of the identification of the rich and the middle class with the BJP (Sridharan 2016, 55). But a significant section of BJP's conven- tional middle-class supporters as well as most upper-class members of minority communities, who have supported the BJP and its allies in 1999 and endorsed the party's economic policies, turned away because they felt that the majoritarian politics of hate and reforms do not go well together (Sridharan 2016). These trends were repeated in 2009 Lok Sabha elections with the BJP losing a further 22 seats, while the Congress gained 61.

Therefore, the new middle has had been a much wider political influence and both coalitions led by the Congress and the BJP have been vying for their support by lending uncritical support for the market reforms measures in order to court the middle-class support (Kumar 2013). The manifestos of the Congress and the BJP in 2004, 2009, 2014 and 2019 parliamentary elections reveal both the parties' eagerness to secure the middle-class support.

While the Ayodhya movement was a game-changer for the BJP, angry with the appeasement politics and rampant corruption during the Congress rule,[29] the middle class comprising professionals cutting across industries, businessmen and the intelligentsia turned hostile to the Congress and viewed the party with suspicion in its fight against corruption. It is not only the BJP's numerical strength in Parliament and the state legislatures that have been growing but also the acceptance of Hindutva ideology in all sections of society, including among people of Indian origin overseas, at all levels has been growing simultaneously. Substantive changes occurred in the country's policy norms, both domestically and externally, during the BJP-led NDA's six-year regime (1998–2004). Despite its electoral defeats in two consecutive elections (2004 and 2009), the BJP-led NDA witnessed the emergence of an acceptable political–religious nationalism capable of successfully challenging the secular origins of the Congress and the Indian state. The BJP emerged as a true mass party and national alternative to the Congress.

The arguments here address the BJP's ascent to power and legitimacy while in government, and the way in which it provided Sangh Parivar supporters with the opportunity to influence the normative basis of domestic politics such that the public opinion generally tilted towards Hindutva. However, the BJP-led NDA safeguarded the fundamental principles enshrined in the Indian Constitution such as

---

[29] Former Prime Minister Rajiv Gandhi' famous remark in 1985 that only 15 paise of every rupee meant for the welfare of the poor reaches them indicates the level of corruption.

equality, secularism, religious tolerance and plurality, while sidestepping its original principles concerning the swadeshi. Although BJP's political rise almost came to a halt for a decade (2004–2014), its spectacular rise in the 2014 Lok Sabha elections under the leadership of the then Gujarat Chief Minister Narendra Modi indicates fluidity of Indian political culture and ambivalence of the middle-class support to political parties. We discuss the causes for the BJP's victory and Modi's policies and moving the political ground towards the Right in the last five years in the next chapter.

CHAPTER 5

# Middle Class and Narendra Modi

## Introduction

The 2014 parliamentary election is termed as 'historic' for its overwhelming mandate received in the Lok Sabha for the first time since 1984. Two outcomes are notable in these elections: first, the BJP scripted the most spectacular electoral triumph in the history of independent India; and second, the performance of the Congress Party was disastrous and the party was reduced to its worst-ever performance in the general elections since Independence. The BJP made significant inroads in many sections of the society as well as geographical areas that were not a part of the party's traditional bastions. Most of the political analysts analysing the election results indicated at two strong pointers. First, the proliferation of scams and increased political corruption and second, emerging aspirations of the middle class and their frustration with the existing political scenario during the UPA II regime.

The BJP encashed on middle-class aspirations and rural India's resurgent hopes. The narrative was that there was a leader who came from the middle class and understood their aspirations. The narrative focused on national pride and the proliferation of political corruption. Under the leadership of Narendra Modi, the BJP's strength had increased from 116 to 282 in the 543 elected members of the

Lok Sabha; the first time in history that the BJP had enjoyed an absolute majority. The 2014 general election was considered as one of the most extraordinary elections in India's history and will remain unforgettable for a long period.

Chief Minister Narendra Modi's emphatic victory in Gujarat legislative assembly elections of 2012, the third time in a row, brought him to the centre stage of national politics. On 14 September 2013, six months ahead of the 2014 general election, the BJP formally announced Narendra Modi as its prime-ministerial candidate. Modi's anointment came after several weeks of back-room manoeuvrings at the behest of the RSS and amidst stiff opposition from veteran party leader L. K. Advani (defeated prime-ministerial candidate in 2009; Reddy 2013).[1]

A combination of factors worked in favour of Modi to emerge as the party's prime-ministerial candidate. Banking on his image as an efficient administrator and a powerful and compelling orator, he ran a high-voltage campaign focusing on the failures of the UPA II government and attacking the dynastic leadership of Congress. The backing of influential sections of corporate India for his pro-business leadership, his proximity with RSS and with religious heads, and already established presence in the social media embraced by the new middle class provided Modi considerable lead over other candidates having prime-ministerial ambitions.

The announcement of Gujarat's longest-serving chief minister as prime-ministerial candidate has struck a chord with the middle class. Traditionally, the Hindu upper castes and the middle class by economic stratification formed the major chunk of the BJP voters. As the chief minister, Modi wooed the middle class, and the high growth of the state economy has lifted a vast number of the population out of poverty. Class-based voting patterns have contributed to the success of Narendra Modi, not only because he has capitalized on the support of the middle class, traditionally the pro-BJP, but also because he has

---

[1] L. K. Advani shot off a two-paragraph letter to the BJP President Rajnath Singh expressing his 'anguish' over his style of functioning. Mr Advani skipped a meeting of the Parliamentary Board, the highest decision-making body of the party, which had taken a decision to announce Narendra Modi as the party's prime-ministerial candidate.

attracted large sections of the emerging 'neo-middle class' (Jaffrelot 2014a, 19). Modi called the people who came out of poverty as 'neo-middle class', an aspiring social category that wanted to join the rank of the middle class.

The size of the new middle class, as we noted in earlier chapters, had expanded enormously since the introduction of economic reforms in the early 1990s. This new middle class was fiercely articulating issues, and it was not afraid or embarrassed to aggressively project its ambitions, was sceptical of the two-decade-old ways of running the coalition government and found a new hero, Narendra Modi. Modi had emerged with a bold, right-wing narrative in a country with a socialist past. Besides numerical strength, the middle class is electorally more impactful relative to its size because of its social capital and opinion-shaping character (Deshpande 2003). In fact, expansion of the new middle class and rise of Modi's political career grew parallel to each other since the 1980s.

The success of Modi's narrative among the new middle class, particularly in urban areas, is not surprising if one looks at his developmental policies in Gujarat. 'The Modi regime's adoption of the global language of neoliberalism—good governance, growth/investment, and development—that was well understood by policymakers, investors, and middle-class consumers at home and abroad' (Kaur 2015, 327). Modi acquired a larger than life image—a messiah of development. Most in the industry concluded that the 2002 communal riots were an aberration that was now past. Industry leaders were as keen as Modi that Gujarat should not get a bad name as the home to riots and disorder. Of course, Modi ran a tightly controlled state government and prevented a recurrence of communal riots after 2002.

Modi's tenure in the state was marked by a galloping of Gujarat economy, the fastest growing among India's states. Under Modi, Gujarat became an economic dynamo (Kaplan 2009). Gujarat secured top rank as the country's most economically free state in 2005 (Saran 2005).[2] The stamp of approval by a report carrying the imprint

[2] In 2005, the Rajiv Gandhi Institute of Contemporary Studies and the German funding agency Friedrich Naumann Stifung brought out a report

of the Rajiv Gandhi Foundation, chaired by the Congress Party chief Sonia Gandhi, created a political controversy. Similar kudos awarded to the state from *India Today*, the magazine which began the annual *State of the States Report* from 2003 and regularly featured Modi's Gujarat on top of the evaluation list of various parameters.

Indeed, Modi's credibility as a prime-ministerial contender rested largely on his reputation for the excellent economic management of his own state. The 'Vibrant Gujarat', billed as Indian Davos, a biannual investment summit being hosted since 2003, acquired altogether new character once Ratan Tata,[3] India's most respected businessman, Reliance Industries Ltd Chairman Mukesh Ambani and Adani Group Chairman Gautam Adani joined the 'praise Modi chorus'. On the whole, his 12-year-long innings as the chief minister was, in the minds of many voters, synonymous with prosperity, development and good governance—qualities that exit polls suggested were at the forefront of voters' minds in 2014 (Vaishnav 2017, xi).

We made an attempt here to understand the reasons for the Congress losing the support of the middle class. The BJP's campaign, which was different from earlier ones, led to an unprecedented scale of the party's victory. The middle-class support to the BJP and Modi in the changed social and economic scenario, particularly in the Hindutva context, contributed to the party's victory.

## Did the Congress Ignore the Middle Class?

The first wave of economic reforms unleashed during the Congress government under P. V. Narasimha Rao and Manmohan Singh (1991–1996) played a vital role in the expansion of the new middle class. Later, the size of the class expanded exponentially owing to high growth rate[4] during the UPA I headed by the Congress (2004–2009).

authored by economist, Bibek Debroy and Laveesh Bhandari titled, *Economic Freedom for States of India*.

[3] Tata set up its Nano car project in Gujarat after it was thrown out of West Bengal. Tata has given credit to Modi for establishing the car plant in Gujarat.

[4] A decade under the UPA saw the Indian economy grow by an average 7.6 per cent; 8.3 per cent excluding 2012–2013 and 2013–2014. Significantly, between

The vast majority saw their incomes go up significantly enough to improve their living style and realized the dreams of joining the new middle class. This new middle class was the beneficiary of a new knowledge economy. Unfortunately, the Congress party which has been historically the centrist party has struggled to grasp its own contributions to the economy and expansion of the new middle class. The first family of Congress and its intellectual support networks did not understand changes in Indian society. Focusing largely on the poor, the Congress tended to ignore the middle class and lower middle classes who were deemed to have become insistently aspirational. (Khare 2014, 223).

It is in this new middle class that the BJP and Modi saw a green pasture for a new nationalist wave and non-corruption argument. During the 2014 elections, the Congress was not successful to reach out to this new demographic that had emerged during its own rule. Besides the Congress' failure to tap the development aspirations, its campaign did not go beyond *roti* to *shiksha, bijli, sadak aur paani* (education, electricity, road and water). The society has changed a lot during a decade-long rule (2004–2014) of the UPA led by the Congress. The voter in 2014 had become richer and more confident than in 2004 and 2009 and was unlikely to be satisfied with a minimum wage guarantee and free doles. The UPA policies not only alienated the middle class but also the poor, as the nation had moved from the welfare ethos to an aspirational ethos. As Tewari (2014) puts it, 'children of MGNREGA no longer sought subsistence but were itching to claim their place in the middle class of India'.

The credit for swelling the ranks of the middle class should go to the two terms of UPA regime under Manmohan Singh which pursued economic liberalization, opening up new opportunities to raise the income levels of the aspiring families. But the Congress failed to tap their sentiments and that provided an ideal platform for Modi to tap it to his electoral advantage. Yogendra Yadav, political analyst and national president of the Swaraj India, argues that 'Narendra Modi's

2004–2005 and 2011–2012, the ratio of Indians below the official poverty line fell from 37.2 per cent to 21.9 per cent, which was much sharper than the decline from 45.3 per cent to 37.2 per cent over a longer period from 1993–1994 to 2004–2005.

politics represents the intersection of caste, class and educational privilege of the Indian middle class'. Moreover, 'Indian nationalism was a dominant middle-class construct, which has found voice in Modi's brand of Hindutva' (Mustafi 2013). Ultimately, the neo-middle class that was the product of the past decade proved to be the Grand Old Party's gravedigger (Damodaran 2014).

Since 1989, new communal, caste and class dynamics, mainly the rise of the middle class, together with the apparent budding of a 'new social block' and the materialization of aspirational voting in 2014 have eroded the Congress base (Farooqui and Sridharan 2016). Modi believed to have figured out that India has moved from being a middle-aged, poor country to young, lower-middle-class income country that strongly believes it can get rich quick and emerge as one of the global leaders. Lower-income middle-class groups are more or less connected to middle-class dreams through their televisions and mobile phones and want more. He has won over the business community and the middle class with the promise of minimum government, maximum governance, promoting private and foreign capital investment, focusing on fast growth rate rather than government welfare spending, emphasizing infrastructure investment, service delivery and ease of doing business. As the 2014 results indicated, Modi emerged as the champion of the new middle class which form the core issue of discussion in this chapter.

One of the notable features of the 2014 general election was that it was conducted on nine separate polling days staggered over five weeks (from 7 April to 12 May 2014). In 2014, the electoral register had grown to 834 million, an increase of 100 million voters over the 2009 general elections. The numbers on the rolls exceeded the entire population of North America or Europe and Russia combined (Chawla 2019, 3–4). As many as 66.38 per cent of the electorate had cast their ballots in favour of one of 8,521 candidates representing 464 political parties in 927,533 polling stations in 29 states and 7 union territories (or areas administered directly by the national government). The election witnessed a record voting, highest in India's post-Independence electoral history, beating the record of 1984 when 64.01 per cent of Indians voted in the aftermath of Indira Gandhi's assassination.

## The Campaign Struck a Different Chord

The 2014 election campaign of the BJP was unique in many ways. For the first time, the BJP projected a chief minister of the state as the prime-ministerial candidate in national elections. It was for the first time after Nehru and Indira Gandhi that a person, Narendra Modi, with his sharp nationalist Hindutva messaging and towering presence, emerged bigger than the party (Subrahmaniam 2019). Being the star campaigner in the elections, Modi attended more than 5,000 election rallies/events while travelling more than three lakh kilometres across India (NDTV 2014). Modi commenced his election campaign nearly a year ahead of polling and followed his own unique style of connecting people wherever he addressed the public meetings. Modi's campaign was professional and in sync with the anxieties and aspirations of young Indians. The campaign was also a subject of much public debate and produced some important scholarly works (Khare 2014; Price 2015; Sardesai 2014). This is also the first elections where the ruling party (Congress) has called other parties to join hands with it to stop the opposition's, Narendra Modi's, march towards Delhi.

The personalization of the BJP election campaign was reflected in the downplaying of the party apparatus and coalition politics. The party's campaign in 2014 was different from the one during the NDA under Vajpayee which was more of the collegial character. It was more of a presidential form of a campaign, turning it into Modi versus others. Lack of opposition unity, the stark contrast in the image of the then Prime Minister Manmohan Singh as a soft, indecisive and pliable leader against a strong, decisive and incorruptible Narendra Modi proved effective in clinching a decisive mandate in favour of the BJP.

The Modi-centric campaign coined some slogans which became very popular; some of them are *achhe din aane waale hain* (good days are coming), *sabka saath, sabka vikas* (participation of all, for the development of all), *na khaoonga, na khaane doonga* (neither will I indulge in corruption, nor allow anyone else to indulge in it), and *abki bar Modi sarkar* (this time, Modi government). While the 'Nehruvian consensus' embedded with the secular socialist state (Guha 2007) dominated the Congress regime, Modi's rhetoric of good times signalled a decisive rightward shift to a capitalist dream world submerged in Hindu cultural nationalism that the aspiring middle class rooted for (Kaur 2015). The focus on combating corruption, development of basic infrastructure such as roads, electricity, water supply, e-governance, easy land acquisition for industrialists, which had been the hallmark of the Modi government in Gujarat, became talking points especially in the context of his bid for power to head the Indian government.

Modi hammered at the 'dynasty model' of the Congress and coined a slogan *maa–beta ki sarkar, nahi chalegi* (mother–son's government will not run). The slogan provided a perfect pitch for the BJP to attack the Congress and the Nehru–Gandhi family. The BJP's prime-ministerial candidate appealed to the electorate to challenge the old arrangements revolving around the dynasty rule for the last four decades. The timely publication of Sanjaya Baru's *The Accidental Prime Minister* (2014) threw light on the dynastic control and power play at the PMO during the reign of Manmohan Singh. Calling for a change and asking people to vote for the BJP at a rally on 2 February 2014, in Meerut, Uttar Pradesh, Modi thundered at the SP government headed by Akhilesh Yadav and asked voters,

> Do you get power 24 hours a day? If your mother is unwell can you switch on a fan? If your son has exams can you turn on the light so he can study? When the British were here they saw the people of Meerut as enemies … but your own government? Why does Meerut not get roads, railways, and an airport? What has Meerut done? What is Meerut's crime?[5]

This kind of audience-connecting speeches saw spontaneous applause and cheers. Many even chanted 'Modi Modi', and he acknowledged them and 'bowed' his head. The chant of 'Modi Modi' became an icon of the campaign and gave birth to the term 'bhakt' for the BJP sympathizers.

[5] https://www.indiatoday.in/india/narendra-modi-s-speeches/story/narendra-modis-speech-at-meerut-rally-on-feb-2-2014-181003-2014-02-14 (accessed on 6 July 2015).

Calling voters *bhaiyo aur behno* (brothers and sisters), at least a dozen times during his speech, Modi dubbed the UPA government as 'remote-controlled' and 'lame', as he raised the pitch for a strong and stable government at the Centre. 'Who has been in power most of these last 55 years?' he asked, using the utterances of UPA chief in a different context.

> 'If power is poison, who has taken the most? Who has a stomach full of poison? Who is vomiting it out now? It is Congress, the party which divides and rules, which pits one religion against another, states against states, which is breaking the country'…. 'We need the politics of development, so the poor need welfare, the young get jobs, mothers and sisters get respect'. He pauses, then calls out: 'Time is running out… Promise me you will change this nation': 'Vote for India'. (Burke 2014)

Modi is a great orator and often called one of the best orators in the world. During the election campaign, Modi clearly knew how to connect well with their audiences by raising specific regional issues. He could keep a huge crowd in the grip of his hands through his rhetoric. He delivered speeches, almost all of which he perceived himself after consulting widely, without notes but with great precision, weaving the personal and the political, the local and the national, the emotional with the policy content. Lance Price (2015, 10–11) argues that the Blairs, Thatchers, Clintons and Barack Obama, all knew how to impress their audience but none of them ever engaged a crowd with such fervent, visceral passion as Modi. Another author and a senior fellow at the Centre for a New American Security, Robert D. Kaplan (2009), says, 'I have met Jimmy Carter, Bill Clinton, and both Bushes. At close range, Modi beats them all in charisma. Whenever he opened his mouth, he suddenly had real, mesmerizing presence'. He seems enthralled by his persona at times, at his accomplishments, intelligence and shrewdness.

Besides his organizational skills inherited from his past role as a *pracharak* (canvasser) in RSS, Modi knew how to galvanize huge crowds by resorting to sarcastic formulas and plays on words. A well-prepared presidential-style campaign by Modi, fuelled by seemingly unending reserves of financial support, provided a fillip to the BJP by infusing new life in the party and enthused the activists of the party that otherwise had looked drifting and listless a year ago (Suri and Palshikar 2014, 39). He mixes regional languages with Hindi and English and speaks cleverly appropriating popular discontent with existing governments. Humour too is a key to his communication as it drives home the party's propaganda. He derides the complex bureaucratic mechanisms that have come to characterize the UPA regime. Wherever he visits, Modi refers to names of local deities and local heroes at the beginning of his speech and waves at crowd, wearing local hats and shawls presented to him by party workers.

## Historic Mandate

The sensational sweep and scale of the BJP's electoral victory was undoubtedly the direct result of the strong upsurge in the popularity of the prime-ministerial candidate, Modi. The Gujarat chief minister was clearly the master of the 'Modi wave' that had caught the imagination of the large sections of the India's voters which had given the BJP-led NDA an unprecedented and historic mandate. With the BJP winning a majority (282 seats) on its own, a remarkable paradigm shift had taken place in the trajectory of India's parliamentary politics. Breaking the trend of the last three decades in which no party was to pull off a runaway victory, the BJP came to power, free from the pressure of coalition politics (*The Hindu* 2017, 258). The Congress, which led the UPA and had ruled the country for 10 years, crashed to ignominious defeat with a mere double-digit figure (44 seats) in parliament, its worst electoral tally since Independence.

The BJP's victory is significant for many reasons. For the first time since the Rajiv Gandhi-led Congress party registered a thumping victory in 1984 in the elections held a few weeks after the assassination of his mother and incumbent Prime Minister Indira Gandhi under a sympathy wave, India voted to a political party (BJP) to the Lok Sabha with the absolute majority only in 2014. The NDA won 336 seats (38.3 per cent votes), while the BJP alone won 282 seats, enough for a majority of its own. The BJP polled 31.1 per cent of the votes in 2014 against 19 per cent votes in 2009. With 31.1 per cent of the votes, the BJP managed to win almost 52 per cent of the seats in the Lok Sabha. In Uttar Pradesh alone, the BJP won an all-time high 71 seats out of 80 seats. Amit Shah, a trusted lieutenant of Modi, brilliantly worked out a strategy to win Uttar Pradesh by identifying winnable candidates and organizing rallies on a grand scale. The Congress, which was reduced to its total tally of 44 seats, received just 19.3 per cent votes polled. The party failed to even open its account in 14 states.

This is the first time that political party other than the Congress has come so close to being pan-Indian in terms of its geographical reach. Although the BJP was able to muster the support of Muslim voters in some pockets in some states, the fact remains that the party did not have even a single member in the Lok Sabha from the Muslim community that constitutes 14.2 per cent of the country's population (as per the 2011 Census of India). For the first time since Independence, Uttar Pradesh did not elect a single Muslim to the Lok Sabha despite 55 candidates being fielded by the non-BJP parties.

The victory of the BJP excited many because they felt that it was a victory for 'economic freedom'. The Janata Party's victory in the 1977 elections was seen as political freedom, while the 2014 election result was seen as economic freedom from 'policy paralysis' (Panagariya 2014). After leading the BJP's resounding victory in the elections, Narendra Modi became the 14th Prime Minister of India on 26 May 2014.

## Unique Modi-fied Effect

Modi has many firsts to his credit. For the first time, a politician who had never been part of national politics led the main opposition party in the 2014 elections to a resounding success. Not having been a part of the earlier NDA government, Modi was a complete outsider for Delhi's political culture. He is also the first prime minister to have been born in independent India. He was the first BJP leader who was projected as its prime-ministerial candidate well before elections and successfully won the majority of seats in the Lok Sabha. For the first time, the Congress abandoned an incumbent prime minister (Manmohan Singh) as its campaign leader and projected only a dynastic figure, Rahul Gandhi.

Modi takes pride in being India's first OBC prime minister from a low-income background. But this claim was contested by H. D. Deve Gowda, prime minister during 1996–1997 (Aji 2015), who belonged to the dominant Vokkaliga community in Karnataka. Modi also takes pride in the fact that he made a living by selling tea in his younger days. Modi's meteoric rise—from an ordinary tea seller to one of the longest-serving chief ministers in the country and somebody who dared to challenge the most powerful political family in the Indian politics—was a story that captured the imagination of the Indian electorate, including many traditional Congress supporters. Modi rarely addresses rallies in English and does not have a formal educational background steeped in the Western tradition, which makes him more 'common' than many of his political rivals, particularly the Gandhis (Palit 2015).

Modi is also the most abused politician in the country since he became the chief minister of Gujarat in 2001. Leaders of the Opposition parties called him 'Hitler' and 'fascist' soon after the 2002 communal carnage in Gujarat. During the 2007 Gujarat assembly elections, the then Congress President Sonia Gandhi called Modi *maut ka saudagar* (a merchant of death). No day passed without abusing him during the 2014 election and later during his five-year prime minister's term. A former minister, Mani Shankar Aiyar, mocked him by calling him a *chaiwala* (tea seller). He vouched publicly that this *chaiwala* can never become the prime minister of India. Further, he called Modi disparagingly *neech* (most backward) and *feku* (liar).

Delhi Chief Minister Arvind Kejriwal called Modi 'a coward and psychopath' during the 2014 election campaign[6]. Congress Vice-President Rahul Gandhi taunted him as saying *suit-boot ki Sarkar* (a

[6] https://timesofindia.indiatimes.com/city/delhi/Modi-a-coward-and-a-psychopath-Arvind-Kejriwal-following-CBI-raid/articleshow/50181493.cms (accessed on 16 December 2015).

government for the rich and corporates). Congress leader Randeep Surjewala condemned the 'authoritarian' rule of Modi and linked the prime minister to Aurangzeb saying, 'Delhi Sultanate's "dictator" Modi who is crueller than Aurangzeb'.[7] Congress politician Salman Khurshid refers Modi as *napunsak* (impotent) for not putting to stop anti-Muslim violence in Gujarat 2002. Referring to the alleged scam in the Rafale deal, Rahul Gandhi said about Modi, *chowkidar chor hai* (the watchman is a thief), in 2019. Modi is also compared to strong figures from contemporary world history such as Margaret Thatcher, Vladimir Putin, R. T. Erdogan as they are by their arch determinism to direct the course of history (Kapila 2016, 40–41).

Noted intellectuals and litterateurs such as late U. R. Ananthamurthy and Girish Karnad had expressed their doubts and reservation about Modi becoming the prime minister. Jnanpith awardee and acclaimed Kannada writer U. R. Ananthamurthy has said he will not live in India with Narendra Modi as its prime minister, and this triggered angry reactions from the BJP which said he was free to leave India. The saffron brigade dismissed them as the 'shouting brigade of the Congress'. The former Prime Minister H. D. Deve Gowda said he would give up his Lok Sabha seat if Modi gets more than 273 seats in the elections. But Gowda on the last day of the 16th Lok Sabha said that Modi asked him to continue as he was one of the senior members of the House.

With all this abusive language, Modi stuck to his campaign not taking any serious note of this derogatory language, but focused more on his brand. He touched sensitive chords and failures during the earlier years to encash on them and push forth his version of nationalism. He never forgot to end his speech with a *Bharat Mata ki Jai* and giving a kind of new life to the slogan along with *Vande Mataram*. This stuck the needed connection to the hearts of the voices and that made the concoction of a new Modi-fied effect.

---

[7] https://www.thehindu.com/news/national/emergency-talk-to-divert-attention-cong/article24264856.ece (accessed on 2 August 2019).

## The Congress Gets on Back Foot

Rahul Gandhi was proclaimed 'Newsmaker of the Year' in 2009 by *India Today* on the cover of its issue on 4 January 2010, and the Congress–UPA victory in the 2009 parliamentary elections was attributed to him. Sanjay Baru (2014), however, preferred to credit the victory to the image of Manmohan Singh. Rahul Gandhi was projected as the future leader and prime-ministerial candidate of the Congress. In an editorial column, Editor-in-Chief Aroon Purie writes, 'Until 2009, Rahul was in the shadow of his mother as a politician and public figure. For the first time in the year, he seemed to find his own voice and his own style'. Rahul's leadership was appreciated by the magazine for giving 'a blood-rush of youthfulness to India's oldest political tradition and made his party dream differently. Defying politics-as-usual, he embodied the kinetics of change' (Prasannarajan 2010). The Congress chose to put full emphasis on projecting Rahul and spearheading campaign with him at the forefront.

The 'Prince of Purpose' that promised of a change never took off (Prasannarajan 2010). In less than two years the Congress-led UPA II was in disarray. The 'Brand Rahul' was badly damaged in the Uttar Pradesh Assembly elections in 2012, and earlier the Rahul-led Congress lost in Bihar as well.[8] Congress Vice-President Rahul Gandhi led an indefensibly uninspiring campaign and had miserably failed to rally a young and impatient electorate. He also made crucial mistakes during his speeches, and, with less effective public-speaking talent, he could not carry with him the younger middle class.

Senior Congress leaders privately expressed their unhappiness with Rahul Gandhi's leadership, but they were unable to express feelings openly. There was a lack of convergence between party and government, and between party president/vice-president and leaders of the party. There has been a colossal failure of the UPA to consolidate and expand itself as a political force. Bifurcation of existing Andhra Pradesh into two states—Telangana and Andhra Pradesh—decimated

[8] In the 403-member Uttar Pradesh Assembly, the Congress won just 28 seats and secured fourth place.

the party further.[9] It not only lost control of the two state governments but had also lost the throne in Delhi.

The ruling UPA coalition scored badly on a range of issues, the major ones being inflation, corruption, lack of development and unemployment. Increase in prices of all types of commodities and food items had a severe blow on the common people. Frequent hike in fuel (diesel and petrol) prices hit hard the middle-class professionals who use vehicles on a daily basis for commuting from home to office and back. Lack of collective focus, absence of objective analysis of the candidates' strength, and campaign that largely focused on preventing Modi or the BJP coming to power cost the party heavily. But the 'Team Rahul believes "absent and silent" PM has dented Congress's chances'.[10] At the same time, the famous long-drawn fast by Anna Hazare, the anti-corruption crusader who took the nation by storm, also left a precipitating effect on hatred towards the Congress and UPA on the minds of the voters.

The Congress found itself in a dilemma as its Prime Minister Manmohan Singh made an announcement that he was retiring at the end of his term and would not be in contention for the third term. By January 2014, at the fag end of his second term, Manmohan Singh, sensing the humiliating defeat UPA II would get in the general election that year said, 'I do not believe that I have been a weak prime minister. I honestly believe that history will be kinder to me…' (Chengappa 2019b). This worked to the advantage of the BJP as it went into the election with a clear face—its prime-ministerial candidate—while the ruling Congress-led UPA was unable to project a face to lead its campaign (Syal and Shastri 2014, 79). The perception that Rahul Gandhi was interested only in 2019 elections has not gone well with the Congress electorate and the cadre was not enthused. Devoid of serious national issues, Rahul Gandhi raked up the issue

[9] In 2009 Lok Sabha elections, the Congress won 33 Lok Sabha seats in Andhra Pradesh, which helped the Congress to cross the magic figure of 200. The Congress drew blank in Andhra Pradesh, while it won just two seats in Telangana in 2014.

[10] https://timesofindia.indiatimes.com/news/Team-Rahul-believes-absent-PM-has-dented-Congress-chances/articleshow/33145667.cms (accessed on 5 April 2019).

of 'Modi marriage' as a political issue[11], which reflected his political immaturity. The Congress did not make it a fight between two ideologies and parties; instead, it concentrated its attack on Modi, making it a Rahul Gandhi versus Narendra Modi contest. This has become apparently an unequal contest on every count.

In its second term (2009–2014), the UPA government faced serious image crisis vis-à-vis charges of massive corruption at the highest levels. As corruption appeared to grow, many middle-class citizens became wary of state-led solutions to the economic issues facing the country (Chhibber and Verma 2014, 51). The rising public anger as a result of the UPA's 'policy paralysis' stalled economic growth and, worst of all, the disclosure of Nira Radia Tapes,[12] the series of corruption scandals such as the coal scam, the 2G spectrum scam, the Commonwealth Games scam, the Adarsh Housing Society scam, Congress' President Sonia Gandhi's son-in-law Robert Vadra's alleged involvement in fraudulent land deals.

It is argued that 'the discretionary power the state has with respect to land is the single biggest source of corruption' in India (Mehta 2010). Owing to the active judiciary, cabinet ministers, bureaucrats and top corporate executives involved in scams were landed up in jail. All these scams created a desire for change, especially among the youth and middle-class Indians who saw Modi as the leader symbolizing their aspirations of high economic growth unshackled from red tape and corruption. The voters began to trust his poll slogan: *na khaoonga, na khaane doonga.*

---

[11] https://indianexpress.com/article/india/politics/modi-mentioned-wife-in-poll-affidavit-after-sc-order-on-full-disclosure/ (accessed on 10 September 2016). Following the Supreme Court order and later the ECI's order in September 2013, making it mandatory for candidates to fill all columns in their affidavits fully, Modi mentioned his wife Jashodaben for the first time in an election affidavit in 2014 while filing nominations to contest elections from Varanasi and Vadodara. Later, Modi's brother issued a statement describing the marriage as 'child marriage'. Modi always left the column for information on marital status in his affidavit blank, making the space with short dash. This is the first time that he has publicly acknowledged the existence of his wife.

[12] Nira Radia Tapes exposed the tale of a messy nexus between sections of the corporate crowd, the media, politicians, lawyers and other power-brokers.

The list of scams and scandals associated with the UPA II was bewildering in its length and complexity. Political scientist Zoya Hasan, who studied ups and downs in the fortunes of both the Congress and the BJP, particularly in Uttar Pradesh, argues that in 2014 'people wanted the Congress out'. According to her, those who most hoped to see the back of the party were 'the corporate sector, the media, the middle classes, upper castes and so on', but, overall, people were 'pretty disgusted with indecisive leadership, dual power centers, and policy paralysis' (quoted in Price 2015, 69). The middle class was convinced that during the UPA II, the government had fraudulently used 'their' taxes to satisfy Sonia Gandhi's insistence to provide for the welfare of the 'poor'. The middle classes were deeply resentful of how the Congress made the government 'waste' their hard-earned profits and bonuses on a social agenda. Modi had zeroed in on the corruption theme to tap resentment among middle-class members who had enthusiastically voted for Manmohan Singh in 2009 (Khare 2014, 206–207).

It was the middle class that developed a more intimate feeling of being denied their due entitlements as citizens, consumers and voters, and was quick to take ownership of anti-corruption activism spurred by the perception, furthered by mainstream media, that corruption was an attempt to steal the assets of the tax-paying public (Philipose 2019, 36, 50). 'That is why the social contract between the liberal state and the middle classes is broken' (Sassen 2013). News reports, opinion pieces and editorials in the print media during UPA II had a larger focus on corruption and siphoning off funds.

It was the narrative on 'corruption' that encouraged civil society groups and activists to make a run on the UPA II. India against Corruption (IAC) campaign in 2011 was directed primarily at the Congress to whittle away its credibility. Anna Hazare, a former army truck operator and now a Gandhian social activist, became the 'anti-corruption' movement's mascot. Arvind Kejriwal,[13] former Indian

---

[13] Arvind Kejriwal later transformed the anti-corruption movement into a political party called Aam Aadmi Party (AAP), and it was formally launched on 26 November 2012. Later, Kejriwal contested the Delhi Assembly elections and became the chief minister of the AAP government in Delhi.

Revenue Officer, who had already won a Magsaysay Award and was the organizational man behind the IAC, worked out a strategy and mobilized energy behind Anna. Some critics termed the high-profile IAC campaign 'funded by corporates',[14] while others described it as 'a self-righteous middle-class uprising' (*The Economist* 2011).[15] The campaign had a pan-India impact. The Anna movement, and later the Kejriwal-led high-decibel campaign against corruption through his political party, AAP, had shaken the entire swathe of the electorate—from the upper middle class to the poorest of the lot—out of its helpless acceptance of misgovernance and nepotism as 'facts of life' (Khare 2014, 31). 'India disillusioned with passive ruling establishment erupted in a moral rage in a year of multiple injustices' (Prasannarajan 2013a). Although AAP was part of the IAC movement, it was Modi who reaped its electoral harvest due to the lack of grassroots organizational machinery for AAP. The latter could benefit from the movement only in Delhi and partly in Punjab where it had an organizational base. As for the rest of the country, it was Modi and the BJP which tapped the public angst and scored huge electoral gains.

Because corruption fed into the everyday conversations of the newspaper-reading middle class, Modi had built a national mood of anger against the 'corrupt' Congress and targeted and reached out to the original Manmohan Singh constituency—the middle and upper-middle class who valued discipline, integrity and accountability in public life. He targeted the urban voters and youth who had voted for the Congress in the 2009 election and who had enough reason to be disappointed and feel cheated. The middle class felt the need for a strong hand to deal with corruption, and they found in Modi an ideal leader for it. It is widely believed that exposure of the Congress scams by AAP leaders also helped the BJP to achieve its political goals.

It was not just a plain sentiment of anti-incumbency among the electorate, particularly the middle class that brought the UPA

---

[14] Social activist and author Arundhati Roy called Anna Hazare a corporate mascot, and his allies Arvind Kejriwal and Kiran Bedi operate NGOs funded by US foundations (Smith 2014).
[15] This is the description of Manu Joseph, former editor of *Open*, an Indian weekly magazine.

government down on its knees. The Congress failed to recognize the significance of the demographic shift and the emergence of a sizeable section the Indian middle class. This demographic shift is significant because middle-class voters are more likely to be aware of the discourse around state regulations and thwarted business development. They are more likely to believe that subsidies can be economically harmful and burden to the state exchequer. The UPA's policy of 'reforms with a human face', an alternative set of policies such as Food Security Act, Employment Guarantee Act, designed to protect the poor, did not benefit the middle class and new middle-class Indians.

Of all, Congress leader and former minister Mani Shankar Aiyar's remarks mocking Modi's prime-ministerial ambitions has backfired the party immensely. When he strode out from the AICC meeting on 17 January 2014, he jumped in with both feet and told the waiting TV crew, 'I promise you in this 21st century, Narendra Modi will never become the prime minister of this country. He won't. If he wants to come and sell tea here we can make some room for him'. Even Jammu and Kashmir Chief Minister Omar Abdullah, an ally of the Congress, said such mockery of the humble background of Modi would not help the UPA's prospects in any way. Aiyar refused to apologize and instead blamed the media for the controversy.

Reacting to Aiyar's comments, the BJP said that remarks illustrate the Congress party's 'poor thinking'. Leader of the Opposition in the Rajya Sabha Arun Jaitley tweeted: 'The strength of Indian democracy will be proved when a former tea vendor defeats a dynasty representative. Let this be the battle of 2014' (Bhatnagar and Ramachandran 2014). Modi said, 'People who are ruling at the Centre don't know what poverty is all about, but I know it'. The Gujarat chief minister has said that he was born in a poor family and lived in poverty. 'I have sold tea at the railway station and in running trains…those selling tea in trains know more about railways than the minister', Modi said at a rally in Patna.[16] Modi told several times that during his childhood

---

[16] https://indianexpress.com/article/india/politics/modi-can-never-become-pm-can-sell-tea-mani-shankar-aiyar/ (accessed on 15 January 2015).

days, he used to help his father, Damodardas, to run a tea shop at Vadnagar railway station in Gujarat.

Once it came to be known that the remark had badly backfired, the Congress tried to find that Modi had been exaggerating his own *chaiwala* story for electoral benefit. Modi, who belongs to Ganchis,[17] listed among the OBCs, made optimum use of his humble social origins. The *chaiwala* comment by Congress leader helped the BJP to evolve a concept, popularly known as *chai pe charcha*, which roughly translates as 'a discussion over a cup of tea'. 'NaMo Tea Parties' had been tried out in the electorally critical state of Uttar Pradesh. The word 'NaMo' is referred to Narendra Modi. The carefully crafted 'NaMo' tag also appeals to the traditional Hindus—the BJP's main vote bank—because of its religious connotation, as the Sanskrit word *namo* is used as a salutation reserved for the Hindu gods. The BJP and the RSS leaders had been meeting academics, students, lawyers and other middle-class professionals over tea for discussion. These *chai pe charchas* not only provided additional media publicity for Modi but also helped the BJP gain maximum benefits by galvanizing party workers and supporters.

## Modi Meets Aspiration of New Middle Class

The market for politics in India has changed considerably in the last decade thanks to the new growing and powerful segment of voters— the new middle class—that does not conform to the traditional boundaries of voters. The unsatisfied needs of the new middle-class voters created an opportunity for a new generation of politicians to position themselves appropriately on the national scene and gain the support of this segment (S. Singh 2017). Old politics and old politicians are at loss to understand the sentiments and sensibilities of the new middle class. The new middle class in India is demanding greater accountability and are challenging regimes seen as corrupt, out of touch and which form obstacles to a better future. An urban middle class in India wanted to aspire for a better life. But the indecisive UPA government led by the Congress in sync with scams, rampant

---

[17] Ganchis were traditional traders in the business of extracting and selling oil.

corruption and crony capitalism distanced itself from improving economic conditions of the people.

But why did the upper-middle- and middle-class vote for the BJP disproportionately in 2014? How did Modi manage to draw such overwhelming support? How did the Modi factor dominate the mind space of this middle class? Disgusted with the UPA regime, India's aspirational middle class, maybe less ideologically driven and more focused on gaining social and economic status, supported Narendra Modi seeking positive changes in the lives. The new middle class kept its hopes on a leader 'who can deliver' and a leader who symbolized their aspirations. The 2014 election was the first since Indira Gandhi's demise when leadership became a decisive factor. Equally significant was that voters were prepared to seek a leader bypassing regional, caste and family loyalties. He appealed urban-class-eroded caste identities and increased religiosity.

The Congress leadership was proved to be ineffective and directionless which added sheen to the BJP's projection of Modi as a decisive, effective and experienced leader. The rise of Modi as the central figure, around whom the BJP's campaign revolved, made the elections something of a plebiscite on the leader rather than a choice of candidates in constituencies. This development was weakly countered by the Congress and its young and inexperienced leader, Rahul Gandhi (Syal and Shastri 2014, 77). Modi's dominance in the campaign practically eclipsed the more routine discussions around local issues, state-level configurations and the socio-economic alternatives that parties offered (Suri and Palshikar 2014, 39–49). Moreover, Modi was perceived to be opposed to reservations, a major issue among the merit-oriented middle class since the Mandal agitation. For the upper-caste middle class, he demonstrates that OBCs can succeed in life without positive discrimination and can even reject this policy as counterproductive (Jaffrelot 2014b). And when the results were announced, parties, media and scholars across the world were unanimous in giving credit to Modi for the BJP's victory.

Modi struck a chord with the first-time voters. On 6 February 2013, Modi addressed students at Delhi's Shri Ram College of Commerce and spoke about the need for speed in government decision-making and about the need to improve the skill of the youth to accelerate economic growth. That speech won him many admirers. Modi's aim was to create a 'technology-driven society' through 'technology-driven development', which galvanized the young voters, who along with aspiring middle class identified with the BJP's prime-ministerial candidature. His messages attracted even those disinterested in politics. Many argue that it's Modi and not the BJP that won 2014. As against this, the Congress also tried the trick of accepting the young middle class by making Rahul Gandhi a young icon of the party. But some of his interactions with young college students were disastrous. For example, his interaction with students of Mount Carmel College in Bengaluru in 2015. Rahul Gandhi's attempt to corner Modi over his flagship schemes such as 'Make in India' and 'Swachh Bharat' boomeranged during his interaction with students.

The impact of issues pertaining to the economy on electoral outcomes has been a subject of considerable debate. With Modi's image as a pro-market leader, as he has encouraged private business and industry in his home state of Gujarat, the election saw an articulation of free-market economy in the name of development by the BJP. The party was able to project its position as distinct from the half-hearted measures initiated by the Congress in liberalizing the economy. The BJP, which had virtually abandoned its swadeshi leanings during its rule (1998–2004), had taken a clear pro-business line during the election. The RSS head Mohan Bhagwat is said to have unambiguously supported market-led economic growth soon after Modi's nomination to the post of the prime minister (Kanwal 2013). This suggests that the RSS has shed some of its *swadeshi* principles. This change in stance allayed middle-class fears about the direction of the economy and helped divert attention away from the public scrutiny over the 2002 Gujarat violence that Modi has never been totally able to distance himself from (Shani 2007). The middle class and the new middle class hugely endorsed the BJP's policy stance and 'revolted' against the sorrowful welfare policies coupled with mal-governance and corruption that India witnessed during the UPA II.

Therefore, voters took a clear rightward shift on issues related to the role of the state in the economy. Chhibber and Verma (2014) call it 'a decisive shift in the middle ground of politics'. It is argued that the administrative failures of the UPA government in managing the economy and Modi's image as a market-friendly, pro-business leader played a catalytic role in the emergence of the economic right as an electoral force that rallied behind the BJP. The BJP manifesto proclaimed that India, instead of remaining a market for the global industry, should become a global manufacturing hub. It promised to create a conducive, enabling environment for doing business in India. It stood for a strong manufacturing sector to bridge the demand–supply gap and making India a hub for cost-competitive labour-intensive mass manufacturing industries (BJP 2014).

The middle class voted for Modi not only for 'negative' reasons such as corruption and dynastic politics during the UPA regime but also for the 'positive' reasons. The positive reasons are that the middle class perceived that Modi functioned like a modern-day CEO by laying emphasis on the positive results and often allegedly put rules and normal norms in the backburner (Dev 2012). Modi's clean image and proven track record in Gujarat as its chief minister for three terms had already created a positive perception among the middle class cutting across state boundaries and caste barriers. His success in bringing more dynamism into the bureaucracy, ramping up the infrastructure and irrigation network in Gujarat, drawing mega investment projects for rapid industrialization was perfectly in sync with the perception of the middle-class youth about development-generating employment opportunities. His success in making Gujarat the only industrialized state which could provide 24 × 7 power to industries and rural masses in the first decade of this millennium when most of the states were facing huge power outages was showcased as a testimony to his ability in delivering what he promises. Gujarat was exporting power to states such as Rajasthan, Punjab, Haryana and even Karnataka during that period. In contrast to Modi's regime in Gujarat, the 10-years UPA regime doled out subsidies liberally with focus on welfare orientation than creating social assets that could act as engines of development to lift the economic standards of the people.

The middle class swayed by Modi's 24 × 7 work culture and him being a hard taskmaster. He made people believe that the primary duty of the government official is to serve people. The people moved by his commitment towards curbing corruption, pro-people governance, farmers' concerns, the minimal intervention of the government. His pro-business approach won him support from the new middle class which trusts in the private sector to modernize the economy. He was the first leader in independent India to spell out a vision for promoting prosperity rather than combating poverty. In his election campaign, the word inequality was not heard even once (Hasan 2016, 144).

The middle-class women members too are swayed by Modi's lifestyle and work culture.

> To the typical middle class, small town, rural and urban women, he's (Modi) is a rock star. He's got cult popularity. Because he doesn't smoke, he doesn't drink, he is very straight, very focused, very committed, hard-working, non-corrupt, and industrious. They love all that about him. (Price 2015, 197)

Modi has no relationship to speak of with his blood relatives and advertises this as part of his incorruptibility. His discipline and the devotion to work are commendable and even Modi's critics, such as Shashi Tharoor, acknowledge that he is a workaholic whose tireless energy amid a punishing schedule is remarkable. But it is also odds at with his BVLGARI glasses, Movado watch and Montblanc pen. He emerged as a style icon in his own right, sporting tailored kurtas, designer waistcoats, Western suits and fashion accessories like hats. For him, they symbolize his commitment to modernization, ambition and good quality products (Philipose 2019, 181). Modi tattoos, Modi kurtas, Modi suits, Modi T-shirts and fabrics have found their way into the market during the 2014 and 2019 elections, and the middle-class activists wore them during the campaigns.

Modi's effort is, indeed, to 'always look distinct and stand out in a crowd'. Modi was able to attract the support because of his appeal to the electorate to vote in favour of the BJP candidates and give him a chance to be *chowkidar* (security guard) in the parliament to guard the nation as well take care of the people. At a rally in Rajasthan on 19 November 2013, Modi thundered, 'I promise that if the BJP comes to power, the party will ensure that it plays the role of a *chowkidar* and will not allow anyone's *panja* (Congress's hand) to play with their money'.[18]

## Middle Class-Centric Social Engineering

Did high turnout of middle-class voters help the BJP to come to power? How Modi-centric campaign and appeal to the middle class enabled him to win the general elections? What kind of strategy did the BJP and Modi adopted for mobilizing voters from the middle class and from the OBCs, particularly in urban areas? Was the BJP able to draw into its coalition those who would like the minimal state intervention in the economy? Is the change in the social composition of the middle class, which comprise a large number of OBCs after economic liberalization, extended support to the BJP? We will make an attempt to answers these questions.

In 2014 general elections, the BJP has been largely successful at reaching out to social groups with which it had not shared a past affinity. With this, the BJP created new ideological groupings that support the party beyond caste boundaries, attracted a new social grouping amid the country's churning demographic changes (Rukmini 2019, 49). The research has found that the middle class supported the BJP and its leader Modi in large numbers. Noting the importance of middle-class voting in 2014 elections, E. Sridharan (2014, 72–76) argues that there has been a significant 10 per cent increase in the voter turnout by the upper middle class and the middle class. The voting percentage of this class increased from 58 per cent in 2009 to 68 per cent in 2014. By contrast, the poor voter turnout increased only by 3 per cent from 57 per cent in 2009 to 60 per cent in 2014. Turnout by the poor people at 60 per cent is significantly less than the

[18] https://www.outlookindia.com/newswire/story/will-be-chowkidar-wont-let-panja-play-with-people-modi/817794 (accessed on 7 June 2016).

68 per cent turnout by the two richer classes. In terms of class-wise party preference, 70 per cent of upper and middle class preferred the BJP and 37 per cent of upper and middle class preferred the Congress in 2014. While only 24 per cent of the poor preferred to vote for the BJP, about 31 per cent among the lower-class voters voted for the BJP (Sridharan 2014).

As discussed earlier, the BJP and new middle class have grown parallel to each other since mid-1980s. Traditionally, social conservatives, many of whom are upper caste, and belonged to the middle class, voted for the Jana Sangh, the predecessor of the BJP. The BJP began with a base among the upper and intermediate castes, succeeded in winning over sections of the OBC groups in the 1990s and now has firmly entrenched itself in both upper and OBC communities. In the 1990s, the BJP brought to the forefront OBC leaders such as Kalyan Singh, Uma Bharti, Vinay Katiyar, Shivraj Singh Chouhan, Sushil Kumar Modi and Gopinath Munde. For the past two decades, leaders from middle and backward castes became the face of the party at the state level too. M. Venkaiah Naidu (a Kamma) and Bangaru Laxman (a Dalit) from Andhra Pradesh became party presidents. The social engineering adopted by the BJP saw the party increase its vote share in the Hindi belt in the Lok Sabha elections in the 1990s.

As argued earlier, the 'BJP's new social bloc' supported the BJP in the 1990s, and the party has emerged as the single largest in 1996, 1998 and 1999 general elections. The BJP has created a 'new social bloc', a new coalition of various social groups that lays claims to political power. The 'new social bloc' is formed by the convergence of traditional caste-community differences and class distinctions— urban rich and middle classes, upper castes and rising landed peasant castes—moving towards the BJP (Yadav et al. 1999). Radhika Desai (2002) provides a similar argument saying this social block put its weight behind the BJP either directly or via their regional parties as NDA coalition partners of the BJP in many states. The expanded middle class of the old and new middle class are everywhere the social bases for right-wing politics, including its more authoritarian forms (Desai 2016, 71).

In addition to OBC middle-class support, the BJP's augmented its social base by moving beyond the so-called 'caste Hindu' groups and acquiring a fair amount of support among Dalits and Adivasis, although their support was uneven to the BJP in different states. The BJP's Dalit vote base largely came from the upwardly mobile sections. Alliance with Ram Vilas Paswan's Lok Janshakti in Bihar, Ramdas Athawale's Republic Party of India in Maharashtra and Udit Raj (he quit the BJP after being denied a ticket in 2019) in Delhi also helped the BJP to secure Dalit votes. With this, the BJP has undergone an internal transformation and managed to win over large sections of Hindu voters in 2014.

The BJP has learnt a bitter lesson from its defeat in 2004, after its much-hyped 'India Shining' campaign. The BJP perhaps sensed the steady change in perception towards economic reform policies and development. Perhaps, understanding a change in the perception of the people towards market reforms, in 2014, the BJP added in its manifesto a new term, 'neo-middle class', in addition to the middle class. The manifesto too speaks of the rise of the neo-middle class and their growing aspirations. As stated in its manifesto, the party saw the emergence of a new middle class in India—those who have risen from the category of poor and are yet to stabilize in the middle class. The members of this neo-middle class want amenities and services of a certain standard from the government but also feel that they are not up to the mark. Hence, they resort to the private sector for provisions related to education, health and transport. As more and more people move into this class, their expectations for better public services have to be met (BJP 2014, 17–18).

Members of the OBCs, who have supported the BJP the most during the 2014 election, did not belong to the poor. Members of this class emerged from the category of the poor and are trying to join the middle class. The class needs practical support and cooperation. These urban OBCs are former peasants who have migrated to cities or who have been incorporated in the rapid process of urbanization that the country has been witnessing during the last two decades. Commercial establishments, residential complexes, entertainment industry, multiplexes, malls and retail industries, cab services, food restaurants and so on provided jobs to lakhs of graduated youth and skilled personnel who migrated to urban areas from rural India. These employees might not earn salaries like government first- or second-grade staff, but their jobs have lifted several families out of poverty and enabled them to enter the rank of the lower middle class, which in turn helped in expanding the size of the middle class.

The Modi campaign raised the hopes of gaining private-sector jobs in the industrial and service sectors among the migrating and newly urbanized OBC and lower-caste voters, who 'aspire to join the ranks of the middle class and in Modi they found an embodiment of their aspirations' (Philipose 2019, 253). Citing the Centre for Study for the Developing Societies (CSDS) Lokniti data, Jaffrelot (2014a, 27) argues that OBCs are differentiated according to class so far as their voting pattern is concerned. While only 28 per cent of the poor OBCs have voted for the BJP, the 'lower' OBCs have supported the party more massively at 37 per cent. OBCs supported Modi because 'Modi has done vikas in Gujarat' and because 'Modi was a decisive administrator'. In fact, the share of OBCs in today's middle class is sizeable (Sheth 1999, 2502–2510). The saffron party, therefore, tapped the anxieties and aspirations of the new entrants to the middle class.

During the electoral campaign, Modi explicitly went on referring to his humble caste background. During a speech at Muzaffarpur, Bihar, he mentioned his low-caste origin and said, 'I am confident that the coming decade is of Dalits, backward classes, Scheduled Castes, Scheduled Tribes and other weaker sections of the society' (Varma 2014). He said that the BJP was no longer an upper-caste party. Sharing a stage with Ram Vilas Paswan, the Dalit leader who re-joined the NDA after quitting 12 years ago in protest against the communal riots in Gujarat, which happened under Modi's tenure, and Rashtriya Lok Samata Party chief Upendra Kushwaha, another OBC leader, who had also joined the NDA, in Muzaffarpur, Bihar, on 3 March 2014, Modi spoke of his own lower-caste origins.

In Kerala's Kochi in March 2014, after inaugurating the centenary celebrations of Kayal Sammelan (lake meeting), organized by Kerala Pulayar Maha Sabha, Modi played a Dalit card and said he is 'victim of untouchability from his school days' (Philip 2014). He said that in the last century, those who had brought changes in the country were either from the backward community or had dedicated their lives for the Dalits. He also touched the local grouse of the backward community by claiming that their social reformer Ayyankali was not properly honoured for his contributions (Philip 2014). No doubt, he identified himself humbly as a small man, but from the land of Mahatma Gandhi and Sardar Patel.

## Middle Class, Hindutva and Nationalism

Of course, Modi remains strongly committed to Hindutva. Modi wooed voters saying that the Third Front and the Congress party are hiding behind secularism to avoid questions on development. The pan-Indian middle classes were horrified at the idea of the 'Third Front'. At a rally in Kolkata, he described the argument as an attempt to 'turn India into a third-rate country'.[19] Modi seems to firmly believe that secularism was a model unworthy of constitutional status. Indeed, Modi's comments even reflect those made on several occasions by RSS leaders, who have been repeatedly stressing that their ultimate aim is the recognition of India as a Hindu State, in which secularism lies not at the Constitution's bedrock, but entirely outside the document's aims and purposes.

The political culture of the Hindu middle class is more and more imbued with ethno-religious connotations. Sometimes, Modi even launches development programmes after visiting temples located nearby towns. For instance, he launched the 'Digitized SHG Member Transaction' programme for enabling cashless transactions for the members having RuPay cards, after offering prayers at Shri Manjunatha Swamy temple at Dharmasthala in Karnataka on 29 October 2017 (Figure 5.1). Apart from visiting and offering prayers at various famous temples, Modi would start his speech by paying respect to the local deities. He never forgets to mention names of leaders of

---

[19] https://www.thehindu.com/news/national/modi-takes-on-third-front-parties/article5656819.ece (accessed on 6 June 2017).

Figure 5.1 *Prime Minister Narendra Modi Offers Prayers at Shri Manjunatha Swamy Temple at Dharmasthala in Karnataka on 29 October 2017*
Source: Press Information Bureau.

the region who fought against the British rule. Everywhere in India, plebeians who experience some upward social mobility, especially when they come from 'a low-caste background, adhere more strongly to the ritualistic forms of Hindu practice' (Saavala 2010). But it also reflects the influence of years of Hindutva politics and the fear of Islamism, especially after the terrorist attacks (on Parliament in 2001 and the Akshardham temple complex at Gandhinagar, Gujarat, in 2002) in the first decade of the 21st century.

The new Indian middle class, like its counterparts in all emerging economies, subscribed to the rites of aggressive nationalism. A new national self-confidence expressed itself as a chauvinistic assertion, especially vis-à-vis our two neighbours—China and Pakistan. In the aftermath of the 26/11 Mumbai terror attack, sections of armed forces and the intelligence community kept fuelling the national rage, pushing the political leadership to rise to the challenge of teaching Pakistan a fitting lesson. Militarized posturing and jingoist talks went down well with the middle class and its media sites (Khare 2014, 22). During the two terms of the UPA government, the number of terrorist attacks increased. The Congress was perceived as having failed to deliver on security issues (Sharma 2015, 22). The middle class pinned strong hopes on Modi to protect 'Mother India'. In fact, Pakistan, which figured prominently in Modi's speeches during the last three Gujarat state elections campaigns as the base of transnational terrorists striking India, was part of the BJP campaign too (Venugopal 2017).

By drawing a contrast between the treatment given to Hindu refugees from Pakistan and those from Bangladesh, Modi says that when some Bangladeshis infiltrate, leaders indulge in the vote bank politics, while when refugees from Pakistan chant *Bharat Mata ki Jai*, nobody cares about them. This anti-Pakistan narrative kicked up a huge controversy when the BJP candidate from Nawada, Bihar, said that 'those who are against Modi should go to Pakistan' (Faizan 2014). Inflammatory speeches by Hyderabad-based All India Majilis-e-Ittehadul Muslimeem leader Akbaruddin Owaisi, 'We (Muslims) are 25 crore and you (Hindus) are 100 crore. If you remove police for 15 minutes we will show our strength' (*agar pandra* [15] *minute police ko hatale, hum hamara himmat dikayenge*) gone viral on social media.[20] Such high communal speeches by Hindu and Muslim leaders had created a wedge between the two communities.

Anti-Pakistan formulations had been popular with the BJP supporters since the Jana Sangh. Out of 438 candidates contesting on BJP ticket, only seven belonged to the Muslim community. The 16th Lok Sabha has the lowest number of Muslim MPs (23). This is because religion-based differences in voting preferences became sharper in

---

[20] https://timesofindia.indiatimes.com/city/hyderabad/Akbaruddin-in-trouble-for-hate-speech/articleshow/17803821.cms (accessed on 19 June 2018).

2014. While turnout among Hindus went up from 58 per cent in 2009 to 68 per cent in 2014, the Muslim turnout remained the same at 59 per cent. Out of the 87 seats where Muslims are over 20 per cent of the population, the BJP won 43 as against 15 seats in 2009 (Sardesai and Gupta 2019, 64).

During the campaign, Modi tried to exploit majoritarian sentiments by polarizing religious communities. He gave some Hindutva flavour to the campaign, Modi continued to attack the Congress as a party pampering Muslims but doing nothing for them. When he sought to deride Rahul Gandhi as a princeling, he never used the Hindi term *rajkumar* (prince), preferring the Persian and Urdu *shehzada* (prince), as if to further damning Rahul Gandhi by association with Islamic terminology.[21] At a public meeting in the coastal town of Mangaluru (Karnataka), Modi accused the UPA government of providing ₹50 crore subsidy for setting up slaughterhouses and for promoting meat export in the framework of a 'pink revolution'.[22]

The RSS network, a traditional asset of the BJP, played a very important role in Modi's victory. On only two occasions, the RSS fully engaged in parliamentary elections: once in 1977 for the Janata Party and then again in 2014 for the BJP (Andersen and Damle 2018, 3).[23] The RSS's leadership supported Modi partly because RSS found that, among the top BJP leaders, he was the only one with compelling reasons to be unambiguously opposed to Sonia Gandhi and her government. Congress leader and Home Minister P. Chidambaram's statement on 'saffron terror' has not amused the BJP and RSS.[24]

---

[21] https://www.ndtv.com/india-news/narendra-modi-mimics-shehzada-rahul-gandhi-at-chhattisgarh-rally-541195 (accessed on 6 March 2014).

[22] https://www.thehindu.com/news/national/karnataka/modi-picks-on-centre-for-promoting-meat-export/article4677494.ece (accessed on 7 June 2014).

[23] This does not mean that RSS has not been involved in other elections, but those two elections were the only ones in which it permitted its *pracharaks* and other higher-level officials to take part in the campaigns (Andersen and Damle 2018, 3).

[24] https://www.ndtv.com/india-news/saffron-terrorism-a-new-phenomenon-says-home-minister-chidambaram-428832 (accessed on 7 March 2018).

The BJP argued that the UPA and Congress leaders were raising the bogey of Hindu terror to distract public attention from Bofors and 2 G scams. Congress leader Digvijaya Singh, who used the phrase 'Hindu terror', clearly has the blessings of Sonia Gandhi, the BJP argued (Parashar 2011). In the 2019 election campaign, Mr Singh said that he had not coined the phrase 'Hindu terror'. The BJP argued that Chidambaram and Digvijaya Singh are calling the RSS as 'saffron terror' and 'Hindu terror' to please Congress President Sonia Gandhi, who is a dedicated Christian and hence unsympathetic to Hindu interests and sentiments. All these made the Sangh Parivar oppose the UPA government and made efforts to vote it out of office.

Modi contested from Vadodara in Gujarat and from Varanasi, the 'capital' of Hinduism in Uttar Pradesh. During his campaign in Varanasi, Modi turned spiritual and said, 'I don't think anyone has sent me here or I have come here. I feel Mother Ganga has called me to Varanasi'.[25] He visited Kashi Vishwanath and Sankat Mochan before addressing the crowd, but, on stage, while the conch shells were blown, he declared that he had 'come from the land of Somnath to seek the blessing of Baba Vishwanath' (Verma 2013). He spoke of the need to resurrect the Ganga, 'the lifeline of Varanasi', and 'exhorted the voters of UP to help usher in Ram Rajya' (Verma 2013). In his speeches, he made several references to Lord Ram without mentioning the building of a temple at Ayodhya. In the section 'Cultural Heritage' of the 2014 Election Manifesto, the BJP simply mentioned that the BJP would 'explore all possibilities within the framework of the Constitution to facilitate the construction of the Ram Temple in Ayodhya'. Interestingly, this section also mentioned 'Ram Setu', 'Ganga River', and 'necessary legal framework to protect cow'.

To sum up, Narendra Modi emerged as BJP's prime-ministerial candidate on the background of a few very strong catalytic events. The failures of the UPA government to tackle rising prices and inflation were irritating phenomena for the middle class. The new middle

[25] https://timesofindia.indiatimes.com/news/Narendra-Modi-files-nomination-says-Ma-Ganga-has-called-me-to-Varanasi/articleshow/34147322.cms (accessed on 10 June 2015).

class was emerging strongly under the shadow of liberalization, and all well-educated youth had met with their aspirational salaries. The corruption and scams were repeated both in visual and print media and were discussed almost continuously. The Congress did not have any charismatic leader and resorted to abusive language instead of maintaining dignity as the most responsible party of the nation. The success story of Gujarat under Chief Minister Modi was used as a major groundwork and the nationalist spirit which extinguished after the Kargil war was fuelled. Modi's oratory skills did not have a match among other parties, and his tall promises were swallowed by the public even though some of these were not feasible. Instead of countering Modi, the opponents started blaming Electronic Voting Machines (EVMs) for disastrous results.

A distilled viewpoint emerged that the middle class, agitated against various issues, went on a virtual war path during the UPA regime opposing its 'policy paralysis', corruption, nepotism, inflation, unemployment, pampering the undeserving and minorities surpass-ing their legitimate stakes. The middle class voted for the BJP and its leader Narendra Modi with the desire to put an end to the prevailing ills in the political economy. Exit-poll data, from small and big cities, reveals that the middle classes overwhelmingly supported the BJP. Modi and the BJP gamed its election campaign to the perfection by tapping aspirations of this agitated mass and social groups aspiring to gain the middle-class status. By raising the popular slogans during the campaign, Modi unraveled his political narratives, providing corruption-free governance and faster economic development by strongly asserting national pride. The Congress leadership proved unproductive and incompetent before the BJP's projection of Modi as a strongman, decisive and experienced leader. With Modi swearing-in as the Prime Minister, the time became ripe to deliver promises made during the election campaign—to accelerate the economic develop-ment and to make India a world power led by this supporting mass.

# CHAPTER 6

# Manoeuvring the Middle Class

## Introduction

Narendra Modi came to power in 2014 with a strong promise of giving *achhe din* to the people of India. Modi developed his appeal by putting the focus on what the people urgently needed—development orientation, better governance, more socio-economic opportunities and death knell of the black economy. He pledged to voters to end corruption with his slogan *na khaoonga, na khaane doonga*. His major election plank was that he would bring back billions of dollars of 'black money' stashed abroad and would be sufficiently large to put ₹15 lakh into the bank accounts of every Indian citizen. He promised two crore jobs a year for unemployed youth. Among the other promises were *sabka saath, sabka vikas* (participation of all, for the development of all) and that he would be a *chowkidar* to guard the nation and take care of the people shaken by the terror attacks sponsored by Pakistan jihadist groups. Modi assured the business community that he would transform the investment climate by improving India's ranking in the World Bank's 'Ease of Doing Business' and give more money to farmers, more for their produce and revive agriculture. He promised the middle class, which was struggling to meet daily needs owing to high price rise in the necessities, to contain the inflation. Most of his promises connected directly to the aspirations of middle-class Indians who wanted to lead a fairly stable daily life by accessing basic facilities and a luxurious life during vacations.

Having won the 2014 elections on the back up of several promises, there was a flurry of activities in the ensuing five years with schemes and reforms launched to address many social and economic issues. Did these schemes align with promises made in the 2014 elections? Did these schemes achieve their desired objectives? What was the impact? Did Modi's policies benefit the middle class and the poor? How Modi's policies were different from the previous UPA regime? Were the policies and day-to-day administration transparent, accountable and effective in moving the country further into the developed world? People seek answers to these questions and an attempt is made here to deliberate on these.

## Tethering the Corruption: Attempting a Steep Climb

In the backdrop of India's anti-corruption movement, the entire middle class considered that they were the victims of corruption, particularly during the UPA II rule. Increasingly, it began to see the state as a promoter of corruption and as being inefficient while the market was seen as rewarding merit and performance. Full-scale liberalization introduced in the early 1990s should have curtailed corruption, but the opposite happened despite several institutional bodies and laws.[1] Modi focused on internalizing the empowering methodology by saying *badal sakta hai* (things can change) rather than the passive *chalta hai* (it's okay) attitude which is prevalent in bureaucracy.[2] With the motto of removing red tape and replacing it with red carpet, the Modi government brought in reforms to change the work culture. In

---

[1] Some of the bodies/laws are the Prevention of Corruption Act, 1988, an independent Central Vigilance Commission, the Comptroller and Auditor General, the Judges (Inquiry) Act, 1968, the Whistle Blowers Protection Act, 2012, the Prevention of Money Laundering Act, 2018, and the Benami Transactions (Prohibition) Act, 2016.

[2] https://pibindia.wordpress.com/2017/08/16/ (accessed on 8 June 2018).

an interview with *The Times of India*, Modi spoke on different issues related to administration, economic growth and elections. About work culture, Modi said,

> Not only change in work culture, but also destroying Congress culture was a key challenge. Learning new things is easy but unlearning (old habits) is a tough thing. Here people had to unlearn practices that Congress left behind and unlearning practices of 70 years was a tough thing. But I can say with confidence that we have succeeded in removing Congress culture from our system. When I talk about Congress culture, I refer to policy paralysis, corruption, nepotism, presence of middlemen, departments working in silos, projects being delayed etc. (Kalra, Diwakar and Deshpande 2019)

Attempting to reign corruption, his government followed two pronged approaches. First, sorting the problem technologically by reducing direct cash payment and linking every transaction to the Permanent Account Number (PAN) or Aadhaar card, thereby bringing transparency in all monetary transactions. Second, connecting and spreading the tax network through PAN cards helped to track many who escaped the tax net. This was supplemented by the introduction of the Goods and Services Tax (GST) that threw out the cascading effect in direct taxation and pilferage.

## Administrative Reforms to Plug Leakage

The new government brought in a new set of administrative reforms and developed a new kind of political culture in governance by introducing transparency and accountability in the delivery of public services, awarding contracts and cracking down pilferage of funds and fake beneficiaries. Modi government's 'zero tolerance to corruption' approach, as well as 'minimum government and maximum governance' approach resulted in the simplification of the governance model. The government abolished the system of attestation/authentication by government servants for submission of certificates. It abolished personal interviews for lower grade government jobs to ensure that avenues for corruption and nepotism were removed and merit was respected; it weeded out inefficient public servants with doubtful integrity above the age of 50 years, prematurely. In 2019, the government forced 49 senior tax officials of the Indian Revenue Service to take early retirements on the grounds of non-performance. During 2014–2019, 312 officers of Groups 'A' and 'B' were recommended for compulsory retirement (Mishra 2019a). Prosecution of over 80 public servants, including four IAS officers, under the Prevention of Corruption Act, is pending with the government.[3]

On the basis of merit, the government appointed professionals, largely from the private sectors, as joint secretaries. This is perhaps the first time that a large group of experts with domain knowledge entered the government.[4] Many serving IAS officers saw this decision as power threatening and shadowing their hegemony. It has also been argued that this marks the 'privatization of the IAS' and the beginning of the end of a 'neutral and impartial' civil service (Bhattacharya 2018). In the banking sector, the Banks Board Bureau (BBB), the apex body for the selection of whole-time directors of state-owned lenders, has identified 75 senior management personnel of public sector lenders to take over leadership roles in the future. Modi approved the constitution of the BBB in 2016 to make recommendations for the appointment of senior bank officers.[5]

The selection of Justice P. C. Ghose as the first Lokpal has come nearly after a delay of five years. Nevertheless, people welcomed it as a milestone in the cause of fighting corruption in high places. The entire credit for enacting this law during the UPA regime must be given to Anna Hazare's movement against corruption. It may be unrealistic to expect any dramatic impact on the lives of the common people, but

---

[3] https://www.thehindu.com/news/national/sanctions-for-prosecution-of-over-80-officials-awaited/article29035803.ece (accessed on 1 October 2019).

[4] https://timesofindia.indiatimes.com/india/9-professionals-selected-as-joint-secys-in-biggest-lateral-induction-into-govt-service/articleshow/68857597.cms (accessed on 8 June 2019).

[5] https://www.thehindubusinessline.com/money-and-banking/bbb-identifies-75-senior-officers-for-leadership-roles-in-psbs/article26884969.ece (accessed on 21 April 2019).

the Lokpal and other members work as deterrence and have a historic responsibility to live up to popular expectations.[6]

Public grievance redressal is said to be the cornerstone of any well-governed democracy. A Centralized Public Grievance Redress and Monitoring System (CPGRAMS), a portal under the Department of Administrative Reforms and Public Grievances, was activated to address public grievances in the delivery of services. Although the portal was not directly related to corruption, it tracked malpractice and corruption in the supply of LPG cylinders. This has not only ensured timely delivery of cylinders to beneficiaries but has also increased LPG coverage across the nation from 55 per cent in December 2014 to 93 per cent in March 2019 under the Ujjwala Yojana (Jaitely 2019). Indian Railway has gone for 100 per cent e-procurement through a single web portal to ensure transparency, accountability and to eliminate corruption. Other departments as well have initiated similar steps that sealed one huge pilferage point in corruption.

JAM—Jan Dhan, Aadhaar and Mobile—trinity refers to the GoI's initiative to link Jan Dhan bank accounts,[7] mobile (cell phone) numbers and Aadhaar cards. This is said to be a game changer in pugging the leakage of government subsidies. Hitherto, that was a source of unaccounted money for generations. JAM-linked direct benefit transfer (DBT) of welfare and subsidies to 103.5 crore beneficiaries cover over 430 schemes across nearly 60 ministries. It largely eliminated fake beneficiaries and middlemen under pensions, the public distribution system, LPG distribution and the Mahatma Gandhi National Rural Employment Guarantee Act (MGNREGA). DBT saved more than ₹1.25 lakh crore for the nation. Much of the DBT savings came from cleaning up LPG subsidies. About 3.79 crore

---

[6] https://www.thehindu.com/opinion/editorial/lokpal-at-last/article26572294.ece (accessed on 15 March 2019).

[7] Under the Pradhan Mantri Jan Dhan Yojana, 35 crore bank accounts were opened and deposits have grown over 2.5 times during 2016–2019 to ₹98,400 crore. Public sector banks stand to earn ₹5,000 crore due to the increasing quantum of deposits placed in Jan Dhan accounts. https://www.thehindu.com/business/Industry/public-sector-banks-long-term-strategy-on-jan-dhan-begins-to-pay-off/article26967981.ece (accessed on 1 May 2019).

'duplicate, fake/non-existent, inactive' LPG connections were eliminated, and 2.2 crore consumers stopped claiming the subsidy. Total savings on this count until March 2018 stood at over ₹42,000 crore. Similarly, the government saved nearly ₹30,000 crore in food subsidy after deletion of 2.75 crore 'duplicate and fake/non-existent' ration cards; the Ministry of Rural Development saved over ₹16,000 crore on wages after eliminating fake or ineligible beneficiaries under MGNREGA.[8] The BHIM (Bharat Interface for Money), a mobile application, facilitates e-payments directly through banks and can be used on all mobile devices. Collectively, the JAM and BHIM application have provided for a smart government where subsidy flows reach the beneficiary in a timely and effective manner, eliminating pilferages on the way.

E-NAM (National Agriculture Market) was launched on 14 April 2016, as an online trading platform for agricultural commodities in India, for helping farmers to get better prices and provide facilities for smooth marketing of their produce. The market transactions stood at ₹36,200 crore by January 2018, mostly intra-market. E-NAM brought in transparency in licensing, commissions and market fees and auctions. PRAGATI (Pro-Active Governance and Timely Implementation)—an ICT-based multi-modal platform—was used extensively for expediting pending/delayed projects. The 28th PRAGATI meetings have seen a cumulative review of infrastructure projects with a total investment of ₹11.75 lakh crore. These projects spread over several states.[9] Projects pending for more than three decades have been cleared. Applying for or renewing a passport is easier now. With the online submission of applications and quicker police verification, passport offices across the country are now able to issue passports in just four to five days. The Income Tax refund is deposited in bank accounts as soon as the scrutiny gets over. The

[8] https://www.thehindubusinessline.com/economy/policy/dbt-savings-may-touch-40000-crore-in-fy19/article24187145.ece (accessed on 20 June 2018).

[9] Prime minister's interaction through PRAGATI (26 September 2018). https://www.narendramodi.in/pm-s-interaction-through-pragati-september-2018–541611

Modi government has also tightened the regulatory net around NGOs which used to receive funding from overseas during the UPA regime.[10]

Most of India's black money has been invested in real estate. Removal of black money and corruption in the realty sector certainly helps the middle class more than the upper class. For tackling black money and corruption in the realty sector, the government brought out the Benami Transactions (Prohibition) Amendment Act, 2016 and the Real Estate (Regulation and Development) (RERA) Act, 2016. Both legislations are aimed at bridging the trust deficit between builders and consumers.

Under the Benami Act, the Income Tax Department has already filed several cases against finance companies, government officials and property developers for their alleged involvement in *benami* deals. The Karnataka–Goa IT department provisionally attached 12 properties under the prohibition properties act.[11] The RERA, 2016 was enacted not to address the problem of corruption; rather, it focuses on greater transparency, accountability and financial discipline in the real estate sector. The state governments would form RERA authority to address grievances of customers. Addressing the CREDAI Youth Conference 2019 in New Delhi, Modi expressed concern over the credibility of the sector and asked developers to improve their image that had been impacted by defaults by some builders. Despite being the chief driver of the economy and the second-largest job provider in the country, the real estate sector is suffering from a credibility deficit among homebuyers and therefore need to improve its image in the eyes of the middle class. Demonetization curbed the use of black money in the sector.

Allocation of coal and spectrum witnessed massive scams under the UPA regime. The NDA government auctioned these in a transparent manner and ensured immense gains for the nation. The auction of

---

[10] https://economictimes.indiatimes.com/news/politics-and-nation/ngo-crackdown-has-foreign-fund-inflows-plunging-40-since-modi-govt-era-report/articleshow/68342585.cms?from=mdr (accessed on 2 May 2019).

[11] https://www.ndtv.com/india-news/foreign-assets-worth-rs-800-crore-unearthed-by-karnataka-goa-it-department-2011958 (accessed on 9 June 2019).

FM radio fetched ₹1,000 crore to the state exchequer.[12] Previous 2G auction enriched select few companies while the NDA government's spectrum auction fetched ₹1.09 lakh crore for the nation. The coal auctions fetched the government ₹3.45 lakh crore.[13] The Comptroller and Auditor General (CAG) had, in a report tabled in Parliament in 2012, pegged the loss to the national exchequer at ₹1.86 lakh crore on account of improper allocation of coal mines during the UPA II. All these were the probable avenues of corruption that got blocked and avoided huge losses to the government.

The introduction of IT, however, has helped to plug leakage of subsidies, crackdown corruption and ensure attendance of staff. But owing to political compulsions, the Modi government has not been able to live up to its much-talked principle of 'minimum government, maximum governance'. When Modi assumed office, the size of the council of ministers was just 44, the smallest one for decades although the administrative reforms commission has regarded 10 per cent of the total membership of the Lok Sabha (i.e., 54 ministers, including cabinet ministers) to be the ideal size. The National Committee to Review the Working of the Constitution recommended the number of ministers 'be fixed at the maximum of 10% of the total strength of the popular House of the Legislature'. But even its recommendation was tweaked a bit to fix the ceiling at 15 per cent (Guruswamy 2004). On 7 July 2004, the 91st Amendment to the Constitution, limiting the size of the Council of Ministers at the centre and the states to no more than 15 per cent of the numbers in Lok Sabha or the state legislature, came into effect (Guruswamy 2004). The government of Prime Minister Manmohan Singh had 78 ministers. After the first cabinet reshuffle, Modi increased his council of ministers from 44 to 76. In 2018, the cabinet size reached 80. There are 543 MPs in the Lok

[12] https://www.hindustantimes.com/india/coal-spectrum-auction-helped-curb-corruption-pm-modi/story-qYP0D49stcHrp1GwRHUrcM.html (accessed on 18 August 2016).

[13] https://economictimes.indiatimes.com/industry/indl-goods/svs/metals-mining/coal-auction-to-get-rs-3-45-lakh-crore-rs-36k-crore-saving-via-dbt-government/articleshow/52492694.cms (accessed on 30 May 2016).

Sabha, which means there can be 81 ministers. The opposition parties say that Modi's minimum government has reached the maximum permissible size.

## Plugging Pilferages in Banking

In recent years, instances of financial frauds have been regularly reported in India. It's not just businessmen facing charges of corruption. Several bank officials came under the scanner of probing agencies of the government such as the CBI and the Enforcement Directorate (ED) for their alleged involvement in frauds. The non-performing assets (NPAs) too have increased during 2014–2019, although it can be argued that NPAs were recognized during this phase while they were essentially created during the UPA regime when there were relatively more easy lending norms by banks (Sabnavis 2019). Modi terms 'phone banking' for such relaxed banking norms. The frequency, complexity and cost of banking frauds have increased manifold resulting in a very serious cause of concern for regulators, such as the Reserve Bank of India (RBI).

An IIM Bangalore study says that during 2010–2013, public sector banks (PSBs) in India have lost a total of ₹22,743 crore on account of various banking frauds. The report says that public sector bank employees were involved in most of these frauds (Singh et al. 2016). A total of 2,480 cases of fraud involving a huge sum of ₹31,898.63 crore rattled 18 PSBs in the first quarter of 2019–2020 fiscal.[14] According to the RBI's annual report dated 31 March 2018, during 2017–2018, PSBs accounted for 92.9 per cent of the amount involved in frauds.[15]

Legislations such as the Prevention of Money Laundering Act (PMLA), 2018; the Fugitive Economic Offenders Act, 2018; the Black

[14] https://www.thehindubusinessline.com/money-and-banking/18-public-sector-banks-hit-by-2480-fraud-cases-of-rs-32000-cr-in-q1-rti/article29367793.ece# (accessed on 10 September 2019).

[15] https://economictimes.indiatimes.com/wealth/personal-finance-news/public-sector-banks-are-much-easier-to-defraud-than-private-sector-ones-heres-the-proof/articleshow/65592437.cms?utm_source=contentofinterest&utm_medium=text&utm_campaign=cppst (accessed on 10 June 2019).

Money (Undisclosed Foreign Income and Assets) and Imposition of Tax Act, 2015; the Benami Transactions (Prohibition) (Amendment) Act, 2016; the Real Estate (Regulation and Development) Act, 2016; the Insolvency and Bankruptcy Code (IBC), 2016 were introduced to curb banking frauds, black money, tax evasion and bankruptcy. India signed double taxation avoidance agreements (DTAA) with more than 80 countries. DTAA will promote investment flow and curb tax evasion. All these reforms provided a strong shield against corrupt leakages and became a deterrent to such practices.

Among all scams, the biggest one, involving ₹12,000 crore, happened in the Punjab National Bank (PNB). The main accused of the scandal was a billionaire jeweller Nirav Modi and his uncle Mehul Choksi. The PMLA, 2002 was amended in 2018 to enable attachment and confiscation of assets located outside the country.[16] Under the Act, ED attached 41 properties worth ₹1,210 crore in the name of 'absconding' Choksi and his associated firms. The central agency attached housing flats, office premises and land properties in different places under the PMLA in connection with alleged fraud in the PNB. The CBI and ED have registered two FIRs each to probe the case. The ED attached properties worth ₹147 crore of Nirav Modi under the Act.[17] Both Choksi and Nirav Modi left India before criminal cases were lodged against them. Both allegedly cheated PNB to the tune of ₹12,000 crore.[18]

A Special Court under PMLA had issued non-bailable arrest warrants against Choksi, his nephew Nirav Modi and Neeshal Deepak Modi, owner of Firestar Diamonds, in March 2018. At least six PNB staff and an equal number of Choksi and Modi employees have been

[16] Under the 2002 Act, the government could act on properties within the country. With the new amendment, probe agencies can take action on properties held overseas by money launderers equivalent to the 'proceeds of crime' committed.

[17] https://realty.economictimes.indiatimes.com/news/regulatory/ed-attaches-nirav-modis-properties-worth-rs-147-crore/68167788 (accessed on 26 February 2019).

[18] https://www.thehindu.com/news/national/mehul-choksis-properties-are-money-laundering-assets-pmla-authority/article24847325.ece (accessed on 1 November 2018).

arrested so far. That acted as a deterrent and fear caught the fraudsters in their ways.

In August 2018, the GoI had sacked Usha Ananthasubramanian on the penultimate day of her job as MD and CEO of Allahabad Bank for alleged involvement in the PNB fraud. Ananthasubramanian was MD and CEO of PNB between August 2015 and May 2017. Vijay Mallya's Kingfisher Airlines had borrowed over ₹9,000 crore from various banks[19] including SBI, PNB, IDBI and Bank of Baroda. Mallya left India on 2 March 2016 and went on hiding in London, and the GoI is fighting for his extradition. All these banking scams allegedly happened during the Congress-headed UPA II regime.

In another major banking scandal, the Serious Fraud Investigation Office (SFIO), an investigation arm of the Ministry of Corporate Affairs, framed charges against Infrastructure Leasing and Financial Services Ltd (IL&FS) Chairman and Managing Director Hari Sankaran and CEO Ramesh Bawa for their role in diverting ₹17,500 crore from the company to make the accounts of certain borrowers and group companies look healthy.[20] The board took charge at parent IL&FS after the irregularities at the group came to light and said nearly 90 per cent of IL&FS's gross loss were NPAs at the end of December 2018. In another scam amounting ₹4,355 crore in the Punjab & Maharashtra Cooperative Bank (PMCB), thousands of depositors have been left in the lurch and three stressed deposit holders died. The PMCB's former managing director Joy Thomas was arrested.[21]

Chanda Kochhar, the first woman to head India's second-biggest private sector bank, ICICI, stepped down from the position in October 2018 following alleged irregularities in granting huge loans to her

[19] https://www.businesstoday.in/current/economy-politics/vijay-mallya-says-he-didnt-borrow-single-rupee-it-was-kingfisher-airlines/story/298229.html (accessed on 7 December 2018).

[20] https://economictimes.indiatimes.com/news/company/corporate-trends/ilfs-financial-services-ex-ceo-had-direct-role-in-diverting-rs-17-5k-cr/articleshow/68883125.cms (accessed on 15 April 2019).

[21] https://www.thehindu.com/news/cities/mumbai/ex-md-of-punjab-maharashtra-cooperative-bank-arrested/article29597302.ece (accessed on 10 October 2019).

relatives during her nine-year chief executive tenure.[22] In another case, the CBI filed FIR against Rotomac Pens promoter Vikram Kothari for allegedly defaulting on loans amounting to ₹3,695 crore to seven nationalized banks. The scam began in 2008 during the UPA era.[23]

Under the Fugitive Economic Offenders Act, 2018, the CBI and the ED are pursuing legal actions to bring back 28 Indians, including six women, living abroad, who have been charged for financial irregularities and criminal offences.[24] The list included Vijay Mallya, Nirav Modi, Mehul Choksi and Jatin Mehta. India had signed extradition treaties with nearly 54 countries.[25] The Opposition is blaming the Modi government for these frauds and alleged that all those duped the banks fled the country during the BJP rule.

Anti-bankruptcy laws passed by the Modi government have made many crony capitalists pay back their loans and divested many of their companies. For the first time in our history, we are seeing many who looted our banks taken to bankruptcy with the recovery of around 45 per cent of the amount. 'Phone-banking' has now become a thing of the past. Banks were forced to recognize their loans and were recapitalized (Pai 2019). No doubt, all these efforts are commendable. But, Modi's promise of 'bringing back' to India 'within 100 days' the billion dollars of 'black money' stashed abroad by tax evaders, corrupt politicians and officials remained only as election rhetoric.

Under the PMLA, the ED has attached properties worth ₹54 crore belonging to Karti Chidambaram, son of former Finance Minister P. Chidambaram, in India, Spain and the UK, following investigations into money laundering cases related to INX Media. In the case, Chidambaram, who served as the union home minister, was arrested

---

[22] https://economictimes.indiatimes.com/industry/banking/finance/banking/icici-bank-accepts-ceo-chanda-kochhars-early-retirement/articleshow/66068242.cms (accessed on 5 October 2018).

[23] https://www.livemint.com/Companies/vBvxbqXc0DFcIPWq6R57GJ/CBI-registers-FIR-against-Rotomac-promoter-for-Rs800-crore-b.html (accessed on 20 February 2018).

[24] https://www.thehindu.com/news/national/list-of-fugitive-economic-offenders-living-abroad/article24600603.ece (accessed on 17 August 2019).

[25] https://mea.gov.in/leta.htm (accessed on 11 December 2019).

and imprisoned in Tihar jail for 106 days and later released on bail on 4 December 2019. On 18 October 2019, the CBI filed a charge sheet against 14 accused, including Chidambaram and his son Karti. Armed with a PMLA court order declaring former liquor baron and once known as 'king of good times' Vijay Mallya a fugitive economic offender, the ED has kicked off the process of compiling a list of immovable property estimated at ₹1,200 crore and shares worth ₹11,000 crore for confiscation.[26] Arrest of Karnataka Congress leader and former Minister D. K. Shivakumar and former Ranbaxy promoters Shivinder Singh and his bother Malvinder Singh on allegations of money laundering cases and cheating indicated that no one is above the law.[27]

The criminal case under the PMLA was filed by ED against AgustaWestland chopper scam accused Gautam Khaitan on the basis of a case lodged by the IT department against him under the provisions of the Black Money (Undisclosed Foreign Income and Assets) and Imposition of Tax Act, 2015. The ED claims to have identified six undeclared foreign bank accounts in Singapore maintained by Gautam Khaitan.[28] British national Christian Michel, the alleged middlemen in the ₹3,600 crore AgustaWestland VIP chopper scam was extradited to India on 4 December 2018, from the United Arab Emirates. The deal was signed during the UPA II in 2010. The deal was scrapped on 1 January 2014 for supplying 12 AW-101 VVIP choppers to the IAF over alleged breach of contractual obligations and charges of kickbacks of ₹423 crore paid by it to secure the deal.[29] As per the CBI, bribe was

[26] https://economictimes.indiatimes.com/news/politics-and-nation/bolstered-by-pmla-order-ed-gets-moving-on-attaching-vijay-mallyas-assets/articleshow/67413233.cms (accessed on 7 January 2019).

[27] https://economictimes.indiatimes.com/industry/healthcare/biotech/healthcare/ex-ranbaxy-promoters-malvinder-shivinder-singh-arrested/articleshow/71533389.cms?from=mdr (accessed on 10 November 2019).

[28] https://economictimes.indiatimes.com/news/politics-and-nation/ed-identifies-gautam-khaitans-six-undeclared-singapore-accounts/articleshow/68714481.cms (accessed on 4 April 2019).

[29] https://www.ndtv.com/india-news/agustawestland-case-accused-rajeev-saxena-says-i-am-not-under-any-pressure-2000597 (accessed on 8 June 2019).

paid to the middlemen and Indian officials and money was transferred through bank accounts in the UK and the UAE.

Another big strike on corruption was the IBC, 2016, that provided the most effective reforms with the potential of transparency and expeditiously resolving India's overwhelming NPAs riddle. With a strict 180+90 days 'resolve or liquidate diktat', the Code has received appreciation from the Indian industry as well as from the World Bank and IMF. It has contributed to the country's significant jump in 'Ease of Doing Business' ranking from 142 in 2014 to 63 in 2020. The Code provides a timeline of 180 days to conclude a corporate insolvency resolution process, extendable by one-time extension up to 90 days. Probably no other country in the world mandates a time-bound resolution. The Code aims to protect the interests of small investors and make the process of doing business less cumbersome.

Once the resolution process starts, the board cedes control of the company and insolvency professionals, and with the help of professional advisors starts managing the company. Under the law, the Insolvency and Bankruptcy Board of India (IBBI) was established on 1 October 2016 and is responsible for the implementation of the Code. More than 12,000 cases have been filed since the implementation of the IBC.[30]

Undue delay in the IBC process is starting to hurt banks, already weighed down by steep provisioning and litigation costs. Moreover, about half of the cases under the Corporate Insolvency Resolution Process (CIRP) have crossed the 180-day timeline, which is worrying (Merwin 2019).[31] The Supreme Court order on 3 April 2019, quashing the RBI's circular of bad loans issued on 12 February 2019,[32] is a setback to the evolving process for debt resolution. Business tycoons

---

[30] https://www.thehindubusinessline.com/money-and-banking/over-12000-cases-filed-after-implementation-ofibc-setting-up-of-nclt/article 26636316.ece (accessed on 26 March 2019).

[31] On an average, cases under the IBC are being dragged for more than 300 days.

[32] The circular had forced banks to recognize defaults by large borrowers with dues over ₹2,000 crore within a day after an instalment fell due; and, if not resolved within six months after that, they had no choice but to refer these accounts for resolution under the IBC.

from power to aviation and real estate will now have more room to negotiate loan repayments with lenders even after payments become overdue.[33] The voiding of the circular could slow down and complicate the resolution process for loans aggregating to as much as ₹3.80 lakh crore across 70 large borrowers, according to data from the rating agency ICRA. The RBI circular was aimed at breaking the nexus between banks and defaulters. The Supreme Court ruling will bring some relief to the founders of many companies who were at risk of being pulled into bankruptcy proceedings.[34]

## Rafale Agreement

In the midst of the Modi government's claim that there was no corruption in the last five years, the troubling questions about the purchase of 36 Rafale fighter jets have persisted despite a clean chit of sorts from the Supreme Court. The Congress and some leaders who served as ministers in the Vajpayee government see the scam in an overall escalation in the price of each jet in 2016 deal struck by the Modi government. The Modi government's deal was to purchase 36 fighters as opposed to the original 126. The deal with the French Government has been a subject of heated claims and counterclaims on favours shown to facilitate the Anil Ambani-owned Reliance Defence Ltd to get the offset contracts from Dassault Aviation. Ammunition for the second charge came from an unexpected quarter with the former French President Francois Hollande stating in an interview that it was India that suggested the Anil Ambani-owned Reliance Defence Ltd as one of the offset partners for the deal,[35] the charge strongly rejected by the Modi government. The deal was debated in the Parliament and outside extensively, as the Opposition, Congress and other parties,

---

[33] https://economictimes.indiatimes.com/news/company/corporate-trends/supreme-court-ruling-on-rbi-circular-to-give-tycoons-reprieve-on-55-billion-of-bad-debt/articleshow/68699252.cms (accessed on 3 April 2019).

[34] https://www.thehindubusinessline.com/opinion/a-bank-merger-that-will-not-pay-off/article25040612.ece (accessed on 26 September 2018).

[35] https://www.thehindu.com/opinion/editorial/the-plane-truth/article25022234.ece (accessed on 24 September 2019).

alleged that the aircraft was arbitrarily purchased for nearly $3 billion to its benchmarked price by the cabinet committee on security led by the prime minister. The Opposition has been demanding a probe on the deal through a Joint Parliamentary Committee. The government has done everything to ensure no probe takes place.

The amendments to the Prevention of Corruption Act, 2005 had come under severe criticism (Yadav 2016). Through changes in the Act, investigating agencies have been barred from even initiating inquiry or probe into the allegation of corruption without prior approval of the government. Effectively, this empowers political masters to decide whether they wish to allow a corruption probe against a public servant or not. Further, under the new law, any benefit that is not economic, that is indirect or that cannot be proven to be intentional fraud will not be considered as corruption. This would frustrate the people's confidence to fight corruption in cases which may not involve the payment of a bribe, as it may be done for other considerations like pleasing political masters for rewards (Bhardwaj and Johri 2019). Further, the BJP government had not operationalized the Whistle-Blowers Protection Act, 2014, by not formulating rules and thereby denied protection to whistle-blowers who fight corruption in high places in the government.

Further, the Modi government also did not take steps to pass the Grievances Redress Bill, 2011, which was lapsed after the dissolution of the Lok Sabha in 2014. The Bill was piloted by the UPA II to check petty corruption in the day-to-day delivery of basic services in health, education or the public distribution system. The Bill would have empowered the public to fight against corruption. Modi's lack of political will to take necessary measures to curb corruption has given credence to slogans like *chowkidar chor hai* (Bhardwaj and Johri 2019), and Rahul Gandhi used the slogan widely during the run-up to the 2019 election campaign to fetch votes for the Congress.

The government's interference in the functioning of the CBI and bypassing of rules in the removal of erstwhile CBI Director Alok Verma, and appointment of an Interim Director M. Nageswara Rao, has largely damaged the image of the government as well as the premier investigating agency in the fight against corruption in high places. The lack of transparency in the electoral bond scheme, passed as a Money Bill in Parliament, prevents citizens from finding out who is funding political parties. It is alleged that donations worth hundreds of crores of rupees can be made anonymously. Unsurprisingly, the largest benefactor of the electoral bonds scheme has been the ruling party (BJP; ₹210 crore) in 2019. The BJP government's proposal to introduce amendments to the RTI Act and to undermine the independence of the Information Commissioners of the Central Information Commission has also come under intense public scrutiny. These amendments were eventually dropped following public outcry.

The RBI too has not lived up to the peoples' expectations in maintaining transparency, and it continued to deny information relating to inspection reports and other material sought by the RTI petitioners. Following this, the Supreme Court on 26 April 2019 ordered the RBI to disclose its annual inspection reports of banks, along with the list of wilful defaulters and information related to them under the RTI. The Apex Court ordered the RBI to 'withdraw its disclosure policy', which it said is in violation of an order passed by the court in December 2015 directing the central bank to disclose information under the provisions of the RTI act. The RBI has repeatedly tried to stonewall multiple requests seeking information ranging from the names of wilful defaulters on bank loans to the tune of hundreds of crores of rupees.[36]

The exit of two RBI Governors—Raghuram Rajan and Urjit Patel—in a short span of time has caused some sorts of embarrassment for the government. The Congress alleged that the Modi government has humiliated the RBI governors and undermined the integrity of institutions by appointing persons from the RSS background. The government has nominated Swadeshi Jagaran Manch's S. Gurumurthy as a part-time director of the RBI.[37]

---

[36] https://www.thehindu.com/opinion/editorial/no-more-leeway/article26974275.ece (accessed on 29 April 2019).

[37] https://www.thehindubusinessline.com/money-and-banking/govt-appoints-s-gurumurthy-on-rbi-board/article24632242.ece (accessed on 9 August 2018).

## Quota and the Middle Class

Reservations in recruitments had been the irritating point for the higher caste groups among the middle class. They always remind that B. R. Ambedkar had put a timeline for reservation; however, it has not only overstepped that timeline but has also been extended to many new social groups. The demands are also continuing with new caste groups seeking reservation. The middle class and the media had strongly opposed granting reservation of 27 per cent to OBCs under the Mandal Commission report in 1990 by the V. P. Sing government. In 2019, both media and middle class have not protested at all when the Parliament approved the 124 Constitutional Amendment Bill to provide 10 per cent reservation in jobs and education for the economically weaker sections, including the upper castes. Although some described it as a quota for the middle class (Yadu 2019), majority of the MPs, cutting across political parties, supported the Bill, although they accused the government in its timings and intention. The decision termed as 'Modi's Mandal Movement' has been perceived as a 'desperate' attempt to woo non-Dalit and non-OBC voters for the 2019 general elections. The RSS and the Republican Party of India, a party of Dalits and a NDA ally, also supported the quota. With the RSS supporting the quota, the increased convergence is seen between the Sangh Parivar and the government on several policy matters.

It is argued that the Modi government, after the bad performance of the BJP in the 2018 assembly elections held in five states, particularly in the Hindi belt comprising Chhattisgarh, Madhya Pradesh and Rajasthan, decided to come out with a sop of 10 per cent quota for upper castes that had apparently voted against the BJP in these states (Misra 2019). The Opposition termed the decision as an 'eyewash' just before the 2019 elections as the government had failed on all fronts, including providing jobs to youth. Nobel laureate economist Amartya Sen has criticized the quota and said it as a 'muddled thinking' that raises serious questions about its political and economic impact.[38]

---

[38] https://www.hindustantimes.com/india-news/10-quota-for-economically-weaker-sections-a-muddled-thinking-says-amartya-sen/story-UKjB2BAn-puHewpVa50iXUI.html (accessed on 10 January 2019).

Whom will the new 10 per cent quota apply to? The eligibility criteria laid down in the Bill to qualify for the reservation are not meant for those who are economically weak. To all those who are not covered in the existing quotas and have an annual family income below ₹8 lakh or agricultural land below five acres are eligible. There are also other criteria to become eligible under this quota. In fact, eligibility criteria for 'economic weakness' have been formulated in such a way that it appears to cover almost all Indians barring the top upper crust of maybe 3 per cent (Misra 2019). By and large, people either belonging to a lower middle class or middle class are expected to get the benefit. The majority of jobs would go to these sections as they have a definite advantage of having better school education and higher studies. These sections pay income tax as well.

The Narasimha Rao government in 1991 had decided to provide 10 per cent quota to the poor or economically backward among other sections of the people who are not covered in any of the existing schemes of reservation. In its landmark 1993 judgement in the Indra Sawhney versus Union of India case, the Supreme Court said that the total number of reserved seats could not exceed 50 per cent of what was available and that the constitutional scheme for reservation, economic backwardness alone could not be a criterion. The Bill passed by the Modi government overshoots the 50 per cent quota and takes the total to 60 per cent. However, the government is confident of passing the legal test. The 10 per cent quota is an attempt to shift the discourse on quota politics from caste to class.

## Middle Class and Housing

The NDA government under Modi has been trying to bring a positive change in the real estate sector for the benefit of the middle class and houseless people. Falling interest rates on housing loans and reduction of GST on housing construction materials largely benefited the middle class. The government has launched an affordable housing scheme and that has helped realized the dreams of lakhs of people who had been toiling hard for years to buy their own house. The slowdown in the real estate market has also brightened the buyer's faces. Demonetization has led to a correction in the prices of housing properties, and Modi responded to the Opposition's criticism that *notebandi* (demonetization) hurt the economy, saying he was being targeted as influential people in the real estate close to the Congress had been hurt.[39] Three to four years ago, the rates of property were skyrocketing. In such circumstances, a salaried, general working-class person could only dream of buying a house at a reasonable price. Under the affordable housing schemes, new affordable houses, which were meant for the lower-middle-class groups of the society, were built.[40]

It is the vision and dream of the Modi government that the citizens of the country will have their own houses by 2022—India's 75th year of independence. To facilitate and promote this vision, the government is trying to encourage builders who are launching projects that fall under the affordable housing scheme—houses that cost from ₹10 lakhs to ₹30 lakhs—available to the lower and middle-income groups. Under this scheme, home loans are being made available at subsidized rates. This has led to the rise in demand for houses/flats falling in the price band of ₹10–30 lakhs. As a result, builders are launching projects mostly falling under the affordable housing scheme in Punjab, Rajasthan, Uttar Pradesh and Haryana.[41]Through the scheme, the government aims at subsidizing the construction of 2.95 crore rural houses and 1.2 urban houses by 2022 (Johari 2019).

Modi has asked the developer community to target the 'neo-middle class' as a large number of people were emerging out of poverty. He [Modi] asked,

> Now is the time, the target should be on neo middle-class category, whose aspirations need to be understood as they are a large market

[39] https://timesofindia.indiatimes.com/elections/lok-sabha-elections-2019/madhya-pradesh/news/pm-modi-fires-back-at-opposition-forcefully-defends-demonetisation/articleshow/69065981.cms (accessed on 27 April 2019).

[40] https://economictimes.indiatimes.com/wealth/real-estate/owning-a-house-no-longer-a-dream-thanks-to-affordable-housing-scheme-enabling-everyone-to-own-a-house-under-the-affordable-housing-scheme/articleshow/57626989.cms?from=mdr (accessed on 17 March 2017).

[41] Ibid.

waiting to be tapped for the sector. ...Real estate sector plays a catalytic role in providing employment. Do you get enough respect? Who is responsible? (Ramnani 2019)

The government has provided a credit-linked scheme, which could provide savings worth ₹5–5.5 lakh on housing loans for the middle class. Since the introduction of RERA, close to 35,000 real estate projects and 27,000 organizations have been registered under it.

In fact, the tax sops announced in the interim budget 2019 will benefit both the developers and the middle-class homebuyers. The move to exempt people earning up to ₹5 lakh from payment of income tax will benefit the housing sector as the surplus will find its way into real estate. The government argues that the youth will get encouragement to buy houses because of this income tax exemption. Under the new GST structure that came into effect from 1 April 2019, normal under-construction houses will attract GST at 5 per cent against the earlier 12 per cent. Similarly, the levy on affordable homes will attract 1 per cent against the earlier 8 per cent.

Moreover, interest rates on housing loans up to of ₹50 lakh have fallen from 10.15 per cent in May 2014 to about 8.5 per cent in April 2019 that could save the borrower up to ₹15 lakh in 25 years. To boost purchase of second homes, the government has announced capital gains up to ₹2 crore could be rolled over for investment in two housing units from the current single unit. It also exempted tax on notional rent on a second self-occupied house. The government extended 100 per cent reduction of profit under Section 80 IBA of the Income Tax Act to housing projects approved until March 2020.

## Inflation Conundrum

Inflation is a very sensitive issue for the middle class, and this class responds very quickly. Inflation was at its peak during the end of the years of UPA II. During the 2014 campaign, a popular slogan was *bahut hui mehengai ki maar/abki baar, Modi sarkar!* (Enough of being hit by price rise; this time Modi government). The Modi government seems to have lived up to the slogan and gave priority for containing inflation. But naysayers are always sceptical of the progress made by this government, so we let the numbers do the talking instead.

Double-digit inflation had choked the middle class and the poor. Prices of food and fuel spiralled uncontrollably in the UPA II regime. Inflation is a hidden and unfair tax on the poor and the middle class. Inflation declined from 10 per cent in 2009–2014 to an average of about 4.5 per cent in 2014–2019. In fact, the last three years' average is much lower. It was close to 2.7 per cent in March 2019. An analysis by credit rating agency Crisil shows that food inflation measured by the consumer index rose only 0.1 per cent in 2018–2019. The last time annual food inflation had fallen below 1 per cent was in 1999–2000.[42] Prices of subsidized and non-subsidized LPG cylinder have been lowered.[43]

In his interim budget speech on 1 February 2019, Finance Minister Piyush Goyal said, 'If we had not controlled inflation, our families would have been spending around 35–40 per cent more today on basic necessities such as food, travel, consumer durables, housing, etc.' Food prices moved south in the last five years. Economists cite bumper crop, low demand, low global prices and muted impact of increased MSP are major factors for low food prices.

India's economy sustained a GDP growth rate of 7.5 per cent, remaining the fastest in the world. The GDP growth during the UPA II was 6.7 per cent. During Modi's term, India's GDP is estimated to have grown over ₹76 lakh crore, with lower inflation, lower fiscal deficit and lower current account deficit (CAD)—all implying quality of growth. Conversely, the UPA II consistently had a high fiscal deficit, high inflation and high CAD, rocking the very foundations of our economy (Pai 2019). Low inflation filters into interest rates, and, consequently, a lower inflation rate environment facilitates more credit activity.

---

[42] https://timesofindia.indiatimes.com/business/india-business/food-inflation-falls-to-lowest-level-since-1991/articleshow/68870152.cms (accessed on 22 April 2019).
[43] https://www.ndtv.com/business/lpg-gas-price-lpg-gas-cylinder-here-s-how-much-an-lpg-gas-cylinder-will-cost-the-consumer-this-month-2033474 (accessed on 7 May 2019).

However, in 2019–2020, India's GDP growth fell to 5 per cent. The GDP was 4.5 per cent in the second quarter of the 2019–2020, a six-year low. The slowdown in economic growth has taken away from India the tag of the world's fastest-growing major economy to China. There are a number of factors behind this economic slowdown, including slowdown in private consumption, investment and export and lack of credit growth and demand in the market.[44] The Modi government has taken a number of measures, including cut in corporate tax to 22 per cent from 30 per cent for existing companies and to 15 per cent from 25 per cent to new manufacturing companies, and issued directions to banks to increase lending.

The middle class benefitted from the Unnat Jyoti by Affordable LEDs for All (UJALA) scheme. Rarely is a middle class or lower middle class attracted to long-term gains by purchasing an LED bulb priced at ₹350–400 for lighting their homes for a few hours in the night. They prefer an incandescent bulb costing ₹10 rather than costly LED bulbs. Approximately 35 crore LED bulbs have been distributed leading to a cost saving of ₹18,341 crores annually (GoI 2019a). The poor and middle-class families benefited from the reduction in electricity bills. Had the subsidy was given instead of bulbs, it would have captured the headlines in the media, claimed Modi.[45]

Launched in 2015, the scheme saved 45,119 million-kilowatt hour of energy every year. The Modi government expanded the scheme and benefited from the economy of scale as it halved the price of each bulb. The government has reduced the prices of LED bulbs to ₹38 per unit, which was around ₹350 earlier. Due to this scheme, India's share in the global LED market has increased to 12 per cent from a mere 0.1 per cent, with the penetration of LED in the domestic

[44] https://www.indiatoday.in/business/story/gross-domestic-product-growth-falls-4-5-per-cent-q2-2019-20-1623733-2019-11-29 (accessed on 30 November 2019).

[45] https://economictimes.indiatimes.com/industry/energy/power/21-crore-led-bulbs-distributed-to-save-rs-11000-crore-pm-narendra-modi/articleshow/57024047.cms (accessed on 11 April 2019).

market rising to 10 per cent from 0.4 per cent.[46] As part of the direct benefit of the UJALA scheme to people and the industry, annual LED domestic production increased from 30 lakh bulbs to over 6 crore bulbs, simultaneously creating 60,000 jobs.[47]

## Wooing for Good Health

Another usual worry of the middle-class voter is their expenditure on health and hospitals. This gives equal political mileage as much as any other subsidy or welfare programme gives. Health insurance coverage and reduction in the cost of hospitalization is certainly a very delicate point on the agenda of the middle class.

Cardiovascular Diseases (CVD) are a major cause of deaths in India, which is about 25 per cent of total deaths. Out of these, 90–95 per cent CVD deaths happen due to coronary artery diseases. In a major relief to lakhs of cardiac patients belonging to the middle class and the poor, the GoI has slashed the prices of life-saving coronary stents by up to 85 per cent by capping them at ₹7,260 for bare-metal stents (BMS) and ₹29,600 for drug-eluting stents (DES) variety in February 2017.[48] The maximum retail price (MRP) of BMS and DES was fixed at ₹7,623 and ₹31,080, respectively, inclusive of taxes. Earlier, the average MRP for BMS was ₹45,000, and, for DES, it was ₹1.21 lakh.[49]

A research paper from Maharashtra doctors and high-ranking bureaucrats shows that the use of DES among the poor cardiac patients ballooned to 70 per cent from 40 per cent after reduction of

[46] https://economictimes.indiatimes.com/industry/energy/power/eesl-distributes-30-cr-led-bulbs-helped-save-rs-15k-cr-annually/articleshow/64234103.cms (accessed on 19 May 2018).

[47] Ibid.

[48] https://economictimes.indiatimes.com/industry/healthcare/biotech/pharmaceuticals/heart-of-the-matter-coronary-stents-get-cheaper-by-up-to-85/articleshow/57150821.cms (accessed on 1 March 2018).

[49] Ibid. In line with the wholesale price index of calendar year 2018, NPPA has hiked prices of stents by 4.2% from April 1, 2019.

prices (Iyer 2019). The capping of the prices will result in saving of ₹80,000–90,000 per piece and gross relief of ₹4,450 crore a year for cardiac patients. Coronary stents are included in the National List of Essential Medicines (NLEM) in July 2015. In case of violations of the ceiling prices, the National Pharmaceutical Pricing Authority has been empowered to recover the over-charged amount along with 15 per cent rate of interest. The ceiling of prices is one of the ways of promoting 'Make in India' as the market size of locally made stents is roughly 30 per cent. However, the industry opposed the capping of prices saying that such a decision has the potential to block innovations and limit access to world-class medical care and options for deserving patients.[50]

Medicines constitute a substantial proportion of the out-of-pocket expenses in Indian households. In order to address this issue and to end the 'medicine mafia', the GoI launched the Jan Aushadhi (Medicine for the Masses) Scheme (JAS) to provide cheap generic medicines to patients. These medicines are provided through 3,600 Jan Aushadhi Kendras, established across the country. Over 850 generic medicines are available at Kendras and their price is 50–90 per cent less than the market price. A generic drug has the same active ingredient as an original branded drug but is less expensive as it does not include the cost of research and development. Modi says, 'Due to illness, the financial burden is immense for the poor and the middle class. Our constant endeavour is to ensure affordable healthcare to every Indian' (Santra 2018). Essential medicines brought under the price control regime are giving customers total benefit of more than ₹1,000 crore a year in India (Santra 2018).

JAS has given a jolt to the uncontrolled medicine prices across all the therapeutic category of medicines in India. However, not all JAS prices are lower than branded medicines.[51] It has been observed that lack of awareness in the public, lack of support for JAS, poor supply chain and poor marketing techniques, and doctors not prescribing

---

[50] https://www.firstpost.com/india/govt-cuts-coronary-stent-prices-by-85-percent-in-major-relief-to-cardiac-patients-3283142.html (accessed on 2 May 2017).

[51] For example, the cheapest branded cefuroxime axetil (500 mg) (antibiotic) in the market is almost three times cheaper than its JAS price.

generic medicines are the major constraints faced by the JAS, leading to its below-average success. But, industry insiders believe that blanket implementation of price control of medicines and medical devices contributed to a drastic fall in foreign direct investment (FDI) in the medical device sector. The FDI had fallen from $439 million in 2016 to $66 million in 2018.[52] But it is argued that FDI generally falls in all sectors of the economy during the election year owing to uncertainty about the general election result.

The mega health insurance scheme called Ayushman Bharat was launched to provide a health insurance cover of ₹5 lakh. The scheme, described as 'Modicare' by the media, is expected to cover 10 crore poor and lower-middle families (50 crore people). Over 16 lakh beneficiaries have been admitted in hospitals since the announcement of the scheme in 2018. The centre spent ₹952 crore on the scheme in less than one year. Nearly 15,000 hospitals have been empanelled under it. Lauding the 'Modicare', the UK-based medical journal, *The Lancet*, said, 'Narendra Modi is first prime minister to prioritize universal health coverage as part of his political platform under the "Ayushman Bharat"'.

Richard Horton, editor-in-chief of *The Lancet* said that the prime minister has grasped the importance of health not only as a natural right of citizens but also as a political instrument to meet the growing expectations of India's emerging middle class. He goes on to add that the Congress President Rahul Gandhi was 'yet to match Modicare'. 'Rahul Gandhi seeking to resurrect the Congress and proved that India's greatest political dynasty still has something to offer, despite his promise to help lower castes, tribal communities and rural poor, is yet to match Modicare', Horton (2018) said.

The opposition parties have called Ayushman Bharat a lifesaver for the private sector, rather than for the poor. Medical practitioners opined that the hospital insurance component of the programme, namely the Pradhan Mantri Jan Aarogya Yojana (PMJAY), envisages extensive partnership with the private sector, from healthcare provisioning to insurance administration and from private hospitals

[52] https://www.thehindu.com/news/national/price-controls-hurting-fdi-in-medical-devices-sector/article26924501.ece (accessed on 24 April 2019).

to third-party administrators. A problematic model of public–private partnership envisaged under PMJAY makes it vulnerable to allegations of unduly favouring the private sector. As these measures aim at expanding access to care under PMJAY, diverting public investment from public hospitals to the private sector entails an increasing circumscription of the scope of the public healthcare to a limited segment of the population, while private health spending caters to the rest (Bhaduri 2019). Already the NITI Aayog's public–private partnership guidelines on non-communicable disease (NCD) management, which invites the private sector to build and run NCD units in district hospitals, is too heavily loaded in favour of the private sector while all risks are to be borne by the government (Prabhu 2017a).

## Looking at the Mirror Image

The launch of the Swachh Bharat Mission (SBM) and the declaration of International Yoga Day by the UN are other initiatives related to health that have been largely appreciated by the middle class. The SBM initiative was launched with a mission mode on Gandhi Jayanti in 2014. The prime minister grabbed the nation's attention by picking up a broom (Figure 6.1). Modi embraced Mahatma Gandhi by using his glasses as a symbol of the SBM. More than nine crore toilets were built and coverage of rural sanitation has risen to 98 per cent from about 40 per cent in 2014.[53] According to the WHO report, the SBM Gramin will result in preventing more than three lakh deaths due to diarrhoea and protein-energy malnutrition during 2014–2019. The SBM will create the greatest long-term impact on people's lives.[54]

No other prime minister in the past had given as high a priority to SBM as Modi has. Amidst a hectic schedule with the visiting Chinese President Xi Jinping to India on 12–13 October 2019, Modi cleaned the shores of the Kovalam beach during his morning stroll, in line

[53] https://economictimes.indiatimes.com/news/politics-and-nation/over-9-crore-toilets-constructed-under-swachh-bharat-kovind/articleshow/67773723.cms (31 January 2019).
[54] https://www.thehindu.com/sci-tech/health/who-thumbs-up-for-swachh-bharats-rural-component/article24595986.ece (4 August 2018).

Figure 6.1 *Prime Minister Narendra Modi Offering* Shramdaan *(Voluntary Work) on the Occasion of the 'Swachhta Hi Seva' Abhiyan in New Delhi on 15 September 2018*
Source: Press Information Bureau.

with his pet SBM. Clad in black T-shirt, the prime minister walked along the sand and picked the trash of used plastic bags, bottles and other filth. His plogging at a beach in Mamallapuram in Tamil Nadu lasted for over 30 minutes and received widespread praise from people from all sections of the society.[55]

Bollywood superstar Amitabh Bachchan, an icon of the Indian middle class, has been associated with 'Banega Swachh' Indian campaign. President Ram Nath Kovind said that the television commercials featuring *darwaja band to bimari band* (use toilets to shut

---

[55] https://www.asianage.com/india/all-india/131019/pm-modi-s-plogging-wins-praise-and-jibes.html (accessed on 13 October 2019).

the door on diseases) by the actor had inspired crores of people.[56] The campaign brought discussion about cleanliness and sanitation to the mainstream. In a bid to scale up the coverage and encourage cities to actively implement mission initiatives, the Ministry of Urban Development provided a periodic ranking of cities across India to judge the performance of the city civic body. The scheme largely revolved around the persona of Modi. The prime minister's personal involvement, his websites and Twitter feeds, his walkathon on the campaign were intended to enhance national awareness of the scheme. However, ground-level reports from some areas show implementation failures—toilets were built in a hurry with no proper water supply or drainage system resulting in unusable toilets. The quality of construction in Bihar and Odisha is poor at places where village heads did not involve beneficiaries (Verma and Sengupta 2018). It was found that even when toilets are built, people continue to defecate in the open because the toilets do not have water connections.

## GST: Elimination of Cascading Irritations

One of the major sources of unaccounted money (black money) was the multi-stage indirect commodity and service taxation. Avoidance was very easy and, generation of unaccounted money through 'speed payment' was almost institutionalized. UPA I and II deliberated on bringing in GST but did not show sufficient courage due to the fear of backlash in elections.

Arguably, the greatest policy achievement of the BJP-led NDA regime and one of the greatest fiscal policy reforms in Indian economic history was amending the Constitution to implement the Goods and Services Tax Act. Despite all its early glitches, the magnitude of the GST achievement was coming together of 29 states and 7 union territories and giving up their sovereignty for the larger common good of creating one market in India; improving tax compliance; creating

[56] https://economictimes.indiatimes.com/news/politics-and-nation/over-9-crore-toilets-constructed-under-swachh-bharat-kovind/articleshow/67773723. cms?from=mdr (accessed on 31 January 2019).

a robust revenue base for the country; and creating the fiscal environment for higher investment and growth (Subramanian 2018). It is undoubtedly a relief that the farrago of more than two dozen central and state sales taxes that had previously bedevilled Indian businesses have nearly all been replaced by GST. Billed as 'one nation, one tax', the government has introduced three GSTs (Integrated GST or IGST, Central GST or CGST and State GST or SGST) as well as five slabs of GST—0 per cent (the exempted category), 5 per cent, 12 per cent, 18 per cent and 28 per cent. GST came into effect from 1 July 2017.

The GST's public perception was largely contaminated by demonetization of high-value currencies having preceded it. When the GST came into force, many shops simply pulled down their shutters and did not open for business: They did not know how to cope with the GST that had been imposed on them. Most small business owners, as well as traders and shopkeepers, were not computer-literate and had to scramble to acquire computer literacy and register online on the Goods and Services Tax Network (GSTN). Congress President Rahul Gandhi dubbed GST as a 'Gabbar Singh Tax'—a reference to the notorious dacoit in the blockbuster film *Sholay*. Economist Arun Kumar called it 'Ground Scorching Tax' owing to its complexity and appealed to the GoI to make it a 'Ground Nourishing Tax' (Mishra 2019b). Anti-GST rhetoric was one of the main electoral narratives of the Congress in the 2018 elections in states as well as the 2019 general elections. Many critics of the Modi government pointed fingers at initial glitches in the execution of the GST.

With the convergence of the central and state taxes under GST, the problem of tax on tax (cascade taxation) was solved. Over 1.21 crore businesses have been registered under the GST regime in April 2019. The GST rolled out on 1 July 2017 with 64 lakh tax payers, and the number of business tax payers nearly doubled in just two years. According to the Income Tax Department data, the number of income tax payers increased from 2.88 crore in 2015–2016 to 6.36 crore in 2019–2020 (as on 30 November of both years), an increase of 220 per cent. The number of individual tax payers increased from 2.60 crore to 5.82 crore during the same period. The number of individuals earning more than ₹1 crore a year and paying taxes has increased from 47,000 to 1.07 lakh during the period.

The increase in the number of taxpayers (who hitherto did not bother to pay taxes whatsoever) seems to be a positive fallout of GST giving the state exchequer to fund many ambitious projects for the neo-middle class and poor. This will surely have a positive impact on the middle class once the amount of tax collection from these new taxpayers is stabilized over the next couple of years. The GST collection was an all-time high in the month of April 2019, crossing ₹1.13 lakh crore. The PMLA will become very handy here also to curb fake GST invoices.

After the initial glitches and protests against the implementation of the GST, the GST Council frequently met and rationalized the prices of commodities by lowering taxes, which is another way of saving the middle class and poor consumers. According to research based on consumer expenditure data, a household would be saving ₹320 each month on their monthly expenditure of ₹8,400 on 10 essential items— cereals, edible oil, sugar, chocolates, *namkeen* and sweets, cosmetics and toiletries, washing powder, tiles, furniture and coir products and other household products—owing to reduction of taxes under GST. Earlier, tax on ₹8400 was ₹830, and, in the post-GST scenario, it has been reduced to ₹510 (Sharma 2018). Then Finance Minister Arun Jaitely claimed that the government has given ₹2 lakh crore tax benefit annually to the middle class without raising a single tax. After the introduction of GST, he said tax rates were lowered on over 350 items and 66 types of services. Now, nearly 97.5 per cent of goods attract GST rate either at 18 per cent or below. As on December 2019, a total of 18 goods are in the 28 per cent slab, the highest tax rate.

The Modi government has argued that due to GST, the tax burden on both businessman and consumer has reduced.

From the traders' perspective, GST has brought transparency. Many indirect taxes like octroi, sales tax, entry tax etc. were abolished. One has been free from maintaining different sets of documents. In GST traders have to evaluate their taxation on their own … traders having turnover less than Rs 40 lakh are excluded from

GST net. If we consider GST from common consumers' perspective as GST has reduced tax burden, as people are able to save four per cent a month. On essential goods, there is only zero to five per cent GST. The GST was reduced on more than 80 items like food grains, sugar, curd, idli-dosa batter, washing power, footwear, sewing machine, furniture, electrical appliances, television and mobile phones.[57]

Most of these items, indeed, are used by middle-class households.

## Demonizing the Demonetization

On 8 November 2016, in a dramatic nationally televised speech, Modi announced that two high denomination currencies of ₹500 and ₹1,000 would cease to be legal tender, that is, they would not be accepted as a government-certified means of payment. It was an unprecedented move that no country in recent history had made in normal times (Subramanian 2018, 94). The decision will be remembered for a long time by the present Indian generation. This unconventional decision was termed as a 'black swan' event in Indian history (Sanyal 2018). These high-value currencies accounted for 86 per cent of all the currency in circulation in India. The declared objective of the unexpected shock-and-awe announcement was to fight 'black money' or, put another way, cash made from tax evasion, crime and corruption. The prime minister declared that his announcement would not only rid the nation of black money, but it would also render worthless the counterfeit notes that were reportedly printed by Pakistan to fuel terrorism against India. The decision has prompted fierce and widespread debate. Based on their ideological groundings, proponents and opponents have argued on specific aspects of the policy.

Unlike the previous demonetization (1978), the Modi government's action has created an enormous impact. It took time for many people, caught in the political crossfire on the decision between the Leaders of the Opposition and ruling parties, to comprehend what exactly were the

[57] https://www.narendramodi.in/pm-modi-s-interview-to-sakal-media-group-544488 (accessed on 6 March 2019).

implications (Goradia 2019a). Demonetization was a major electoral plank for opposition parties to target the BJP in all elections held so far. Opposition parties observed the first anniversary of demonetization as a 'black day'. Congress members lamented for not having made public the Parliamentary panel report on demonetization. The BJP which has 17 members in the 31-member panel, opposed the release of the report.

No doubt, withdrawal of high-value currencies from the circulation had caused a severe shortage of cash, causing confusion, chaos and misery to common man for at least two months. It caused suffering to many people: businesses went down and then fuel prices hit a record high across the country, and it also emptied the middle-class pockets. More than a hundred people reportedly died after collapsing in bank queues or committing suicide owing to failure to deposit cash in banks (Dutta 2018). Meera H. Sanyal (2018) provides a comprehensive analysis of the policy, its execution and pitfalls and argues that demonetization destroyed livelihoods of millions in the informal sector, caused enormous distress to farmers, weavers and traders, and forcing many micro, small and medium enterprises (MSMEs) into bankruptcy. The main victims were the poor, house servants, small shopkeepers and the lower middle classes, who rely on cash for their daily activities. The liquidity crisis led to the postponement of weddings, housewarming ceremonies, family tours and so on.

While the Modi government claimed that it was the silver bullet that India needed for eliminating black money, corruption, tax evasion and terror funding. The return of over 99 per cent of the banned high-value notes showed that the government's idea of demonetization dividend was nothing but a mirage (Sanyal 2018). However, we are yet to know how much of this money returned to RBI is actually genuine notes printed in India and what is the share of counterfeit notes from Pakistan. The World Bank (2017) has estimated a sizeable share of counterfeit notes in circulation in India.

Some argue that the market black money has not been dented; counterfeiting and terrorism continues; the credibility of the RBI, banks and currency is damaged; the accountability of the parliament and the prime minister has been eroded; and the social divide has widened

(Kumar 2017). The Opposition has used this experience of hardship to incite people's anger against demonetization and the BJP has used it for appealing for their support terming it as a war on black money. There have been many arguments and counterarguments from both sides.

Modi went to the people, appealing to them to cooperate as the measure was aimed at cracking down corruption and black money. He asked the people to bear with him for 50 days to bring normalcy in currency circulation. The people of India believed him by patiently standing in queues for days and giving him total support. Writing on the first anniversary of demonetization in *The Hindu* on 9 November 2017, S. Gurumurthy, currently a part-time director of RBI, said,

> The black money agenda of demonetization is no failure, though ill-executed. Black money of Rs 45,000 crore has been uncovered and Rs 2.9 lakh crore of cash deposits are under tax probe. Following demonetization, there are 56 lakh more assessees, advance tax receipts have gone up by 42% and self-assessment tax raised by 34%. It has also led to an attack on benami properties. Even intelligence agencies note a 50% drop in hawala-related calls post demonetization, nearly 2.24 lakh shell companies have been used for hawala have been uncovered; 35,000 have been found laundering Rs 17,000 crore; one of them, Rs 2,484 crore.

The government claimed that demonetization helped to unearth undeclared assets and identify lakhs of shell companies. The tax base was also doubled. Despite suffering by the people, the BJP gained electoral victory in the Uttar Pradesh assembly elections in 2017 and in the local bodies' elections in Mumbai, Maharashtra, Gujarat and even Odisha. Prime Minister Modi argued that the decision was supposed to have inconvenienced one and all, but was particularly appreciated by the rural populace. The BJP victory in the Uttar Pradesh election in 2017 showed that the poor were convinced by the argument; while many of the rich folk stood to lose their 'ill-gotten wealth', the poor had no such fears. Faced with the scale of the BJP's victory in Uttar Pradesh, leaders of the opposition parties, including BSP supremo Mayawati, have claimed that EVMs were tampered with. They were reluctant to admit that their tactic and strategy could not withstand the Modi wave

(Chawla 2019, 2002–2003). The same leaders of opposition parties did not raise a single word against EVMs when the BJP lost in Hindi heartland states in December 2018.

The poor were willing to overlook their own hardship, knowing that the rich and their ill-begotten wealth were experiencing even greater hardship: 'I lost a goat but they lost their cows' (Gurumurthy 2017). Many middle-class households, who surrendered their LPG subsidies happily for the greater cause, strongly stood with Modi during demonetization only because they trusted his intentions. The average lower-middle-class and poorer people were happy that the rich people had been hit for their ill-gotten wealth. Until then, their impression was that only the poor get punished while the rich get away with the help of their influence and wealth (Goradia 2019b). Modi's populism, direct appeal to the public and personal image of selfless-ness has proved huge political assets in a period of failing policies and economic setbacks. Many weaker sections of the society reacted with stoicism, swayed by the government's assiduous public relations messaging that portrayed their difficulties as a small sacrifice for the nation (Tharoor 2018b, 84, 339).

A major positive development of demonetization is that India gradually started moving towards a 'cashless society', although the idea was not mentioned in Modi's speech on 8 November 2016. The number of debit cards in the country doubled to 94 crore in February 2019 from 42 crore in August 2014. Digital payments have increased nine-fold over the last five years. The total card payments in volume terms stood at 52 per cent of the total retail payments during 2017–2018.[58]

On the flip side, it is argued that demonetization of the bulk of India's currency caused negative consequences for the economy such as loss of jobs, closure of businesses. It is reported that daily-wage workers, a large majority of India's labour force, lost their jobs because

---

[58] https://www.thehindubusinessline.com/money-and-banking/nine-fold-increase-in-digital-payments-over-last-five-years-rbi-governor/article26632268.ece (26 March 2019).

private firms did not have the cash to pay them. Women were much more affected than men when it came to jobs.[59] More than 90 per cent of Indian workers are in what the government describes as informal sectors, including agriculture, construction or home-based activities such as pickling and tailoring, and these are areas that depend on cash. Over 90 per cent of all financial transactions are made in cash, and over 85 per cent of workers are paid their incomes in cash. Moreover, everyday economy was brought to a standstill in the last two months of the year 2016 (Tharoor 2018b). The lack of cash reduced both consumption and demand across the board. A booming economy that had boasted the highest growth rate in the world suddenly became a cash scarce economy. No one disputes that demonetization slowed growth. Rather, the debate has been about the size of the effect, whether it was 2 per cent, or much less. Many other factors affected the growth in this period, particularly higher real interest rate, GST implementation and high fuel prices (Subramanian 2018, 99).

## Did the Employment Sector Suffer under Demonetization?

Local industries such as garments in Bengaluru and Tirupur, footwear in Agra, handloom in north Karnataka have suspended work due to cash shortage. According to the All-India Manufacturers' Organization (AIMO), in the first 34 days of demonetization, micro-small industries suffered 35 per cent job losses and a 50 per cent dip in revenue. The AIMO represents over three lakh MSMEs engaged in manufacturing and export activities.[60]

Did the Modi government create two crore jobs it promised in 2014? Job creation by the Modi government has become the most contested issue in recent years. While the Congress and opposition

[59] https://www.businesstoday.in/sectors/jobs/50-lakh-people-lost-jobs-since-demonetisation-says-azim-premji-university-report/story/337980.html (accessed on 18 April 2019).

[60] https://indianexpress.com/article/india/demonetisation-35-per-cent-job-losses-50-per-cent-revenue-dip-says-study-by-largest-organisation-of-manufacturers-4465524/ (accessed on 9 January 2017).

parties criticized the Modi government for its failure to create the promised employment of two crore a year, the BJP leaders claimed that it has created jobs that it had promised in the 2014 poll campaign.

Unemployment remains one of the biggest problems the country is facing today. According to the Centre for Monitoring Indian Economy (CMIE), demonetization cost India 15 lakh jobs between January and April 2017. The CMIE data between December 2017 and December 2018 put the figure of job loss at 11 million, women lost 8.8 million jobs and men lost 2.2 million (Vyas 2019b). The Labour Bureau's Quarterly Employment Survey for October–December 2017 showed that about 1.25 lakh casual and 46,000 part-time workers were out of jobs.[61] My informal conversations with builders revealed that the construction industry, which employs millions of people, came to a halt nearly for a few months after demonetization.

An unapproved National Sample Survey Organization (NSSO) periodic labour force survey (PLFS) has revealed that India's unemployment has touched 6.1 per cent, which is the highest since 1972–1973. It further said that unemployment was higher in urban areas, at 7.8 per cent, as compared to 5.3 per cent in rural areas of India. In the backdrop of a leaked NSSO data stirring a controversy, the government has rejected the NSSO report terming it an unapproved draft. The Opposition used it as an opportunity to criticize the government. It argued that data are being withheld precisely where experts have flagged problems, such as employment, farmers' crisis and economic growth (Kumar 2019). A total of 108 Indian economists and scientists across the world termed 'economic statistics in a shambles' and alleged that the government machinery is interfering in the functioning of the statistical organizations such as the Central Statistical Office and NSSO.[62]

---

[61] https://www.thehindubusinessline.com/economy/152-lakh-casual-45000-parttime-jobs-lost-postdemonetisation/article9679061.ece (accessed on 3 May 2017).

[62] Economic Statistics in a Shambles: Need to Raise a Voice: An Appeal from 108 Economists and Social Scientists across the World. Press release dated 14 March 2019. https://cdn-live.theprint.in/wp-content/

However, the former director of Infosys Ltd and the Chairman of Manipal Global Institute, Mohandas Pai (2019) countered negative arguments on job creation and said that job creation has been a major success of the BJP government, contrary to the false narratives by biased economists and politicians. The NPS, EPFO, ESI, income tax data and the bourgeoning transport sector alone show the creation of over 4.25 crore jobs during the Modi regime. The truth, however, is that there is not enough credible job data to judge whether the Modi government has actually delivered on the employment front or not. This is largely due to a high percentage (more than 80%) of the informal economy in the country. Moreover, there is no definite way to compare how the Modi government has performed in terms of employment as opposed to the UPA II regime.[63]

Noting different issues regarding the creation of employment in formal and informal sectors, Modi says,

> In the last one year 1.2 crore jobs were created in each month as per the figures of EPFO and ESIC. In the last four years, 55 lakh became members of NPS. Nearly one crore people were benefited through PM's Employment Guarantee Scheme. According to NASSCOM, there is a good momentum of jobs in IT sector. IT sector has only 15% share in entire job market. If this sector has created one crore jobs, then you can think of total number of new jobs created. In the last four years, 17 crore people got loans sanctioned through Mudra loans. Out of them, 4.35 crore are starting business for the first time. It means that nearly four crore people started their business. Small and medium industries have created six crore new jobs as per the CII survey. In last four years, the number of tourists and jobs created through tourism has been

uploads/2019/03/1552578453615_Press-Release-14-3-2019-Economic-Statistics-in-Shambles.pdf

[63] https://www.businesstoday.in/current/economy-politics/budget-2019-job-creation-modi-government-manmohan-singh/story/315847.html (accessed on 1 February 2019).

increase by 50%. Does that not mean, that tourism sector created new job opportunities?[64]

The Modi government claimed that decrease in the number of people living below poverty, increase in FDI, doubling of work in the construction of roads, highways, railways and airports, and houses have created more jobs. Moreover, several start-ups have been established and are operating their business in many sectors of the economy.[65] But Modi's comment that selling *pakodas* (fritters) in the street, something that many unemployed graduates have been reduced to doing, is also a 'job' has drawn flak from the Congress. In his maiden speech in the Rajya Sabha, the BJP President Amit Shah defended the prime minister's comment and said, 'It is better to earn a living selling than being unemployed.'[66]

CMIE Director Mahesh Vyas (2019a) argues that jobs are growing faster at the lower end of the education spectrum and not at the higher end. Over the last three years, between early 2016 and late 2018, 38 million jobs were created for people who had completed primary education, that is, up to 5th standard. This means jobs for the less educated increased by nearly 45 per cent over the last three years. The proliferation of tea, tobacco stalls, e-commerce (delivery boys) and taxi aggregators and the like are generating jobs. Those with a graduate or a post-graduate degree saw the smallest growth in jobs—2.9 million, the growth rate of less than 6 per cent during the same period. Therefore, the quality of Indian jobs is falling. The count of the self-employed has increased by nearly 20 million, a 71 per cent increase.

## Is It a Distressing Point?

The negative perception of demonetization and the initial glitches in the implementation of a new GST, along with anti-incumbency and

[64] https://www.narendramodi.in/pm-modi-s-interview-to-sakal-media-group-544488 (accessed on 25 April, 2019).

[65] Ibid.

[66] https://www.thehindu.com/news/national/selling-pakodas-not-shameful-amit-shah/article22660603.ece (6 February 2018).

an effective Congress party campaign led by Rahul Gandhi, brought the BJP in Gujarat close to defeat in the state assembly elections of December 2017. Modi made the vote a referendum on himself. He dramatically asked his fellow Gujratis to demonstrate their pride in having him, their representative, as the nation's prime minister. It worked; the BJP scraped through with a sharply reduced majority. Many attributed distress in rural economy owing to demonetization, botched implementation of GST and failure to create employment as the major reasons for the BJP's defeat in the Rajasthan, Madhya Pradesh and Chhattisgarh assembly elections in December 2018. During private conversations, Congress and BJP leaders claimed that the middle class had distanced from the BJP owing to its failure to execute the promises made in 2014. Kishore Tiwari, a prominent RSS figure and also a farmer leader from Maharashtra, has demanded that the RSS replace Prime Minister Modi with Union Minister Nitin Gadkari if the BJP wishes to win the 2019 general elections. Many started believing that the BJP had lost the three Hindi heartland states because of its 'arrogant leaders' who took 'devastating' decisions such as demonetization, GST (Gupta 2019). Reducing fuel prices did not help the BJP as the Congress termed it as an 'electoral lollipop', and it demanded the Modi government to bring petroleum products under the GST regime.[67]

Despite controversies over the creation of jobs, initial difficulties in the execution of GST and slowdown of the economy after monetary disruptions, one must not forget that the electorate has continued to reward Modi, until the December 2018 elections in the Hindi heartland. Before losing power in Madhya Pradesh, Rajasthan and Chhattisgarh, the BJP was ruling by itself or with a partner, 21 out of 29 Indian states—the highest such proportion since the Congress held power in 18 states about 25 years ago. The results of the three states challenged Modi and Amit Shah's dream of making the country 'Congress-mukt Bharat' (Congress-free India).

[67] https://www.hindustantimes.com/india-news/fuel-price-cut-an-electoral-lollipop-says-congress-after-another-hike/story-8eOJSbEdIM4MEgX7aq7pNN.html (accessed 1 November 2018).

## Infrastructure: A Key to Woo the Middle Class

White-collared workers and urban elites depend heavily on infrastructure as that impacts their daily routine. It is the key to the decision-making power of the middle class. Infrastructure is arguably one bright spot in the government's record. The speeding up of highway construction, the new Bharatmala and Sagarmala projects, the building or revival of regional airports and regional connectivity, and much work on modernizing and expanding railways are all achievements that the Modi government can claim. The claims of having electrified all of India 'which the Congress had done nothing in 70 years' is exaggerated (Raghotham, Das, and Nayak 2019). The Modi government electrified around 18,000 villages.

The transformation of the Indian Railways, the fourth-largest network in the world, under the Modi-led NDA government could be traced right from Karnataka itself, where at least two long-pending projects were speeded up and completed within a year or so of the new government. The BJP had promised to transform the Indian Railways into a vibrant system by improving its overall performance, adding/increasing new lines, exploiting IT for improving efficiency, connecting hinterlands/ports for speedier freight movement and many more. According to a senior journalist,[68] who has been covering the Indian Railways for nearly two decades, the Modi government meant business when it came to power which was evident when a long-pending new line work was commissioned within two years. The foundation stone of the Bengaluru (Nelamangala)–Hassan (166 km) new line laid by then Prime Minister H. D. Deve Gowda in 1996 was completed during the Modi regime. The new line, besides reducing the railroad distance between Bengaluru and Hassan, also reduced the distance between Bengaluru and Mangaluru when it was commissioned in February 2017.

Similar was the case with line doubling and electrification of the Bengaluru–Mysuru line (130 km). While the doubling work started in the year 2000, it got completed only recently along with electrification after the NDA government came into power. These are the two

[68] This is according to Anil Kumar Sastry, senior journalist with *The Hindu*.

examples of how the NDA government took up railway projects on priority besides augmenting the capacity of existing lines, expanding terminals and introducing ITES in providing various services to passengers and other stakeholders.

The NDA government scrapped the railway budget. It did not venture to hike passenger fares, as has been practised by its predecessors since the same would have a considerable political impact. Working towards enhancing passenger comfort, Indian Railways has introduced 407 new trains while providing high-speed free Wi-Fi facility at over 675 stations. It has installed LED lights in all stations to achieve energy efficiency. Several of its initiatives, including increasing the capacity of online ticket booking, instant grievance redressal of passengers for complaints made through social media, delegation of decision-making powers to general managers of zones and so on have improved the overall efficiency as well as passenger satisfaction, say experts in the railway field.

Currently, the metro rail service operates in 14 cities and its length is 645 km. Informal discussions with commuters revealed that a large number of middle-class professionals have not been using their personal vehicles to travel to offices and return home after operationalization of metro train services in Bengaluru. Projects stuck for decades, such as the Eastern Peripheral Highway around Delhi or Bogibeel bridge, the country's longest rail-cum-road bridge (4.94 km) in Assam, were completed. More than 10,000 km of national highways, with speed limits of 27 km per day, are being built. For the first time, container freight movement has started on inland waterways from Kolkata to Varanasi. Although work is slow, the implementation of 100 smart cities, has improved 'ease of living' of residents of the middle class owing to improved footpaths, developing civic and technological infrastructure in cities such as Bengaluru.

A lot of attention was given to civil aviation. Today, we have 102 functional airports. The period saw the domestic aviation market witnessing double-digit growth for more than four years in a row. Big-ticket announcements like the 'Ude Desh ka Aam Naagrik' (UDAN) scheme and passenger charter meant to give more benefits to the middle-class flying public. Keeping in mind the growing middle class in Tier II and Tier III cities, the government provided a chance to fly at a ticket priced at ₹2,500.[69] Because of UDAN, today even an ordinary middle-class citizen also travels by air. Out of 7.5 lakh seats made available for sale by eight airline operators, 5.24 lakh seats were sold to smaller towns from the launch of the scheme between 27 April 2017 and 1 August 2018.[70] According to industry experts, UDAN provided an impetus to the tourism industry. Within less than a month's time after its inauguration, the Statue of Unity has become one of the major tourist attractions in Gujarat.[71] On the flip side, towards the end of the first term of Modi, all the private airlines were in the red, and Jet Airways grounded all its operations owing to huge debt (Phadnis 2019).

## Trapping of the New Entrepreneurs

India moves up several notches in ease of doing business. It is no mean feat that India has moved up from a low 142 in 2014 to 63 in 2020 in the World Bank's 'Ease of Doing Business' Index. The Finance Minister Arun Jaitley said India seems to have 'cracked the code' in moving up the ranking ladder.[72] But the country still needs to improve under certain sectors such as 'Enforcement of Contracts'. The index has evoked criticism in the past; notably, the 2018 Nobel Prize winner Paul Romer suggested that its methodology was biased.[73]

The Modi government focused on business, self-sufficiency and entrepreneurship, and has unveiled a slew of policy measures such as

[69] Airlines operating under the UDAN scheme have to ensure that prices of at least 50 per cent seats are available at ₹2,500 for one-hour flying.

[70] https://www.thehindu.com/news/national/7-out-of-10-seats-sold-on-flights-to-smaller-cities/article24958449.ece (accessed on 16 September 2018).

[71] https://economictimes.indiatimes.com/magazines/travel/attracting-curious-tourists-to-gujarat-the-statue-of-unity-is-a-must-visit/articleshow/67256257.cms (accessed 27 December 2018).

[72] https://www.thehindubusinessline.com/opinion/editorial/india-moves-up-several-notches-in-ease-of-doing-business-but-grey-areas-remain/article25393786.ece (accessed on 1 November 2018).

[73] https://www.pressreader.com/india/the-hindu-business-line/20181102/281822874802484 (accessed on 10 September 2019).

Digital India, Skill India, Make in India, Startup India, Standup India and Smart Cities. These programmes envisage for digital inclusion of the society at large. While 'Make in India' brought companies such as Apple and Samsung to set up manufacturing units in Tamil Nadu and Uttar Pradesh, thereby creating employment opportunities for many, Mudra Yojana encouraged young entrepreneurs to avail loans without collateral security and discover new avenues of occupation and produce employment opportunities for others. Modi's foreign visits have focused emphatically on wooing investors to various 'Make in India' sectors, and this resulted in an increase in the number of cell phone manufacturing companies in India from 2 in 2014 to 127 in 2019. After China, India has become the second-largest manufacturer of cell phones,[74] which have created more than 4 lakh jobs.[75] Vande Bharat Express, the semi-high-speed train, is a product of 'Make in India'. Similarly, a modern version of the Kalashnikov rifle factory was launched under 'Make in India' on 13 March 2019 in Amethi, Uttar Pradesh.

Under the Mudra Yojana, loans amounting to ₹7.23 lakh crore have been disbursed. The government's claims of job creation now rest on these loans, the logic being that the government has given more than ₹7 lakh crore in loans to entrepreneurs during 2014–2019, and these must have created jobs. With job-seekers becoming job generators, over \$40 billion has come in over the last five years into start-ups, creating 26 Unicorns, 36 Soonicorns, 7 lakh jobs and radically changing India, making it the third-largest start-up ecosystem globally (Pai 2019). Modi says the biggest beneficiary of Mudra Yojana is the middle class. 'If the middle class wants a loan to build a house, they never got relief from banks but after demonetization, people get a relief of ₹5–6 lakh. A start-up ecosystem has been promoted which is

[74] https://economictimes.indiatimes.com/tech/hardware/india-is-now-worlds-second-largest-mobile-phone-producer-ica/articleshow/63566172.cms (accessed on 1 April 2018).

[75] *Quartz India*, 13 July. https://qz.com/india/1326969/mobile-manufacturing-units-in-india-have-jumped-60-fold-under-narendra-modi/ (accessed on 15 July 2018).

being driven by the middle class'.[76] During the 15th Pravasi Bharatiya Divas convention in 2019 in Varanasi, Uttar Pradesh, Modi promised to bring NRI mentors and start-ups on the same platform.

## Playing on the Middle Class's Nationalism

Another major promise of Modi was that he would be *chowkidar* to guard the nation as well as take care of the people shaken by the terror attacks by Pakistan-sponsored jihadi groups. As I noted earlier, Pakistan figured prominently in Modi's speeches during the 2014 general election and 2017 Gujarat state election campaigns. He focused on 'zero tolerance' on national security as cross-border terrorism and illegal infiltration have infested India for decades. The diplomatic maturity shown in the handling of the standoff between India and China over Doklam without losing any ground was appreciated widely. Modi has commended the bravery of the country's armed forces on several occasions saying that the armed forces protect the people from external threats. As promised, the one rank, one pension scheme, or popularly known as OROP, was introduced after waiting for four decades. Bullet-proof jackets are ordered for soldiers and women are being recruited in armed forces through online registration, for the first time. Chinese intrusions too have declined.[77]

After running through a variety of non-military responses to the terrorist strike that happened on 18 September 2016 at an army camp at Uri in Jammu and Kashmir, killing 17 soldiers, the Modi government carried out 'surgical strikes' across the Line of Control (LoC). The operation that began and concluded in the early hours on 27 September 2016 was proclaimed to be a military success with no injuries to the Indian para-military commandos who went across the LoC into Pakistan-occupied Kashmir to attack several locations. Perhaps, this was not the first time India has undertaken cross-LoC operations. But for the first time, the government chose to share

---

[76] Prime Minister Narendra Modi interview to ANI news TV Channel on 1 January 2019.

[77] https://www.thehindu.com/news/national/chinese-intrusions-declined-by-10-this-year-says-official/article24970774.ece (accessed 18 September 2018).

information about the successful surgical strike publicly. Pakistan, of course, has played down the Indian operation, terming it as an act of routine and habitual cross-border shelling. The September 2016 operation has made its way into Bollywood—*Uri: The Surgical Strike* (2019). The Modi government claimed that it has conducted three such surgical strikes over the past five years. With this, Modi set a new paradigm in how India tackled its hostile neighbour.

Two years after the surgical strike, an airstrike was launched against Pakistan. Twelve days after the deadly attack killing 40 Central Reserve Police Force men in the south of Kashmir, Indian armed forces conducted an aerial strike on the Jaish-e-Mohammad's biggest terror-training camp in Pakistan's Balakot on 26 February 2019. In the attack, more than 300 Pakistan militants were said to be killed. The Indian operation was carried out by 12 Mirage-2000 fighter jets unleashing the attacks on the camp based 70 km inside the LoC in the Pakistan province of Khyber Pakhtunkhwa. The following day (27 February), in a tit-for-tat airstrike, Pakistan retaliated causing an Indian warplane to be shotdown and its pilot, Abhinandan Varthaman (wing-commander in the IAF) to be taken prisoner by the Pakistan military before being returned on 1 March 2019. Following the attack, India withdrew the Most Forward Nation status granted to Pakistan and decided not to hold peace talks until the latter took action against terrorists. It is believed that the Pakistan government led by Imran Khan released the pilot in a couple of days following Modi's diplomatic clout at the global level. Astute diplomatic moves by the prime minister have brought nations such as the USA, Israel, Japan and others closer to India, while Pakistan stands isolated.

Both the 2016 surgical strike and 2019 airstrike have become political issues for the ruling BJP and the opposition Congress. The Congress has alleged that the BJP has been using its armed forces to serve political objectives. The entire Opposition alleged that the Modi government's broadcast news of the army's 'surgical strike' against Pakistan was clearly an attempt to impress the electorate in the 2019 general elections. No doubt, Modi did raise the issues related to internal security and airstrikes carried by the Indian armed forces against Pakistan during the 2019 election campaign. Congress leaders blasted the prime minister for repeatedly using the army in its political propaganda. Over 150 military veterans, including some former chiefs, have written to President Ram Nath Kovind protesting the 'politicization' of the armed forces.[78]

Despite political differences, however, leaders across the political spectrum hailed the Indian armed forces' precision in attacking the terror camp in Balakot in Pakistan. It is widely argued that the Modi government had established India's self-respect by conducting surgical and aerial strikes. These two actions taken during the five-year period of the NDA rule had instilled a sense of pride, confidence and hope in Indians within and outside the country. Both events have proved to be the greatest moments of all-round national jubilation. It is simply unimaginable that India could have undertaken such steps in the Congress regime when it was deeply dependent on the support of allies. Several global leaders acknowledged India's rapid strides on the defence front.

## Budget and the Middle Class

Major causes for the BJP's electoral reversals in three major north Indian states (Rajasthan, Madhya Pradesh and Chhattisgarh) in the December 2018 Assembly elections was the shift of the middle-class voters away from the party. The farmers' distress across the country was another reason for the defeat.[79] Farmers held several rallies and passed a vote of non-trust against the Modi government alleging the government's failure to solve their problems.[80]Therefore, there was pressure on the Modi government to announce some relief measures

---

[78] https://timesofindia.indiatimes.com/india/veterans-write-to-president-kovind-express-outrage-over-politicisation-of-armed-forces/articleshow/68853736.cms (accessed on 4 April 2019).

[79] To address farm distress, the government has announced a Pradhan Mantri Kisan Samman Nidhi in 2019 budget to provide direct annul income support of ₹6,000 to each farmer with land holding up to 2 hectares. This would benefit about 12 crore farmers. Before the announcement of elections to 2019, the government had deposited in the farmers bank accounts ₹2,000 as the first instalment.

[80] https://www.thehindu.com/news/national/farmers-pass-a-no-trust-verdict/article24477147.ece (accessed on 21 July 2018).

in the last budget, even if an interim one, before the party went to the Lok Sabha elections. Given the middle class's expanse, just one measure would not have sufficed. So, the finance minister announced a slew of proposals, which were greeted with thumping of desks and vocal cheering from the treasury bench.

Some called the 2019 interim budget 'the middle-class budget that spared the rich' while others called it 'an appeasement budget'. Finance Minister Piyush Goyal said that the 'Congress's Interim Budget gave relief on SUVs of rich, ours will help middle class'.[81] The one major budgetary proposal which most energized the NDA rank and possibly that fall in the middle-class category was the 100 per cent tax rebate for individual taxpayers whose annual income did not cross ₹5 lakh (Singh 2019). Until then, they had to pay 5 per cent as the tax on their income. If one adds the ₹4.75 lakh tax exemptions that one can use by taking advantage of various tax-saving measures related to interest on education, national pension schemes, medical claims, interest on home loans and so on, then practically, for a salaried individual, up to ₹9.75 lakh of taxable income would attract no tax whatsoever.[82]

The potential political reach of this proposal is huge. Close to 30 million taxpayers from the middle class end up saving more than ₹18,000 crore annually. There are other spinoffs. Savings on tax can result in the amount of disposable income and thereby increase purchasing power. The likely increase in consumption expenditure will, in turn, positively impact industrial output, particularly the FMCG sector. The middle class was given a further bonanza by raising the limit of the standard deduction from ₹40,000 to ₹50,000.

As said earlier, second-time home buyers, again an important constituent of the aspirational middle class, would get exemption on

---

[81] https://timesofindia.indiatimes.com/india/no-norms-violated-congress-interim-budget-gave-relief-on-suvs-of-rich-ours-will-help-middle-class/articleshow/67812893.cms (accessed on 3 February 2019).

[82] The figure of ₹4.75 lakh has been arrived at by including ₹1.5 lakh available as tax benefit under Section 80C, ₹50,000 under National Pension Scheme, ₹25,000 under Mediclaim, ₹50,000 as standard deduction and ₹2 lakh as interest tax exemption on housing loan for self-occupied property.

notional rent earned on the second house, benefits from the long-term capital gains tax, and relief on tax deducted at source (TDS) for rental income up to ₹2.40 lakh. These measures would not only encourage more middle-class taxpayers to own a second home, but also revive the housing sector, which is struggling with unsold properties, after demonetization. Further, the tax exemption limit on interest on savings in banks and post offices was increased four-fold, from ₹10,000 to ₹40,000. The government has provided these concessions keeping in mind the middle-class vote bank.

## Sabka Saath, Sabka Vikas aur Sabka Vishwas

The proclaimed social policy of the Modi government is premised on the principle/slogan of *sabka saath, sabka vikas* (participation of all, for the development of all), arguably Modi's most effective slogan, whereby each and every person becomes an important stakeholder in the country's development. Countering the appeasement politics pursued by the Congress government for decades, the Modi government seeks to bring inclusive growth by ensuing collective participation of each individual, group, community and religion in the developmental journey. *Sabka saath, sabka vikas* is also intended to end caste politics and provide an equal opportunity for all in the total development of the country.

Modi says *sabka saath, sabka vikas* is not only an electoral phrase, 'it is our way'.[83] The US Secretary of State John Kerry appreciated the developmental agenda encompassing *sabka saath, sabka vikas* and said it is a great vision…together with all, development for all, that's a concept, a vision that we want to support.[84] To achieve *sabka saath, sabka vikas*, Modi has launched many schemes and set the target for

[83] https://economictimes.indiatimes.com/news/politics-and-nation/sabka-saath-sabka-vikas-is-not-only-an-electoral-phrase-it-is-our-way-says-pm-modi/videoshow/65948626.cms (accessed on 25 September 2018).

[84] https://economictimes.indiatimes.com/news/politics-and-nation/narendra-modis-sabka-saath-sabka-vikas-is-great-vision-john-kerry/articleshow/39216986.cms (accessed on 29 July 2014).

achieving more goals by 2022, the 75th year of India's independence. Among them, major goals are doubling of the farmers' income and housing for all by 2022.

A plethora of welfare schemes were implemented for the welfare of women, farmers, unemployed youth, physically challenged persons, entrepreneurs, unskilled people, the girl child, old-age people, schemes for the middle class, working class, backward regions, urban and rural areas for achieving *sabka saath, sabka vikas*. As Prime Minister Modi has noted frequently, the provision of *bijli* (electricity), *sadak* (roads) and *paani* (water) is non-discriminatory.

Under the inclusive policy, services of many lesser-known persons, who were living in poverty but whose contribution to society was paramount, were recognized and bestowed with the country's civilian awards. For instance, Saalumarada Thimmakka, who planted and grew banyan trees on a 4.5 km highway in Karnataka; Sitavva Joddati, the social activist working for the emancipation and empowerment of women suffering within the Devadasi system in Karnataka; and Sulagitti Narasamma, midwife from the drought-prone Pavagada village in Tumakuru district of Karnataka, who performed more than 15,000 traditional deliveries free of charge for over seven decades were given Padma Shri awards by the Modi government. Until then, their services had been rarely recognized at the national level. Unlike the Congress-led government that used to launch all schemes from the national capital, the Modi government launched schemes from different state capitals for inclusiveness of all regions.

Several bills were passed for social inclusiveness and gender justice. A few prominent bills are the Transgender Persons (Protection of Rights) Bill, 2016, the Constitution (One Hundred and Second Amendment) Bill, 2018, regarding constitution of the National Commission for Backward Classes under the newly inserted article 338 B of the Constitution; the Scheduled Castes and the Scheduled Tribe (Prevention of Atrocities) Amendment Bill, 2018; the Aadhaar (Targeted Delivery of Financial and other Subsidies, Benefits and Services) Bill, 2016; and the Mental Healthcare Bill, 2017.

The first six months of Modi's second term began with a bang—the government focused its energies on realizing the party's long-pending promises. The NDA government succeeded in getting the Triple Talaq Bill passed by the Parliament on 30 July 2019, and the BJP called it a 'victory of gender justice'. Article 370 of the Constitution, which granted the special status to Jammu and Kashmir, was revoked in August 2019 through a Presidential Order and the passage of a resolution in Parliament. The Jammu and Kashmir Reorganization Act, 2019 was passed by the Parliament in August 2019. The Act re-constituted the erstwhile state of Jammu and Kashmir into two union territories, Jammu and Kashmir and Ladakh, with effect from 31 October 2019.

The Modi government cleared the Citizenship (Amendment) Act, 2019 for providing Indian citizenship to a thousands of refugees belonging to Hindus, Sikhs, Parsis, Buddhists, Jains and Christians from three Islamic neighbouring countries—Pakistan, Afghanistan and Bangladesh. The beneficiaries had to have entered India on or before 31 December 2014 and should have faced 'religious persecution or fear of religious persecution' in these Islamic countries. Home Minister Amit Shah also promised to conduct a National Register of Citizenship across the country by 2024 to identify illegal immigrants and take action against them. The opposition parties, including the Congress, saw both these moves as an effort to target the Muslim community, decrying them as attempts towards the creation of a Hindu *rashtra*. Opposition parties and students of Jamia Millia Islamia, Aligarh Muslim University and a few other institutes took it to the streets opposing the Citizenship (Amendment) Act, by terming it 'anti-secular' and being targeted towards the Muslim community. Both Prime Minister Modi and Home Minister Amit Shah said that the opposition parties were misleading the youth and the society.

During the first term, the Modi government increased scholarships by 25 per cent for students to enable students to bring out quality research.[85] A less-known Dalit leader has been appointed the President

[85] The monthly Junior Research Fellowship increased from ₹25,000 in 2014 to ₹31,000 in 2019, while Senior Research Fellowship from ₹28,000 to ₹35,000

Figure 6.2 *Prime Minister Narendra Modi Felicitated Sanitation Workers by Washing Their Feet (a Mark of Respect According to Indian Tradition) in Prayagraj on 24 February 2019*
*Source:* Narendra Modi's Facebook page.

of India. Modi was honoured with Seol Peace Prize for 2018 for fostering global ties and dedicated the prize money ₹1.42 crore to the Namami Gange programme that seeks to stop pollution in the Ganga and to rejuvenate the river. But a gamut of problems still remains.

After offering prayers at the Sangam—the holy confluence of the sacred Ganga, Yamuna and the mythical Saraswati rivers—Prime Minister Modi felicitated sanitation workers by washing their feet in Prayagraj, Uttar Pradesh (Figure 6.2.). At the Kumbh Mela 2019, he participated in the Swachh Kumbh Swachh Aabhaar event and

during the same period.

distributed the Swachh Kumbh Swachh Aabhaar awards to *safaai karmacharis* (sanitation workers). Empowerment, not entitlement, is the hallmark of the Modi government.

However, well-known academicians and public intellectuals such as Amartya Sen, Ramachandra Guha, Kaushik Basu, Arun Kumar and some others from Indian universities are very critical of the Modi government and its policies. Guha (2019) commented that 'since May 2014, the Modi government has launched a surgical strike against science and scholarship and has waged an almost continuous war against the intellect, by wilfully undermining our best universities and research institutes'. Guha (2019) argues that the Modi government takes suggestions from the RSS and makes appointments of heads to the Indian Council of Historical Research and the Indian Council of Social Science Research who lack calibre. He says the government's unrelenting hostility towards the Central University, Hyderabad, and JNU, New Delhi, was based on the views of the RSS student wing, ABVP. Left intellectuals condemned the government for filing the charge sheet in the JNU sedition case against former JNU students Kanhaiya Kumar, Umar Khalid and Anirban Bhattacharya. The case related to the protest march held in the JNU campus to commemorate the hanging of parliament attack convict Afzal Guru on 6 February 2016. The Delhi police registered the case based on the ABVP's complaint. However, the RSS chief Mohan Bhagwat says, 'RSS has its views on national issues but does not interfere in the government's policies and functioning'.[86]

Public intellectuals argue that for the first time, Indian democracy finds itself facing the reality of its top three constitutional positions—president, vice-president and prime minister—all being held by RSS members of the same ideological disposition. It is also true that the BJP became the first governing party in the history of independent India to come to power without a single elected Muslim member of the Lok Sabha. All the three Muslims who have served in the Modi

---

[86] https://www.asianage.com/india/all-india/190918/we-dont-try-to-influence-bjp-only-give-advice-if-its-sought-rss-chief.html (accessed on 20 September 2018).

government are members of the Rajya Sabha. A US panel opined that there is 'overall deterioration of religious freedom conditions in 2018 in India'.[87] Leaving 40 lakh of the 3.29 crore applicants in Assam from the draft National Register of Citizens (NRC) had rocked Parliament proceedings and led to several days of protest in Assam. In the final list that NRC published on 30 August 2019, which was monitored by the Supreme Court, a total of 31,121,004 people have been found eligible for inclusion, leaving exclusion of little over 19 lakh. Retired civil service officers had written to Modi, asking for 'firm action against perpetrators of hate crimes' against minorities in the country.[88]

Intellectuals questioned Modi's pro-Hindutva agenda which has set alarm bells off among minorities, the excess of the 'cow vigilantes' and mob lynching, and subversion of institutions—RBI, CBI, judiciary, universities—largely managed by professionals belonging to the middle class. They criticized the NDA government's policies and argued that the Modi slogan *sabka saath, sabka vikas* has remained only on the paper. In reality, India's minorities are being made to feel 'uncomfortable' by the majoritarian discourse flourished under the BJP. They alleged that ruling party MPs, including ministers, were found uttering Hindu-chauvinist sentiments for creating fear psychosis among minorities and even commenting on changing the Constitution.[89] Controversy over the release of the Hindi film *Padmavat*, the return of awards, *ghar vapsi*, saffronization, re-writing of history textbooks in the BJP-ruled states, renaming of cities (Allahabad as Prayagraj and Faizabad as Ayodhya), lynching, killing of writers/rationalists/activists and so on[90] have entered into political discourse, and allegedly the prime minister has largely remained silent on these issues.

---

[87] https://www.thehindu.com/news/international/us-commission-says-religious-freedom-in-india-deteriorated-in-2018/article27002889.ece (2 May 2019).

[88] https://scroll.in/latest/866697/retired-civil-servants-ask-pm-modi-to-take-firm-action-against-perpetrators-of-hate-crimes (accessed on 2 June 2019).

[89] https://www.ndtv.com/india-news/we-are-here-to-change-the-constitution-says-union-minister-anant-kumar-hegde-in-new-controversy-1792197 (accessed on 1 June 2018).

[90] Writers/activists such as Gauri Lankesh, Narendra Dabholkar, Govind Pansare, and M. M. Kalburgi were killed. Agencies probing these killings are yet

The media has reported several cases of lynching by cow vigilantes. Cow vigilantes assaulted men they accused either of killings cows or transporting cattle to be slaughtered. There have been 117 *gau raksha* (cow protection) related incidents of violence in the country since 2015. As per *Quint*, there have been 88 people killed in lynching since 2015 across India.[91] Observing lynching as 'horrendous acts of mobocracy', the Supreme Court told the Parliament to make lynching a separate offence.[92] The *gau rakshaks* (cow protectors) would not have proliferated without encouragement from the RSS, backed by the BJP governments (Chowdhury 2018). In Tamil Nadu, Assam, West Bengal and other parts of the country, men and women have been lynched on suspicion that they were out to kidnap children.

In many lynching cases, such public concern was created or heightened by warnings that were circulated on social media.[93] In July 2018, the company limited forwarding WhatsApp messages to five chats at a time in a bid to curb rumours. Modi appealed to the people not to take the law in their hands in case they suspect cow slaughter but allow the legal system to do its work, as many Indian states enacted laws and declared slaughtering cattle illegal. By taking all communities into faith, the law enforcement authorities at the local level can contain such incidents. The RSS claimed that isolated incidents of social violence should not be labelled with foreign words like lynching to defame the country.[94]

With all the incidents that widened the gaps between religions and knowing fully well the voices raised by the intellectuals and some stalwarts about the feeling of insecurity, Modi tried to incorporate the

to reveal reasons behind murders of these writers/activists.

[91] https://scroll.in/article/912533/the-modi-years-what-has-fuelled-rising-mob-violence-in-india (accessed on 1 March 2019).

[92] https://www.thehindu.com/news/national/make-lynching-a-separate-offence-sc-tells-parliament/article24446071.ece (accessed on 18 July 2018).

[93] https://www.thehindu.com/opinion/editorial/wave-of-lynchings/article24223296.ece (accessed on 22 June 2018).

[94] https://www.thehindu.com/news/national/rss-chief-says-lynching-is-a-western-construct/article29616428.ece (accessed on 8 October 2019).

Muslims by adding *sabka vishwas* (trust of all) to his slogan. He also saw to it that the Triple Talaq Bill got passed and the Muslim women felt safe under his new regime.

From the above analysis, one can safely conclude that Prime Minister Narendra Modi delivered on some promises and faltered on some others. But the NDA government delivered relatively better results compared to UPA II. Modi made efforts to deliver promises made in 2014. The performance of the government has been sound in cracking down corruption, containing inflation, reducing bank rate of interest on loans, implementing GST, developing infrastructure and improving rankings in ease of doing business. Its track record of execution of demonetization, providing jobs to unemployed youth, addressing farmers' distress has not met the expectations of voters who supported Modi in 2014. Farmers sent messages to the BJP government through electoral verdicts in Rajasthan, Madhya Pradesh and Chhattisgarh. Inaugurating the 9th Vibrant Gujarat Summit on 18 January 2019, Modi admitted that the country needed to create more jobs for its youth.

Before going to elections in 2019, Modi changed the government's narratives towards the middle class by implementing a plethora of development-oriented schemes during his five-year term. The middle class is the biggest beneficiaries of income tax concessions, the Mudra scheme, reduction in prices of commodities and low bank interest rates on housing and education loans. All these reasons contributed to the BJP's spectacular show in the 2019 general elections.

## The 2019 Elections

The 2019 general election is built on poll plank around the narratives of national security, development, corruption, religious nationalism, agrarian distress and unemployment. Modi turned the elections into a presidential-style contest, addressing 142 rallies across the country in the scorching summer heat. The BJP President Amit Shah held roadshows across the country, with special focus on West Bengal and Uttar Pradesh. Modi played on the voters' mind regarding an 'unholy' alliance of the Opposition which is unable to decide on a prime ministerial candidate. Modi kept on asking voters, 'Who do they trust more to deliver on national security and development: him or those he termed the *mahamilavat* (highly adulterated) opposition leaders?' The undercurrent of support he manufactured saw the electorate answer that question in his favour (Chengappa 2019a).

India's airstrikes on terrorist training camps in Balakot in Pakistan in February in response to the Pulwama attack in 2019 bolstered his image as a strong leader willing to take tough decisions to safeguard the country. Modi said he had the gumption to 'enter enemy territory to avenge Pulwama' (*dushman ko ghar mein ghus ke maara*). After the airstrikes, national sentiments have been running high among voters. The attack was claimed by Pakistan-based militant group Jaish-e-Mohammed, whose chief Masoon Azhar was named a global terrorist by the United Nations on 1 May 2019, which is considered a victory for Modi's government.

Besides a last-mile delivery of schemes, it was Prime Minister Modi's image as a doer, of being an incorruptible leader and his ability to convince voters of his sincerity that appealed to the voters. This was one reason why Rahul Gandhi's charges of corruption in the Rafale deal failed to resonate with voters. A high percentage of Modi's supporters continued to view Modi as being honest and having committed no wrongdoing in the Rafale deal. Rahul Gandhi largely focused his campaign around the Rafale fighter aircraft deal and the slogan, *chowkidar chor hai*, that Modi turned on its head to craft his *main bhi chowkidar* (I too am a watchman) campaign.[95] We have discussed this issue in detail in Chapter 8 of this volume.

The middle class has emerged as a key electoral force in India in the 2019 elections too. During a run-upto the campaign, political parties competed with each other to win the support of the middle class, which makes up about 30 per cent of the total electorate. Leaders of the ruling BJP and the opposition Congress party have targeted the middle class with speeches and campaign promises. A 45-page 2019 election manifesto of the BJP has devoted two paragraphs to the middle class

---

[95] https://www.indiatoday.in/elections/lok-sabha-2019/story/narendra-modi-speeches-lok-sabha-elections-1512995-2019-04-29 (accessed on 1 May 2019).

under the section 'Responsive to the Needs of Aspirational Middle Class' (BJP 2019, 33). The manifesto says,

> After providing major tax relief in the budget, we are committed to further revise the tax slabs and the tax benefits to ensure more cash and greater purchasing power in the hands of our middle-income families. We will make all efforts to ensure that our aspirational middle class has access to education, employment opportunities and suitable urban infrastructure for a better quality of life. (BJP 2019)

It reiterated the budget proposal of the rising neo-middle class and the middle class with taxable income up to ₹5 lakh no longer requiring to pay income tax. In contrast, in the Congress manifesto, there is only one reference to the middle class: 'It is the Congress that created India's successful middle class and the new entrepreneurial class' (INC 2019, 7).

As in the past, the abolition of poverty remains the foremost goal of the Congress manifesto. It blamed the five-year tenure of the Modi government for all ills the country is facing. It promised Nyuntam Aay Yojana (NYAY), or Minimum Income Support Programme, to poor families just a few days ahead of general elections in order to wrest the post-Balakot momentum back from the BJP. Under the NYAY, the party guaranteed a cash transfer of ₹72,000 a year to the bank account of a woman of each family that constitutes the poorest 20 per cent of all families (five crore). The promise did not click in the elections.

## Election Results

The outcome of the general election of 2019 is historic in more ways than one. It's a vote for pro-incumbency. It's a vote for a second term for the BJP government. The BJP fulfilled its slogan of *ab ki baar 300 paar* (this time, more than 300 seats) by winning 303 seats. The Congress performed marginally better, from 44 seats in 2014 to just 52 seats in 2019, still not enough to earn the Leader of Opposition post in Lok Sabha, which requires at least 10 per cent seats of the total House strength. The Congress had failed to get even a single seat in 17 states and union territories. As in 2014, the RSS played a stellar role in the BJP's victory. With this victory, Prime Minister Narendra Modi and the BJP President Amit Shah 'get their names inscribed in history books by crafting a spectacular win, decimating a determined opposition and proving traditional political theories wrong' (Mahurkar 2019). The victory shifts the centre of gravity of Indian politics from the liberal centre to the extreme Right. Media leaning towards the Left have started arguing that the victory will move India faster than ever before towards the goal of a Hindu Rashtra (Ramakrishnan 2019, 7).

The election registered the highest-ever voter turnout of 67.47 per cent, 1.03 per cent more than the 2014 figure. The BJP's vote share stood at 37.41 per cent, compared with 19.51 per cent of the Congress. As in 2014, there is not a single Muslim MP elected to the Lok Sabha on the ruling BJP's ticket. The highest number (78) of women MPs were elected in 2019 against 62 in 2014. Of the 78 women MPs, 34 are from the BJP. It is argued that welfare schemes like Ujjwala became popular among women and attracted them to the BJP. However, the support among women beneficiaries of Ujjwala is only moderately higher than the BJP's average vote share (Deshpande 2019).

A combination of factors helped Modi to register the victory. By striking an alliance with strong regional parties and projecting that 'there is no alternative' leadership to challenge Modi, the BJP and the NDA exploited the advantage by leaving the UPA and other state-based parties on the back foot. The superlative organizational machinery of the BJP, commandeered by its president Amit Shah, the micro-level management strategy across the country, commitment to nationalism and Modi's ability to rise above regional and caste identities and his energy to travel across the country and the association with welfare programmes are altogether different from any previous prime ministers. Modi played a card of the aspirational middle class and used social media to appeal to the youth to vote.

Modi called it a mandate from 'New India' in his address to the celebrating party workers on 23 May at the BJP headquarters in New Delhi. His metaphors were also epic: 'Just like Lord Krishna said post the Kurukshetra battle that he was on the side of Hastinapur, 130 crore Indians have today said that they are on the side of India'. Then, Modi said that the mandate laid the foundation for 21st century India, where there would be only two castes. 'The first of these castes would be the poor, and the second those who want to fight poverty' (Hebbar 2019). The emergence of these two castes in this election was the reason for the defeat of parties that espoused casteism. He also promised that his government would respect the bounds placed by the Constitution. After *sabka saath, sabka vikas*, he added one more tenet to his mantra *sabka vishwas*. Modi matched the track record of Nehru and Indira Gandhi and became the third leader to retain power for a second term with a full majority for his party in the Lok Sabha. He bucked anti-incumbency and came back with a far great consensus. The elections result shows the endorsement of the broad direction he has set out in since 2014.

Rahul Gandhi's slogan *chowkidar chor hai* cut no ice, while Modi's constant taunts about *naamdars* fetched votes. The electorate clearly felt no thrill at the prospect of old entitled elites moving in to reclaim their crowns. Voters defeated several candidates of 'dynasts'.[96] In his victory speech, the BJP chief Amit Shah too made the point that people had rejected the Congress for its *parivaarvaad* (dynasticism), *jaativaad* (casteism) and *tushtikaran* (appeasement) (Vij-Aurora 2019). The election also witnessed a number of veterans, who shaped India's political landscape, either bowing out of electoral fray citing age/health reasons or being denied a ticket to contest elections.

The question is why Indian people have chosen Modi for a second term? First, because every political party in the Opposition had one common agenda and that was to remove Modi from power. Such a unanimous Opposition unity was last seen in 1977 against Indira Gandhi's Emergency. But the country's people perceived Modi as the first leader who had risen from the soil and loved his motherland more than everything else. During his five-year tenure, he convinced the

---

[96] Candidates hailing from 'dynasty' that lost elections are Jyotiraditya Scindia, Gaurav Gogoi, Sushmita Dev, Deepender Singh Hooda, Jitin Prasada, Deve Gowda's grandson, Nikhil Kumaraswamy and Milind Deora.

people that he has worked for the people and the country and not for himself (Goradia 2019b). Second, Modi's welfare schemes benefited more than 20 crore families. These welfare schemes subsumed issues such as unemployment. Third, Modi goes beyond narrow politics. All beneficiaries, irrespective of caste and religion, were contacted by the BJP workers on the ground and through specially created call centres. That's the reason the BJP won SC/ST seats and also in constituencies where minorities have a significant presence.[97] The farmers' distress was addressed through the PM Kisan Samman Nidhi Yojana. By giving the poor access to middle-class amenities such as gas cylinders, toilets, electricity, health insurance, Modi has provided a ladder for social upward mobility and they look to him to lead them into a middle-class future (Kripalani 2019). As the findings of the post-poll survey indicate, the NDA was able to win as much support among the poor as it did among the middle and the upper classes (Ranjan, Singh and Alam 2019).

The BJP which has been accused by the Opposition of following a divisive agenda charted new territory by making significant inroads in West Bengal, Odisha and the Northeast. The BJP's votes in West Bengal, once a 'red fortress', went up from 17 per cent in 2014 to 40.3 per cent. The BJP won 18 seats in West Bengal in 2019 against two in 2014. The TMC led by Chief Minister Mamata Banerjee won 22 seats against 34 in 2014. The Left has drawn a blank in its former home. In the Northeast, the BJP-led NDA recorded its best-ever performance where it won 19 of the 25 seats in the eight sister states. In Odisha, the BJP won seven seats in 2019 against just one in 2014. The party made deep inroads in these states to emerge as a main challenger to the ruling parties.

The BJP swept entire North (except Punjab), West and Central India. It did exceptionally well where there was a direct contest with the Congress. The only northern state where the latter had a face-saving result was Punjab where it won eight of the 13 seats. Congress

---

[97] For instance, in Karnataka, the BJP won all seven reserved seats for SC/ST and constituencies dominated by minorities.

performance in the Hindi-speaking states was dismal, despite the fact that it had won the assembly polls in Rajasthan, Madhya Pradesh and Chhattisgarh[98] barely six months before. The Congress could win only three of the 65 seats in these three states where it was hoping to replicate its assembly feat. With the victory in these three states, Modi turned upside down the old argument that a party that wins the state election goes to win a majority of seats of the parliament in the state if Lok Sabha elections are held in less than a year of an assembly victory.

Barring the three southern states, Tamil Nadu, Kerala and Andhra Pradesh, where the BJP was unable to win a single seat, Modi's pan-India appeal saw his party making a clean sweep in many states. The BJP won all seats in Rajasthan (25), Gujarat (26), Himachal Pradesh (4), Uttarakhand (5), Delhi (7) and Haryana (10). In Bihar, the BJP in alliance with the Janata Dal (U), and Lok Janshakti Party won 39 of the 40 seats. In Jharkhand, the BJP sealed an alliance with the All Jharkhand Student's Union (AJSU), and the alliance won 12 out of the state's 14 seats. With the BJP's sweep across the regions, today we are witnessing the rise of a new 'BJP system' in Indian politics. The country witnessed the 'Congress system' in the 1950s and 1960s.

The biggest failure was that of the Mahagathbandhan (Grand Alliance) in Uttar Pradesh, where long-time rivals, SP and BSP, burying their grudges, had come together to form a seemingly formidable caste-based alliance, along with the RLD. The arithmetic of that coalition meant that gamble was loaded against the BJP. But using his personal chemistry backed by solid organizational strength, Modi demolished the alliance (Chengappa 2019a). The alliance won just 15 out of 80 seats. The BJP and its ally Apna Dal managed to cross the barrier of caste loyalties, on which the Mahagathbandhan was based, to win 64 seats in the state.

The biggest upset for the Congress came from Uttar Pradesh as the party President Rahul Gandhi lost the family pocket-borough Amethi

---

[98] In Chhattisgarh, the BJP had taken the calculated risks of replacing all its 10 incumbent MPs with new faces.

to a feisty Smriti Irani of the BJP. Rahul Gandhi entered Lok Sabha by contesting from a minority-dominated constituency Wayanad in Kerala. The Congress retained its lone seat—Sonia Gandhi elected from Rae Bareli. Congress's Priyanka Gandhi Vadra's entry in the political landscape created ripples in the media, but she made no impact on the fate of her party. People preferred to give a decisive mandate for stability, endorsing the BJP lines of a *majboot sarkar* (strong government) instead of a *majboor sarkar* (helpless government) (Vij-Aurora 2019). The major reason for the defeat was the alliance's inability to mobilize beyond their traditional voter bases (Nair 2019). With this, Modi and the BJP ended the era of Mandal and caste-dominated politics, particularly in Uttar Pradesh.

In the West, despite its serious differences with the Shiv Sena, the BJP was able to form an alliance in Maharashtra and was willing to yield more seats than its ally deserved. The BJP–Shiv Sena alliance won 41 seats while the UPA-led alliance secured five seats. In Modi's home state, Gujarat, the BJP repeated its spectacular show by winning all 26 seats. Except in Tamil Nadu, 'the UPA and state-based parties opposed to the BJP seemed unclear on whether their primary focus was to defeat the BJP or protect their own political/electoral spaces' (Palshikar et al. 2019).

The South (except Karnataka) continues to elude the BJP. In Karnataka, Congress and JD(S) alliance met a humiliating defeat in the hands of the BJP. While alliance partners won one seat each, the BJP gained 26 seats, including an independent supported by it. In Kerala, the United Democratic Front led by the Congress won 19 out of 20 seats. The Left Democratic Front secured a solitary seat. In Telangana, out of 13 seats, the BJP won four while the Telangana Rashtra Samiti registered a victory on nine seats. In Andhra Pradesh, the YSR Congress won 22 seats and it also won the Assembly elections. The Chandrababu Naidu-led Telugu Desam Party, which walked out of the Modi government mid-way, secured just three seats. In Tamil Nadu, the DMK-led front cornered 38 of 39 seats and one seat in Puducherry. The AIADMK won one seat—P. Raveendranath Kumar, son of O. Panneerselvam, Deputy Chief Minister of

Tamil Nadu and three times Chief Minister of the state—elected from the Theni constituency.

A few weeks after a crushing general elections defeat, Rahul Gandhi resigned as the President of the INC party, plunging the party into fresh turmoil over its future leadership. UPA chairperson Sonia Gandhi was appointed the interim president of the party until the AICC elected a new president, believing that only a Nehru–Gandhi can keep the party together and can mount a countrywide opposition to the BJP. After the BJP's sweeping victory in Uttar Pradesh in the 2019 general elections, BSP chief Mayawati terminated her party's alliance with the SP. As the Congress became very weak, incumbent legislators in Goa, Karnataka and several other states switched to the BJP. The JD(S) and Congress coalition government, which was facing a bundle of contradictions, collapsed in Karnataka on 23 May 2019, following defection of 17 MLAs of Congress and JD(S). The BJP secured a majority of seats in the Assembly by winning 12 out of 15 Assembly constituencies that went to bi-polls on 5 December 2019.

From the 2019 general elections results, it is widely acknowledged that Prime Minister Modi won the election by effective delivery of some promises made in 2014. The good governance record of the government based on the delivery of welfare schemes is one of the main reasons for the BJP's victory. The government's track record of execution of demonetization and crackdown on corruption proved to be a game-changer in elections as it established Modi's image of being a pro-poor and willing to target the rich and corrupt.

To assuage upper-caste sentiment following tightening of the Dalit atrocity law last year for which the BJP suffered defeat in three states in the Hindi heartland in 2018, the government announced 10 per cent quota for weaker sections of the society, including upper castes. As said earlier, the middle-class members have not opposed the quota as it did in 1990. It is widely argued that the BJP gained middle-class support by announcing several tax concessions to the class in its interim budget before elections. Modi often acknowledged the contributions of the middle class towards economic development and nation-building during his election speeches as well in media interviews. The middle class often eulogized Modi as *vikas purush* (the man for development), although it never lives on someone's mercy as understood by Modi himself.

Owing to his mass appeal, the people cutting across the class trust the prime minister more than any other leader.[99] Former President Pranab Mukherjee praised Modi for his quick learning and mastering of the skill of governance and emerging as a national and international figure.[100] For his leadership, several countries honoured Modi with their highest civilian awards. But Prime Minister Modi continues to elude the media, and, he did not hold a single press conference during his first term in office. In this context, the next two chapters primarily focus on Modi's handling of print and electronic media and his use of social media.

[99] https://www.moneycontrol.com/news/business/india-trusts-prime-minis-ters-office-more-than-supreme-court-parliament-survey-3438221.html (accessed on 1 March 2019).

[100] https://economictimes.indiatimes.com/news/politics-and-nation/prime-minister-narendra-modi-is-a-quick-learner-president-pranab-mukherjee/arti-cleshow/57689610.cms (accessed on 18 March 2019).

# CHAPTER 7

# Managing the Unmanageable
## Media and Modi

## Introduction

Media is definitely a powerful tool during the elections; it played a critical role in shaping the electoral outcome in the 2019 parliamentary elections of India. Political parties, national or regional, political party leaders, election strategists and candidates contesting the elections have recognized the growing importance of mass media as part of their electoral campaign in a rapidly expanding media and changing society. The ECI too utilized the media for creating awareness of voting and ensuring a high turnout of voters during the seven-phase elections. The elections are conducted in the glare of close to 900 television channels, nearly 400 of them are 24×7 news channels and more than a lakh dailies across 20 languages. These channels and newspapers unleashed blistering visual images of the world's largest democracy. There political parties, candidates and their supporters made unprecedented use of advertising on television and in the print and social media during the election to reach out to 900 million voters.

The 17th general elections were estimated to incur a cost of a staggering ₹60,000 crore, more than double that of 2014, making it the most expensive in the world.[1] Many saw the BJP's victory as largely due to its high voltage media campaign. Some have blamed the media for letting the BJP team influence Modi's election coverage while others have argued that TV's obsession with Modi was a result of the convergence between corporate ownership of the electronic media and Modi's close association with the corporate world.

The election has seen many interesting features. However, one of the most abiding political themes in the election was Prime Minister Modi's decision not to address a single press conference. Considering how much Modi criticized his predecessor, Manmohan Singh, for not speaking out on crucial issues, Modi's decision to end his term without an open house with the media is somewhat strange, if not ironic. Possibly, he believed strongly his own statements and lectures as a feeder to the media. Modi, however, had discovered the power of social media platforms like Twitter early and put it to effective use. Modi could address his followers directly and yet choose not to respond to a query. He could engage and disengage with ease, inform and educate, choose to respond personally or royally ignore. He could share his *Mann Ki Baat* on All India Radio (AIR) without the need to engage with journalists. Many believe that Modi's reluctance to engage with the media comes from his days as chief minister of Gujarat. At several public fora, he expressed that the media, particularly the English media, unfairly blamed him for the 2002 Gujarat riots, and, according to a senior journalist and political commentator, Sandeep Phukan,[2] it is this bitter past that might have shaped his present.

Modi shared his thoughts in *Mann Ki Baat* on AIR every month, which has proved to be a simple yet effective way for the prime minister to reach out to the people in the remotest areas of the country. He kept his monthly talk away from politics. He has been naming some outstanding people every month to recognize their service to the people or to appreciate their novel suggestions. In his *Mann Ki Baat*

[1] https://www.newsclick.in/poll-expenditure-Loksabha-2019 (accessed on 5 June, 2019).

[2] Sandeep Phukan is with The *Hindu*, New Delhi, and he has been covering politics for the past two decades.

on 28 January 2018, Modi lauded Sitavva Jodatti, who was conferred Padma Shri for her struggle to eradicate Devadasi culture in Belagavi in Karnataka since the past two decades. Addressing the last episode of the year 2018 (30 December), in *Mann Ki Baat*, Modi called for spreading positive news. 'Spreading negativity is fairly easy', he said and appealed to citizens to share positive news and make 'positivity viral'. On 24 November 2019 *Mann Ki Baat*, Modi thanked the people for the 'spirit of unity' after the Ayodhya verdict.

The *Mann Ki Baat* programme is yet another example of Modi's media savviness, which no other leader had even contemplated in an era of 24 × 7 news channels and at a time when the radio is losing its sheen as a medium of communication. His informal style of delivering his message by choosing the issues with public connect, many a time drawing from the observations and comments made by ordinary citizens or even children in remote areas of the country, compelled even the print media to highlight it, thus ensuring double impact on the masses to create a positive perception about him.

Unlike the 1960s and 1970s, wherein popular participation in elections took place largely through rallies and meetings on vast public grounds, much of the elections in the 21st century are fought on mainstream and social media. The 'old-fashioned' public meetings of Modi, for instance, were made to circulate endlessly on social media platforms. The BJP victory was achieved largely through the narratives built around religious nationalism, and Modi-centric campaign revolved around the massive management of broadcast, online and social media. Modi, whose popularity had skyrocketed after the airstrikes against Pakistan just before the announcement of elections, prominently highlighted national security and corruption-free governance during the five-year rule in his public speeches and media interviews. During his tour of UP on 8 March 2019, he gave out a slogan, *Modi hai toh mumkin hai* (with Modi, everything is possible), stressing on the action he had ordered against Pakistan and his development record.

The airstrikes in Pakistan dominated Modi's speeches as he asked the crowd whether he should have sat quietly after the attack in

Pulwama like the Congress government did after the 26/11 attack. Modi asked the crowd in Ghaziabad, UP, amidst roars of approval:

> If things had to be like the previous government, why did people vote me to power? Doesn't every Indian want to teach a lesson to Pakistan? Shouldn't terrorists be answered in their own language? Do I have your blessings, if I act like this in the future too?[3]

He used highly emotional, slogan-based appeals and a 'verbal radicalism combined with political marketing skills' that not only led to fast dissemination of his message through media but also to emotional identification with the electorate (Sinha 2017). Moreover, commercial media controlled by India Inc. extended support to Modi and projected him as a clean, smart and intelligent leader who was capable of leading 130 crore people fearlessly, while highlighting out of proportion Rahul Gandhi's weaknesses, particularly his actions such as wink in the Indian parliament which did not go well with the Indian public. Modi, who rarely chose to speak in English in public meetings, was trying to connect with the urban middle-class audience that had become politically conscious since the early 1990s.

Like in the 2014 elections, the 2019 general elections marked the spectacle of 'mediated elections', familiar to observers of the American style of mediated democracy. Aided by some pro-media TV channels and dailies, the BJP succeeded in media management and swept into power by a massive majority. The campaign that was backed by massive funding centred upon its Prime Minister Modi successfully dominated the media. This has caused resentment among the opposition Congress, and Rahul Gandhi slammed Narendra Modi as more of a 'publicity minister than a prime minister'.

Generally, the BJP leaders have honed the skills of managing the media and journalists better than its political rivals, which was particularly prominent during the electoral campaign. This was dictated by the fact that the BJP's traditional support base happened to have

---

[3] https://economictimes.indiatimes.com/news/politics-and-nation/modi-hai-toh-mumkin-hai-says-pm-stressing-on-air-strikes-development/articleshow/68329424.cms (accessed on 15 March 2019).

a preponderance of voters who were more educated, upper-caste, wealthy, resided in urban areas, belonged to a higher caste and middle class, thus making a strong media outreach electorally rewarding for the party. Studies (Chhibber 1997) have also found that voters with higher media exposure generally have greater chances of voting for the BJP, and the 2019 election was no different from that. Moreover, in 2014, the media as a platform promoted political discourse which reflected middle-class anger at the economic slowdown and attacked rights-based welfare schemes. The BJP issued a booklet condemning UPA's 10 years as a 'Dark Decade in Governance', and the media routinely described it as a 'wasted decade' or 'the lost decade' (Hasan 2016, 141).

## Emerging Power of the Media

In recent years, media trials have become more important than trials in courts. This is especially true with regard to Modi who had faced more media trials than court trials. Modi, who has emerged as one of the most controversial figures of our times, has many admirers as well as haters. The people, from business to film industry to the common public, admire him as a saviour of India who has the capability to rid the country's polity of corruption and lead it towards a bright future of 'New India'. Modi says that in the New India, everyone will have equal opportunity and aspirations and the wishes of everyone will be fulfilled. New India will be a place where peace, unity and amity will be our guiding force.[4]

On the other hand are those who projected him as the biggest threat to India's secularism, pluralism, democracy and to minorities. They saw Modi from the prism of the 2002 Gujarat riots and called him Hitler, fascist and so on, who had come to dominate the Indian political discourse through subverting democratic institutions. The US-based *TIME* (2019) magazine called Prime Minister Modi 'India's divider-in-chief' and, at the same time, described him as 'India's best

---

[4] PM's *Mann Ki Baat* address on All India Radio on 31 December 2017. http://www.ptinews.com/news/9364552_Votes-of-youths-will-be-bedrock-of-New-India–PM

hope for economic reform' (Bremmer 2019). In 2016, Modi was TIME Person of the Year: Reader's Poll (Haynes 2016). People, who largely embraced the ideology of the Left, are not willing to change their opinion on Modi even after the Supreme Court-monitored Special Investigation Team (SIT) gave him a clean chit, which was endorsed by lower courts and the Apex Court with regard to his role in the Gujarat riots in 2002. Zakia Jafri, the widow of late MP and Congress leader Ehsan Jafri, who was among the people killed by a mob during the riots, filed a petition in the Apex Court challenging the clean chit given to Modi by the SIT. For instance, intellectuals like Anand Teltumbde even said that Modi had 'enacted the carnage of Muslims in 2002'.[5]

*TIME*'s cover page headline 'India's Divider-in-Chief' received vehement support as well as criticism online. Modi did not take that kindly to criticism. Replying to a question on the *TIME* magazine cover story by a TV interviewer, Modi referred to the belongingness of the author's father and said there is no credibility to such an article. Modi is well aware of the fact that his image cannot be dented by the media or the media of Lutyen's Delhi. This he made clear in an interview to *The Indian Express* on 11 May 2019. Modi said,

> *Modi ki chhavi, Delhi ke Khan Market ke gang ne nahin banayi hai, Lutyens Delhi ne nahin banayi hai. 45 saal ki Modi ki tapasya ne chhavi banayi hai. Achchi hai ya buri hai* (Modi's image has not been created by the Khan Market gang, or Lutyens Delhi, but 45 years of his toil… good or bad). You cannot dismantle it. But Lutyens and the Khan Market gang created an image for a former prime minister, 'Mr Clean, Mr Clean'; how did it end up?[6]

With hundreds of TV channels totally devoted to the news business, the visual media had a great job in building or breaking the image of any personality. This is also supported by the print media and social

---

[5] https://www.nytimes.com/2019/02/20/world/asia/india-modi-intellectuals-dissent.html (accessed on 1 May 2019).

[6] https://indianexpress.com/elections/pm-narendra-modi-interview-khan-market-gang-hasnt-created-my-image-45-yrs-of-tapasya-has-you-cant-dismantle-it-5723364/ (accessed on 15 May 2019).

media and message mongering through many mobile phone sources. But it was clear that breaking Modi's image was difficult, and was also not easy to build an image of an equally competent replacement from opposition. Rahul Gandhi could not match the charisma despite his sporting jeans and a T-shirt. He also tried to identify himself with young voters by telling them to call him 'Rahul'. But could not match the very confident and strong image of Modi created by the media, and tempering with that was *namumkin* (impossible).

## Initial Image-Making of Modi

Modi rose from the rank of an unknown *pracharak* of the RSS to becoming the prime minister of India. Before becoming the full-time *pracharak* in 1971, he used to sell tea at Vadnagar railway station, Gujarat, and help his father run a teashop. The evolution of the man and his media strategies, which helped him to become the prime minister of the country, has a long story, which we will discuss here.

In the RSS, Modi graduated from being a *pracharak* to becoming the organizing secretary of the BJP in Gujarat and then moved to the national level. Traditionally, *pracharaks* and organizing secretaries keep themselves aloof from the media. But Modi had perceived the significance of the media early in his life. He executed his out-of-box ideas and media management skills when the BJP President L. K. Advani launched Ram Rath Yatra (chariot procession) in 1990. Hundreds of journalists covered the month-long *yatra*, and it received national and international attention largely owing to the management of the media by Modi. Modi was in charge of the Gujarat leg and was to accompany the procession from Somnath to Mumbai. According to senior journalists who covered the *yatra*, Modi would personally ensure that the media was provided with all facilities to cover the *yatra*. Narrating his early memories with Modi, senior TV journalist Rajdeep Sardesai recalls:

> His (Modi) eye for detail. Every evening, journalists covering the *yatra* would receive a printed sheet with the exact program for the next day. Modi would personally ensure that the media was provided every facility to cover the *yatra*. Fax machines were made available at

every place along the *yatra* route, with the BJP local office bearing all expenses. Modi even occasionally suggested the storyline and what could be highlighted! Micromanagement was obvious skill, one he would use to greater effect later years. (Sardesai 2014, 5)

A year later in 1991, Murli Manohar Joshi roped in Modi while embarking upon the *Ekta Yatra*, which set out from Kanyakumari in December with the objective of unfurling the national flag at Lal Chowk in Srinagar on the Republic Day, 1992. Once again, it was Modi who ensured widespread media coverage to the *yatra* and received appreciation from senior leaders of the party for his 'nose for news' and media management skills. A movie, *PM Narendra Modi*, released after the 2019 parliamentary elections, excellently depicted Modi's role in the *Ekta Yatra*.

The BJP leaders say, apart from managing the media in those days, Modi's role as party spokesperson had also grown in importance. After he was appointed the national secretary (organization) of the BJP in 1998, he moved to Delhi. In the national capital, he made sincere efforts to establish his rapport with reporters and editors of national newspapers and TV channels on a more regular basis. Since ensuring wide media coverage for the BJP leaders was among his responsibilities, he had to organize regular press conferences, a task he recalled during a meeting with media persons in Delhi after he became the prime minister. 'I used to arrange chairs here (BJP office) waiting for you (media). Those were different days when we used to interact freely. I had a beautiful relationship with you and it helped me in Gujarat',[7] he told the assembled editors and reporters at the Diwali *milan* (get together) in 2014. The prime minister recalled his fond relations with the media when he was a BJP office-bearer before going to Gujarat as the chief minister in 2001. Modi freely mixed with a few hundred journalists, including top editors and beat reporters.[8] In this meeting

[7] https://www.thehindubusinessline.com/news/modi-lauds-medias-role-in-spreading-awareness-on-clean-india-campaign/article20896042.ece1 (accessed on 1 March 2015).

[8] Ibid.

with media personnel too, Modi only breaks the ice with media but does not take questions.

His stay in Delhi provided him with an opportunity to project his political narratives and ideological convictions. During the Kargil war with Pakistan in 1999, he was given the responsibility of addressing the media on behalf of the party by the then BJP President Kushabhau Thakre. As a party representative, he was seen on different TV news channels and discussion panels, presenting his viewpoint. When he was asked about the overall situation in Kargil in one TV debate, his response was the centre of every listener's attention: *Chiken biryani nahi denge, bullet ka jawab bomb se diya jayega* (We won't serve them chicken biryani; we will respond to a bullet with a bomb) (Makwana 2015, 144). By 1999, Modi had won the full confidence of Prime Minister Vajpayee and was acting as the party spokesperson. After the 2001 Agra summit between Vajpayee and the then President of Pakistan, General Pervez Musharraf, Modi had been given the task of providing the details of the party's position vis-à-vis Musharraf to the media. Modi met the prime minister soon after the summit meeting was over. He shouldered the responsibility and handled the media remarkably.

In an interview given to Rediff.com's senior correspondent Onkar Singh on 19 July 2001, Modi said, 'What transpired at the meeting is a confidential matter between Prime Minister Vajpayee and myself and hence I cannot talk about it'. When Onkar Singh asked, 'Is Vajpayee on the defensive after the meeting with Musharraf?' Modi gave a sharp reply:

Defensive and offensive are subjective terms. Atalji is not merely a politician but also a statesman. He was very clear about what he was doing before extending an invitation to the Pakistan president. The very fact that Musharraf had to go back without signing the agreement clearly shows that Atalji was not on the defensive, but on the offensive.[9]

[9] https://m.rediff.com/news/2001/jul/19inter.htm (accessed on 1 June 2015).

Modi said that Musharraf was the architect of the Kargil war imposed on India, and we had the capacity to deal with terrorism despite Pakistan's presence. In a reply to a question, 'Is the BJP disappointed that no agreement could be reached at the Agra summit', Mr Modi said,

> Neither the Government of India nor the BJP has said that the talks have failed. In our considered opinion the journey has just begun. As far as the agreements are concerned, we have the agreements signed between India and Pakistan at Simla and Lahore respectively.[10]

This was one of the examples of Modi's ways of handling the media. Usually, Modi does not allow a journalist to get away with disparaging remarks or doubtful assumptions.

That shows Modi handled the media well and made it clear that even as the political spokesperson of the party, he had done it. As general secretary of the BJP in Delhi, Modi was attracting the media's attention.

During the attack on Twin Towers on 11 September 2001 in New York, Modi in a television debate thundered, 'It has taken an attack like 9/11 for India's pseudo-secular media to finally use a word like Islamic terrorism and wake up to the reality of how some groups are misusing religion to promote terror' (Sardesai 2014). Later, after witnessing the involvement of Muslim terrorists in attacks, a few BJP leaders said, 'All Muslims are not terrorists, but all terrorist are Muslims' (Mohsina 2019). As the chief minister of Gujarat, he often used the term 'pseudo-secular'[11] to define the mainstream media to indicate that he had a strong dislike towards national mainstream media for what he perceived as elitist, secular bias and anti-Hindu.

---

[10] Ibid.

[11] 'Pseudo-secular', a term that L. K. Advani had borrowed from Anthony Elenjimittam's 1951 book, *Philosophy and Actions of the RSS for the Hind Swaraj*, and was used widely during the month-long Rath Yatra in 1989.

Modi's statement on the occasion of him being elected the leader of the party in the Gujarat Legislative Assembly that he had come to play a one-day match elicited wide interest and became the subject of much debate in the media. Modi in his first interaction with the press as the chief minister of Gujarat was reported to have announced, 'I have come here to play a one-day match and not here to a play a five-day test' (Chitkara 2003, 216). Later, he went on to deny reports of him comparing his term of office to a 'one-day cricket match'. He said that the remark had been twisted. What he had said when he took office was that there were 12,000 hours to go before the 2002 assembly elections. Just as in one-day cricket, achieving a given run-rate is critical, he had appealed for a better 'work-rate' to fulfil the Government's promises to the people (Patel, Padgaonkar, and Verghese 2002). But Modi transformed himself from a one-day player to be a good test player. He learnt the art of playing a long innings with patience, communication skills and administrative experience.

## Media and Gujarat Riots

Born in a middle-class family, Modi was sworn-in as the chief minister of Gujarat on 7 October 2001, and the event was given wide coverage by the mainstream media. This could be attributed to the fact that it was for the first time that a RSS *pracharak* had made it to the high office of the chief minister. But soon after that, the relationship between Modi and media started deteriorating markedly during and immediately after the February 2002 Gujarat riots.[12] No doubt, both Muslims and Hindus indulged in a lot of violence resulted in killings of hundreds of people of both communities. The Congress, the Left, the socialists, many public intellectuals, national and international journalists and NGOs framed Modi as a polarizing figure without any substantial evidence. National and international media reported extensively on the violence, raised questions about the Gujarat government's

---

[12] The burning of coach S6 of the Sabarmati Express at Godhra in Gujarat, resulting in the deaths of 59 Hindu pilgrims on 27 February 2002, and the communal riots that engulfed the state from the next day.

role, and some blamed Modi for failing to stop the brutality. The BJP and then Home Minister L. K. Advani denied any association of Hindu organizations with the communal riots and attributed it squarely to Muslim fanaticism.

The media seems to be divided on projecting Modi's image after the 2002 riots. While a section of the media painted him as a polarizing figure, a champion of Hindutva, defender of Gujarat pride, another section of the media, which Modi calls 'pseudo-secular', framed him as an abdicator of the constitutional responsibility to protect minorities and complicit in the genocidal violence that ravaged Gujarat. But the local Gujarat media stood behind Modi and his vision of the development. Defending himself against his critics, Modi justified some of the alleged controversial decisions he took soon after the burning of the Sabarmati Express coaches, whether it was the handling of the funerals of the victims of the train attack or the tardy summoning in of the army for maintaining law and order.

Modi began his aversion to media, especially TV channels, which had then echoed the voices of the Congress party, played a key role in creating a distorted discourse on the Godhra riots. These TV channels kept on broadcasting the same images over and over again. For instance, in the 1 March 2002 issue of *The Times of India*, Siddarth Varadarajan wrote, 'While official inquiry will establish the extent to which the attack on the Sabarmati Express was pre-mediated, there can be no doubt about the planned nature of the violence directed against Gujarat's Muslims on Thursday (February 28)' (Kishwar 2014, 206). Modi said, 'None in the media had appealed for peace. Yes, maybe editorials had appeared, but ordinary people did not read editorials'.[13] Modi himself had gone on air and repeatedly called for peace. In his first televised address on DD on 28 February 2002, he spoke on Godhra and made no reference to the riots that were already raging in the state.

Modi, like certain other official spokespersons of parties in Delhi, drew a comparison between media coverage of the Gujarat riots and

---

[13] https://www.outlookindia.com/website/story/meeting-with-narendra-modi/215587 (accessed on 1 May 2016).

the restrained and responsible role of the American media after the 9/11 attack on the World Trade Towers in New York. In the case of the Twin Towers attack, dead bodies were not shown on television or in press photographs.[14] Of course, two episodes were quite different in nature. The Godhra incident has been described by the Congress, Left and public intellectuals in many terms, such as 'inhuman genocide', 'inhuman carnage' and 'massacre'. But Madhu Purnima Kishwar in her study *Modi, Muslims and Media* (2014) highlights the partisan role played by national media and says that it is evident from the fact that the Editors Guild of India appointed a team headed by Dileep Padgaonkar and Aakar Patel to study the media coverage of riots. According to Kishwar (2014), Dileep Padgaonkar and Aakar Patel have been leading members of the Smear Modi campaign. The team in its 254-page report castigated the role of certain Gujarati newspapers, particularly *Sandesh* and *Gujarat Samachar*, for 'provocating and irresponsible' coverage of the Godhra incident and the subsequent riots in the state. But the Guild team had nothing to say about the provocative role of the national TV channels and newspapers in fanning the flames (Kishwar 2014, 298).

Modi has always denied any wrongdoing, and commissions of inquiries and Indian courts have not found any evidence to prosecute him. In an interview in June 2002 to *The New York Times*, Modi offered no consolation to the state's Muslims and expressed satisfaction with his government's performance. His only regret, he said, was that he did not handle the news media better. 'We have 18,600 villages', he said in his office, where a photograph of Gandhi hung on the wall. Celia W. Dugger (2002) observed, 'Ninety-eight per cent of Gujarat was peaceful. Is it not a credit for the administration, the government?' The year 2002 onwards, the relationship with media remained fraught. Since 2002, his aides have routinely requested journalists to present their questions in advance as a condition to secure a formal meeting with him.

A deep-seated feeling of the media's hate campaign against Modi was known when the people of Gujarat, and the entire country, were

---

[14] Ibid.

full of praise for the manner in which the chief minister undertook relief works in the districts of the state that were hit by a devastating earthquake, also known as the Bhuj earthquake, causing unbelievable loss of life and damage on the Republic Day 2001. A Gujarat State Disaster Management Authority (GSDMA) was set up to coordinate all construction and rehabilitation activities efficiently. GSDMA received the Gold Award established by the Commonwealth Association for Public Administration and Management and the UN Sasakawa Award 2003 for outstanding work in the field of disaster management and risk reduction. The English media did not provide publicity on the rehabilitation works undertaken by Modi in a short span of time.

Stung by adverse publicity he has attracted in media both in India and abroad, Modi told journalists to act as a 'honey-bee' rather than a 'fly' while discharging their duty. After inaugurating the Shakti Hall of *Gujarat Samachar*, a bilingual weekly, on 21 August 2003, Modi said,

> I would like to tell my journalist friends that the world is not only of garbage and rubbish. Journalists should not act like flies, carrying dirt from place to place and spreading disease. Rather they should be like the honeybees, which fly from one flower to another, savoring honey and at the same time sting severely in an adverse circumstance.[15]

Modi's media management team has adopted different strategies to achieve an image makeover over the next few years. Modi gradually transformed his image of a 'Hindu Hriday Samrat' (the emperor of Hindu hearts) to a 'Vikas Purush' (man of development). In 2003, he began organizing the Gujarat global investors' conference with a slogan 'Vibrant Gujarat', for attracting investments to the state. Highlighting the buzzword 'Resurgent Gujarat' and 'Gujarat Unlimited', he announced that the government was 'firmly committed to economic reforms'. In 2010, Big 'B' Amitabh Bachchan became the 'brand ambassador' for the state for promoting tourism in Gujarat. NRI

---

[15] https://www.rediff.com/news/2003/aug/20modi.htm (accessed on 1 June 2014).

Gujaratis were urged to change the development profile of the state with investments and were offered transparency and fast-moving files in return, along with subsidies and tax holidays.

Narendra Modi and the Gujarat unit of the BJP witnessed the national media's denunciation of the handling of the 2002 riots as a direct attack on Gujarat and Gujaratis and, by extension, on Hindus and Hinduism. The ruling BJP managed to portray the media coverage of the violence as an attack on Gujarati regional pride, successfully converting it into an emotive election issue (Mehta 2006). Modi said that Mahatma Gandhi had taught Gujarat to fight against injustice.[16] The maligning of Gujarat was to become the central focus of the pre-election *Gaurav Yatra* that Modi had taken out in September 2002, ahead of assembly elections. Just before launching his *Gaurav Yatra*, Modi had said on 28 August 2002, 'I am determined to take out the yatra and tell the world the Gaurav Gatha of five crore people of the state.... Gujarat is not a state of murderers, rapists as the pseudo-secularists, fanatic and power-hungry Congress leaders are attempting to project.'[17]

Despite a demand from a section of the people not to resume *Gaurav Yatra* after the attack on the Akshardham Temple in Gandhinagar on 24 September 2002, which claimed 37 lives and injured 81, Modi set off his *yatra* again. Members of opposition parties expressed concern that the *yatra* would provoke communal passion and Congress President Sonia Gandhi shot off a letter to the then Prime Minister Atal Bihari Vajpayee to persuade Modi to call off the *yatra*. Attack on the Akshardham Temple sentiment fuelled his campaign momentum. Campaigning on the border districts, Modi blamed Pakistan President 'Miya Musharraf' for the attack on the Temple (Pandey 2002). Modi blamed Musharraf for the conspiracy to assassinate him (Bunsha 2002). Six years later, when a 10-member group of Lashkar-e-Taiba attacked Mumbai in 2008, an event referred to as 26/11 in which at least 174 people died and more than 300 people

[16] Available at: https://www.outlookindia.com/website/story/role-of-the-media/218050 (accessed on 5 July 2014).

[17] Available at: vhttps://timesofindia.indiatimes.com/blogs/On-the-bounce/the-marginalization-of-a-secular-gujarati/ accessed on 10 March 2014).

were injured, Modi accused Pakistan of sponsoring terror across the border. In an India TV show hosted by Rajat Sharma, *Aap ki Adalat* (The People's Court), in 2012, Modi told the UPA Prime Minister Manmohan Singh, '*Pakistan ko usi ki bhasha mein jawab dena chaiye. Yeh love letter likhna band kar do*' (Respond to Pakistan in the only language it understands. Stop writing 'love letters to Pakistan').[18]

Modi made sincere efforts to control the way in which the media interpreted his involvement in the 2002 communal violence. In NDTV's *Walk the Talk* interview with senior journalist and editor of *The Indian Express*, Shekhar Gupta, conducted on the Sardar Sarovar dam in April 2004, Modi kept the focus of his conversation on development-oriented subjects like education of the girl child. When asked a question about the riots, Modi maintained that it is sad when anyone is killed—*insan, insan hi hote hai* (a human life is a human life)—but immediately went on to deny the charge that the Gujarat police had killed more Muslims than Hindus during the violence, accusing his interlocutor of having an agenda.

> The state is peaceful and progressing in every field.... But you have an agenda you feel that such a big incident happened in someone's tenure but the media could not get him punished. Until this man is removed from the CM's post, we will not rest in peace, my best wishes to you and in your mission. If I am guilty, you can hang me.[19]

The expression, 'If I am guilty, hang me', became a familiar refrain of Modi in the future. He did not resign and the BJP did not dismiss him.

One of the off-repeated 'proofs' offered by secularists about Modi's alleged hatred of Muslims is that he refused to wear a skullcap offered to him by a cleric during his 2011 Sadbhavana fast in Ahmedabad (Kishwar 2014, 295). If Modi wears all kinds of headgear, why did he refuse to wear a skullcap? Modi visited mosques. He was robed in a green coloured *chadar* (shawl) during a visit to Singapore's iconic

---

[18] The video is available on YouTube: https://www.youtube.com/watch?v=ZH6nn5YF0Ig

[19] vhttps://www.ndtv.com/video/shows/walk-the-talk/walk-the-talk-narendra-modi-aired-april-2004-290236 (accessed on 10 May 2014).

Chulia mosque. It was widely believed that Modi did not wish to make the mistake that L. K. Advani had made on his visit to Pakistan in June in 2005. Advani described the founder of Pakistan as a secular leader. That episode apparently dented Advani's credibility and Modi did not wish to repeat the same.

Replying to the controversy over his refusal to wear a skullcap, Modi invoked Mahatma Gandhi in his defence and said nobody questioned him for never having worn one.

In an interview given to India TV, Modi said, 'If a cap is a symbol of unity then why Mahatma Gandhi didn't wear any'. The Gujarat chief minister added that his vision of a Muslim is that he may be wearing a cap and have a Quran in one hand but there should be a computer in his other hand.... 'Actually a kind of deformity has come in Indian politics where anything can be done for appeasement. My job is to respect all communities, respect the values of all communities but I have to accept my own values. I live with my values. Hence, I don't bluff people by wearing a cap, or getting clicked'.[20]

Instead of easing the decade-old tensions, Modi triggered another controversy by using a dog-centred analogy to describe his abhorrence of violence. According to *Reuters*, Modi responded to a question on whether he regretted the violence by saying,

If someone else is driving a car and we're sitting behind, even then if a puppy comes under the wheel, will it be painful or not? Of course it is. If I'm a chief minister or not, I'm a human being. If something bad happens anywhere, it is natural to be sad.[21]

Modi's comment provoked widespread outrage from political opponents and dominated television news broadcasts. Following his

[20] https://www.indiatoday.in/elections/highlights/story/narendra-modi-skull-cap-mahatma-gandhi-bjp-pm-candidate-188697-2014-04-12 (accessed on May 1, 2015).

[21] https://in.reuters.com/article/narendra-modi-puppy-reuters-interview/modis-puppy-remark-triggers-new-controversy-over-2002-riots-idINDEE96B08S20130712 (accessed on May 8, 2017).

remarks, the then ruling Congress party called a news conference to criticize Modi for quoting the puppy analogy out of context and demanded that he apologized.

The shadow of the riots dogged Modi often enlarged by circumstances over which he had no control, as for instance, when the USA rejected his application for a diplomatic visa in March 2005. The US Consular denied him a diplomatic visa, apparently holding him responsible for the 2002 riots. The US government chose to ignore the verdict of Indian democracy and the elected chief minister a state. After a gap of eight years, 64 MPs of Indian parliament, 25 from the Lok Sabha and 39 from the Rajya Sabha, petitioned the US President Barack Obama to advise the State Department to hold firm to its 2005 decision to deny three-time Chief Minister Modi an entry visa, owing to his alleged association with the 2002 riots.[22]

During 2002–2007, Gujarat witnessed sound economic growth along with several other states (PricewaterhouseCoopers 2010). On the eve of the 2007 assembly elections, Modi was projected as the 'God with a beard', a strong, courageous, 'masculine' leader who had achieved unprecedented growth, under whom the state was number one in India. His power-point presentations, video conferences, 'e-governance', 'broadband telephony' and so on mesmerized the media, multiplying his popularity. Stickers with Modi's photographs were printed on school notebooks, mid-day meals and food packages to flood victims (Shah 2015). This is yet another incarnation of print media initially used in Tamil Nadu.

By the time his first term as an elected chief minister came to an end in 2007, Modi was drawing a firm line between media houses he considered sympathetic to him and those that he had long dismissed as pseudo-secular. Towards the latter, he was adopting a far more combative tone (Philipose 2019, 172). Just before the 2007 Gujarat assembly elections, a three-minute interview of Modi by Karan Thapar, who was then anchoring an interview-based show, *The Devil's Advocate*, on CNN-IBN channel, shook the media world. After a few good words

[22] https://www.thehindu.com/news/national/64-mps-urged-obama-to-keep-visa-ban-for-modi/article4945209.ece (accessed on July 1, 2015).

related to Modi's 6-year-term and the Rajiv Gandhi Foundation's certification declaring Gujarat to be the best administered state and later *India Today* magazine, on two separate occasions, having declared Modi the most efficient chief minister, Thapar came straight to the riots, asking Modi why, despite being an efficient administrator, he is often referred to as a 'mass murderer'. When Thapar went on quoting Supreme Court 2003 and 2004 observations, Modi said,

> *'Apni dosti bani rahe. Bas.* I'll be happy. You came here. I am happy and thankful to you. I can't do this interview.... *Aapke ideas hain, aap bolte rahiye, aap karte rahiye.... Dekho mein dostana sambhand banana chahta hoon* (They are your ideas, you keep speaking.... I want to maintain friendly relations with you). (Thapar 2018)

A major consequence of this interview was that after the party's victory in 2014, the BJP leaders/ministers/spokespersons shut their doors to Karan Thapar's show (Thapar 2018).

Quietly and without any fuss, Modi terminated the interview. The interview in 2007, according to Mukhopadhyay (2013) was a turning point in Modi's media strategy. Modi stopped engaging with a section of mainstream media in India over the riots. Seven years later, on the eve of becoming the prime minister of India, he remarked, 'I was not silent. I answered every top journalist in the country from 2002 to 2007 (on the riots) but noticed there was no exercise to understand the truth'.[23] Modi spun criticisms of himself as attacks on Gujaratis at large, raising slogans of '*garvi* Gujarat' and 'Gujarati *asmita*' (pride). He cultivated allies in Gujarati media and television, which was taking off at this time (Sinha 2017).

If Modi had infuriated the Congress on the Sohrabuddin case,[24] a puerile statement by Congress chief Sonia Gandhi calling Modi *maut*

---

[23] https://www.ndtv.com/elections-news/not-silent-on-riots-but-no-exercise-to-understand-truth-says-narendra-modi-557619 (accessed on July 17, 2018).

[24] Referring to Sohrabbudin, who was killed in an encounter in 2005 by police, Modi had asked a campaign rally what should be done with a man who had hidden AK-47 rifles, was wanted by police and had relations with Pakistan. When the crowd shouted 'kill him, kill him', Modi replied, 'Does my government

*ka saudagar* (merchants of death) in her election speech on 1 December 2007, plus Digvijay Singh's casual invocation of 'Hindu terrorism' at a press conference, gave Modi the opening to raise the issue of national security and terrorism which he was itching to do (Dasgupta 2018). In fact, both remarks have worked to Modi's advantage. Modi himself accused Sonia Gandhi of 'insulting' Gujarat when she spoke of *maut ka saudagar*, and it is the grand old party which is 'hand in glove' with *maut ka saudagar*. Modi said,

> The main conspirator of the Parliament attack case Afzal Guru has been awarded death sentence by the Supreme Court, but the ruling Congress government has not hanged him for the last one-and-half years…. Why is the government of Sonia Gandhi trying to save a terrorist like Afzal Guru? This shows who is with the merchants of deaths.[25]

The ECI served notices to both Modi for his remarks on the Sohrabuddin issue and Sonia Gandhi for her remark 'merchant of death'. Modi replied by saying he was only responding to a remark by Sonia Gandhi who labelled his government 'merchant of death'.[26] Congress leaders defended Gandhi saying that her statement had not specifically named Modi or any BJP leader as merchant of death. The ECI did not pursue the matter against both and they were let off with a mild warning.[27] By accusation, the media was making Modi even stronger.

All the so-called experts and political pundits were proved utterly wrong. In the 2007 Gujarat assembly elections, the BJP with 117 seats emerged victorious, while the Congress finished with 59 seats in the

need Soniaben's (Sonia Gandhi's) permission for this?' The Supreme Court and the ECI pulled up Modi for his remarks (*Reuters* 2008).

[25] https://www.rediff.com/news/2007/dec/02gujpoll3.htm (accessed on 5 June 2014).

[26] https://timesofindia.indiatimes.com/india/Sonia-Gandhi-defends-merchants-of-death-remark/articleshow/2635581.cms (accessed on 20 December 2018).

[27] https://www.rediff.com/news/2007/dec/23gujpoll5.htm (accessed on 14 July 2015).

182-member House. Modi had won the election for the second time against the hate-Modi, hate-BJP propaganda run by all opposition parties, including the Congress. Modi's victory was covered on the front pages of all newspapers. The media had played its positive and negative roles equally well.

After the victory in 2007, the mainstream media gradually reduced its anti-Modi stance and began approving the 'Gujarat model' of development. This was largely owing to Gujarat state's corporate-friendly policy-making, public relations and Modi's own media strategy. Development became the dominant narrative in the media after Tata Motors Ltd decided to manufacture its Tata Nano car in Sanad, Gujarat, in 2008. The high-profile cheap car project was pulled out of Singur, West Bengal, over violent land-related protests led by Mamata Banerjee. The term 'Gujarat model' now began to gain increasing currency not just in the media but also among the experts in the fields of economics, finance and development. Newspaper advertisements under catchy captions like 'Always Enterprising Gujarat' were beginning to appear to attract investment from across the globe.

As the decade progressed, a public-relations machinery was hired for ensuring a sharp image makeover of Modi and improving Gujarat's rankings in ease of doing business. The government hired APCO Worldwide in 2009 to promote Gujarat's biannual business investment summits (Vibrant Gujarat) in India and abroad. APCO Worldwide with its team members spread out in many countries made sure that Modi became a global figure, appearing on the cover of international publications.[28] The *Time* (Asia) covered him in March 2012, under the title 'Modi Means Business'. The magazine praised him for the development of the state that he has been ruling for a decade. The Indian print and visual media provided wide publicity for Modi for appearing on the *Time*'s cover page. The then ruling Congress criticized Modi for hiring APCO Worldwide for his political campaigns and questioned his achievements. But the Washington-based firm had

---

[28] https://economictimes.indiatimes.com/news/company/corporate-trends/how-an-american-lobbying-company-apco-worldwide-markets-narendra-modi-to-the-world/articleshow/17537402.cms (accessed on 10 June 2015).

repeatedly denied any involvement with Modi's political campaigns.[29] Modi himself said that he was in no need of image-makers. 'I have never looked at or listened to or met a PR agency. Modi does not have a PR agency' (Colvin and Bhattacharjya 2013).

While highlighting the 'Gujarat model' of development, the mainstream media largely neglected issues related to malnutrition of women and children, displacement of people, regional imbalances in growth, the welfare of tribal people, poverty and so on. However, the issue of malnutrition in Gujarat came under the media scanner when *The Wall Street Journal* asked Modi in August 2012 why around half of the Gujarati children under five were stunted, or too short for their age. He attributed the high rate of malnutrition to 'beauty consciousness' among young girls who were worried about putting on weight. The US daily, *The Wall Street Journal*, has quoted Modi as explaining the challenge of malnutrition in Gujarat thus,

> Gujarat is by and large a vegetarian state. And secondly, Gujarat is also a middle-class state. The middle class is more beauty conscious than health conscious—that is a challenge. If a mother tells her daughter to have milk, they'll have a fight. She'll tell her mother, 'I won't drink milk. I'll get fat'.[30]

This statement sparked a row in the country, and the Indian media gave it wide coverage. This also provoked some media scrutiny into the reasons for the high malnutrition levels in a state as prosperous as Modi's Gujarat. Modi's answer has drawn widespread criticism and angry outbursts, and the Congress said that Modi insulted all women.[31]

[29] https://economictimes.indiatimes.com/news/politics-and-nation/apco-worldwide-denies-working-for-narendra-modi/articleshow/20826192.cms (accessed on 20 June 2018).

[30] Available at: https://blogs.wsj.com/indiarealtime/2012/08/30/everything-modi-said-on-malnutrition/ (accessed on 20 November 2015).

[31] https://www.ndtv.com/india-news/narendra-modi-under-fire-for-attributing-malnutrition-in-gujarat-to-beauty-conscious-young-girls-498154 (accessed on 20 December 2015).

Unil 2014, both the print and electronic media condoned him non-stop. Positive developments about Gujarat were not covered by the media. With adverse media coverage for all his remarks, he adopted a conscious policy of reward and punishment towards mainstream media houses and journalists. In fact, APCOs brief was not restricted to building Gujarat as an investment destination alone. It was asked to 'gauge the tonality of coverage and identify journalists who can further be Media Ambassadors for Gujarat'.[32]

While approaching the 2012 assembly elections, the media again began comparing Gujarat's economic growth rate with that of the Indian economy. The government claimed that its growth rate of 10.24 per cent during 2002–2012 was much higher than India's growth figure (around 7%). The media was conducting opinion polls, projecting Modi as the country's best chief minister and, as the decade progressed, as the person most suited to be the prime minister of the country. In January 2013, the 'Mood of the Nation' poll conducted by *India Today* brought out an opinion survey that stated Modi as the most preferred choice for the prime minister, with 57 per cent people speaking in favour of Modi, while only 41 per cent supporting Rahul Gandhi, who was then elevated as the vice-president of the Congress. Hailing Modi's transformation, an *India Today* journalist said, 'One of the most captivating transformation sagas in Indian politics, Modi has come a long way from being a ubiquitous office bearer in Delhi to the anti-hero of 2002 riots to the highest priest and practitioner of development politics with a national fan following' (Prasannarajan 2013b). Citing growth figures of the state, *India Today* said that Gujarat is arguably the best-governed state in the country.

## Hat-Trick Hero

The paradigm shift occurred in the media narrative on Gujarat during the decade from 2002 to 2012. During the 10 years as chief minister, Modi has recast himself as a business-savvy, investor-friendly

---

[32] https://indianexpress.com/article/news-archive/politics/the-modi-machine-makeover-gurus/ (accessed on 10 November 2017).

administrator, and a charismatic leader who has presided over a booming economy and lured major foreign and Indian companies to invest in the state, famed for its spirit of entrepreneurship. By providing an efficient and non-corrupt administration, he has electrified all 18,000 villages of Gujarat with a near 24 × 7 power supply (Colvin and Bhattacharjya 2013). His pro-business policies attracted many automobile manufacturing companies. With the higher growth trajectory of Gujarat, the corporate forces redefined the role of national media. The media that developed by advertising-driven business models embraced Modi's ideas of liberalization.

During the 2012 assembly elections, Modi embraced modern technology like no other Indian politician. To counter mainstream media, the NaMo Gujarat TV channel was launched in October 2012, just before the state elections, which broadcasted all his speeches and rallies live across the state. Modi became very active in social media, and it was increasingly used to put across important information, forcing traditional media to regularly reference his Twitter feeds and YouTube posts in the news discourse as part of their political coverage. Campaign managers used 3D projection technology to make appear Modi simultaneously at multiple events. The election 'will be a memorable one since for the first time 3D technology was used, which has never been done in world before',[33] Mr Modi said, referring to the use of 3D Holographic technology to air his poll speeches at different locations simultaneously.

The BJP won 117 seats in the 182-seat state assembly, two less than the 2007 tally. Its closest rival, the Congress party won 61 seats. Unlike the previous Assembly elections, the 2012 elections have been contested on the issues of good governance. Many among the who's who of India Inc. lined up to praise Modi who returned to power as the chief minister for the fourth time, registering a hat trick in the assembly elections.

Although the BJP was evasive on Modi running for the prime minister's chair after the 2012 victory, the media projected him as

[33] https://www.thehindu.com/news/national/narendra-modi-the-leader-with-a-difference/article4221755.ece (accessed on 10 July 2014).

the country's next prime-ministerial candidate. A national magazine, *India Today*, in its headline said, 'Modi rides high on development in Gujarat, New Delhi doesn't seem far now'. But, at his victory rally on the evening of 20 December, the day the assembly elections results were announced, Modi apologized to the people of Gujarat if he had committed any mistake. 'If there has been a mistake somewhere, if I have erred somewhere, I seek apology from you, the six crore Gujaratis', Modi said in his speech given in Hindi that many saw as aimed at reaching out to a wider audience (Bhattacharya 2012). The country's primer news agency PTI noted that 'after 11 long years as Gujarat Chief Minister and his third consecutive success at the hustings, Mr. Modi may have propelled himself as a strong contender as party's candidate for Prime Minister's post in the 2014 Lok Sabha polls'.[34]

*The Guardian* observed that Modi's supporters believe he could become prime minister in 2014. The BJP's leadership has long presented Modi as a potential future prime minister. As supporters danced in front of party offices calling for Modi to become prime minister, party officials dodged questions of his role in the next national elections, expected in 2014.[35] Modi himself made clear that he was thinking of the future. 'No need of looking behind, FORWARD! We want infinite energy, infinite courage, infinite patience', he tweeted. The tweet was interpreted in some circles as a subtle comment indicating his intention to be in the prime-ministerial race.

## Hurricane Election

Modi created history by emerging as the first BJP chief minister to have a third successive win at a time when the party was in dire need of a strong leader to get back to the power at the centre. Recognizing his leadership, top politicians in the BJP, some of the constituents of the NDA, and some outsiders like the AIADMK, attended his swearing-in ceremony. Although the Modi camp had not been able to persuade

---

[34] https://www.thehindu.com/news/national/narendra-modi-the-leader-with-a-difference/article4221755.ece (accessed on 10 July 2014).

[35] https://www.theguardian.com/world/2012/dec/20/gujarat-leader-victory-state-elections (accessed on 19 July 2018).

Bihar Chief Minister Nitish Kumar and other leaders of the Janata Dal (United), a key partner in the NDA, to attend the swearing-in, the presence of Tamil Nadu Chief Minister and AIADMK leader Jayalalithaa more than made up for that failure. For Modi, this was part of his national brand-building, an attestation of his acceptability as prime-ministerial material.[36] On 14 September 2013, the BJP formally announced Narendra Modi as its prime-ministerial candidate, after several weeks of discussions with top BJP and RSS leaders.

Gujarat becoming the most industrialized state and Modi's connections with the Gujarat capital that are deeply connected with their counterparts in Mumbai, India's financial capital and home to some its industrialists, helped him greatly in transforming his image in the corporate media, electronic and print alike during the 2014 election campaign. This corporate support helped him spend on his electoral campaign roughly the same amount as Barack Obama had spent on his campaign (Ahmad 2019, 18). According to Milan Vaishnav, the 2014 elections campaign expenditure was estimated to be $5 billion, a figure that approximates the record-breaking 2012 American elections.[37] It was proved to be the most expensive elections in India's history. Business houses, who flourished under the Modi regime in Gujarat, willingly supported Modi's campaign in all forms—men, material and generous contributions. This made *The New York Times* describe the Indian 2014 elections campaign as 'the greatest show on earth' (quoted in Lance Price 2015).

Ever since the day in 2007 when he walked out of a television interview with Karan Thapar, Modi firmly believed that media, especially a few English-language media based in Delhi, would always be unfair to him. In the run-up to the general elections of 2014, Modi called such journalists 'news traders'. Modi and several of his BJP's senior leaders, besides millions of his diehard followers, were convinced that most, if not all, journalists, certainly those dubbed 'Lutyens media',

---

[36] https://www.thehindu.com/opinion/editorial/modi-and-friends/article4245955.ece (accessed on 14 January 2017).

[37] https://economictimes.indiatimes.com/news/politics-and-nation/2019-general-elections-could-be-worlds-most-expensive-expert/articleshow/68108424.cms (accessed on 1 March 2019).

(the capital's elite, after Edwin Lutyens, who designed New Delhi) have been co-opted into echoing the Congress party narrative and are brazenly corrupt.[38] Such journalists allegedly worked as 'power brokers' and 'courtiers' of the Congress, particularly during the Rajiv Gandhi era. Modi, an outsider to Delhi, demolished the Lutyens media, who believed that they are running the country by interviewing top leaders in the government.

Eventually, the mainstream media dramatically transformed its dominant narratives soon after Modi was declared BJP's prime-ministerial candidate. The print and electronic media, which had condemned Modi without any limit or control for his handling of the 2002 riots, had turned into brazen admirers of his prime-ministerial candidature by 2014. During the 2014 elections, the BJP worked long and hard to engineer a discursive shift. Skilfully deploying the media to erase the taint of narrow ethno-religious nationalism and majoritarian violence, the party redefined its public message in terms of Modi's supposed success with the 'Gujarat model', denoting a commitment to fast-track neoliberalism (Chakravartty and Roy 2015).

One man had come to dominate print and particularly visual media during prime time news. The mainstream media, which was largely owned by corporate houses, devoted themselves to almost fawning dissemination of the Modi message (Tharoor 2018b, 38). Witnessing the control of media by the corporate world, journalist, economist and media commentator Paranjoy Guha Thakurta (2014) argues that never before this big business and industrial groups have so openly advocated the candidature of an individual in the way they extolled the virtues of Mr Modi in the run-up to the elections.

Besides, the presidential style of campaign, Modi's media strategies merged with those of private television channels in a competitive market. Important media houses became open Modi partisans. This led the Congress to keep their panellists out of partisan TV debates during the 2019 elections. In fact, Arnab Goswami, now heading the Republic TV channel, exposed Rahul Gandhi's leadership qualities

[38] https://www.asiatimes.com/2019/03/opinion/behind-narendra-modis-media-phobia/ (accessed on 20 March 2019).

in a *Frankly Speaking Show* on *Times Now* on 27 January 2014. The owner of Zee TV, Subhash Chandra, endorsed Modi and later became a BJP-supported MP. *Dainik Jagran*, the largest circulated Hindi daily, became a Modi supporter (Sinha 2017). The *Dainik Jagran* editorial that greeted Modi's victory with a title '*Janata ka Jawab*' (the people's answer) can be widely seen as the daily's inclination towards Modi's views. In fact, Modi recorded emphatic victory in the Hindi heartland where the newspaper has a major presence.

Modi did not face any press conferences during the run-up to the 2014 elections. But he allowed himself to be open to give interviews to newspapers and television channels that are sympathetic to him. He gave one-to-one interviews to almost all TV channels and dailies. Modi's first interview was with sympathetic India TV, a popular Hindi language 24×7 news channel, in April of 2014. Modi's appearance for a 90-minute talk on India TV's programme *Aap Ki Adalat* hosted by the channel's head Rajat Sharma left the live audience and his supporters spellbound by every statement of his. A controversy ensued as to whether Modi's appearance had been 'stage managed' by his campaign team, but, regardless, the interview was a massive commercial success with the appearance triggering unprecedented Television Rating Points (TRPs) for India TV. In contrast, the leading Hindi news channel *Aaj Tak*, which had aired the first interview with Rahul Gandhi, Congress candidate for the prime minister, had little rating success with its programme (Sardesai 2014, 227–228).

Branding of the Modi campaign and its tagline of '*acche din aane waale hain*' (good times are coming) and catchy slogans such as '*abki baar Modi sarkar*' conveyed that a prosperous future was in store for India if the BJP came into power. He was selling hopes and dreams to the common people of rising from their humble and underprivileged origins to the position of power. Modi narratives remained unchallenged by any other political alternative during the 2014 campaign. The BJP and its supporters' made unprecedented use of advertising on television, which, for the first time, reached almost all 800 million voters, both young and old. A team led by senior BJP leader Piyush Goyal handled the overall media strategy. A special team was formed to handle Modi's campaign in Varanasi. The world's best advertising agencies lent their skills at various levels and handled television, radio and print media campaigns with catchy slogans. Besides the expenditure incurred for advertisement in the mainstream media, the Modi team used holograms and virtual sets to broadcast Mr Modi's speeches across the country, which was unmatched in terms of the sheer scale and spread. Live audiovisual feeds of his public rallies were provided to TV channels free of cost. For portraying Modi as a natural leader and a passionate defender of the oppressed, a comic book titled *Bal Narendra* (Modi as a child) was brought out to tell the tales of Modi's heroism during his childhood days.

Media acted as a double-edged weapon for Modi. Some media persons and journalists, who liked his personality as a strong man and a firm decision-maker, preferred to highlight his image by using lavish quotations from his speeches. Others, who had some issue about the 'not-so-secular' or 'Hindu fanatic' image of Modi, unleashed to paint a tyrannous image of Modi, with well-punched anecdotes. Following Modi's social media presence, a special Congress techno-savvy group also got busy on social media. But all that also helped to build Modi's image, especially because of over-enthusiasm with some of these makeovers, journalists made huge errors quite visible to the general public. As a result, Modi's popularity grew owing to both his admirers and to an equal contribution by his critiques.

Many media houses that were glaring in their support for Mr Modi were very critical of the Congress, UPA government and the then Prime Minister Manmohan Singh, UPA Chairperson and Congress President Sonia Gandhi. Congress leaders became extremely unpopular in the media, largely owing to high inflation, unemployment, rampant corruption, the economic slowdown and the 'policy paralysis' in the government. The English media which has been catering to the ideas espoused by the corporates criticized the UPA government's welfare programmes such as Right to Education, MGNREGA, Right to Work, the Right to Food and dismissed them as populist and wasteful. A study (Rukmini 2018) found that Modi got 2,575 minutes, or 33.21 per cent, of the prime time news telecast. His closest competitor was AAP leader Arvind Kejriwal (10.31%). Rahul Gandhi, who was leading the campaign for the Congress, came a distant third (4.33%).

However, editors of the channels argued that they were merely following the biggest stories of the day. Some, however, privately admitted that the media had gone overboard in its coverage of Modi.

Commenting on the media coverage of 2014 general elections, Paranjoy Guha Thakurta (2014) said,

> A distinctive feature of the general elections was the manner in which large sections of the mass media extended wholehearted support to the candidature of Narendra Modi. The media, in turn, was greatly benefitted by an unprecedented advertising campaign launched to promote Modi—the scale of the campaign was unparalleled in Indian history not only in the traditional media (print, radio, television and outdoor banners) but even more so in the new media (Internet websites, blogs and social media platforms like Facebook and Twitter).

The BJP led by Modi secured a majority (282 seats) in the parliament. The stunning victory in the elections drew mixed reactions from the media in India and across the world, with some hailing the results while others cautioning against it.

## Setting the House

After his electoral victory in 2014, Modi did not change his style and continued with a similar channelling of information at the national level. He had not held a press conference during his five-year tenure as the prime minister (2014–2019). Instead, he conveyed the message to the citizens of the country through his public speeches, the public broadcasting arms—radio and TV—and direct, unfiltered communication with 'the nation' through social media. He addressed the nation every month through *Mann Ki Baat* (talking from the heart) on AIR. In fact, he used the public broadcaster DD to announce the demonetization of high-value currencies on 8 November 2016 and the 'Mission Shakti' operation—an indigenously-built anti-satellite missile that destroyed a live satellite in three minutes, which put India in the space 'super league' on 27 March 2019.

During the Atal Bihari Vajpayee government and subsequently the UPA regime, powerful editors were appointed as media advisor to the prime minister; Modi scrapped such a high-profile post. If there was no opportunity to know the 'prime minister's mind' now through his media advisor, there was also limited opportunity in 'selective leaks'. However, journalists seen to be close to the ruling party continued to benefit from 'exclusive information' whose targets usually were the Opposition leaders. Documents regarding their income tax filing, ED recoveries, *hawala* dealings,[39] land grab allegations all routinely find their way to TV studios who seek accountability from the Opposition more than the government of the day. TV debates questioned Sonia Gandhi's son-in-law Robert Vadra's alleged involvement in money laundering, IT raids on Karnataka Congress leader D. K. Shivakumar's residence, and on several Congress leaders' residences for possessing disproportionate sources of income.

Most of the information that the PMO wanted to be shared was either tweeted or handed out as press release through the Press Information Bureau (PIB). If an issue or a policy decision was very important, then a cabinet minister would brief the media where any query or clarification can be sought. This has been the template of the government's official engagement with the media, argues Sandeep Phukan.[40]

With the absence of a media advisor, there was no point or a person from the PMO for the mainstream media to get more information on news or clarity on the decisions taken by the Union cabinet or the government on different matters. Press conferences at the PMO had ceased. Ministers and bureaucrats had been reportedly told to avoid the media and speak only when Modi offered an 'official line'. In his first address to bureaucrats in 2014, he told them to stay away from journalists (Ray 2014). Access to top civil servants had been severed for journalists, who were now forced to rely more and more on official press releases. There was an overwhelming feeling that bureaucrats

[39] *Hawala* is a popular informal money transfer system, which is also known as underground banking system.

[40] Revealed by Sandeep Phukan, journalist, during discussions in Bengaluru.

who spoke to journalists were being watched. The government and ministers monitored journalists who wrote critical stories on government policies, and most media houses maintained editorial balance while criticizing the actions of the government. Moreover, in the era of 'paid journalism', more and more owners of media organizations were reluctant to stand up against the government.

Modi's aversion to media percolated to his council of ministers, who were once media friendly but were later found avoiding journalists. Indian mainstream media was filled with complaints that Modi was denying journalists the opportunity to engage with complex subjects like governance beyond official statements and limited briefings. Private news outlets said diminishing interaction with the government made their jobs harder. But the sight of journalists falling over each other to take selfies with the prime minister, rather than urge him to answer questions, was at odds with the idea that the media was hostile towards him and his government (Vij 2015). And he had a host of television channels ready to live telecast his speeches at any time during the day. He had any number of newspapers and magazines and news websites that fell head over heels to carry his message. This was a clear indication that 'Indian media needs Modi and Modi doesn't need Indian media'.[41]

It is argued that reportage critical of the government is difficult, since getting an official reaction, particularly to a negative story, is not forthcoming. But several media organizations and websites made attempts to expose shortfalls in the governance, and the promotion of crony capitalism. Many of the big-ticket stories that have attracted national attention—from the Rafale jet deal to environmental concessions given to favour vested corporate interests—were first reported and consistently addressed in the media.[42]

Modi again broke the longstanding convention of journalists travelling with the Indian prime minister on all his foreign tours. Instead of

[41] https://www.dailyo.in/politics/freedom-of-press-boycott-arun-shourie-narendra-modi-bjp/story/1/17775.html (accessed on July 15, 2017).

[42] https://www.newsclick.in/media-credibility-hit-new-low-modi (accessed on 4 May, 2019).

carrying a large contingent of local media on his official aircraft, Modi chose to take a few reporters from news agencies and the state-run DD.[43] During the UPA regime, when Manmohan Singh undertook foreign tours, more than two dozen journalists from print and electronic media used to accompany him. This shows a different style of functioning of the two leaders. While Singh spoke very little during his regime, Modi spoke all the time. Modi gave rousing speeches that made good headlines, unlike his predecessor who could put you to sleep (Vij 2015).

Modi did not speak about limiting access to journalists, but many observers say it may have something to do with his troubled relationship with the media in the past. Modi's ministers, his party's politicians and his vociferous fans on social media regularly blame the media for being biased against their leader. They blame the media for being secularist, elitist, old-establishment elite, beneficiaries of shady financial transactions and so on (Vij 2015). Ministers even abused media personnel. For instance, the Union Minister of State for External Affairs V. K. Singh, a former army chief, described journalists as 'presstitutes'. But later he apologized for using the word but said a small number of people in the media fraternity still deserved to be called that way.[44] It was getting extremely difficult to say or publish anything against Modi in the Indian media. Indian journalists said that they were intimidated, ostracized if they criticized Modi and the BJP.[45]

Self-censorship became widespread across the industry over the past few years. While Lakshmi Chaudhry did not wish to speak about leaving *Firstpost*, she said that the Indian press had always been under a certain degree of control (Trivedi 2016). Neha Dixit, a freelancer, wrote a critical report in a national magazine on alleged child trafficking by RSS affiliates, but she is more cautious now about the kinds of

---

[43] https://www.firstpost.com/politics/why-pm-narendra-modi-is-not-taking-journalists-on-board-air-india-one-1626221.html (accessed on 10 March 2016).

[44] https://www.indiatoday.in/india/story/presstitutes-vk-singh-media-minister-external-affairs-journalists-248178-2015-04-11 (accessed on 10 May 2016).

[45] https://in.reuters.com/article/india-politics-media-analysis/indian-journalists-say-they-are-intimidated-ostracised-if-they-criticise-modi-and-the-bjp-idINKBN1HY0AQ (accessed on 30 May 2018).

stories she takes on. Dixit was charged in a criminal complaint with promoting communal disharmony, a charge that carried a penalty of up to five years in jail. For several days, both she and her husband were the subject of online threats.[46] Therefore, there is immense pressure on journalists of both print and electronic media to toe the government line.

In June 2017, the CBI raided the promoters of NDTV, yet another indication that the government of the day is intolerant of media dissent and is quite amenable to use the law selectively to silence it. Although the central government disagree that the raids were an attack on freedom of speech or an attack on the freedom of the press, journalists and former editors, including some present and past MPs, spoke out against the raids and condemned the attack on the freedom of the press. Seeing all these developments, many media managements began to tone down criticisms against the government, and, even if criticisms were made, they are written carefully and balanced with a lot of coverage for the government.

Some Left intellectuals grabbed headlines for alleging that the 'democracy is under threat' under Modi after the nationwide crackdown of rights activists, civil society members and prominent citizens on 30 August 2018 for their alleged Maoist links. Noted writer and actor Girish Karnad too staged a protest in Bengaluru by holding a placard 'Me too urban Naxal', opposing the crackdown of rights activists. Media highlighted these anti-government sentiments in full details, but the details of the cases under which arrests were made remained covered in the eyes of media.

It is argued that the restriction of free speech is not unique to the Modi era. Press freedom came under the scanner during a 21-month Emergency (1975–1977). In 1989, the Rajiv Gandhi government banned Salman Rushdie's *The Satanic Verses* in response to protests by Muslims. Many sedition cases were filed during the UPA I and

---

[46] https://www.washingtonpost.com/world/asia_pacific/in-modis-india-journalists-face-bullying-criminal-cases-and-worse/2018/02/13/e8176b72-8695-42ab-abd5-d26aab830d3e_story.html?noredirect=on&utm_term=.ca9cca61fbcc (accessed on 10 March 2018).

UPA II regimes. All these were neither protested so vehemently against by the liberals nor did the media take cognizance of that.

However, media has not refrained from publishing the opposition party's criticisms or allegations against the Modi government. Rahul Gandhi's jibe at Modi leading a *suit-boot ki sarkar*, a reference to the prime minister wearing a monogrammed suit during Barack Obama's 2015 visit to India made headlines on the front pages of all dailies. His other remark 'Gabbar Singh Tax', a reference to botched implementation of GST also made headlines on front pages. Moreover, cartoons and jokes lampooning Modi's 56-inch chest were released on various platforms. To be fair, the mainstream media did a wide range of stories on adverse consequences of demonetization. But this newfound critical voice of the media was largely silenced after the 2017 assembly elections in Uttar Pradesh which the BJP won by a landslide. The mandate was projected by the government as public endorsement of demonetization (Pillai 2019).

The Modi government has been under attack not only from the opposition parties but also from public intellectuals and academic scholars. Prime Minister Modi's assertion during a TV interview in 2018 that selling *pakodas* was a form of employment came under severe criticism from the Congress and its youth wings across the country. With a stagnant job market, for once, the middle class too felt betrayed by Modi by making such as a comment.

Modi was one of the most effective communicators during his first tenure. He seemed to believe that he did need to meet the media because he had succeeded in dragooning certain TV channels and newspapers into toeing his line. When a student asked the prime minister in February 2018 whether he was nervous about the 'examination' he faced in 2019, he laughed off the question. 'If I was your teacher', he said, 'I would guide you towards a career in journalism because only journalists can ask such convoluted questions' (T. Singh 2018). Before the elections, some commentators had expressed doubts over Modi's ability to win the 2019 elections, particularly after the saffron party's defeat in the Hindi belt in December 2018 assembly elections. The Bengaluru-based *Deccan Herald* published a full-page story on

30 December 2018, saying 'The NaMo sheen has worn off, and questions are being asked' with the main headline 'Is Modi a liability for BJP in 2019?', which proved wrong. The following section discusses the media's role in the 2019 general elections.

## Decisive Win under Democracy

The 2019 elections campaign was built upon poll plank around the narratives of religious nationalism. Of all the slogans coined during the election, the *chowkidar*, a Hindi slogan, became a dominant theme in the poll campaign and in the media narratives. After a few scams in banks' lending to corporates, the Congress President Rahul Gandhi raised allegations of favouritism and price escalation in the Dassault Rafale deal and started taking a jibe at Modi saying *chowkidar chor hai* in almost all public rallies during the 2018 assembly elections to four states and later during the 2019 general elections. The slogan captured public imagination so well that in every rally, Rahul had to only begin to say *chowkidar* and the crowd erupted into *chor hai*. He had extended an unconditional apology to the Supreme Court for unintentionally and inadvertently linking the court order in the Rafale review plea to his *chowkidar chor hai* political jibe against Prime Minister Modi. Modi, very intelligently, transformed the jibe to say that *chor hi chowkidar se darta hai*, which was a smart use of the insult.

In 2014, Modi, who had extensively referred to himself as a *chowkidar* inferring that he would not allow any corruption and promised that he would serve the country, not as a prime minister but as a watchman, countered Gandhi's slogan by coining *main bhi chowkidar* (I too am a watchman) in the 2019 campaign, for his supporters, implying that everyone is a fighter against corruption. Modi even changed the name of his official Twitter handle from 'Narendra Modi' to 'Chowkidar Modi'. This encouraged not only the BJP President Amit Shah, ministers and other BJP leaders to change their Twitter profile names by adding a prefix *chowkidar*. Modi turned every abuse hurled against him into ornaments. During an audio interaction with nearly 25 lakh *chowkidars* (security guards) on 20 March 2019, Modi said, 'I have a habit and I urge you to cultivate it, of turning abuses thrown at you into an ornament and go forward (*gaali ko gehna banakar aagey badhein*)'.[47] At the end of his public speeches, Modi had to say 'doctors, engineers, teachers, bankers...' and the crowd erupted into *chowkidar*. Modi said *chowkidar* was nothing but trusteeship advocated by Mahatma Gandhi. Any attempt on Rahul Gandhi's part to now call *chowkidar a chor* would mean he was insulting all the people. In fact, the word *chowkidar* was the most frequently used word in Modi's speeches in the 2019 election (Rampal 2019).

Targeting Modi, opposition parties, particularly the Congress, raised issues such as the 45-year-high unemployment rate, farmers' distress, an alleged scam in the Rafale deal, alleged tampering of EVMs, and projection of the Modi government working for the growth of crony capitalists. To attract the attention of international media, Rahul Gandhi played domestic politics abroad during his visit to Germany and the UK in August 2018. During his interactive session at the London School of Economics, Gandhi accused Prime Minister Modi of being unpatriotic for misusing public anger over the country's 'job problem'.[48] Gandhi even threatened that a united opposition would not allow Prime Minister Modi to sleep until he announced a farm loan waiver. Economists such as Kaushik Basu, Raghuram Rajan and Arun Kumar wrote articles and went to media and criticized Modi's demonetization and GST.

Political commentators and journalists loyal to the Congress and non-BJP parties abused Modi every day during television channels' prime time news, and they question the development work done by Modi in the five-year rule. The development outcomes in terms of construction of highways, housing, electrification, bridges, railway networks and delivery of social welfare schemes and non-corruption of the Modi government were visible on the ground. For instance, seven crore households had been provided clean LPG gas connections under the Ujjwala scheme; 1.54 crore houses were built under the Pradhan

[47] https://www.thehindu.com/elections/lok-sabha-2019/i-turn-abuse-into-ornaments-narendra-modi/article26593387.ece (accessed on 20 March 2019).

[48] https://www.thehindu.com/news/national/in-europe-rahul-gandhis-singu-lar-target-is-narendra-modi/article24782055.ece (accessed on 26 August 2018).

Mantri Awas Yojana; and nearly 5.6 lakh villages had become ODF during 2014–2019 (GoI 2019). But the media maintained steady silence on these issues. Issues related to Hindutva, EVMs, Pulwama, Rafale deal, unemployment, IT raids, GDP data, the fake news, JNU, urban Naxals and communal polarization got more air time. On many days, commentator or analysts are invited to TV studios to criticize or praise Modi's policies. Political analysts such as Tanveer Ahmed, Abdul Razak, M. C. Abbas, Majeed Memon, Yogendra Yadav, Ajoy Bose, Ashutosh, John Dayal, Saba Naqvi and Tehseen Poonawala were more or less regular on national TV channels.

Modi, who was ever ready to give interviews to unbiased 'real' journalists, started his 2019 campaign by giving a long interview to Smita Prakash, editor of Asian News International on the very first day of the new year (1 January 2019). The interview served Modi well. It was telecast on every news channel. The Hindi channels alone garnered around six million impressions, according to an audience-research body (Donthi 2019). Rahul Gandhi called the ANI editor pliable, and the BJP demanded an apology from Rahul for mocking the interviewer. In the Parliament, Rahul termed the one-and-half-hour interview as 'stage managed'.

It is argued that the ANI editor provided another platform to Modi to attack the Congress, and lead the audience towards believing that the Indian political system was only a contest between him and the opposition, or more like a Modi versus Rahul Gandhi cricket match.[49] During the run-up to the elections, Rahul had arranged a long interview with NDTV, but that did not add any positive narratives and focused more on highlighting how he did not get to the core of the questions. The result was very simple for voters—a confident personality versus a not-so-confident fumbling leader.

However, all these narratives began to change in the political circles and in the media after the killing of 40 CRPF personnel in Jammu and Kashmir on 14 February 2019. The media extensively debated and showed the images of airstrikes in Pakistan for several

[49] https://thewire.in/politics/narendra-modi-ani-interview-questions (accessed on 1 March 2019).

days. India's airstrikes on Balakot in Pakistan is one issue that made a strong impression in the voters' minds. People felt strongly about how the Modi government retaliated after the unfortunate incidents of Uri and Pulwama. In almost all speeches, Modi mentioned Pakistan and terrorism sponsored by it across the border. The mind of Modi was so pre-occupied with Pakistan while addressing a public meeting in Gujarat's Jamnagar that he said 'Karachi' instead of 'Kochi' while mentioning the virtues of the Centre's flagship Ayushman Bharat scheme.[50] However, the prime minister immediately realized the error and corrected himself saying that his mind was preoccupied with Pakistan those days. Anti-Pakistan speeches by Modi during the election campaign drew maximum cheers and claps.

Questions by the Opposition trying to seek proof of exact damage and casualty in airstrikes in Balakot were portrayed as unpatriotic and targeted at questioning the credibility of the armed forces by the BJP and Modi. The Opposition criticized Modi for what they saw as his politicization of the armed forces as he tried to ride a patriotic wave into a second term in office at the general elections. The Uttar Pradesh Chief Minister Yogi Adityanath's description of the Indian Army as *Modi ji ki sena* (Modiji's army) during an election rally[51] and Rajasthan Governor Kalyan Singh's statement that the BJP should emerge victorious and 'we are all BJP workers. We want Modiji to become the PM once again. It is important for the country'[52] have not gone well with the Opposition and were given wide coverage by the media. Several political leaders crossed the 'Lakshman Rekha' and have made headlines for their controversial remarks during the elections. The statements range from communal and sexist to the usual political mud-slinging being reported in the media.

[50] https://www.indiatoday.in/india/story/mind-pre-occupied-with-pakistan-pm-modi-on-mixing-kochi-with-karachi-1470167-2019-03-04 (accessed on 6 March 2019).

[51] https://economictimes.indiatimes.com/news/elections/lok-sabha/uttar-pradesh/at-poll-rally-yogi-adityanath-calls-indian-army-modi-ji-ki-sena/articleshow/68672270.cms (accessed on 5 April, 2019).

[52] https://www.financialexpress.com/elections/bjp-should-emerge-victorious-india-needs-pm-modi-rajasthan-governor-kalyan-singh/1527213/ (accessed on 10 June 2019).

Congress leader Sam Pitroda's reaction to the media on the BJP's charge that Rajiv Gandhi was linked to the 1984 riots sparked off a major controversy. Rajiv loyalist Pitroda said *hua toh hua* (It happened, so what?) for the anti-Sikh riots in 1984.[53] This spoiled the party's chances in the national capital where thousands of Sikhs were killed after Indira Gandhi's death in 1984. The remark reflects the arrogance of the opposition party, Modi said while addressing a rally at Ratlam in Madhya Pradesh. He said that *hua to hua* are not just three words but reflect the arrogance of the Congress. While they (Congress leaders) were saying *hua toh hua*, the people of the country were saying 'enough is enough', said the prime minister.[54] The Congress distanced itself from the remark. Pitroda as the main ideologue could not read and tap the voters' mood.

In a counter-attack to the BJP, the Congress said unlike the saffron party, the 'Congress has shown the moral and political courage to punish people and leaders accused of violence in 1984'.[55] But the BJP fielded Sadhvi Pragya Singh Thakur, the accused in the 2008 Malegaon blast case, in the Bhopal constituency. She defeated Congress stalwart Digvijaya Singh and entered the Parliament. But she became a 'controversial MP' after she stirred up a row with her remarks on Nathuram Godse in the Lok Sabha in November 2019. She termed Godse, the one who killed Mahatma Gandhi, a 'deshbhakt' and her party BJP distanced from her remarks and she was removed from the Parliament panel on defence. Later, Sadhvi Pragya Singh Thakur tendered an apology in the Parliament.

Unlike the previous elections, the ECI has come under scrutiny for its 'little action' on most of the complaints filed with it regarding the

[53] https://www.indiatoday.in/elections/lok-sabha-2019/story/sam-pitroda-amit-shah-1984-riots-sikh-controversy-rajiv-gandhi-congress-bjp-1521499-2019-05-10 (accessed on 8 June 2019).

[54] https://www.ndtv.com/india-news/lok-sabha-elections-2019-hua-toh-hua-remark-shows-arrogance-of-congress-pm-modi-2036806 (accessed on 15 May, 2019).

[55] https://economictimes.indiatimes.com/news/politics-and-nation/congress-distances-from-pitrodas-comment-on-1984-riots-asks-leaders-to-be-sensitive/articleshow/69271923.cms (accessed on 12 May 2019).

violation of the Model Code of Conduct. In a letter addressed to the President of India, a group of 66 former bureaucrats expressed their 'anguish' over the conduct of the election watchdog, saying the poll panel suffered from a 'crisis of credibility'.[56] In *The Asian Age*, veteran writer A. G. Noorani (2019) noted, 'EC seems biased towards Modi' and argued that 'the EC seems to obey no rules except its own'. The Congress approached the Supreme Court pleading to hear its petition on the EC's ongoing silence on complaints regarding vitriolic speeches and the misuse of armed forces as a propaganda by Prime Minister Modi and the BJP President Amit Shah. The Congress alleged that BJP leaders' speeches were tantamount to a 'tacit endorsement' of their conduct.[57] Former Chief Election Commissioner S. Y. Quraishi (2019) suggested that the 'EC must act touch'. Finally, after receiving innumerable complaints, the EC cracked its whip and banned Uttar Pradesh Chief Minister Yogi Adityanath and BSP chief Mayawati from the campaign for 72 and 48 hours, respectively, for violating the model code of conduct. Later, the EC also gave directives to release Modi's biopic *PM Narendra Modi* after elections and it attracted the media attention in the heat and dust of the campaign.

The controversies relating of cow vigilantism, beef row, Durga Puja–Muharram row in West Bengal, seeking votes on the basis of caste and similar other issues helped the rise of Hindutva. On these issues, Modi had a verbal duel with West Bengal Chief Minister Mamata Banerjee, BSP leader Mayawati, Rahul Gandhi and many other leaders, and media continued to highlight these verbal spats.

Although he did not face a single press conference during 2014–2019 as the prime minister or during the elections, he and his party did organize a slew of one-on-one interviews where Modi was asked tough questions: from fielding a terror accused in the Lok Sabha elections to demonetization. Unlike his predecessor Manmohan Singh, Modi has given more than two dozen interviews to print and electronic

---

[56] https://www.bloombergquint.com/elections/is-criticism-of-election-commission-justified (accessed on 14 April 2019).

[57] https://web.dailyhunt.in/news/india/marathi/kashmir+times-epaper-kashmirtimes/india+s+wild+elephant-newsid-115602103 (accessed on 4 June 2019).

media owned by different groups. But it is argued that Modi has given interviews only to fawning media channels or those who have agreed to let their questions pass through the PMO's strict vetting process in advance.[58] However, the main objective of these interviews were to reach a targeted audience and ensure maximum outreach. This was in sharp contrast to Modi's approach in the last five years, during which he has not addressed a single press conference and given only a few interviews to media while relying largely on social media, his radio show *Mann Ki Baat* and public meetings for outreach. Interviews were given to the Hindi publications targeting the Hindi heartland, and regional language dailies having one or more publications. Modi has given interviews to TV channels having more than one media outlet. In fact, an influential section of the news media turned cheerleaders in the 2019 election (Prasad 2019).

Among all TV interviews, Modi's soft interview to Bollywood actor Akshay Kumar on 24 April 2019 was more candid and was watched by millions of people. During the interview at the prime minister's residence, Modi spoke a lot about his life and experiences. Dubbed as an apolitical interview, Modi spoke about his love for mangoes, his childhood days, sleeping hours, clothing style, food, retirement plan, his friends in the Opposition and so on. The aim of this interview was to attract viewers who were interested in knowing about the prime minister's life and, at another level, to portray Modi as a workaholic, a management guru and a down-to-earth leader whose heart beat for the common people.[59]

The Congress called a news conference to react to the interview. Its president, Rahul Gandhi, posted a *shayari* on Twitter, taking a dig at Modi. His sister, Priyanka Gandhi Vadra, referred to the prime minister as 'chief publicity minister'. The effort of the so-called interview was to cast an inward light on Modi's personality, characteristic traits and personal journey to make the prime minister appear more

[58] https://thewire.in/politics/narendra-modi-ani-interview-questions (accessed on 3 March 2019).

[59] https://www.firstpost.com/politics/oppositions-ire-to-narendra-modis-interview-by-akshay-kumar-is-the-reaction-of-outsmarted-defeatists-6518361.html (accessed on 1 May 2019).

human—a more rounded and three-dimensional figure far removed from the political caricature that abounds. In almost all TV and print interviews, Modi expressed confidence that the BJP would win more seats than before, saying he is seeing an 'unprecedented' pro-incumbency wave.[60]

Modi is perhaps the first Indian prime minister in independent India's history to finish his first five-year tenure without a single, open interaction with the press. The Congress party found his monthly talks on radio and social media messages as nothing more than the 'monologue'. The media expected that they would get a chance to interact with Modi during the launch of the BJP manifesto on 8 April at the party headquarters, but they were left disappointed as he left the venue without facing any question at the 90-minute function. On the concluding day of the campaign on 18 May 2019, Modi addressed media persons during a party-held press conference at the BJP headquarters. It was the first time that the prime minister was at a press conference amid several demands and challenges by the opposition parties in the last five years. He thanked the voters for ensuring peaceful elections. But he did not take any questions at the press conference and diverted them to BJP chief Amit Shah to answer the questions. 'Party president would answer the questions', Modi said. The opposition criticized Modi's press conference as the last episode of *Mann Ki Baat* on television instead of the radio.[61]

Modi's management of media was in a way unique in its style and methodology. He did not face or call any press conference but occasionally used to leave or release very interesting information that would lead to some chosen media houses. These were immediately picked up by others, and he used to be covered both by favourable and unfavourable media. As a final consequence, he managed to stay longer with the media than his competitors. The sharp criticisms he faced on the Rafale deal died down no sooner the election campaign was over, and

[60] https://theprint.in/politics/narendra-modis-rare-interview-blitzkrieg-10-print-4-tv-channels-in-20-days/222875/ (accessed on 1 May 2019).

[61] https://www.news18.com/news/politics/oppn-takes-swipes-at-pm-modi-for-not-taking-questions-at-press-conference-2146115.html (accessed on 10 June 2019).

voters felt that it was more of a campaign material than the truth. He smartly managed the media, instead of letting the media manage him. Had Karan Thapar succeeded in getting an answer, it would not have helped Modi; but the walkout by the Gujarat chief minister certainly made headlines and that was really shrewd management of media.

Newspapers also dedicated their pages to announce Prime Minister Modi's spectacular comeback. *The New Indian Express* had a picture of the prime minister with party President Amit Shah with a headline 'TRIPLE TON' to say the BJP hit triple century by winning 303 MPs. *The Indian Express* had a picture of the prime minister with the headline 'Modi 2.024'. The headline referred to Modi's return to power for the next five years. The *Hindustan Times*, in its special edition for the elections, featured Prime Minister Modi with his fist raised, referring to the BJP's win as 'NaMoMent'. *The Times of India* played on Prime Minister Modi's campaign slogan *main bhi chowkidar* for its headline, which reads, 'Chowkidar's Chamatkaar'. *The Hindu* had on its front page Prime Minister Modi with the BJP President Amit Shah with the headline, 'India Gives Modi a High Five'. *The Hindu Business Line* brought the issue with the front-page headline 'Modi 2.0: Bigger and Broader', while another business daily *Mint* came out with the headline 'Together We will Build a Strong and Inclusive India' indicating Modi's new slogan *sabka saath, sabka vikas, sabka vishwas*.

Magazines too devoted all pages to Modi's victory. While *Outlook* brought out an issue with a cover page titled 'Narendra Modi: Conquerer in Chief', *India Today* had a cover page titled 'The Republic of Modi'. *Frontline* too had a similar cover page saying 'Republic of the Right'. *The Week* has its cover page title 'Wow! And How! Modi Wins Vote for a Strong India', while *Open* had a title 'Narendra Modi: India's Choice'. Foreign media too provided wide coverage to Modi's victory.

Overall, one can conclude that the relationship between media and Modi is a highly complex one, with deeply entrenched political and corporate interests. Unfortunately, the media, supposedly the fourth pillar of democracy, had been reduced to a site for discussing issues largely rhetoric between Rahul Gandhi and Narendra Modi during the election campaign. Modi used the media for creating awareness about flagship schemes and issues related to health and the environment. He is the first politician from India to appear on the hour-long 'Man vs Wild' show with noted adventurer Bear Grylls in Discovery TV. The special episode was aired in more than 180 countries on the night of 12 August 2019. Modi used the show to create awareness about safeguarding the environment.

However, Modi, who used the media extensively during the election period, did take a U-turn after assuming power by avoiding the media to the maximum extent. Further, he had asked his colleagues in the government to hold press conferences and interact with media personnel only when required. This strategy has been honed to perfection by Bollywood celebrities. The big stars refuse to give one-to-one interviews or talk to media until there is some film that's about to be released. Then they are willing to talk to all media personnel who can be trusted to focus their questions on areas that the stars are willing to talk about. Modi used the Bollywood star strategy extremely well during the run-up to the 2014 and 2019 general elections (Jagannathan 2016, 82–83). He declined to talk to media until the declaration of election and then during the peak of the election campaign, he gave interviews only to TV channels and newspapers he trusted.

Early on as the chief minister, particularly after the 2002 riots, he bypassed the mainstream or conventional media using one-way radio addresses, stage-managed TV events and social media. The next chapter discusses the use of social media tools by Modi and its consequences on the mainstream media and the public at large.

# CHAPTER 8

# Modi's Ride to Power on Social Media

## Introduction

As we approach the new decade of this century, the Internet proliferation, growth of digital technologies, and online social media bridged distances and provided us platforms where we could speak and be heard. Social media is no longer just a virtual space to connect with friends and family members. The expanding social media is changing the political dynamics of India. Although the mainstream media comprising television and newspapers continued to play a major role in shaping the opinion of the electorate during elections in India, Internet penetration, growth of digital technologies and online social media platforms have challenged its dominance. Social networking sites have become a major space for political activities and discourse often leading to heated and polarized conversations (Lokniti-CSDS 2019). Social media helped break down information barriers between politicians and voters, allowing voters to better understand the candidates and the issues they were promoting.

India's impressive growth in IT powered the expansion of social media. For escaping the gatekeeping by the mainstream media as well as realizing the significance of the social media in the campaign, political parties are increasingly becoming tech-savvy. The use of social media is important to grasp the pulse of the people, especially the literate middle-class urban youth. Without digital media, it was very difficult for any individual or party to reach out to the electorate and influence their opinions in a short span of time. Social media, therefore, demolished the walls that once stood tall between the politicians and the voters, making the free flow of information possible. The new media has not only brought a change in the older forms of media but has also become the cause of the disappearance of some old media such as telegram services. A social media campaign by the ECI enhanced awareness among voters and about voter registration.

When the Internet in India was thrown open to the public in 1995 and subsequently to private operators, it was embraced largely by the urban, educated, primarily the English-speaking middle class. With increased Internet penetration, social media networks and messaging apps have become more and more accessible to the common public, especially to those on the margins. Smartphone ownership, increased availability of bandwidth, cheap data plans and increased awareness driven by government programmes are clearly key drivers of the growth of the social media. Deepening of the Internet is contributing to reducing the digital gap between rural and urban India. There are about 604 million Internet subscribers in India (Telecom Regulatory Authority of India [TRAI] 2019). India's mobile universe doubled from 600 million in 2010 to 1,200 million subscriptions in 2019. More significantly, the country's broadband user base went up from zero in 2010 to 600 million in 2019 (Roy 2019b). Robin Jeffrey and Assa Doron (2013) in their 'cell phone nation' study argue that the cheap mobile phone is probably the most disruptive communication device in history, and, in India, its potential to stir up society is breathtaking. The BJP used the data, technology and social media outreach to come to power in 2014 and 2019.

Factors such as literacy, increased incomes, growth of the working class and middle class, reducing prices of cell phone devices as well as call per minute contributed increased use of cell phones by people of all sections. Social media platforms such as Facebook, Twitter, WhatsApp, Instagram, YouTube and so on provided an alternative to mainstream Indian media, which has provided poor representation to marginalized sections of the society. Owing to its multiple uses (photo albums, music machines, databases, radios, flashlights and browsing), cell phones might even have become a bigger necessity than toilets in rural India (Mahapatra 2019).

In India, Facebook claimed a user base of 260 million, higher than the USA (190 million), while Twitter users increased from 11.5 million in 2013 to 34.4 million in 2019. Increased users were one of the factors that made Facebook clinch $19 billion deal to acquire the messaging service WhatsApp in 2014. India is the biggest WhatsApp market in the world, with estimated users increased to 300 million. The citizens linked through notebook computers, personal digital assistant devices and Internet-enabled cell phones became active on social media. Political parties and candidates have been extensively using social media since the country's mediatized national elections in 2014.

## Modi's Early Sojourns with Social Media

Modi is the first prominent politician to acknowledge the power of social media in India. He used social media penetration to sidestep and attack traditional media, which he had often and publicly declared to be unfair to him after the 2002 Gujarat riots. Through messages on social media, Modi built his own powerful online brand, allowing him to transcend a controversial past and emerge as a techno-savvy Indian leader who spoke directly to his electorate and supporters. Him messaging on Twitter, or for that matter on any communication platform, was a one-way process—highly disciplined and focused on building support for his policies and himself. He responded to issues raised by the public on his own terms rather than being dependent on the news media.[1] This direct and unmediated communication between the leader and the people led to wider popular acceptance

[1] https://indianexpress.com/article/india/pm-modis-note-ban-tweets-one-way-public-address-study-demonetisation-4930487/ (accessed on 10 March 2018).

of authority exercised by the leader and, in a way, dissolved the 'high command culture'.

Modi communicated to the public through social media, especially Twitter, his favourite medium. Modi joined Twitter in 2009, and, today he is the most-followed world leader on social media. While Modi has 48.1 million Twitter followers in his handle @narendramodi and 29.3 million followers in his @PMOIndia handle (totalling 77.4 million). US President Donald Trump comes second with 61.1 million Twitter followers. Modi has 43 million Facebook and 23.9 million Instagram followers and lakhs of followers on YouTube and other social media tools. Rahul Gandhi of Congress joined Twitter in April 2015, a relative newcomer, and had 9.84 million followers in June 2019. While Rahul's messaging on Twitter is largely around three things—attack on Modi, farmers and job crisis—Modi tweets about a wide array of issues from the government's new development initiatives to politics.

Unlike older politicians who found it difficult to make a transition from mainstream media to social media, Modi has been an agile adapter to changing media technologies. In the 1990s, he had adapted to the computer, and a cell phone was his constant accessory. His Internet habit started, he said, in the late 1990s, when he discovered it was the best way to keep in touch with what was happening in his home state of Gujarat. Modi claims he was the first to use a digital camera during India's 1999 elections.

Modi felt that the growing social media is the most suitable form of media to reach out to the public. He wrote in his blog on 12 May 2014, 'We have to profusely thank social media—it has caused the downfall of manufactured lies and half-truths at a very nascent stage' (Asha and Rani 2014, 19). After his swearing-in as the chief minister of Gujarat in 2001, a personal English website was established.[2] The website offered insightful facts and graphics that positively contributed to the NaMo campaign. Modi logged in to Facebook and Twitter in 2009, and, from a slow start, his number of followers grew steadily. It was after declaring his intention to become prime minister in 2012 that

[2] www.narendramodi.org

he became active on the platform, tweeting 'faulty' economic policies and bad governance of the UPA II.

After a victory in the Gujarat Legislative Assembly elections in 2007, Modi moved out of the Hindutva agenda and began projecting the 'Gujarat model' of development. Modi's online image has been carefully presented. He used social media to project himself as a man of modernity with tradition, who represented values and globalized vision. His images with Apple laptop and cell phone, reading an Obama biography, playing golf, walking with lions, meeting foreign leaders, hosting film stars and sports heroes circulated in the media and social media, marking the transition from an RSS *pracharak* to a modern politician. He is a modern person, who began with according importance to society with the slogan 'Swachh Bharat'. His election campaign theme of 2014 was development, which implied modernization. The social media campaign was largely contributed to the visual brand building of Modi, which was continued since his second term as chief minister of Gujarat (Kaur 2015).

Besides hiring top-notch consulting and advertising agencies for his brand building, various social media outlets were used to show Modi with his mother to project that he respects elders. Images of his development initiatives were shown in social media to recast him as a development hero. During the elections, online products featuring Modi, including laptop bags, T-shirts, caps and even an Android-based smartphone, were found in the market. These images were used to show how Modi was different from other politicians of his or of the previous era. In all social media tools, he was attempting to communicate with middle-class families across the country to suggest he was working towards improving the image of India and the well-being of Indians.

## Sadbhavana with Twitter: Both towards Winning Post

The year 2012 was known for many landmark achievements in Modi's political career. *TIME*, one of the world's leading news magazines, had Modi on its cover page with a story titled 'Modi Means Business' in its issue of 26 March 2012. This clearly indicated pro-business leadership of Modi, and he steadily was moving from the main Hindutva plank to a developmental agenda with the Gujarat model of development as the showcase. In the same year on 17 September, he completed a record 4,000 days as the chief minister of Gujarat. British High Commissioner James Bevan held a meeting with Modi on 22 October 2012 to discuss business and investment that ended the UK's 10-year diplomatic boycott imposed on him for failing to stop the Gujarat riots. The same year, Gujarat went to polls and Modi registered an emphatic victory, third in a row.

Since the Gujarat assembly elections of 2012, Modi started focusing on expanding his base in social media platforms. First, on 31 August 2012, Modi addressed a range of issues during an online webcam chat which drew attention across India and the globe (Sharma 2016). He answered the questions raised by NRIs, who were his admirers and supporters. The initiative to mobilize more and more people to follow him on social media often worked in tandem with the BJP's intellectual cells across Gujarat. Second, Modi used his blog to inform the public of the significance of Sadbhavana Yatra, 2011–2012, where he covered almost the entire state, ostensibly to promote social harmony. Third, his Google Hangout session with Bollywood actor Ajay Devgn on 31 August 2012, who had then released *Tezz* and *Bol Bachchan* films, had drawn wide attention. Google plus hosted a hangout session with Chief Minister Modi in preparation for the 2012 assembly elections and was broadcasted on YouTube. This was the first for a major politician in India to appear on a live interactive session. The endorsement by the film star, who had a million followers then, was a mega success. The hashtag #ModiHangout became the first viral event on Modi's social media. It was viewed by many young middle-class voters. Fourth, Modi follows many celebrity Twitter accounts from the field of film and sports, including megastars Amitabh Bachchan, Rajinikanth, Akkineni Nagarjuna and Mahendra Singh Dhoni. Modi's following were accompanied by photographs, which were retweeted many times. While a team of young professionals and trusted officials facilitated his significant presence on social media, he crafted his own electoral media plans.

Until the 2012 assembly elections, the entire focus of Modi supporters on Facebook and Twitter was on the development projects of Gujarat and the government's achievements. Apart from using a diverse digital platform, attention was paid to ensure synchronization of the message with real developments taking place on the ground to gain widespread publicity. The Gujarat model of development was effectively showcased.

Soon after the 2012 Gujarat election victory, there was a strong emphasis on projecting Modi as the prime-ministerial candidate. A Facebook campaign titled '*Ek Hi Vikalp Modi*' was launched, projecting Modi as the only option at the national level to take on the Congress (Dutta 2013). His supporters held up posters that said, 'This is the trailer, watch the film in 2014' and 'CM in 2012, PM in 2014' and even 'Hit & Fit for PM'[3] sending out a clear message that he was ready to move on towards the national capital.

Modi's win generated a debate in the media on his possible projection as the BJP's prime-ministerial candidate in the 2014 general elections. The Congress played down the victory and treated him as a state leader sans pan-India appeal. The speculation ended on 9 June 2013, when Modi was elevated to Chairman of the BJP's 2014 election campaign, which confirmed him as the candidate for prime minister. Disappointed with the party's decision, veteran leader L. K. Advani resigned from the BJP's decision-making body, exposing deep rifts in the party. However, he later withdrew the resignation on the intervention of the RSS. Modi tweeted on this occasion too, saying that he talked to Advaniji on phone and urged him to revert his decision of resigning from the BJP's committee. Almost a week later, on 16 June 2013, JD(U) leader and Bihar Chief Minister Nitish Kumar pulled out of a 17-year-old alliance with the BJP after the party's decision, opposing the appointment of Modi as the BJP head to campaign the general elections.

On 10 June 2013, Modi tweeted, 'Spoke to Rajnath ji. In such a short time cannot reach the Parliamentary Board Meeting but will

---

[3] https://www.ndtv.com/assembly/bjps-big-gujarat-win-narendra-modi-to-get-third-term-as-chief-minister-508068 (accessed on 5 March 2016).

stand by whatever decision the Board takes'. A few days later, Modi sent a series of messages referring to 'seeking the blessings' of Advani and party president Rajnath Singh. This marked a new, national phase in Modi's social media discourse. By July 2013, he had tweeted only about meeting two former Presidents A. P. J. Abdul Kalam and the then President Pranab Mukherjee (Pal 2015). Twitter accounts in various Indian languages were set up to translate Modi's tweets. On 4 July 2013, Mr Modi, one among the prolific politicians on Twitter, crossed 1.8 million followers, and he eclipsed Congress leader and parliamentarian Shashi Tharoor as the country's most 'followed' politician on Twitter and multiplied his lead several times soon thereafter.[4] On 14 September 2013, the BJP formally announced Modi as its prime-ministerial candidate. On Modi's birthday on 17 September 2013, his handle, @narendramodi, 'followed' a number of Twitter accounts.

With barely a few months left for the 2014 general elections, Modi in order to accelerate his party's run towards the Delhi throne, flagged off the 'Run for Unity' marathon, a mega event on the 63rd death anniversary of Sardar Vallabhbhai Patel, the country's Iron man, at Vadodra in Gujarat (15 December 2013). He tweeted, 'Statue of Unity Movement is a tribute to the ideals & values of Sardar Patel. It is a dream to unite our nation & draw the world to India'. The marathons were held at over 1,000 locations. Following Modi's appeal in print, electronic and social media to participate, the event witnessed participation from over 40 lakh people in different parts of the country. Modi managed to convert a marathon run into a major mobilization event for the BJP and to mobilize resources for constructing a 182-feet 'Statue of Unity', a fitting tribute to the towering figure of (Sardar Vallabhbhai Patel) of unity in the country.[5] The statue built in the Narmada district was inaugurated by Prime Minister Modi on 31 October 2018, the 143rd birth anniversary of Patel (See Figure 8.1).

---

[4] https://blogs.wsj.com/indiarealtime/2013/07/05/meet-modis-social-media-men/ (accessed on 6 August 2014).

[5] http://archive.indianexpress.com/news/modi-flags-off-run-for-unity-marathon-appeals-not-to-view-event-politically/1207860/ (accessed on 30 March 2015).

Figure 8.1 *Prime Minister Narendra Modi and Other Dignitaries at the Dedication of the 'Statue of Unity' to the Nation, on the Occasion of Rashtriya Ekta Diwas at Kevadiya in Narmada District of Gujarat on 31 October 2018*
Source: Press Information Bureau.

The erection of the 'Statue of Unity' was viewed as creating an alternative discourse on a nationalist movement that would bypass the Nehru–Gandhi family and claim Vallabhbhai Patel as the Iron Man who unified India. In his article 'Tribute to a Great Unifier', Modi (2018) described Patel as the 'maker of the modern India'.

The Congress alleged that the BJP was trying to 'hijack' the legacy of freedom fighters and national heroes like Patel as they had no leaders of their own to celebrate.[6] The Congress social media handler Ramya (Divya Spandana) took a jibe on Twitter at the prime minister by posting a photograph of Modi standing at the feet of Patel statue with the caption, 'Is that bird dropping?', which led to a huge backlash on social media from the saffron party.[7]

Modi ended the year 2013 on a victory note. Borrowing the words of Mahatma Gandhi, Modi tweeted '*Satyamev Jayate*! Truth alone triumphs', after a magistrate court in Ahmedabad on 26 December 2013 gave him a clean chit in the 2002 communal violence in the state. The court rejected a petition against Modi filed by widow Zakia Jafri, whose husband and former Congress MP Ehsan Jafri was among 68 people killed in the Gulberg Society in Ahmedabad by a mob on 28 February 2002. Jafri had challenged the closure report of the Supreme Court-appointed SIT that said there was no prosecutable evidence against Modi.

The BJP termed the order 'a moral victory for the BJP and Narendra Modi'.[8] The BJP leader Arun Jaitley tweeted, 'Modi goes into the 2014 campaign untainted by the propaganda. The verdict has proved that propaganda can never be a substitute for truth'.[9] In February 2012, the SIT said that there was no prosecutable evidence against Modi and filed a closure report indicating its inquiry has ended. The court verdict provided much-needed relief to Modi who wanted his leadership to be accepted by a larger section of the people. The Nanavati Commission report tabled in the Gujarat State Legislative Assembly on 11 December 2019, 17 years after the riots shook the state, also gave Modi a clean chit.

---

[6] https://www.theweek.in/news/india/2018/10/31/An-election-gimmick-a-treason-congress-reacts-to-Statue-of-Unity.html (accessed on 2 January 2019).

[7] https://www.deccanherald.com/national/divya-spandana-posts-701047.html (accessed on 2 November 2018).

[8] https://www.ndtv.com/cheat-sheet/narendra-modi-will-not-face-charges-in-2002-riots-tweets-satyamev-jayate-545805 (accessed on 19 March 2016).

[9] Ibid.

For the BJP too, the year 2013 ended on a happy note. The party secured victories in assembly elections in Madhya Pradesh, Rajasthan and Chhattisgarh. The middle class, for long a non-entity in Indian elections, surfaced strongly saying that it wanted to be heard. Effective, non-corrupt governance had been the mantra of this voting class, and it helped defeat incumbent Congress party chief ministers in Rajasthan and Delhi. The incumbent BJP chief minister of Madhya Pradesh, Shivraj Singh Chouhan, was elected for the third time because he was viewed as efficient and clean.[10]

## The 2014 Lok Sabha Campaign

The Lok Sabha elections 2014 witnessed the emergence of acronyms 'NaMo' that has a meaning in north Indian languages as 'bowing with respect'. The media brigade led by the committed RSS workers did not take much time to ride on this newfound talisman. Everywhere, and in all respects, it was used freely and firmly to establish the Modi identity. The elections were dubbed the first 'social media election' in India (Ali 2014). *The New York Times* called Narendra Modi 'The Social Media Politician' (Willis 2014), and his election campaign was compared to Obama's 2008 Presidential campaign in its effective use of social media. The UK's *Financial Times* labelled Modi 'India's first social media prime minister'—a tag that Modi and his *bhakts* have flaunted numerous times during the last five years, especially while comparing him to his predecessor, Manmohan Singh, whose lack of public communication became the butt of jokes.[11] Even the Congress used 'NaMo' acronym in their speeches thereby recognizing its identity though inadvertently.

According to Facebook data, from the day elections were announced (6 March) to the day polling ended (12 May), 29 million people in India had put out 227 million posts, comments, shares and likes on its sites in the specific context of the elections, with an

[10] https://qz.com/155439/the-five-real-winners-of-indias-state-election-results/ (accessed on 10 July 2018).

[11] https://thewire.in/politics/acche-din-kab-aayenge (accessed on 8 June 2018).

additional 13 million making 75 million interactions involving Modi. On the day of counting of votes and poll results, Modi's photo with his victory wall message generated more than a million likes and shares (Das 2014). According to the data shared by Twitter, from 1 January to 16 May 2014, the day results were announced, an estimated 58 million tweets, specifically related to the elections, were generated.[12] The 2014 elections have been widely considered as India's first Twitter election.

Modi aggressively launched his political campaign on social media tools. His Twitter account became a key vehicle of his messaging. In addition to his Twitter page, Modi or his personal social media cell ran a Facebook page, a YouTube channel, a LinkedIn, Pinterest, Instagram and Tumblr accounts, and posted his messages, speeches, photographs of public rallies and so on. Indeed, in his entire 2014 campaign, Modi did not believe in holding press conferences, and journalists had to rely on Twitter to get soundbytes from Modi. The campaign on social media was directed at the upwardly mobile middle and upper-class youth who were disgusted with the 'policy paralysis' and 'non-performing' UPA II politicians and looked at Modi as an alternative.

From the early days of the BJP's election campaign, more attention was given to young and first-time voters, including those in the rural areas. Besides, efforts of the All India Bharatiya Yuva Morcha headed by Anurag Thakur, who was at its helm for six years, a special committee was created for mobilizing the group. This committee was headed by another youth face of the party, Muralidhar Rao, who had emerged as the recognizable face in the party because of his remarkable skills as student organizer (Torri 2015, 65). Assuming that the youth would vote for him, Modi called upon the youth to exercise their vote. He tweeted in this regard on 23 April: 'I particularly call upon my young friends to go & vote in large numbers. The youth of India must show the way!' A few weeks later (11 May), the tone grew louder: 'My special request to the youth – go out and vote and take your family and friends along to the polling booth!' Each tweet of this

---

[12] https://www.socialsamosa.com/2014/05/twitter-elections-data/ (accessed on 20 May 2017).

kind helped to increase voter turnout, especially from the neo-middle class, who were hitherto complacent towards elections.

Modi's clever use of digital media space as a forum of public relations and dominance over media, in general, was a key factor contributing to his convincing win in the general elections. Modi used social media to reach out to first-time voters in the age group of 18–23 years, which were around 150 million or almost 15 per cent of the total electorate. Knowing well the social media's significant role in mobilizing people in the IAC movement led by Anna Hazare in Delhi, Modi used such media to attract the young generation, which was quite comfortable with smartphones and was continually present on social media platforms. According to a study, 50 per cent of the population was below the age of 25, while 65 per cent was below the age of 35.[13] This demographic group was either studying in colleges or employed in various companies. Modi tapped this tech-savvy youth by using diverse social networking tools with updated trends and topics and catchy slogans such as 'abki baar, Modi sarkar', five words, that resonates with the voters. The catchphrase 'NaMo' soon found space all over the social networking sites, campaign pamphlets, hoardings, print and digital media advertisements, posters and wall writings.[14] The two themes that are dominating in Modi's tweets through all the nine phases of the campaign were 'youth' and 'development' (Pal, Chandra, and Vydiswaran 2016).

Through the deployment of communication technologies and apps, efforts were made to spread out party's policies, create faith in the electorate about the party's idea of growth and inspire youth to participate in the election process. The BJP received 39 per cent support from the first-time voters against 19 per cent of Congress.[15] Therefore, the

[13] https://www.digitalvidya.com/blog/social-media-politics/ (accessed on 23 March 2018).

[14] https://indianexpress.com/article/india/india-others/man-behind-ab-ki-baar-modi-sarkaar-is-spice-jet-co-owner/ (accessed on 25 May 2017).

[15] https://economictimes.indiatimes.com/news/politics-and-nation/election-results-2014-maximum-first-time-voters-supported-bjp/articleshow/35311341.cms?from=mdr (accessed on 23 June 2016).

2014 election was probably the first parliamentary election that was decided not on caste, religion and region, although they played some role but by a combination of young first-time voters and the urban and semi-urban middle class. In fact, the BJP borrowed a strategy to reach out to youth from the AAP's 2013 campaign. In turn, the AAP learnt from the BJP's 2014 media campaign in order to win the Delhi assembly elections in 2015.

Modi dominated the Twitter conversations. He was mentioned in 11.1 million tweets (out of 58 million tweets) between 1 January and 12 May 2014.[16] His interviews, speeches and manifesto promises were tweeted regularly, through his personal Twitter account and those of the party and followers. Unlike the Gujarat assembly elections where the Hindutva appeal had always ensured electoral victories, Modi broadened his political appeal in the general elections and, besides the Hindutva plank, issues related to corruption, black money, national security, policy paralysis and economic slowdown were increasingly used in public rallies and tweets. He turned towards development issues, showcasing Gujarat's model of development.

Modi used his Twitter to set the political agenda. Usually, the ruling party sets the agenda during the election, but, in the 2014 election, Modi set the agenda on his Twitter and gave chance for attack to the opponents, particularly the Congress. The Opposition failed to set a counter-narrative and was often seen playing along the lines released by the agenda dictated by the BJP in the campaign. Referring to the lack of a proactive role of the ruling Congress, he made two tweets, 'Usually ruling party sets agenda of the election but in this campaign ruling party was neither proactive nor responsive, it remained reactive' (12 May 2014). 'Campaigning for 2014 elections is reaching its final stages but no Congress leader has talked about any developmental issues. Very sad' (6 May 2014). These tweets

[16] https://economictimes.indiatimes.com/news/politics-and-nation/modi-dominated-twitter-conversations-during-lok-sabha-polls-features-11-million-times-on-twitter/articleshow/35137369.cms?from=mdr (accessed on 26 May 2018).

clearly indicated a weak ruling UPA led by the Congress, which was embroiled already in several scandals. Another tweet by Modi (26 March)—'Give us 60 months to serve you. We don't want to enjoy power but want to be Chowkidars who will guard people's money'—has been widely covered in the print media. Modi exposed Congress's commitment to bring black money back by tweeting 'Why is Congress hesitant to bring back black money? Because they know who it belongs to ... NDA will bring back every Paisa that is stashed abroad' (30 March). He highlighted 'policy paralysis' during the UPA II regime by tweeting '2014 Lok Sabha Elections is a contest between good governance agenda of NDA and the misgovernance and corruption of UPA' (30 March).

During the campaign, Modi has relentlessly attacked the Congress party. 'Freedom from dynasty politics, nepotism, corruption, communalism, divisions in society, poverty ... this is what Congress Mukt Bharat is' (12 January 2014). He kept referring to Rahul Gandhi as 'Rahul baba': 'The way Rahul Baba is making statements with a dash of comedy in them, I think the TV show of Kapil Sharma may soon have to shut shop' (27 April). It was re-tweed 10,830 times. A number of personal attacks included a reference to the foreign origin of Sonia Gandhi and the naming of schemes and institutions, public grounds, parks, museums and so on after the Gandhi family. After a decade-long rule, the Congress was found 'out of sync' with the electorate. Congress leaders were stuck only at the 2002 riots and calling him *chaiwala*. These proved counter-productive.

Modi played the caste card to hit back at the Congress after Priyanka Gandhi Vadra said Modi was indulging in *neech rajniti* (low-level politics). Giving her comments a caste spin, Modi tweeted, 'As I belong to a socially backward section, they consider my politics to be neech rajniti... Some people cannot see that it is due to the renunciation, sacrifice and hard work of people of backward castes that the country has reached its current heights' (6 May). Modi invoked his OBC background as a part of a strategy to seek the support of backward castes. It was the same tactic that was used to counter Mani Shankar Aiyar's statement that Modi was a *neech aadmi* (lowly man) during the Gujarat assembly election in 2017.

## 'Tweet' and 'Selfie' Revolution

Among the youngsters, Twitter, Facebook and WhatsApp had made a strong establishment. This along with 'selfies' kept the young Indians engaged in a larger part of the day. The smart move by the BJP campaign managers, and also by Modi, was to ride on this wave, capture and turn it towards his advantage: He did that and tweeting selfies was yet another strategy. On 30 April 2014, a selfie tweet that went viral showed an image of Modi at a polling booth with his inked finger holding up a lotus icon: 'Voted!' Thousands of Modi's followers and supporters came back to post their inked fingertips in response to a single tweet from Modi (Rapoza 2014). After casting his vote, he clicked a selfie and attacked the Congress, saying nothing can now save the 'mother–son' government.[17] However, the ECI took serious note of the violation of the electoral laws, under which no person can display any election matter or address a meeting in a polling booth on the day of the election. But the selfie was a BJP game plan to involve young people by inviting them to post their selfies after voting. Modi later explained that 'the selfie was a natural reaction and just for social media. It was part of what I was always doing and the youth of the nation were in my mind when I did it'. Adding, 'Our message got the attention it deserved to keep the election momentum going' (Price 2015, 171–178). Rao (2018) calls this 'selfie nationalism', a clear break from Mohandas Gandhi's advocacy of 'spiritual nationalism'.

Modi's campaign team was largely comprised of non-politicians, mainly young middle-class professionals and corporate honchos well versed with technology and social media. Teams led by Mumbai-based technology entrepreneur Rajesh Jain; political strategist Prashant Kishor and his Citizens for Accountable Governance, a media and publicity company; IT expert Hiren Joshi; and another IT expert Arvind Gupta, who headed the BJP's IT cell, ran the campaign in a coordinated way to achieve the target 'Mission 272 plus'. This group played a major role in conducting the whole campaign, in producing

---

[17] https://www.indiatoday.in/elections/gujarat/story/narendra-modi-voting-vadodra-seventh-phase-of-elections-bjp-congress-191010-2014-04-30 (accessed on 5 May 2014).

talking points to Modi and in putting together and distributing *Moditva*, a book collection of Modi's speeches (Torri 2015, 66).

While Joshi, who has been managing Modi's blogs, websites and Twitter and Facebook accounts, Prashant Kishor and his team, which later regrouped as the Indian Political Action Committee (I-PAC) in 2015, supervised many programmes such as 'Run for Unity', 'Chai pe Charcha' (discussions over tea), 'Manthan' (churning). It's not easy for product brands to go from regional to national levels. Team Modi worked hard to transform Modi's image from a regional brand as the three-time chief minister of Gujarat to a national-level prime-ministerial candidate, establishing a connection between Modi and the youth of the nation, and to enable Modi to communicate in English with the politically aware urban population (Pande 2014). The team focused on building Modi's image as a self-made, strong, able, efficient, inspiring and incorruptible leader. The BJP's IT department claimed that the social media campaign influenced 30–40 per cent of the overall seats in the election (Kapoor and Dwivedi 2015).

The BJP's IT Cell, supported by US-trained software professionals, was established as the National Digital Operations Centre at the party headquarters in New Delhi in July 2013. The centre not only used digital technology in 2014 elections but also recruited more than a million 'vote mobilizers' who campaigned for the BJP and Modi. The IT team identified 155 key urban constituencies, known as the 'digital seats' because, that were the most exposed to media and 'connected' (Mahurkar and Pradhan 2014). Up to 40,000 tweets were sent daily during the campaign. IT expert Arvind Gupta described some of the IT team's tactics as 'multi-media carpet-bombing' (Sardesai 2014). The innovative campaign built around the slogan '272 plus', supported by lakhs of volunteers involving online professionals speaking different languages, ensured Modi's victory. Thus, the media has moved from 'manufacturing consent' to 'manufacturing dissent' against the existing government before it returns to create consent (Hasan 2014). The BJP and Modi registered a spectacular victory in the elections. Modi tweeted on 16 May 2014: 'India has won. *Bharat ki vijay, achche din aane wale hain'*. As on 24 June 2019, it was retweeted 114,029 times and was marked as India's most-shared tweet.

During the election campaign, Modi's tweets and other messages on the social media were largely followed by the 'Internet Hindus' comprised of young, often urban, middle-class/upper-middle-class followers of Hinduism residing in India and abroad. The 'Internet Hindus' aggressively supported Modi's right-wing political views on social media platforms (Mohan 2015). Internet Hindus dominates 'every social media discussion and every online forum' (Pradhan and Sriram 2013).

## Tweet from Prime Minister's Seat

After becoming the prime minister, Modi used his millions of followers on Twitter and social media for ensuring better governance and reform. Many ministries used social media sites to push transparency, participative governance and reduce corruption. Crowdsourcing ideas, picking up trends, seeking inputs on policies and seeking feedback on union budget were done through social networks. In fact, keeping in line with Modi's vision of creating a digitally empowered nation, a large number of leaders, organizations, ministries and the defence wings made their presence felt online. Officials started believing that digitalization has not only made proceedings more transparent for the citizens but has also helped authorities keep a tab on the progress of their work. Since digitalization has bridged the gap between citizens and the government, a lot of information and data now reach the authorities first hand.

Prime Minister Modi saw social media as some form of direct democracy where a leader could hear directly from his people. Using social media, he conveyed important policy decisions to the citizens. The communication hub of Ministry of Information and Broadcasting helped to generate content, track trends and roll out publicity campaigns for government programmes. The ministries of railways, health, textiles, human resource development, defence, PMO India, Indian Space Research Organization (ISRO) and other major organizations are followed on social networking platforms. The social media in governance has not only eliminated the middleman but people personally reached out to authorities concerned with their grievances. Late

Sushma Swaraj (the then minister of external affairs) earned public trust when she responded to citizen's appeals for her ministry's services on Twitter. She successfully solved the irritating issues easily and became the most responsible minister. Her tweet, 'Even if you are stuck on Mars, Indian Embassy there will help you', became very popular.

In the first year (2014) itself, we saw a flurry of campaign launches by Modi, including the Digital India campaign, the 'Pradhan Mantri Jan Dhan Yojana' (prime-ministerial people's fund scheme), the 'Make in India' global initiative, the 'Clean India' campaign, and the 'Beti Bachao, Beti Padhao' scheme that ensures the rights of female children. Tweets and hashtag usage reflects support for specific initiatives: #SwachchBharat, #MakeInIndia, #StartUpIndia, #JandDhan, #SelfieWithDaughter and so on. Modi's Twitter account shows that he used celebrities' names and popularity on Twitter to promote his schemes by posting selfies with film and sports stars, foreign dignitaries or enlisting them to participate in his campaigns. Modi's Twitter handle @narendramodi and PMO Twitter handle @PMOIndia work in synchronicity to inform millions of followers of his and his government's activities (Rodrigues and Niemann 2017). Under the hashtag #MannKiBaat, Modi solicits content for his monthly radio monologue and asks for feedback.

Moving forward, Modi launched the 'Narendra Modi Mobile App' (NaMo) on 17 June 2015, and it has become a major tool for the prime minister to obtain feedback from the citizens on various welfare schemes and developmental projects. The app allows users to share news related to Modi, receive updates and take part in polls. In one of the party's parliamentary meetings, Modi remarked that he greeted party MPs on his personal app almost every day, but did not get a response (Hebbar 2018). The app allows the users to know about Modi's style of governance, the initiatives and achievements of the government. To promote e-governance, in February 2018, tech entrepreneur Arvind Gupta, who headed the BJP's IT Cell in the 2014 election campaign, was appointed as the CEO of MyGovIndia, an innovative platform to build a partnership between citizens and the government with the help of technology growth and development. On 25 October 2018, Modi launched the *Main Nahin, Hum* (not

I, we) portal, which works on the theme 'self4society' to enable IT professionals and organizations to bring together their efforts towards social causes and service to society, on one platform. Many IT firms registered on the portal.

## Vanguards of Swadeshi

Modi developed a style of using a software, not only the Twitter handle but also the soft chords in the minds of a typical middle class. Invoking the spirit of the Gandhian era of 'Clean Bharat' and reverting to yoga, were the two important nodes on which we struck emotionally with people. By popularizing yoga, Modi's first major achievement was the UN decision on 11 December 2014 declaring 21 June as the 'International Day of Yoga'. The prime minister welcomed the UN decision and tweeted: 'Elated! Have no words to describe my joy on the UN declaring 21st June as "International Day of Yoga". I fully welcome the decision'. Since 2015, the International Day of Yoga is celebrated annually on 21 June across the globe.

Modi has been participating in Yoga Day celebrations every year since 2015 (Figure 8.2). Modi led Yoga Day celebrations and performed *asanas* (exercises) at a ground in Ranchi on 21 June 2019. Yoga has been embraced by many—the rich and middle-class families—in their quest to stay fit and healthy. The Modi government, through the International Yoga Day celebrations, has been encouraging more people to embrace the fitness routine. 'We should make efforts to take yoga from cities to villages, tribal areas. Yoga is above religion, above faith, above everything'.[18] Modi congratulated Yoga Day award winners and posted the congratulatory messages on Twitter in Spanish, French, Arabic, Russian, Japanese and English.[19] A set of followers celebrates Modi's identification with aspects of Hindu culture, such as with Yoga and his religious fasts or visits to temples.

---

[18] https://www.indiatoday.in/india/story/yoga-above-everything-make-integral-part-life-narendra-modi-1553821-2019-06-21 (accessed on 22 June 2019).
[19] https://www.dailypioneer.com/2019/india/modi-congratulates-yoga-day-award-winners.html (accessed on 26 June 2019).

Figure 8.2 *Prime Minister Narendra Modi at Yoga Day celebrations at the Forest Research Institute, Dehradun, Uttarakhand on 21 June 2018*

*Source:* Press Information Bureau.

The Swachh Bharat or Clean India Mission is another ambitious programme by the Modi government. Since its launch, Modi's message on the Clean India Mission remained sharp, including his tweets and YouTube videos related to the topic. A study by Rodrigues and Niemann (2017) says that 'the campaign was part of the BJP's election manifesto, tapping into the desire of educated youth and middle classes to see the economic growth in the country manifested in basic amenities for all and cleaner communities'. In the first year of its launch, Modi extensively posted tweets about events related to the SBM. Modi engaged celebrities from film, sports, business and fellow politicians in the campaign to boost visibility. Celebrities wielding brooms for Clean India has received wide publicity in social media and created awareness among the public about the mission objectives. Moreover, 'these celebrities are also social media influencers or Twitterati, who are followed by millions on Twitter. Every time Modi added a 140-character message on Twitter about a launch of an event or congratulating a celebrity's efforts in the Clean India effort, mainstream media reported it as a news story' (Rodrigues and Niemann 2017).

Several phone apps were launched by the central and local government departments in 2015 (e.g., the Swachh Delhi App by the New Delhi government). On the mission's success, Modi tweeted: 'Swachh Bharat Mission will save lakhs of lives and result in over 14 million more years of healthy living ... fascinating observations by the @WHO study on India's strides in cleanliness and sanitation' (4 August 2018). In another tweet, the prime minister said, 'Swachh Bharat Abhiyan has brought every Indian together. It has become a people's movement and there has been remarkable progress across all states, including in toilet construction and becoming ODF' (23 June 2018). On 10 October 2014, Facebook co-founder Mark Zuckerberg, who was on a two-day visit to India, met Prime Minister Modi in New Delhi. Modi posted photographs of meeting Mark Zuckerberg on Facebook as well as on the PMO Twitter handle. 'Had a wonderful meeting with Facebook CEO Mr. Mark Zuckerberg ... I spoke to him about Swachh Bharat Mission. Mr. Zuckerberg shared that Facebook would assist the Government of India in the Clean India mobile application. This will surely give an impetus to Swachh Bharat Mission'.

In the initial days of 2014, the #achhedin has acquired prominence in the mainstream and social media. On some days, the #achhedin hashtag framed thousands of tweets and posts; on dull days, it continued to record its presence a few hundred times. The Twitter saw a surge of messages on *achhe din* (good days) when a growth rate accelerated, a fall in inflation and an increase in FDI flows. But a year later, Congress and AAP leaders and supporters posted links to Modi's videos from the past, where he holds positions totally contrary to those he professed. Opposing Modi's policies, Rahul Gandhi said *achhe din* has come only for the prime minister and not the *aam aadmi* (common citizen) who are groaning under unprecedented price rise. In September 2015, at a rally in Odisha, Rahul Gandhi took a dig at the NDA government for trying to dilute the Land Acquisition Act, 2013 and said, 'Farmers and labourers had reposed faith in Modiji, who assured of ushering in "achhe din".[20] But after becoming the prime minister, he forgot them in just two days. Where are the "achhe din" for farmers?' Rahul in another tweet (23 December 2016) said, 'Congress is best at Governance. Excellent Congress track record and truth speaks louder than *jumlas*. India misses INC in power'. Congress-affiliated handles on Twitter also question Modi's growth claims, lampooning his unorthodox policies as #Fekunomics and #Jumlanomics (Sinha 2017).

## Twitter Diplomacy: Reaching out of Indian Borders

Modi used Twitter in building diplomatic relations too. Modi has never missed a chance to pose for selfies with important political leaders around the world. Modi started the 'selfie craze' in India by tweeting his selfies and encouraging visitors to take them. Photographs of Modi hugging world leaders are posted on his Twitter, and his Facebook page reposted them as an affirmation that Modi had stature on the global stage. The prime minister's visit to the USA, address to the UN's General Assembly on 27 September 2015 and his meetings with Internet barons, Mark Zuckerberg (Facebook), Shantanu Narayen (Adobe), Satya Nadella (Microsoft) and Sundar Pichai (Google) have gone viral on the social media. He made public tweets to world leaders, including Vladimir Putin, Stephen Harper, Obama, Shinzo Abe and David Cameron. Modi did a series of live tweets and pictures from meetings with leaders from neighbouring countries. Modi took a selfie outside the Temple of Heaven with China's premier Li Keqiang in May 2015, which he posed on Twitter, attracting a lot of media attention, including a comment about how he had found a way through China's 'Great Firewall' which restricts access to the Internet (Whitehead 2016, 169). The social media turned frenzy over 'Howdy, Modi' event at Houston, the USA, in September 2019.

However, Modi's surprise visit to Pakistan drew flak. Modi's clip threatening Pakistan on the India TV show *Aap Ki Adalat* hosted by

---

[20] https://www.indiatoday.in/india/story/where-are-achhe-din-rahul-mocks-modi-government-262249-2015-09-10 (accessed on 10 October 2016).

Rajat Sharma in 2012 was juxtaposed with pictures of his surprise visit to Pakistan and meeting with Prime Minister Nawaz Sharif on 25 December 2015 (Sinha 2017). 'Spoke to PM Nawaz Sharif & wished him on his birthday', Modi tweeted. Sharif turned 66 on 25 December 2015. Sharif had invited Modi to attend the marriage of his granddaughter Mehrun Nisa at the Sharif's Raiwind palatial residence. However, when Nawaz Sharif was arrested on 13 July 2018 on charges of corruption, the Congress lost no time and tweeted, 'Nawaz Sharif has been arrested on corruption charges. We'd like to know what his dear friend, PM Modi, has to say about this', along with a photograph of the two holding hands during the Indian prime minister's visit to Pakistan in December 2015. The Congress tweet was not liked by all. The National Conference Vice-President Omar Abdullah said that Congress's tweet about 'Modi and Nawaz Sharif was disappointing'.[21] During tours abroad, particularly in the USA, Modi has successfully raised India's profile at the global level which has impressed many. But at the same time, the Congress and Left scholars accused Modi of using foreign tours and foreign policy to project the country as a 'Hindu power' with his nationalistic Hindu pride' narrative, especially to the Indian diaspora.

## Surgical Strikes and Demonetization

Two prominent developments in the second half of 2016—'surgical strikes' against militants across the Line of Control in Pakistan administered Kashmir and demonetization of high-value currencies—dominated the discussion on social media networking. The surgical strike was a retaliatory measure taken by the NDA government on the intervening night of 29–30 September 2016 in response to the Uri attack that had killed 17 Indian soldiers in the same year. Indian Twitter celebrated 'Modi's punishment for Pakistan'.[22] MPs, leaders,

---

[21] https://www.dailypioneer.com/2018/sunday-edition/omar-calls-congress-tweet-about-pm-modi-sharif-disappointing.html (accessed on 20 July 2018).

[22] https://www.indiatoday.in/india/story/indian-army-surgical-strikes-pakistan-twitter-343889-2016-09-29 (accessed on 28 June 2018).

workers and supporters of the BJP used social media to congratulate Modi for successfully carrying out the surgical strikes against Pakistan.

Initially, the Congress congratulated the Indian Army with Rahul Gandhi's tweet: 'The Congress Party and I salute the Indian Army and our jawans for acting valiantly to defend our country & our people. Jai Hind' (29 September 2016). However, it quickly changed its track and repeatedly asked for its proof, even claiming that it was 'fake'. Rahul Gandhi accused Prime Minister Modi of using surgical strikes for political gain.[23] The Congress made similar attacks against Modi when armed forces conducted airstrikes against Pakistan in 2019.

The government's decision to withdraw currency notes of ₹1,000 and ₹500 denomination has quite obviously created a storm on social media; while some welcomed it, others opposed it. Modi has made several tweets on the day of the announcement and later. 'A historic step to fight corruption, black money and terrorism' (8 November). 'Our fight against corruption & black money will continue. We can't tolerate these evils any more' (13 November). Besides leaders of the ruling parties, Bollywood celebrities, business leaders and cricket stars congratulated Modi and hailed the decision. Nearly five lakh conversations on demonetization on Twitter & Instagram accounted for 6 of the top 10 trending topics, and Prime Minister Modi garnered half of the trending topics. #IamwithModi and #Modi were the topics that made up for 19 per cent of the conversations within the top 10 trends.[24]

Rahul Gandhi emerged as the biggest critic of Modi's decision on demonetization. He became the voice of all those who were not convinced with the BJP government's rationale behind the decision. He made a series of tweets and led the party's protest to highlight difficulties faced by the people. The CPI, CPI(M), JD(S), BSP, SP, Trinamool Congress and other parties have bitterly criticized the decision. West Bengal Chief Minister Mamata Banerjee tweeted: 'This

[23] https://www.indiatoday.in/india/story/surgical-strikes-ds-hooda-congress-modi-1405130-2018-12-08 (accessed on 5 June 2018).
[24] https://bestmediainfo.com/2016/12/demonetization-how-the-nation-reacted-on-twitter-instagram/ (accessed on 5 May 2017).

is a financial chaos and disaster let loose on the common people of India…'; 'Withdraw this draconian decision' (8 November 2016). As the Modi government was celebrating one year of the demonetization, Rahul Gandhi led the party's protest against the note ban and tweeted: 'Demonetization is a tragedy. We stand with millions of honest Indians, whose lives & livelihoods were destroyed by PM's thoughtless act' (8 November 2017). Several opposition parties unitedly protested against the note ban calling it a 'reckless' and 'thoughtless' move by the central government.

Although the Congress made demonetization a major polls issue since 2016, Modi convinced the citizens that he has worked for the country and not for himself. Modi tweeted, '125 crore Indians fought a decisive battle and WON. #AntiBlackMoneyDay' (8 November 2017). The people kept faith in Modi who said demonetization was done in the national interest, not for political gains.

## Second Political Tsunami: NaMo Wave II

Well before the 2019 elections were to be declared, the Opposition fortified its strategy and did not hesitate to use Modi's methodology, including using the 'Prashant Kishor strategy', and forged alliances even with the erstwhile political rivals such as Akhilesh Yadav and Mayawati. Priyanka Gandhi Vardra changed from jeans and top makeover to new saree-clad attire to compare with her grandmother late Indira Gandhi. Even the colour of sarees she wore had a resemblance to those commonly used by her grandmother.

The 2019 Lok Sabha elections were contested with ferocious competitiveness in the dusty bylanes of urban and rural India. The elections witnessed feisty fights in the supercharged atmosphere of social media platforms, Twitter and other networking sites. Conversations around #MainBhiChowkidar of the BJP and the NYAY scheme of the Congress gained momentum during the election period. National security, religion, jobs, agriculture, taxes and trade were the top five election conversations during the period. Of all, however, *chowkidar* has emerged as the most talked-about poll-related topic on all social media networks.

The word *chowkidar* was not only the most spoken word in public rallies by both the Congress and the BJP but also the top trending word on Twitter. In the Indian political discourse, the word has come to mean much more than its literal meaning since Modi used this after he became the prime minister in 2014. The Congress has since been trolling him. The slogan of *achhe din aayenge* (good times will come) was countered and the new punch line emerged: *Chowkidar chor hai* (watchman is a thief). Rahul Gandhi was repeating the slogan *chowkidar chor hai* at his rallies across the country, accusing the prime minister of being involved in irregularities in the Rafale deal which was the main cannon that misfired many salvos.

Countering Rahul's 'chowkidar chor hai' campaign, Modi tweeted 'Your Chowkidar is standing firm & serving the nation. But, I am not alone. Everyone who is fighting corruption, dirt, social evils is a Chowkidar. Everyone working hard for the progress of India is a Chowkidar. Today, every Indian is saying - #MainBhiChokidar' (15 March 2019). The very next day, he added the *chowkidar* as a prefix to his name on Twitter making it 'Chowkidar Narendra Modi'. Following his footsteps, the BJP president Amit Shah, Union Ministers Piyush Goyal, Suresh Prabhu, Harsh Vardhan, Dharmendra Pradhan and J. P. Nadda also added *chowkidar* as a prefix to their names on Twitter.

Data shows that both the hashtags #MainBhiChokidar and #ChowkidarPhirSe ruled Twitter on 16 and 17 March. While #MainBhiChokidar received around 1.5 million mentions on Twitter, #ChowkidarPhirSe received around three lakh mentions. The #ChowkidarChorHai received hardly 1.63 lakh mentions, which is about 10 per cent of the number of times #MainBhiChokidar got mentioned. The BJP provided fitting replies to Rahul Gandhi's allegations on Rafale, and, on 3 March, Modi blamed the Congress for delays in procuring Rafale aircraft which, he argued, led to a less than ideal response when Pakistani fighter aircraft bombed Indian soil on 27 February 2019. An Indian fighter plane was shot down and a pilot, Abhinandan Varthaman, was captured by Pakistan.[25]

---

[25] https://scroll.in/article/916924/chowkidar-narendra-modi-on-social-media-bjp-takes-congress-corruption-charges-head-on (accessed on 25 March 2019).

The Twitter battles were on. For calling him *shauchalaya ka chowkidar* (watchman of toilets), Modi hit out at the Congress saying, 'I wear their abuse as a badge of honor'. 'They said I do chowkidari of shauchalaya (toilets). They think they are insulting me but their gaali (abuse) in my gehna (ornament). For me, shauchalaya represents the honour of our mothers and sisters who do not have to face problems because of open defecation', the prime minister said while addressing a rally in Maharashtra.[26]

Taking a jibe at Modi, Delhi Chief Minister Arvind Kejriwal too criticized the prime minister on the *chowkidar* slogan and had asked the people to vote for the BJP only if they wanted to make their children a *chowkidar* and not doctors and engineers. While *chaiwala* or tea seller jibe against Modi from former minister and Congress leaders Mani Shankar Aiyar was the dominant theme in 2014, the *chowkidar* counter-offensive was the major narrative in the 2019 elections that ensured Modi to the PMO again. Remarks made by the ruling BJP and the opposition Congress and other parties on issues such as GST, Modi calling Rajiv Gandhi 'Bhrashtachaari No. 1' (corrupt no. 1) for his alleged involvement in the Bofors deal, Modi and the West Bengal chief minister's involvement in a verbal war over chants of 'Jai Shri Ram' during the campaign, all have been discussed extensively on the social media platforms. Modi could garner the best out of the worst ever criticism that he faced, and the mood of the nation has become clear.

As the exit polls showed Rahul Gandhi's slogan *chowkidar chor hai*, which refers to the Rafale jets controversy, did not resonate in the countryside, as rural Indians were more concerned about unemployment, inflation, farming distress and terrorism. The prediction by the exit polls suggested that the Congress got it all wrong and the issues like the NYAY, unemployment and alleged 'arrogance' of Prime Minister Modi raised by it during the election campaign failed to impress voters.[27]

[26] https://www.indiatoday.in/elections/lok-sabha-2019/story/pm-modi-in-maharashtra-chowkidar-of-toilets-1491143-2019-04-01 (accessed on 5 April 2019).

[27] https://economictimes.indiatimes.com/news/elections/lok-sabha/india/exit-polls-indicate-congress-issues-of-corruption-welfare-may-not-have-clicked/articleshow/69411897.cms?from=mdr

Social media was abuzz with status and tweets brimming with patriotism after the airstrikes on Balakot, Pakistan, on 27 February. Memes took the centre stage on many Facebook pages with hilarious taunts on Pakistan's poor defence mechanism. Hashtags such as #SurgicalStrike2, #IndiaStrikesBack, #JoshIsHigh and #ModiPunishesPak among others were seen trending on Twitter and Facebook. Many took to their Instagram handles as well as WhatsApp status to praise the efforts by the Indian Air Force.[28]

The airstrikes were turned into an occasion to showcase the personal bravado of Modi. During the election campaign in Ahmedabad in March, Modi said in reference to the Balakot airstrike, whose casualties were under dispute, 'It is my nature to avenge every wrongdoing' (Bhattacharjee 2019). The airstrike was turned into a hyper-masculine ethic of nationalism.

Like in 2014, Modi used Twitter to urge politicians cutting across parties, spiritual gurus, Bollywood stars, and badminton players to encourage high voter turnout. A tweet targeted at badminton players P. V. Sindhu, Saina Nehwal and Kidambi Srikanth read, 'The core of badminton is the court and the core of democracy is the vote. Just like you smash records, do also inspire a record-breaking voter turnout. I request you to increase voter awareness & motivate youth to vote in large numbers' (13 March 2019). Modi also focused his attention on Bollywood and his selfie with film stars on 10 January 2019 has become the selfie of the year (Figure 8.3). Young Bollywood stars flew from Mumbai to Delhi to meet the prime minister. A photograph taken with many of the celebrities had gone viral in all of the social media platforms. Two months after that meeting, on 14 March, Modi tagged everybody, Aamir Khan, Shah Rukh Khan, A. R. Rahman, Karan Johar and Akshay Kumar, in a series of tweets, urging them to encourage their fans to vote.

The NaMo app became a major campaign tool for the BJP. The party had used it for conducting a large-scale survey to assess the popularity and achievements of incumbent MPs, distributing ticket,

---

[28] https://timesofindia.indiatimes.com/city/patna/balakot-air-strikes-trending-on-social-media/articleshow/68175317.cms (accessed on 2 July 2019).

Figure 8.3 *Bollywood Stars with Prime Minister Narendra Modi in New Delhi on 10 January 2019*

*Source:* Narendra Modi's Facebook page.

allocating tasks to its members online instead of sending physical letters and circulars. With more than 10 million downloads since its launch in 2015, the NaMo app has turned into an open platform for ensuring large-scale citizen engagement, first-hand feedback and flow of the system for party workers. The app also provided key input to the BJP in finalizing its candidates for the elections. The party started selling Modi-branded merchandizes through the app.[29] NaMo branded saree and sweet stores also followed.

[29] https://m.economictimes.com/news/elections/lok-sabha/india/new-engagement-platform-namo-app-a-big-campaign-and-feedback-tool/article-show/68474625.cms (accessed on 25 March 2019).

Modi has not only led his party to a sensational victory in the 2019 Lok Sabha elections but also ruled the social media. As the BJP secured more than 300 seats, he tweeted: 'The people of India became Chowkidars and rendered great service to the nation. Chowkidar has become a powerful symbol to safeguard India from the evils of casteism, communalism, corruption and cronyism'. 'Now, the time has come to take the Chowkidar Spirit to the next level. Keep this spirit alive at every moment and continue working for India's progress. The word "Chowkidar" goes from my Twitter name but it remains an integral part of me. Urging you all to do the same too' (16 May 2019). The Opposition was stuck with the manipulation of EVMs that did not hold any water even on common sense as the exit polls predicted almost the same.

Modi thanked Indian voters and BJP workers for their hard work during the campaign by tweeting, 'Thank you India! The faith placed in our alliance is humbling and gives us strength to work even harder to fulfil people's aspirations. I salute every BJP Karyakarta for their determination, perseverance & hardwork. They went home to home, elaborating on our development agenda'. Throughout the election process, Modi was the most talked-about figure. Riding on a massive Modi wave sweeping through most parts of India, markets cheered, as the benchmark BSE Sensex touched 40,000 for the first time and NSE Nifty breached the 12,000 level. The rupee appreciated 14 paise to 69.51 against the US dollar.

## Dark Side of Social Media: Fake News and Abusiveness

Moving on the negative side of social media, one can see 'rampant pro-liferation of disinformation and hate speech' on social media networks (Muralidharan 2019). Jokes and cartoons on Rahul Gandhi, Sonia Gandhi, Mayawati and Modi were common features in all groups. Political parties who lost elections used social media to spread reports of electoral malpractice by the BJP to delegitimize its victory, although these charges remained unproven. 'Internet Hindu Warriors' posted anti-Muslim, anti-opposition tweets, morphed photos and videos, jokes and cartoons, which were then liked or retweeted. Thus, Twitter became not just an arena for circulating and endorsing official information on Modi but also a vast reservoir of half-truths and untruths, fake news, rumours and slander against Modi's opponents. Many people have been booked or arrested for 'insulting' Modi (Piyasree Dasgupta 2018). Many blame Modi's followers, who have emerged as a majoritarian, casteist troll army for inciting hatred of caste and religious minorities (Soundararajan 2018). Fake news and malicious campaigns were followed by both sides.

In view of fake news and bad happenings owing to social media, Modi urged the BJP workers to desist from spreading 'dirt' on social media, emphasizing that the issue was not about ideology but behaviour that did not indicate a decent society. During a video interaction with the BJP workers and volunteers from Varanasi, his Lok Sabha constituency, Modi said, 'It is about 125 crore Indians ... and everybody should train themselves to never spread dirt through social media'. 'The *swachhta abhiyan* or cleanliness drive is not just about sanitation but also about mental purity', he said and asked the people to share good things around them on social media.[30] In an interview to *The Times of India* on 12 August 2018, Modi said, 'I want to make it clear lynching is a crime, no matter the motive', and send a strong warning to the perpetrators of crime.

Despite the prime minister's appeal, social media is used to fan violence against minority religious and ethnic groups. Fake news sometimes even led to mob violence and lynching. Although Modi warned about lynching, it was alleged that the prime minister remained silent on nation-wide lynching and attacks on Muslims over alleged beef eating and cow slaughter. Further, our media sees every debate in the binary: 'Are you with Modi or against Modi?' The people who challenged Modi's actions on social media ended up being angrily branded as 'anti-national' or 'anti-Hindu, and sometimes subjected to vile threats (Chaturvedi 2017).

[30] https://www.thehindu.com/news/national/dont-spread-dirt-on-social-media-narendra-modi-tells-bjp-workers/article24812216.ece (accessed on 30 August 2018).

It is interesting that the entire print and electronic media went bi-polar with only a few exceptions. Many of the news channels were clearly divided into two groups: one pro-Modi and another anti-Modi. They expressed sentiments very sternly and some of them had to face consequences as well. The bi-polar division of media and intellectuals as well as public figures did not happen in Indian political history so sharply, as we can see today.

Journalists expressing anti-Modi views were extensively trolled. Journalist Swati Chaturvedi (2016) in her book *I am a Troll* exposed the role of trolling by the saffron party's cyber squads. The Uttar Pradesh police coerced journalist Prashant Kanojia who was arrested for allegedly tweeting a video of a woman claiming to be in a relationship with Uttar Pradesh Chief Minister Yogi Adityanath in June 2019. Later, with the intervention of the Supreme Court, the journalist was released.[31] Journalists took out a march to the Parliament in Delhi condemning the arrest of the journalist. *The Times of India* (13 June 2019) in its editorial termed the arrest of the journalist as an 'Assault on Media' and highlighted the authorities' failure to uphold the constitutional guarantees like the freedom of the press. *The Hindu* (12 June 2019) in its editorial 'Thin-Skinned Masters' said that arbitrary arrest for a social media post reflected a disregard for law and liberty. During the run-up to the 2019 elections, West Bengal police arrested a BJP youth-wing leader for a meme mocking Chief Minister Mamata Banerjee. Historian Ramachandra Guha, who posted a picture eating beef in the BJP ruled Goa on Twitter, received threatening phone calls. Soon after, Guha was targeted by right-wing trolls. Later, he deleted the photo.[32]

As we noted in the previous chapter, Modi indirectly wields influence on the media. Comedian Shyam Rangeela—whose video imitating Prime Minister Modi (with a mimicked version of Rahul Gandhi making a 'guest appearance') went viral on social media—has

---

[31] Ordering the release on bail of arrested journalist Prashant Kanojia, the Supreme Court observed that 'we are not appreciative of the manner of his tweets, but we are bothered about his arrest and incarceration' (Rajagopal 2019).

[32] https://www.thenewsminute.com/article/after-beef-tweet-historian-ramachandra-guha-allegedly-gets-threat-calls-93114 (accessed on 15 June 2019).

alleged that Star Plus, a leading Hindi-language television channel, refused to telecast his act on its reality show 'The Great Indian Laughter Challenge'.[33] It is believed that he was told that he could record his mimicry of Rahul Gandhi but not Modi. Multi-language actor Prakash Rai has not been offered a role by Bollywood since he started speaking out against Modi.[34]

As the Opposition argued, Modi, who could identify with Indians of all castes and classes, has been maintaining silence on the issues related to poverty, free press, judiciary and legislative processes and India's plural religious traditions. 'Modi's Twitter is unequivocally Hindu with few references to major non-Hindu religious holidays and no reference to non-Hindu religious figures' (Rao 2018, 11). The focus of his social media messages is on achieving prosperity and growth and not removing poverty. There are no photographs of poor people or Modi among the poor (Rao 2018). Modi sees India's national and political life as synonymous with a Hindu religious order and this was reflected in tweets related to gods, saints and seers. He never mentions about secularism in his tweets.

It is found that people had a difficult time differentiating correct information and 'fake news'. There were reports of vested interests using Facebook and WhatsApp to spread 'fake news' and tailored content to sway voters. In May and June 2018, more than 20 people were lynched based on fake posts or rumours floating on social media platforms, particularly on WhatsApp.[35] Owing to the seriousness of the issue, just before the 2019 Lok Sabha elections, the ECI convened a meeting with representatives of social media firms to try to find ways of how content on social networking sites and apps that violated the election code of conduct could be deleted. Facebook disabled more

[33] https://thewire.in/media/the-great-indian-laughter-challenge-narendra-modi-shyam-rangeela-akshay-kumar-rahul-gandhi-video (accessed on June 10 2018).

[34] https://theprint.in/politics/bollywood-hasnt-offered-a-role-since-i-spoke-against-modi-prakash-raj/55059/ (accessed on 10 March 2018).

[35] https://www.thehindu.com/opinion/op-ed/should-whatsapp-be-held-accountable-for-lynchings/article24463841.ece (accessed on 20 July 2018).

than two billion fake accounts worldwide in May 2019.[36] Although the companies owning these digital platforms did take some steps in this direction, it was too late then.

WhatsApp functioned as a conduit for hoaxes and jokes. In June 2016, fake news broke out on WhatsApp groups, and other social media, that the UN cultural agency had awarded Prime Minister Modi the title of 'best prime minister in the world'. Another fake news claiming that UNESCO has declared India's national anthem, 'Jana Gana Mana', the 'Best National Anthem in the World' has gone viral. The fake message that the RBI had declared the ₹10 coin invalid spread through WhatsApp in 2016.[37] Hopefully, over time, people will learn to take responsibility for what they share on social media.

It is also argued that social media such as Facebook no longer remained unbiased media network. Facebook co-founder Mark Zuckerberg met Modi on a couple of occasions both in the USA and in India, and this made many to believe that it became a platform for the country's ruling party (BJP) that has huge resources to spend on disseminating its propaganda. Sam and Thakurta (2019) explain, 'How Facebook is distorting democracy in India'. They show that Facebook and its companion platforms, WhatsApp and Instagram, are promoting the interests of the country's ruling BJP and augmenting its own right-wing majoritarian agenda' (xxii–xxiii). The opposition parties, including Trinamool Congress, has accused Facebook of being 'de facto' campaigner of the BJP in the 2019 elections. TMC leader and MP Derek O'Brien told the Parliament that 'Facebook censored anti-BJP content and its Delhi office was an extension of the BJP IT cell'.[38] The issue assumed importance because, in 2018, the CBI instituted a preliminary inquiry to determine whether the UK-based

[36] https://timesofindia.indiatimes.com/business/international-business/why-the-world-that-you-are-living-in-feels-so-fake/articleshow/69749654.cms (accessed on 12 June 2019).

[37] https://www.indiatoday.in/india/story/top-ten-fake-news-that-we-almost-believed-in-2016-modi-best-pm-declared-unesco-359619-2016-12-26 (accessed on 28 December 2016).

[38] https://www.thehindu.com/news/national/fb-censored-anti-bjp-posts-derek-obrien/article28137506.ece (accessed on 27 June 2019).

Global Science Research and Cambridge Analytica illegally harvested and misused the data of Indian Facebook users. Therefore, one can safely conclude that social media is a double-edged sword.

However, contrary to reports of the BJP using its strong social media presence to improve its performance in the 2019 general election, the Delhi-based Centre for the Study of Developing Societies and Lokniti survey report highlighted the limited role of social media as a key influencing factor for voting choices in the elections. It said that the BJP's vote share lead over the main opposition Congress among social media users was actually lower than 2014. Although the survey did establish a relationship between social media usage and BJP voters, showing that voters with high exposure to social media were most likely to have voted for the saffron party, with the BJP's vote share dropping among those with low or no exposure. However, it also stated that voters with high exposure account for only one-tenth of the electorate, while those with no exposure make up 64 per cent. The study highlights that the BJP would have won the 2019 elections even if social media was taken out of the equation. In fact, the BJP's social media advantage over its principal rival, the Congress, actually declined between 2014 and 2019.[39]

In general, one can safely conclude that the social media played an important role in the BJP's victory in the 2014 and 2019 general elections, although it's only a part of the overall strategy. After Modi's victory, all political parties and leaders started embracing social media tools for projecting their images and political campaigning. Of all parties, the BJP extensively used social media by forming teams comprised of IT experts and enchased its potential for reaching out to the middle class and youth. Social media brings down walls between leaders and the electorate. It emerged as a platform to question and criticize the ruling leaders of the country.

After the victory, Modi continues to use social media and e-governance tools to engage citizens in the administration. Social

---

[39] https://www.thehindu.com/news/national/role-of-social-media-as-influencer-of-voting-choices-overhyped-csds-study/article27819723.ece (accessed on 15 June 2019).

media has become a source of information for the government; Modi uses his app and other tools to inform the public about the government's policies. Social media tools are also used to gather citizens' viewpoints and opinions on political manifestoes, budget and other policy matters. Modi's marketing techniques during elections have become case studies in several universities and business schools, and students have been studying how digital marketing may create such a big effect. The moot question is how far citizens' viewpoints and opinions feed into policymaking. This needs to be investigated. Moreover, further research is required to test the effectiveness of Modi's social strategy in the election campaigns as well as in governance. This research has provided some insights into the relevance of social media in the election campaigns as well in the delivery of services. Going forward, with significant digital divide in India, we believe that further research is needed to study the growth of online and social media and their role in shaping political preferences in national elections in India.

# Epilogue

Indian political process underwent a sea change after liberalization and new market forces entering the scenario. A huge swarm of young professionals as voters emerged due to demographic dividend and new opportunities. This class of new voters included the educated middle class, young professionals with strong aspirations for the process of statecraft, clean governance and new emerging nationalism. It required a political acumen to trap their aspirations and no other political leader in modern India identified these aspirations of the emerging middle class other than the BJP's prime-ministerial candidate for the 2014 elections, Narendra Modi.

Modi identified himself with the full understanding of taste, temper and temptations of the middle class which has grown enormously over the years and have started exercising the political clout. He caught up with the tune of the present Indian social moorings and cultural trades. Very imaginatively, he plugged the middle classes' desperate bid for good governance, edgy nationalism and anger against rampant corruption in public. This class admired his distinctive oratory, the pauses, mannerism and the unique left-hand clap, besides his immaculate wardrobe.

The middle class as well as the general public viewed Modi as an admirable and strong leader, wise, clever and good strategist, humble, Hindu, non-corruptible nationalist, and a hard-working candidate for prime ministership. They saw in him an effective believable leader, a nationalist who defends Mother India against enemies both within and outside. The concoction was apt and voters en masse were eager for change to better governance for good development. This fish-net was attractive enough to get unprecedented haul of new voters.

The success of Modi's right-wing narrative was endeared by the middle class in the parliamentary elections of 2014 and 2019, and subsequent several elections to sub-national governments. The middle class welcomed economic reforms unleashed by Modi as the chief minister of Gujarat for 12 long years and later as the prime minister of India. The liberalization of the Indian economy unleashed materialism after decades of state-controlled economy; people have come to accept the fact that they don't really bother about religious tolerance or privatization as drivers of the economy as long as politicians expedite economic growth and enable the market-led consumerism. Modi understood the trends in the global economic pattern well, embraced social media ahead of other leaders and positioned himself as a man who delivers without compromising the national interest. He demonstrated a body language that evoked confidence among the voters, and they even sustained changes such as demonetization, implementation of GST, one rank, one pension for retired armed forces personnel, direct benefit transfer, constitutional status to OBC Commission, abolition of Article 370 and 35A, abolition of triple talaq, implementation of the Citizenship (Amendment) Act, 2019, despite the opposition's inexplicable resistance. One nation, one flag, and one Constitution became a reality under the Modi government.

In the 2019 elections, Narendra Modi wrested a powerful victory for the BJP through countless meetings, rallies and speeches, and has acquired a global profile. His presence in electioneering across the length and breadth of the country by far surpassed his political opponents. He has been one of the most talked-about leaders around the world. The successive second term for the prime minister underscores that middle-class people willingly endorsed his policies. And they backed the most criticized GST and demonetization decisions by giving unparalleled mandate in Uttar Pradesh and in subsequent assembly polls. It is clear that the middle class stood rock solid behind his policies. All exit poll surveys, from the big cities to the urbanizing states, vindicated that the middle classes voted overwhelmingly for the BJP, particularly in the last two general elections.

The 2019 election was marked by deep Hindu nationalist narratives and a massive advertisement blitz. Modi managed to project the Congress as a 'ma–beta party' that was appeasing the minorities, soft towards Pakistan-based terror and obstructing the majoritarian Hindu nationalist interests, values and sentiments. The BJP succeeded in making inroads in West Bengal and north-eastern states by imploding the middle-class sentiments aided by aggressive coverage in the media. One must acknowledge the elections verdict as an endorsement of middle-class aspirations. If the 16th general elections catapulted the BJP as the primary pole of Indian politics, the 2019 elections established it firmly as an overarching hegemon.[1] The voters felt that there was no alternative to Modi. The election verdict will make the government more stable and stronger in the days to come.

Modi spelled out his mission to build a new India by envisaging development of all sections of the people across the nation (*sabka saath, sabka vikas, sabka vishwas*). Without some understanding of events that unfolded during the last three decades or so, it would be wrong to judge the political scenario merely through media commentaries or reports. Modi has been very frequently communicating his ideas to the people of the country through social media. He also often communicates through huge political rallies that are televised. He speaks fluently in Hindi and English. Whether it is his monthly radio programme, *Mann Ki Baat*, Twitter or Facebook messages and photographs, the prime minister is an amazingly effective communicator. Social media is the primary tool for communication for almost all ministers in Modi 2.0. All the cabinet ministers have Twitter accounts. He does not fumble in vocabulary and radiates the confidence that the middle-class voters anxiously look for.

The Modi government showed the commitment to the principle of 'reform, perform and transform' and achieved some goals up to last-mile delivery during his first tenure. People are hoping that many big-ticket programmes and services that were initiated and delivered during 2014–2019 will be further accelerated by simplifying procedures, incentivizing performance, cracking corruption and making the best use of technology. The first budget (2019–2020) of the Modi 2.0 presented by Finance Minister Nirmala Sitharaman spelled out various initiatives and allocated funds to tackle several

---

[1] https://www.thehindu.com/opinion/editorial/for-a-rediscovery-of-india/article27226762.ece (accessed on 1 June 2019).

chronic issues in the economy through incremental steps, instead of opting for a spectacular announcement route. The budget had many announcements that could benefit the middle-class income earners, particularly the buyers of affordable houses. The government has listed infrastructure development as one of the top priorities that will benefit the middle class in the long run.

While 2014 was a mandate for hope and aspiration, the 2019 mandate is about confidence and acceleration (Kalra, Diwakar, and Deshpande 2019). In the first term, Modi consolidated his position; in his second term, he is implementing long-pending agendas of the party: abrogation of Article 370, the Citizenship (Amendment) Act, 2019, and the construction of the Ram temple at Ayodhya. After his second consecutive victory, and a bigger mandate, Modi is even stronger and everything now is in his control. The Opposition, indeed, is in a state of disrepair.

Politics apart, we hope that the Modi government will identify specific areas to focus in the economy to tackle the bottlenecks to India's growth and accelerate it to drive the country's development journey towards becoming a global leader. The opportunity is ripe for now to use the available prowess for transforming the Indian economy into a $5 trillion economy and lift millions of people out of poverty. If he can pull this off, he would surely go down in history as one the strongest leaders the country has seen.

# Bibliography

Advani, L. K. 2008. *My Country My Life*. New Delhi: Rupa & Co.

Ahmad, Aijaz. 2019. 'India: Liberal Democracy and the Extreme Right'. *Frontline*, 7 June, 14–26.

Ahmad, Faizan. 2014. 'Those Opposed to Narendra Modi Should Go to Pakistan, BJP Leader Giriraj Singh Says'. *The Times of India*, 20 April. Available at https://timesofindia.indiatimes.com/news/Those-opposed-to-Narendra-Modi-should-go-to-Pakistan-BJP-leader-Giriraj-Singh-says/articleshow/33971544.cms

Ahmad, Imtiaz, and Helmut Reifeld. 2001. 'Introduction'. In *Middle Class Values in India and Western Europe*, edited by Imtiaz Ahmad and Helmut Reifeld, 1–17. New Delhi: Konard Adenauer Foundation, Social Sciences.

Aji, Sowmy. 2015. 'I was India's First OBC PM, Not Narendra Modi: H. D. Deve Gowda'. *The Economic Times*, 13 July. Available at https://economictimes.indiatimes.com/news/politics-and-nation/i-was-indias-first-obc-pm-not-narendra-modi-h-d-deve-gowda/articleshow/48047326.cms

Ali, Idrees. 2014. 'Social Media Played Big Role in India's Election'. *Voice of America*, 6 June. Available at https://www.voanews.com/silicon-valley-technology/social-media-played-big-role-indias-election

Amoranto, Glenita, Natalie Chun, and Anil Deolalikar. 2010. 'Who are the Middle Class and What Values do They Hold? Evidence from the World Values Survey'. ADB Economics Working Paper Series, No. 229. Available at http://library.umac.mo/e_resources/org_publications/b17697098.pdf

Andersen, Walter K., and Shridhar D. Damle. 2018. *The RSS: A View to the Inside*. Gurgaon: Penguin/Viking.

Aristotle. 1999. *Politics*. Translated by Benjamin Jowett. Kitchener: Batoche Books. Available at https://socialsciences.mcmaster.ca/econ/ugcm/3ll3/aristotle/Politics.pdf

Asha, K., and Usha Rani N. 2014. Usage of Social Media in the 2014 Indian General Elections: A Review of Modi Factor and IT Czar's Digital Trail. *Journal of Media and Social Development* 2 (2): 18–22.

Atterberry, Adrienne. 2012. *Nationalism on the Net: Exploring the Ideology of India's Bharatiya Janata Party*. Media Studies thesis 11, Lee Syracuse University. Available at https://surface.syr.edu/cgi/viewcontent.cgi?article=1010&context=ms_thesis

Austin, Granville. 1966. *The Indian Constitution: Cornerstone of a Nation*. New Delhi: Oxford University Press.

Awasthi, Dilip. 1992. 'Ayodhya: The Final Countdown'. *India Today*, New Delhi, 31 July.

Balakrishnan, Pulapre. 2007. 'The Recovery of India: Economic Growth in the Nehru Era'. *Economic and Political Weekly* 42 (45–46): 52–66.

Banerjee, A., and E. Duflo. 2011. *Poor Economics: A Radical Rethinking of the Way to Fight Global Poverty.* New York, NY: PublicAffairs.

Banerjee, A., and E. Duflo. 2008. 'What is Middle Class about the Middle Classes around the World?' *The Journal of Economic Perspectives* 22 (2): 3–28.

Banerjee, Sumanta. 1991. 'Hindutva: Ideology and Social Psychology'. *Economic and Political Weekly* 26 (3): 85–97.

Barro, Robert, J. 1999. 'Determinants of Democracy'. *Journal of Political Economy* 107 (6), 158–183.

Baru. Sanjaya. 2014. *The Accidental Prime Minister: The Making of Manmohan Singh.* New Delhi: Penguin.

Basu, Amrita, and Atul Kohli. 1998. *Community Conflicts and the State in India.* New York: Oxford University Press.

Basu, Kaushik. 2004. *India's Engaging Economy: Performance and Prospects in the 1990s and Beyond.* New Delhi: Oxford University Press.

Baviskar, Amita, and Raka Ray. 2016. *Elite and Everyman: The Cultural Politics of the Indian Middle Class.* New Delhi: Routledge.

Baviskar, Amita. 2009. 'Breaking Homes, Making Cities: Class and Gender in the Politics of Urban Development'. In *Displaced by Development, Confronting Marginalisation and Gender Injustice*, edited by Lyla Mehta, 59–81. New Delhi: SAGE Publications.

———. 2016. 'Cows, Cars and Cycle-Rickshaws: Bourgeois Environmentalists and the Battle for Delhi's Streets', In *Elite and Everyman. The Cultural Politics of the Indian Middle Classes*, edited by Amita Baviskar and Raka Ray, 391–318. New Delhi: Routledge.

Bayly, Christopher Alan. 2012. Development and Sentiment: Sarvepalli Gopal and the Political Thought of Nehru's India. First Dr S Gopal Annual Memorial Lecture, delivered at King's College, London.

Beteille, Andre. 2001. 'The Social Character of the Indian Middle Class'. In *Middle Class Values in India and Western Europe*, edited by Imtiaz Ahmad and Helmut Reifeld, 73–85. New Delhi: Konard Adenauer Foundation.

———. 2002. 'Hierarchical and Competitive Inequality'. *Sociological Bulletin* 51 (1): 3–27.

———. 2007. 'Classes and Communities'. *Economic and Political Weekly* 42 (11): 945–952.

Bhaduri, Soham. 2019. 'By Right or by Policy'. *Deccan Herald*, Bengaluru, 24 April.

Bhalla, Surjit S. 2007. The Middle Class Kingdoms of India and China. Washington, DC: Peterson Institute for International Economics.

Bhardwaj, Anjali, and Amrita Johri. 2019. 'The Government's Anti-Corruption Scorecard'. *The Hindu*, Chennai, April 29.

Bhatnagar, Gaurav Vivek, and Smriti Kak Ramachandran. 2014. 'Mani Shankar Takes Flak for "Tea Seller" Jibe at Modi'. *The Hindu*, 18 January.

Bhatt, C., and P. Mukta. 2000. 'Hindutva in the West: Mapping the Antinomies of Diaspora Nationalism'. *Ethnic and Racial Studies* 23(3), 407–411.

Bhattacharjee, Manash Firaq. 2019. 'Modi Battling for Modi'. *The Wire*, May 2. https://thewire.in/politics/modi-battling-for-modi

Bhattacharya, Amitabha. 2018. 'Reforming the Civil Services'. *The Hindu*, Chennai, 9 August.

Bhattacharya, Ananya. 2018. 'India's Phenomenal Mobile Manufacturing Boom in One Chart'. *Quartz India*, 13 July. Available at https://qz.com/india/1326969/mobile-manufacturing-units-in-india-have-jumped-60-fold-under-narendra-modi/

Bhattacharya, D. P. 2012. 'Modi Rides High on Development in Gujarat, New Delhi Doesn't Seem Far Now'. *India Today*, Ahmedabad, 21 December. Available at https://www.indiatoday.in/gujarat-assembly-elections-2012/story/gujarat-assembly-poll-2012-narendra-modi-wins-hat-trick-124888-2012-12-21

Bhattacharya, Malini. 2005. 'Culture'. In *The Changing Status of Women in West Bengal, 1970–2000: The Challenge Ahead*, edited by Jasodhara Bagchi, 186–192. New Delhi: SAGE Publications.

Bhishkar, C. P. 2014. *Pt. Deendayal Upadhyaya Ideology & Perception. Part 5: Concept of The Rashtra*. New Delhi: Suruchi Prakashan.

Birdsall, N. 2010. 'The (Indispensable) Middle Class: Or, Why It's the Rich and the Rest, Not the Poor and the Rest'. Working Paper 207, Center for Global Development, Washington, DC.

Birdsall, N., Carol Graham, and Stefano Pettinato. 2000. 'Stuck in the Tunnel: Is Globalization Muddling the Middle Class?' Working Paper No. 14, Center on Social and Economic Dynamics.

Birdsall, N., N. Lustig, and C. Meyer. 2013. 'The Strugglers: The New Poor in Latin America?' Center for Global Development Working Paper, Center for Global Development, Washington, DC.

Bjorkman, J. W. 1980. 'Public Law 480 and the Policies of Self-Help and Short-Tether: Indo-American Relations, 1965–80'. In *The Regional Imperative: The Administration of the US Foreign Policy Towards South Asian States under Presidents Johnson and Nixon*, edited by Lloyd I. Rudolph and Susanne Hoeber Rudolph. New Delhi: Concept.

BJP. 2014. *Election Manifesto*. New Delhi: BJP.

———. 2019. *Sankalp Patra, Lok Sabha 2019*. New Delhi: BJP.

Blau, Peter, and Otis Duncan. 1967. *The American Occupational Structure*. New York: Wiley.

Bose, Mihir. 1999. '1960's: India's Changing Phase'. *India Today*, 30 November.

Bose, Prasenjit. 2018. 'A Bank Merged that will Not Pay Off'. The *Business Line*, Chennai, 26 September.

Bottomore, T. B. 1965. *Classes in Modern Society*. London: Allen and Unwin.

Bourdieu, Pierre, Alain Accardo, and Susan Emanuel. 1999. *The Weight of the World: Social Suffering in Contemporary Society*. California: Stanford University Press. Available at http://voidnetwork.gr/wp-content/uploads/2016/08/The-Weight-of-the-World-Social-Suffering-in-Contemporary-Society-by-Pierre-Bourdieu-and-others.pdf

Bourdieu, Pierre. 1996. *Distinction: A Social Critique of the Judgement of Taste*. Translated by Richard Nice. Cambridge, MA: Harvard University Press.

Brandi, C., and M. Buge. 2014. 'A Cartography of the New Middle Classes in Developing and Emerging Countries'. Discussion Paper 35, German Development Institute.

Brass, Paul. 1980. 'The Politicization of Peasantry in a North Indian State: I & II'. *Journal of Peasant Studies* 7–8 (4–1): 395–426, 3–36.

———. 1984. *Caste Faction and Party in Indian Politics*. New Delhi: Chanakya.

Braverman, Harry. 1974. *Labor and Monopoly Capital: The Degradation of Work in the Twentieth Century*. New York: Monthly Review Press.

Bremmer, Ian. 2019. 'Modi is India's Best Hope for Economic Reform'. *TIME*, 9 May.

Brosius, Christiane. 2010. *India's Middle Class: New Forms of Urban Leisure, Consumption and Prosperity*. New Delhi: Routledge.

Bunsha, Dionne. 2002. 'The Modi Road Show'. *Frontline* 19 (21). Available at https://frontline.thehindu.com/static/html/fl1921/stories/20021025006900900.htm

Burke, Jason. 2014. 'Narendra Modi: India's Saviour or its Worst Nightmare?' *The Guardian*, 6 March. https://www.theguardian.com/world/2014/mar/06/narendra-modi-india-bjp-leader-elections

Burris, Val. 1986. 'The Discovery of the New Middle Class'. *Theory and Society* 15 (3): 317–349.

Burrows, Mathew. 2015. 'The Emerging Global Middle Class, So What?' *The Washington Quarterly* 38 (1): 7–22.

Carchedi, G. 1977. *The Economic Identification of Social Classes*. London: Routledge & Kegan Paul.

Carter, Bob. 1985. *Capitalism, Class Conflict, and the New Middle Class*. London: Routledge & Kegan Paul.

Chakrabarti, Dalia. 2010. 'D.P. Mukerji and the Middle Class in India'. *Sociological Bulletin, Indian Sociological Society* 59 (2): 235–255.

Chakraborty, Sunandan, Joyojeet Pal, Priyank Chandra, and Daniel M. Romero. 2018. 'Political Tweets and Mainstream News Impact in India: A Mixed Methods Investigation into Political Outreach'. Available at http://www.priyankc.com/files/chandra_p10.pdf

Chakravartty, Paula, and Srirupa Roy. 2015. 'Mr Modi Goes to Delhi: Mediated Populism and the 2014 Indian Elections'. *Television & New Media* 16 (4): 311–322.

Chancel, Lucas, and Thomas Piketty. 2017. 'Indian Income Inequality, 1922–2015: From British Raj to Billionaire Raj?' Working Paper Series

2017/11, World Equality Lab. Available at https://wid.world/document/chancelpiketty2017widworld/

Chandra, Bipan. 1984. *Communalism in Modern India*. New Delhi: Vikas.

Chatterjee, Partha. 1992. 'A Religion of Urban Domesticity: Sri Ramakrishna Calcutta Middle Class'. In *Subaltern Studies VII: Writings on South Asian History and Society*, edited by Partha Chatterjee and Gyanendra Pandey. Delhi: Oxford University Press.

———. 1993. *The Nation and its Fragments: Colonial and Postcolonial Histories*. Princeton, NJ: Princeton University Press.

———. 1994. *Nation and its Fragments: Colonial and Post-Colonial World*. New Delhi: Oxford University Press.

———. 2003. 'Are Indian Cities Becoming Bourgeois at Last?' In *Body. City: Siting Contemporary Culture in India, 170–85*, edited by Indira Chandrashekhar and Peter C. Seel. New Delhi: Tulika Books.

Chatterji, Joya. 2002. *Bengal Divided: Hindu Communalism and Partition, 1932–47*. Cambridge: Cambridge University Press.

Chaturvedi, Swati. 2016. *I Am a Troll: Inside the Secret World of the BJP's Digital Army*. New Delhi: Juggernaut Books.

———. 2017. 'General Narendra Modi and His Troll Army'. *The Wire*, 8 September. https://thewire.in/politics/narendra-modi-twitter-trolls-free-expression

Chawla, Navin. 2019. *Every Vote Counts: The Story of India's Elections*. Noida: HarperCollins Publishers.

Chawla, Prabhu. 1988. 'Rajiv Gandhi Government Withdraws Infamous Defamation Bill'. *India Today*, 15 October. Available at https://www.india-today.in/magazine/special-report/story/19881015-rajiv-gandhi-government-withdraws-infamous-defamation-bill-797786-1988-10-15

Chengappa, Raj. 2019a. 'The Republic of Modi'. *India Today*, 3 June.

———. 2019b. 'The Decade in Review'. *India Today*, 23 December.

Chhibber, Pradeep, and Rahul Verma. 2014. 'The BJP's 2014 Modi Wave: An Ideological Consolidation of the Right'. *Economic and Political Weekly* 49 (39): 50–56.

Chhibber, Pradeep. 1997. 'Who Voted for the Bharatiya Janata Party?' *British Journal Political Science* 27 (04), 619–659.

Chibber, Vivek. 2003. *Locked in Place: State-Building and Late Industrialization in India*. Princeton, NJ: Princeton University Press.

Chitkara, M. G. 2003. *Hindutva Parivar*. Delhi: APH Publishing Corporation.

Chitra, Rachel. 2018. 'Bengaluru has 3rd Most Startups Globally'. *The Times of India*, Bengaluru, 26 October.

Chopra, R. 2006. 'Global Primordialities: Virtual Identity Politics in Online Hindutva and Online Dalit Discourse'. *New Media Society* 8 (2): 187–206.

Chowdhury, Amirta Basu Roy. 2016. 'Globalization, and the rise of NMC: Construction of New Gender roles in Bengali Print Advertisement, 1991–2010'. A paper presented at seminar on *The Middle Class in World Society*, Institute for Social and Economic Change, Bengaluru, December 16–17.

Chowdhury, Prasenjit. 2018. 'Act, before It's too Late'. *Deccan Herald*, Bengaluru, 7 August. Available at https://www.deccanherald.com/opinion/main-article/a-huge-step-backward-752309.html

Cohen, S. 2002. *India, Emerging Power*. New Delhi: Oxford University Press.

Colvin, Ross, and Satarupa Bhattacharjya. 2013. 'Special Report: The Remaking of Narendra Modi'. *Reuters*, July 12. Available at https://in.reuters.com/article/india-modi-gujarat-bjp/special-report-the-remaking-of-narendra-modi-idINDEE96B00Y20130712

Corbridge, Stuart, and John Harriss. 2000. *Reinventing India: Liberalization, Hindu Nationalism and Popular Democracy*. New Delhi: Oxford University Press.

Corey, Lewis. 1935. *The Crisis of the Middle Class*. New York: Cevici Friede.

Crawford, Gordon. 2006. 'The World Bank and Good Governance: Rethinking the State or Consolidating Neo-Liberalism?' In *The IMF, World Bank and Policy Reform*, edited by Alberto Paloni and Maurizio Zanardi. London: Routledge.

Dahl, R. A. 1971. *Polyarchy: Participation and Opposition*. New Haven: Yale University Press.

Dahrendorf, R. 1959. *Class and Class Conflict in Industrial Society*. London: Routeldge & Kegan Paul.

Damodaran, Harish. 2014. 'Modi and the New-Middle Class'. *The Hindu Business Line*, Chennai, 25 May. Available at https://www.thehindubusinessline.com/opinion/columns/harish-damodaran/modi-and-the-neo-middle-class/article20780912.ece1

Dandekar, V. M. 1998. 'Nature of Class Conflict in Indian Society'. In *Contemporary India: G R Bhatkal Memorial Lecturers 1975–95*, edited by Sadanand Bhatkal, 39–69. Bombay: Popular Prakashan.

Das, Ankhi, 2014. 'How "Likes" Bring Votes: Narendra Modi's Campaign on Facebook'. *Scroll.in*, 19 May. Available at https://scroll.in/article/664756/how-likes-bring-votes-narendra-modis-campaign-on-facebook

Das, Gurcharan. 2002. *India Unbound*. New Delhi: Viking.

Das, Shaswati, and Alekh Archana. 2018. 'Rotomac Bank Fraud: CBI Files FIR Against Scam Worth ₹3695 Crore'. *Live Mint*, New Delhi, 20 February.

Dasgupta, Piyasree. 2018. 'What Happens to the People Arrested for Insulting Modi?' *Huffington Post*, 13 February. Available at https://www.huffingtonpost.in/2018/04/23/what-happens-to-the-people-arrested-for-insulting-modi_a_23417412/

Dasgupta, Swapan. 2012. 'A Half-Turn in History'. *Outlook*, 17 December.

———. 2018. 'The Modi Phenomenon'. *Seminar*. Available at https://www.india-seminar.com/2008/581/581_swapan_dasgupta.htm

Davis, Richard, H. 1996. 'The Iconography of Rama's Chariot'. In *Making India Hindu: Religion, Community, and the Politics of Democracy in India*, edited by David Ludden. Delhi: Oxford University Press.

Desai, A. R. 1981. *Social Background of Indian Nationalism*. Bombay: Popular Prakashan.

Desai, Meghnad. 2016. 'India as Hindu Nation–and Other Ideas of India'. In *Making Sense of Modi's India*, edited by Hasan Suroor, 7–22. New Delhi: HarperCollins Publishers India

Desai, Radhika. 2002. *Hindutva's Gujarat: The Image of India's Future, Slouching towards Ayodhya*. New Delhi: Three Essays Press.

———. 2016. 'The Question of Fascism'. In *Making Sense of Modi's India*, edited by Hasan Suroor, 56–79. New Delhi: HarperCollins Publishers India.

Deshpande, R. 2019. 'Gender Wise Politics: To What Extent Did Women's Vote Contribute to the BJP's Spectacular Victory?' In *The Times of India*, 18 July. Available at https://timesofindia.indiatimes.com/blogs/toi-edit-page/gender-wise-politics-to-what-extent-did-womens-vote-contribute-to-the-bjps-spectacular-victory/ (accessed on 16 January 2020).

Deshpande, Satish. 2003. *Contemporary India: A Sociological View*. New Delhi: Penguin Books.

Dev, Nirendra. 2012. *Modi to Moditva: An Uncensored Truth*. New Delhi: Manas Publications.

Dobbin, Christine. 1972. *Urban Leadership in Western India: Politics and Communities in Bombay City 1840–1885*. New York: Oxford University Press.

Donner, Henrike. 2008. *Domestic Goddesses: Maternity, Globalization and Middle-Class Identity in Contemporary India*. Aldershot: Ashgate.

Donthi, Praveen. 2019. 'How ANI Reports Government's Version of Truth'. *The Carvan*, March.

Dorschner, John P. 2015. 'The Myth of the Indian Middle Class'. *American Diplomacy*. Available at http://americandiplomacy.web.unc.edu/2015/09/the-myth-of-the-indian-middle-class/

Dubey, S. 1992: 'The Middle Class'. In *India Briefing 1992*, edited by L. Gordon and P. Oldenburg, 137–164. Boulder: Westview and the Asia Society.

Dugger , Celia W. 2002. 'Religious Riots Loom Over Indian Politics'. *The New York Times*, 27 July. Available at https://www.nytimes.com/2002/07/27/world/religious-riots-loom-over-indian-politics.html

Durant, Will. 1930. *The Case for India*. New York: Simon & Schuster. (Re-issued in a limited edition by Stand Book Stall, Mumbai.)

Dutt, R. C. 1950. *The Economic History of India under Early British Rule: From the Rise of the British Power in 1757 to the Accession of Queen Victoria in 1837*. New Delhi: Routledge.

Dutta, Prabash K. 2018. 'Demonetisation: What India Gained, and Lost'. *India Today*, 30 August. Available at https://www.indiatoday.in/india/story/demonetisation-what-india-gained-and-lost-1327502-2018-08-30

Dutta, Sagnik. 2013. 'Trending Modi'. *Frontline*, 17 May. Available at https://frontline.thehindu.com/cover-story/trending-modi/article4669744.ece

Easterly, W. 2001. 'The Middle Class Consensus and Economic Development'. *Journal of Economic Growth* 6 (4): 317–335.

Easterly, W., and R. Levine. 2001. 'What have We Learned from a Decade of Empirical Research on Growth? It's Not Factor Accumulation: Stylized Facts and Growth Models'. *World Bank Economic Review* 15 (2): 177–219.

Echeverri-Gent, John. 2002. 'Politics in India's Decentered Polity'. In *India Briefing: Quickening the Pace of Change*, edited by Alyssa Ayres and Philip Oldenburg. New York: M. E. Sharpe.

Ehrenreich, B., and J. Ehrenreich. 1979. 'The Professional Managerial Class'. In *Between Labor and Capital*, edited by P. Walker, 5–45. New York: South End Press.

Elst, Koenraad. 2001. *The Saffron Swastika: The Notion of Hindu Fascism*. New Delhi: Voice of India.

Engineer, Asghar Ali. 1991. 'Communal Riots Before, During and After Lok Sabha Elections'. *Economic and Political Weekly* 26 (37): 2135–2138.

Erikson, Robert, and John H. Goldthorpe. 1992. *The Constant Flux: A Study of Class Mobility in Industrial Societies*. New York: Oxford University Press.

Ernst & Young, 2013. *Hitting the Sweet Spot: The Growth of the Middle Class in Emerging Markets*. London: Ernst & Young. Available at https://www.ey.com/Publication/vwLUAssets/Hitting_the_sweet_spot/%24FILE/Hitting_the_sweet_spot.pdf

Farooqui, Adnan, and E. Sridharan. 2016. 'Can Umbrella Parties Survive? The Decline of the Indian National Congress'. *Commonwealth and Comparative Politics* 54 (3): 331–361.

Farrell, Diana, and Eric Beinhocker. 2007. 'Next Big Spenders: India's Middle Class'. McKinsey Global Institute, 19 May. Available at https://www.mckinsey.com/mgi/overview/in-the-news/next-big-spenders-indian-middle-class

Fernandes, Leela. 2000. 'Restructuring the New Middle Class in Liberalising India'. *Comparative Studies of South Asia, Africa and the Middle East* 20 (1): 88–104.

———. 2004. 'The Politics of Forgetting: Class Politics, State Power and the Restructuring of Urban Space in India'. *Urban Studies* 41 (12): 2415–2430.

———. 2006. *India's New Middle Class: Democratic Politics in an Era of Economic Reform*. London: University of Minnesota Press.

Ferreira, F. H. G., J. Messina, J. Rigolini, L.-F. Lopez-Calva, M. A. Lugo, and R. Vakis. 2013. *Economic Mobility and the Rise of the Latin American Middle Class*. Washington, DC: World Bank. Available at https://www.lampadia.com/assets/uploads_documentos/467a3-english-report-midclass.pdf

Fletcher, P. 2013. 'Africa's Emerging Middle Class Drives Growth and Democracy'. *Reuters*, 10 May. Available at www.reuters.com/article/us-africa-investment-idUSBRE9490DV20130510

Frank, Robert H., and Philip J. Cook. 1995. *The Winner-Take-All Society*. New York: The Free Press.

Frankel, R. Francine. 1988. 'Middle Class and Castes in India's Politics: Prospect for Political Accommodation'. In *India's Democracy: An Analysis of Changing State–Society Relations*, edited by Atul Kohli. New Delhi: Orient Longman.

Freitag, Sandria B. 1989. *Collective Action and Community: Public Arenas and the Emergence of Communalism in North India*. Berkeley, CA: University of California Press.

Fukuyama, F. 1993. 'Capitalism and Democracy: The Missing Link'. In *Capitalism, Socialism, and Democracy Revisited*, edited by L. Diamond and M. F. Plattner, 94–105. Baltimore, MD: The Johns Hopkins University Press.

———. 2012. 'The Future of History: Can Liberal Democracy Survive the Decline of the Middle Class?' *Foreign Affairs* 91 (1): 53–61.

———. 2014. *Political Order and Political Decay: From the Industrial Revolution to the Globalization of Democracy*. London: Profile Books.

Fuller, C. J., and H. Narasimhan. 2007. 'Information Technology Professionals and the New-Rich Middle Class in Chennai (Madras)'. *Modern Asian Studies* 41 (1): 121–150.

Gallagher, Mary E. 2002. 'Reform and Openness: Why China's Economic Reform have Delayed Democracy?' *World Politics* 54 (3): 338–372.

Ganguly-Scrase, R., and Timothy J. Scrase. 2016. 'Privatization, Profit and the Public: The Consequences of Neoliberal Reforms on Working Lives'. In *Elite and Everyman: The Cultural Politics of the Indian Middle Classes*, edited by Amita Baviskar and Raka Ray, 300–323. New Delhi: Routledge.

Ghosh, Jayati. 2002. 'VRS—The Voluntary Retirement Scandal'. *People's Democracy* 26 (37). Available at https://archives.peoplesdemocracy.in/2002/sept22/09152002_eco1.htm (*People's Democracy* is a weekly organ of the CPI (M), New Delhi).

Gill, Rajesh. 2005. *State, Market and Civil Society: Issues and Interface*. Jaipur: Rawat Publications.

Glassman, R. M. 1995. *The Middle Class and Democracy in Socio-Historical Perspective*. (Vol 10). Leiden: E. J. Brill.

Godbole, Madhav. 1996. *Unfinished Innings: Recollections and Reflections of a Civil Servant*. New Delhi: Orient Longman.

GoI. 2019a, 5 July. *Budget Speech 2019–20*. New Delhi: Ministry of Finance, Government of India.

GoI. 2019b. *Union Budget 2019–20*. New Delhi: Ministry of Finance, GoI.

Goldthorpe, J. H. 1987. *Social Mobility and Class Structure in Modern Britain* (2nd edition). Oxford: Clarendon Press

Gopal, Sarvepalli. 2014. *Jawaharlal Nehru: A Biography* (Vol 3, 1956–1964). New Delhi: Oxford University Press.

Goradia, Prafull. 2019a. 'Dissecting Demonetization and Middle Class'. *The Pioneer*, 11 March. Available at https://www.dailypioneer.com/2019/columnists/dissecting-demonetisation.html

———. 2019b. 'Modi, the Faith Keeper'. *The Pioneer*, 25 May. Available at https://www.dailypioneer.com/2019/columnists/modi–the-faith-keeper.html

Gould, H. A. 1986. 'A Sociological Perspective on the Eighth General Election in India'. *Asian Survey* 26 (6): 630–652.

Graham, Bruce. 1990. *Hindu Nationalism and Indian Politics: The Origins and Development of the Bharatiya Jana Sangh.* Cambridge: Cambridge University Press.

Guha, Ramachandra. 2000. 'Indira Gandhi Put Democracy on Hold with Emergency but Never Thought She Erred'. *India Today*, 3 July.

———. 2005. 'They Too Wrote Our History'. *Outlook*, 22 August. Available at https://www.outlookindia.com/magazine/story/they-too-wrote-our-history/228341

———. 2007. *India After Gandhi: The History of the World's Largest Democracy.* London: Macmillan.

———. 2019. 'Surgical Strike against Science and Scholarship'. *The Telegraph*, 27 April. Available at https://www.telegraphindia.com/opinion/surgical-strike-against-science-and-scholarship/cid/1689471

Gupta, Dipankar. 2000. *Mistaken Modernity*. New Delhi: HarperCollins Publishers.

Gupta, Smita. 2019. 'Wooing Voters in 2019: Some Takeaways from December 2018'. *The Hindu Centre for Politics and Public Policy*, Chennai. Available at https://www.thehinducentre.com/the-arena/current-issues/article25806981.ece

Gupta, Surojit. 2019. 'Food Inflation Falls to Lowest Level since 1991'. *The Times of India*, New Delhi, 14 April. Available at https://timesofindia.indiatimes.com/business/india-business/food-inflation-falls-to-lowest-level-since-1991/articleshow/68870152.cms

Gurumurthy, S. 2017. 'Demonetisation: The Great Reset, A Year Later'. *The Hindu*, Chennai, 9 November.

Guruswamy, Mohan. 2004. '91st Constitutional Amendment: Not Quite Adequate'. *The Hindu Business Line*, Chennai, 20 July. Available at https://www.thehindubusinessline.com/2004/07/20/stories/2004072000251100.htm

Gunadasa, Saman, and Kranti Kumara. 2017. 'India's 1-percent Grabs Nearly a Quarter of All Income'. *World Socialist Web*, 6 November. Available at https://www.wsws.org/en/articles/2017/11/06/indi-n06.html (accessed on 8 January 2019).

Hansen, T. B. 1999: *The Saffron Wave: Democracy and Hindu Nationalism in Modern India.* Princeton, NJ: Princeton University Press.

Hansen, T. B., and Christophe Jaffrelot. 2001. *The BJP and the Compulsions of Politics in India.* Delhi: Oxford University Press.

Hardgrave, R. L. (1993). 'India: The Dilemmas of Diversity'. *Journal of Democracy* 4 (4): 55–68.

Harvey, David. 2005. *A Brief History of Neoliberalism.* New York: Oxford University Press.

Hasan, Mushirul. 1997. *Legacy of a Divided Nation: India's Muslims since Independence.* Boulder, CO: Westview Press.

Hasan, Zoya. 2001. 'Changing Political Orientations of the Middle Classes in India'. In *Middle Class Values in India and Western Europe*, edited by I. Ahmad and Helmut Reifeld, 152–170. New Delhi: Social Science Press.

———. 2004. *India Elections 2004: A Setback for BJP's Exclusive Agenda*. New Delhi: JNU. Available at https://www.sciencespo.fr/ceri/sites/sciencespo.fr.ceri/files/artzh.pdf

———. 2014. 'Manufacturing Dissent: The Media and the 2014 Election'. *The Hindu Centre for Politics and Public Policy*, Chennai, 2 April. Available at https://www.thehinducentre.com/verdict/commentary/article5843621.ece

———. 2016. 'Collapse of the Congress'. In *Making Sense of Modi's India*, edited by Hasan Suroor, 138–155. New Delhi: HarperCollins Publishers India.

Haynes, Douglas E. 1992. *Rhetoric and Ritual in Colonial India: The Shaping of a Public Culture in Surat City, 1852–1928*. Berkeley, CA: University of California Press.

Haynes, Suyin. 2016. 'Narendra Modi Leads Julian Assange in TIME's Person of Year Poll'. *TIME*, 24 May. Available at https://time.com/4582014/narendra-modi-julian-assange-person-of-the-year-poll/

Hebbar, Nistula. 2019. 'A Mandate from a New India, Modi'. *The Hindu*, New Delhi, 23 May. Available at https://www.thehindu.com/elections/lok-sabha-2019/a-mandate-from-a-new-india-modi/article27227566.ece

———. 2018. 'Narendra Modi to Party MPs: What's up? *The Hindu*, New Delhi, 3 January.

Heiman, Rachel, Carla Freeman and Mark Liechty. 2012. *The Global Middle Classes: Theorizing Through Ethnography*. SAR Press.

Hollingshead, August B. 1959. 'Book Reviews. The Black Coated Worker: A Study in Class Consciousness: David Lockwood'. *American Journal of Sociology* 65 (1): 115. Available at https://www.journals.uchicago.edu/doi/abs/10.1086/222644?mobileUi=0

Horton, Richard. 2018. 'The New Politics of Health in India'. *The Lancet*, 11 September. Available at https://www.thelancet.com/journals/lancet/article/PIIS0140-6736(18)32211-6/fulltext

Huntington, S. 1991. *The Third Wave: Democratization in the Late Twentieth Century*. Norman: University of Oklahoma Press.

INC. 2019. *Congress will Deliver, Manifesto, Lok Sabha Elections 2019*. New Delhi: INC.

*India Today*. 1992. 'PV Narasimha Rao's Family Members are Ambitious, Quirky and Naïve'. *India Today*, 30 September.

Iyer, Malathy. 2019. 'Study Reveals Price Cut Ups Use of Drug-Eluting Stents'. *Sunday Times of India*, Bengaluru, 14 April.

Jaffrelot, Christophe. 1996. *The Hindu Nationalist Movement and Indian Politics, 1925 to the 1990s*. Gurgaon: Viking.

———. 2003. *India's Silent Revolution: The Rise of Lower Castes in North India*. London: C. Hurst & Co. Publishers Ltd.

Jaffrelot, Christophe. 2007. *Hindu Nationalism: A Reader*. Princeton: Princeton University.

————. 2008. 'Why Should We Vote? The Indian Middle Class and the Functioning of the World's Largest Democracy'. In *Patterns of Middle Class Consumption in India and China*, edited by Christophe Jaffrelot and Peter Van der Veer. New Delhi: SAGE Publications.

————. 2014a. 'The Class Element in the 2014 Indian Election and the BJP's Success with Special Reference to the Hindi Belt'. *Studies in Indian Politics* 3 (1): 19–38.

————. 2014b. 'Modi of the Middle Class'. *The Indian Express*, 24 March. Available at http://indianexpress.com/article/opinion/columns/modi-of-the-middle-class/

————. 2015. 'The Modi-Centric BJP 2014 Election Campaign: New Techniques and Old Tactics'. *Contemporary South Asia* 23 (2): 151–166.

Jaffrelot, Christophe, and Gilles Verniers. 2009. 'India's 2009 Elections. The Resilience of Regionalism and Ethnicity'. Available at https://www.research-gate.net/publication/40903310_India's_2009_Elections_The_Resilience_of_Regionalism_and_Ethnicity

Jaffrelot, Christophe, and Peter Van der Veer. 2008. *Patterns and Middle Class Consumption in India and China*. New Delhi: SAGE Publications.

Jagannathan, R. 2016. 'Who Is the Real Narendra Modi: A 'Communal Czar' or an 'Inclusive Icon'?' In *Making Sense of Modi's India*, edited by Hasan Suroor, 80–88. New Delhi: HarperCollins Publishers India.

Jaitely, Arun. 2019. Part-9: The NDA Government's Economy Report Card vs. Its Predecessors. Facebook, 19 March. Available at https://m.facebook.com/notes/arun-jaitley/agenda-2019-part-9-the-nda-governments-economy-report-card-vs-its-predecessors/980481652140383/

Jani, Pranav. 2002. 'Karl Marx, Eurocentrism, and the 1857 Revolt in British India'. In *Marxism, Modernity and Postcolonial Studies*, edited by Crystal Bartolovich and Neil Lazarus, 81–100. Cambridge: Cambridge University Press. Available at https://epdf.pub/marxism-modernity-and-postcolonial-studies.html

Jayal, Niraja Gopal. 2004. 'A Malevolent Embrace? The BJP and Muslims in the Parliamentary Election of 2004'. *India Review* 3 (3): 183–209.

Jeffrey, Robin, and Assa Doron. 2013. *Cell Phone Nation: How Mobile Phones Have Revolutionized Business, Politics and Ordinary Life in India*. New Delhi: Hachette India.

Jenkins, Rob. 2000. 'Appearances and Reality in Indian Politics: Making Sense of the 1999 General Election'. *Government and Opposition* 35 (1): 49–66.

Jha, Prem Shankar. 2002. *The Perilous Road to the Market: The Political Economy of Reform in Russia, India and China*. New Delhi: Rupa & Co.

Jodhka, Surinder S., and Aseem Prakash. 2016. *The Indian Middle Class*. New Delhi: Oxford University Press.

Johari, Aarefa. 2019. 'The Modi Years: How Close is India to Affordable Housing for All?' *Scroll.in*, 20 February. Available at https://scroll.in/article/913188/the-modi-years-how-close-is-india-to-affordable-housing-for-all

Johnson, Dale. 1982. *Class and Social Development: A New Theory of the Middle Class*. Beverly Hills, CA: SAGE Publications.

Joshi, Sanjay. 2001. *Fractured Modernity: Making of a Middle Class in Colonial North India*. Delhi: Oxford University Press.

———. 2017. 'India's Middle Class'. Available at http://asianhistory.oxfordre.com/view/10.1093/acrefore/9780190277727.001.0001/acrefore-9780190277727-e-179

Kalra, Rajesh, Diwakar, and Rajeev Deshpande. 2019. '2014 was a Mandate for Hope and Aspiration, 2019 is bout Confidence and Acceleration'. *The Times of India*, New Delhi, 18 April. Available at https://timesofindia.indiatimes.com/india/2014-was-a-mandate-for-hope-and-aspiration-2019-is-about-confidence-and-acceleration-pm-modi/articleshow/68920680.cms

Kamath, M. V., and Kalindi Randeri. 2009. *Narendra Modi: Architect of a Modern State*. New Delhi: Rupa & Co.

Kanwal, Rahul. 2013. 'RSS Views Now More Aligned with Modi's? Mohan Bhagwat Says Sangh not Opposed to FDI, Liberalisation'. *India Today*, 2 November. Available at https://www.indiatoday.in/india/story/rss-mohan-bhagwat-narendra-modi-fdi-bjp-216245-2013-11-02

Kapila, Shruti. 2016. 'Conservatism and the Cult of Individual in a Populist Age'. In *Making Sense of Modi's India*, edited by Hasan Suroor, 40-55. New Delhi: HarperCollins Publishers India.

Kaplan, Robert, D. 2009. 'India's New Face'. *The Atlantic*. Available at https://www.theatlantic.com/magazine/archive/2009/04/indias-new-face/307332/

Kapoor, K., and Y. Dwivedi. 2015. 'Metamorphosis of Indian Electoral Campaigns: Modi's Social Media Experiment'. *International Journal of Indian Culture and Business Management* 11 (4): 496–516. Available at https://pdfs.semanticscholar.org/4d2a/7206b488a672e756022f8a9cf670c15e1019.pdf

Kapur, Devesh, and Milan Vaishnav. 2014. 'Being Middle Class in India'. *The Hindu*, Chennai, 9 December. Available at https://www.thehindu.com/opinion/op-ed/being-middle-class-in-india/article6673580.ece

Kapur, Devesh, Neelanjan Sircar, and Milan Vaishnav. 2017. 'Slippery as Ever: It's not Ideology but Aspiration that Derives India's Middle Class—Politicians Take Note'. *Quartz India*, December 4. Available at https://qz.com/india/1140621/indias-middle-class-is-driven-by-aspiration-not-ideology-politicians-take-note/

Katju, Manjari. 2003. *Vishva Hindu Parishad and India Politics*. Hyderabad: Orient Longman.

Kaur, Ravinder. 2015. 'Good Times, Brought to You by Brand Modi'. *Television & New Media* 15 (4): 323–330.

Kaviraj, Sudipta. 1991. 'On State, Society and Discourse in India'. In *Rethinking Third World Politics*, edited by J. Manor, 72–99. Harlow: Longman.

———. 1997. 'Filth and the Public Sphere: Concepts and Practices about Space in Calcutta'. *Public Culture* 10 (1): 81–113.

Kelly, M. P. 1980. *White-Collar Proletariat*. London. Routledge & Keganpaul.

Kenny, C. 2011. 'Where Is the Virtue in the Middle Class?' (Unpublished paper). Center for Global Development, Washington DC.

Keynes, John Maynard. 1936. *The General Theory of Employment, Interest, and Money*. London: Palgrave Macmillan.

Khair, Tabish. 2018. 'The Useful Disease of English'. *The Hindu*, Chennai, 30 September. Available at https://www.thehindu.com/opinion/columns/the-useful-disease-of-english/article25083993.ece

Kharas, Homi. 2010. 'The Emerging Middle Class in Developing Countries.' OECD Development Centre Working Paper No. 285, OECD, Paris. Available at https://www.oecd.org/dev/44457738.pdf

———. 2017. 'The Unprecedented Expansion of the Global Middle Class: An Update'. Global Economy and Development Working Paper, 100. Available at https://www.brookings.edu/wp-content/uploads/2017/02/global_20170228_global-middle-class.pdf16

Kharas, Homi, and Geoffrey Gertz. 2010, March. *The New Global Middle Class: A Cross-Over from West to East*. Washington, DC: Brookings Institution, March. Available at https://www.brookings.edu/research/the-new-global-middle-class-a-cross-over-from-west-to-east/

Kharas, Homi, and Kristofer Hamel. 2018, 27 September. *Future Development: A Global Tipping Point: Half the World is Now Middle Class or Wealthier*. Washington, DC: Brookings Institution. Available at https://www.brook-ings.edu/blog/future-development/2018/09/27/a-global-tipping-point-half-the-world-is-now-middle-class-or-wealthier/

Khare, Harish. 2014. *How Modi Won It: Notes from the 2014 Election*. New Delhi: Hachette.

Khilnani, Sunil. 1997. *The Idea of India*. New Delhi: Penguin Books.

Khurana, Suanshu. 2014. 'Man Behind "Ab Ki Bar Modi Sarkar" is Spice Jet Co-owner'. *The Indian Express*, New Delhi, 20 May. Available at https://indianexpress.com/article/india/india-others/man-behind-ab-ki-baar-modi-sarkaar-is-spice-jet-co-owner/

Kim, Yoosuk. 2006. 'Indian Electoral Politics and the Rise of the Bharatiya Janata Party' (MSc thesis). Department of Political Science, Florida State University Library, USA. Available at https://diginole.lib.fsu.edu/islandora/object/fsu:181249/datastream/PDF/view

Kishwar, Madhu Purnima. 2014. *Modi, Muslims and Media*. New Delhi: Manushi Publications.

Klingender, F. D. 1935. *Condition of Clerical Labour in Britain*. London: Martin Lawrence Ltd.

Kochanek, Stanley A. 1976. 'Mrs. Gandhi's Pyramid: The New Congress'. In *Indira Gandhi's India: A Political System Reappraised*, edited by Henry C. Hart. Boulder, CO: Westview Press.

Kochhar, Rakesh. 2016. 'A Global Middle Class: Is more Promise than Reality'. Paper presented at a seminar on *The Middle Class in World Society*, Institute for Social and Economic Change, Bengaluru, 16–17 December.

Kohli, Atul. 1988. 'State–Society Relations in India's Changing Democracy'. In *India's Democracy*, edited by Atul Kohli, 305–318. Princeton, NJ: Princeton University Press.

———. 2004. *State-Directed Development: Political Power and Industrialization in the Global Periphery*. New York: Cambridge University Press.

Kosambi, D. D. 1946. 'The Bourgeoisie Comes of Age in India'. *Science and Society* 10: 392–398.

Kothari, Rajni. 1964. 'The Congress "System" in India'. *Asian Survey* 4 (12): 1161–1173.

———. 1993. *Growing Amnesia: An Essay on Poverty and the Human Consciousness*. New Delhi: Viking.

Kripalani, Manjeet. 2019. 'Elections 2019: Making Indian Middle Class'. *Gateway House*. Available at https://www.gatewayhouse.in/india-elections-2019/

Krishna, Anirudh, and Devendra Bajpai. 2015. 'Layers in Globalising Society and the New Middle Class in India: Trends, Distribution and Prospects'. *Economic and Political Weekly* 50 (5): 69–77.

Krishnan, Sandhya, and Neeraj Hatekar. 2017. 'Rise of the New Middle Class in India and its Changing Structure'. *Economic and Political Weekly* 55 (22): 40–48.

Krueger, O. Anne. 2002. *Economic Policy Reforms and the Indian Economy*. New Delhi: Oxford University Press.

Kumar, Arun. 2017. *Demonetization and the Black Money*. Delhi: Penguin.

———. 2019. The Problem with Cherry-Picking Data. *The Hindu*, 24 April. Available at https://www.thehindu.com/opinion/op-ed/the-problem-with-cherry-picking-data/article26925274.ece

Kumar, Ravinder. 1987. 'Introduction'. In *Myth and Reality: The Struggle for Freedom in India, 1945–47*, edited by A. K. Gupta. New Delhi: Manohar.

Kumar, Shashikant. 2015. 'The Rural Middle Class: The Nature of Social Change in Charotar (Anand, Gujarat)'. In *The Trajectory of India's Middle Class: Economy, Ethics and Etiquette*, edited by Lancy Lobo and Jayesh Shah, 184–197. Newcastle upon Tyne, UK: Cambridge Scholars Publishing.

Kumar, Vidyarthi. 2013. 'Moditva Emerging Stronger'. *Power Politics* (July): 15–16.

Lahiri, Ashok. 2014. 'The Middle Class and Economic Reforms'. *Economic and Political Weekly* 49 (111): 37–44

Lakha, Salim. 1999. 'The State, Globalization, and Indian Middle Class Identity'. In *Culture and Privilege in Capitalist Asia*, edited by Michael Pinches. New York: Routledge.

Lash, Scott, and John Urry. 1987. *The End of Organized Capitalism*. Madison, WI: University of Wisconsin Press.

Lau, L. 2010. 'Literary Representations of the "New Indian Woman": The Single, Working, Urban, Middle Class Indian Woman Seeking Personal Autonomy'. *Journal of South Asian Development* 5 (2): 271–292.

Liechty, Mark. 2003. *Suitably Modern: Making New Middle Class Culture in a New Consumer Society*. Princeton, NJ: Princeton University Press.

Lipset, S. M. 1959. 'Some Social Requisites of Democracy: Economic Development and Political Legitimacy'. *American Political Science Review* 53 (1): 69–105.

———. 1960. *Political Man: The Social Basis of Politics*. New York: Doubleday.

Loayza, Norman, Jamele Rigolini, and Gonzalo Llorente. 2012. 'Do Middle Classes Bring Institutional Reforms?' Policy Research Working Paper 6015, World Bank, Washington, DC.

Lobo, Lancy, and Jayesh Shah. 2015. *The Trajectory of India's Middle Class, Economy, Ethics and Etiquette*. Newcastle upon Tyne, UK: Cambridge Scholars Publishing.

Lockwood, David. 1958. *The Blackcoated Worker*. London: Allen & Unwin.

Lokniti-CSDS. 2019. *Social Media and Political Behaviour*. New Delhi: Lokniti-CSDS.

Lopez-Calva, L. F., Jamele Rigolini, and Florenica Torche. 2011. 'Is There Such Thing as Middle Class Values? Class Differences, Values and Political Orientations in Latin America'. Policy Research Working Paper No. 5874, World Bank, Washington DC.

Madan, T. N. 1987. 'Secularism in Its Place'. *The Journal of Asian Studies* 46 (4): 747–759.

———. 1991. *Religion in India*. New York: Oxford University Press.

Madland, David. 2011. 'Growth and the Middle Class'. *Democracy: A Journal of Ideas* 20 (Spring). Available at https://democracyjournal.org/magazine/20/growth-and-the-middle-class/

Mahapatra, Richard. 2019. 'Development News, Polarisation and Social Media in Times of Lok Sabha Polls'. *Down to Earth*, 16 April. Available at https://www.downtoearth.org.in/blog/general-elections-2019/development-news-polarisation-and-social-media-in-times-of-lok-sabha-polls-64002

Mahurkar, U. 2019. 'Modi, Shah Reign Again'. *India Today*, 3 June.

Mahurkar, U., and K. Pradhan. 2014. 'Meet the Men behind Modi's Audacious Election Campaign'. *India Today*, 24 February.

Makwana, Kishor. 2015. *MODI Common Man's PM*. New Delhi: Prabhat Prakashan.

Malhotra, Inder. 2003. *Dynasties of India and Beyond*. New Delhi: HarperCollins Publishers.

———. 2014. 'The Rise of "Mr Clean"'. *The Indian Express*, 24 November.

Mallet, S. 1975. *The New Working Class*. France: Bertrand Russell Peace Foundation for Spokesman Books.

Mandhana, Niharika. 2014. 'Narendra Modi's Elections Win Heralds New Era in India'. *The Wall Street Journal*, 17 May. Available at https://www.wsj.com/articles/vote-counting-begins-in-indias-national-election-1400210643

Mankekar, D. R., and Kamla Mankekar. 1977. *Decline and Fall of Indira Gandhi*. New Delhi: Vision Books.

Mankekar, Purnima. 1999. *Screening Culture, Viewing Politics: An Ethnography of Television, Womanhood and Nation in Postcolonial India*. Durham, NC: Duke University Press.

Marx, Karl. 1863. *Theories of Surplus Value* (Part 2). Moscow: Progress Publishers.

Marx, Karl, and Friedrich Engels. 1968 [1848]. *The Communist Manifesto*. Moscow: Progress Publishers.

Mathur, Nita. 2010. 'Shopping Malls, Credit Cards and Global Brands: Consumer Culture and Lifestyle of India's New Middle Class'. *South Asia Research* 30 (3): 211–231.

Mazzarella, William. 2004. 'Middle Class'. Available at https://www.soas.ac.uk/south-asia-institute/keywords/file24808.pdf

McKinsey Global Institute. 2007. 'The Bird of Gold: The Rise of India's Middle Class'. Available at http://www.mckinsey.com/mgi/publications/india_consumer_market/index.asp

McLane, John R. 1977. *Indian Nationalism and the Early Congress*. Princeton, NJ: Princeton University Press.

Mehta, Gautam. 2019. 'Hindu Nationalism and the BJP's Economic Record'. In *The BJP in Power: Indian Democracy and Religious Nationalism*, edited by Milan Vaishnav. Carnegie Endowment for International Peace. Available at https://carnegieendowment.org/2019/04/04/hindu-nationalism-and-bjp-s-economic-record-pub-78720

Mehta, Nalin. 2006. 'Modi and the Camera: The Politics of Television in the 2002 Gujarat Riots'. *Journal of South Asian Studies* 29 (3): 395–414.

Mehta, Pratap Bhanu. 2010. 'It's Land, Stupid'. *The New Indian Express*, 19 August. Available at https://indianexpress.com/article/opinion/columns/its-land-stupid/

Mehta, Vinod. 2012. *The Sanjay Story*. New Delhi: HarperCollins.

Merwin, Radhika. 2019. 'The IBC Conundrum'. *The Hindu Business Line*, 15 April.

Meyer, Christian, and Nancy Birdsall. 2012. 'New Estimates of India's Middle Class'. Technical Note, Center for Global Development.

Mills, C. Wright. 1956. *White Collar: The American Middle Classes*. London: Oxford University Press.

Mishra, Richa. 2019a. 'Is It Fair to Ask Bureaucrats to Retire Early?' *The Hindu Business Line*, Chennai, 29 August. Available at https://www.thehindubusinessline.com/specials/people-at-work/is-it-fair-to-ask-bureaucrats-to-retire-early/article29281155.ece (accessed on 16 January 2020).

———. 2019b. 'Time to Soften GST Blown on MSMEs'. *The Hindu Business Line*, Chennai, 15 April.

Misra, B. B. 1961. *The Indian Middle Classes, Their Growth in Modern Times*. London: Oxford University Press.

Misra, Satish. 2019. 'Who Will Gain from 10% Reservation for EWS?' *Observer Research Foundation*, 14 April. Available at https://www.orfonline.org/expert-speak/who-will-gain-from-10-reservation-for-ews-47312/

Modi, Narendra. 2018. 'Tribute to a Great Unifier: Sardar Vallabhbhai Patel Can Justly be Regarded as the Maker of Modern India'. *The Times of India*, 31 October.

Mohan, Sriram. 2015. 'Locating the "Internet Hindu": Political Speech and Performance in Indian Cyberspace'. *Television & New Media* 16 (4): 339–345.

Mohsina, Nazneen. 2019. 'Political Opportunism in India: Exploring Islamophobia'. *The Diplomat*. Available at https://thediplomat.com/2019/05/political-opportunism-in-india-exploiting-islamophobia/

Mooji, Jos. 2005. *The Politics of Economic Reforms in India*. New Delhi: SAGE Publications.

Moore, Barrington. 1966. *Social Origins of Dictatorship and Democracy: Lord and Peasant in the Making of the Modern World*. Boston, MA: Beacon Press.

Mosley, P., J. Harrigan, and J .F. J. Toye. 1991 *Aid and Power: The World Bank and Policy-Based Lending* (vols. I & II). London: Routledge.

Mukerji, D. P. 1948. *Indian Culture: A Sociological Study*. Bombay: Hind Kitabs Ltd.

———. 1958. *Diversities*. New Delhi: People's Publishing House.

———. 1979. *Sociology of Indian Culture*. Jaipur: Rawat Publications.

Mukhopadhyay, Nilanjan. 2013. *Narendra Modi: The Man, the Times*. New Delhi: Westland Publications Ltd.

Munshi, K. 2014. 'Community Networks and the Process of Development'. *The Journal of Economic Perspectives* 28 (4): 49–76.

———. 2016. 'Caste and the Indian Economy'. In *Development in India*, pp. 13–37. New Delhi: Springer. Available at http://www.histecon.magd.cam.ac.uk/km/Munshi_JEL1.pdf

Muralidharan, Sukumar. 2019. 'News, Social Media and Voter Influence'. *The Hindu Business Line*, Chennai, 21 June.

Mustafi, Sambuddha Mitra. 2013. 'What Makes Narendra Modi a Middle Class Hero?' *The New York Times*, 16 May. Available at https://india.blogs.nytimes.com/2013/05/16/what-makes-narendra-modi-a-middle-class-hero/

Myrdal, Gunnar. 1968. *Asian Drama: An Inquiry into the Poverty of Nations*. Middlesex: Penguin Books Ltd.

Nagesha. 1994. 'Middle Class in India: Its Constitution and Politics' (MPhil dissertation). Mangalore University, Karnataka.

Nair, Preetha. 2019. 'In Which BJP Takes All'. *Outlook* 59 (21): 32–23.

Nair, Sobhana K. 2018. 'Better to Sell Pakodas than be Jobless: Shah'. *The Hindu*, 6 February.

Nayak, Pulin B. 1991. 'On the Crisis and Remedies.' *Economic and Political Weekly* 26 (34): 1993–1997.

Nayar, B. R. 2003. 'Globalisation and India's National Autonomy'. *Commonwealth and Contemporary Politics* 41 (2): 1–34.

*NDTV*. 2014. 'From Narendra Modi's team, Some States: 437 rallies, 5827 events, 3 lakh kms'. *NDTV*, 9 May. Available at https://www.ndtv.com/

elections-news/from-narendra-modis-team-some-stats-437-rallies-5827-events-3-lakh-kilometres-560938.

Neubert, Dieter. 2014. 'What is "Middle Class"? In Search of an Appropriate Concept'. *Meta Journal* 2: 23–35. Available at https://meta-journal.net/article/view/1330/2095

News18. 2019. 'Oppn Takes Swipes at PM Modi for Not Taking Questions at Press Conference'. News18, 20 May. Available at https://www.news18.com/news/politics/oppn-takes-swipes-at-pm-modi-for-not-taking-questions-at-press-conference-2146115.html

Nicolaus, M. 1970. 'Proletariat and Middle Class in Marx: Hegelian Choreography and Capitalist Dialectic.' In *For a New America: Essays in History and Political Studies on the Left 1959–1967,* edited by James Weinstein, and David W. Eakins. New York: Vintage.

Noorani, A. G. 2009. 'Essay: BJP's Democracy Deficit'. *Frontline* 26 (20): 80–85.

———. 2019. 'EC Seems Biased Towards Modi'. *The Asian Age*, Mumbai, 5 May. Available at https://www.asianage.com/opinion/oped/050519/election-commission-seems-biased-towards-modi.html

Oberoi, Harjot S. 1994. *Construction of Religious Boundaries: Culture, Identity and Diversity in the Sikh Tradition.* Delhi: Oxford University Press.

Oesch, D. 2003. 'Labour Market Trends and the Goldthorpe Class Schema: A Conceptual Reassessment'. *Swiss Journal of Sociology* 29 (3): 241–262.

Ogden, Chris. 2012. 'A Lasting Legacy: The BJP-Led National Democratic Alliance and India's Politics'. *Journal of Contemporary Asia* 42 (1): 22–38.

Oza, Rupal. 2006.' Showcasing India: Gender, Geography, and Globalization'. 26 Signs. Available at https://pdfs.semanticscholar.org/e100/7f8c38b7ee18761515f7a9a9dfea48f8c77e.pdf

Ozturk, Ayse. 2016. 'Examining the Economic Growth and the Middle-Income Trap from the Perspective of the Middle Class'. *International Business Review* 25 (3): 726–738.

Pai, Mohandas T. V. 2019. 'Here's How PM Narendra Modi Transforming India'. *Financial Express*, 2 March. Available at https://www.financialexpress.com/opinion/heres-how-pm-narendra-modi-transforming-india/1502842/

Pal, Joyojeet. 2015. 'Banalities Turned Viral: Narendra Modi and the Political Tweet'. *Television & New Media* 16 (4): 378–387.

Pal, Joyojeet, and Lia Bozarth. 2018. 'Is Tweeting in Indian Languages Helping Politicians Widen Their Reach?' *Economic and Political Weekly* 53 (25), June. Available at https://www.epw.in/engage/article/tweeting-indian-languages-helping-politicians-widen-reach

Pal, Joyojeet, Priyanka Chandra, and V. G. Vinod Vydiswaran. 2016. 'Twitter and the Rebranding of Narendra Modi'. *Economic and Political Weekly* 51 (8): 52–60.

Palit, Amitendu. 2015. 'Economics in Narendra Modi's Foreign Policy'. *Asie. Visions* 77. Available at https://www.ifri.org/sites/default/files/atoms/files/asie_visions77_0.pdf

Palshikar, Suhas. 2001. 'Politics of India's Middle Classes'. In *Middle Class Values in India and Western Europe*, edited by Imtiaz Ahmad and Helmut Reifeld, 171–193. New Delhi: Social Science Press.

———. 2004. 'Majoritarian Middle Ground?' *Economic and Political Weekly* 39 (51): 5426–5430.

Palshikar, Suhas, Sanjay Kumar and Sandeep Shastri. 2019. 'Post-Poll Survey: Explaining the Modi Sweep across Regions'. *The Hindu*, Chennai, 26 May. Available at https://www.thehindu.com/elections/lok-sabha-2019/post-poll-survey-explaining-the-modi-sweep-across-regions/article27250054.ece

Panagariya, Arvind. 2014. 'Towards Economic Freedom'. *The Times of India*, New Delhi, 17 May.

Pande, Shamni. 2014. 'Just the Right Image'. *Business Today*, 08 June. Available at https://www.businesstoday.in/magazine/case-study/case-study-strategy-tactics-behind-creation-of-brand-narendra-modi/story/206321.html

Pandey, A. 2007. 'Communalism and Separatism in India: An Analysis'. *Journal of Asian and African Studies* 42 (6): 533–549.

Pandey, Gyanendra. 1990. *The Construction of Communalism in Colonial North India*. New Delhi: Oxford University Press.

Pandey, Sanjay. 2002. 'Modi Attacks Musharraf Again'. *The Times of India*, 6 October. Available at https://timesofindia.indiatimes.com/india/Modi-attacks-Musharraf-again/articleshow/24394650.cms

Pandit, Rajat. 2019. '150 Retired Officers Write to President Kovind over "Politicisation" of Forces'. *The Economic Times*, Bengaluru, 4 April.

Panikkar, K. N. 2009. 'Communal Recipe'. *Frontline* 26 (20): 86–89.

Panini, M. N. 2015. 'Embourgeoisement and the Middle Class in India'. In *The Trajectory of India's Middle Class: Economy, Ethics and Etiquette*, edited by Lancy Lobo and Jayesh Shah, 14–39. Newcastle upon Tyne, UK: Cambridge Scholars Publishing.

Parashar, Sachin. 2011. '"Saffron Terror", a UPA Conspiracy: Gadkari'. *The Economic Times*, 9 January. Available at https://economictimes.indiatimes.com/news/politics-and-nation/saffron-terror-a-upa-conspiracy-gadkari/articleshow/7245499.cms?from=mdr

Parkin, Frank. 1979. *Marxism and Class Theory: A Bourgeois Critique*. London: Tavistock Publications.

Patel, Aakar, Dileep Padgaonkar, and B. G. Verghese. 2002. *Editors Guild Fact Finding Mission Report: Rights and Wrongs: Ordeal by Fire in the Killing Fields of Gujarat*. New Delhi.

Perappadan, Bindu Shajan. 2019. 'Price Controls Hurting FDI in Medical Devices Sector'. *The Hindu*, Chennai, 23 April.

Pezzini, Mario. 2012. 'An Emerging Middle Class'. *OECD Observer*. Available at http://oecdobserver.org/news/fullstory.php/aid/3681/An_emerging_middle_class.html

Phadnis, Ashwini. 2019. 'What Took Off in Domestic Aviation, and What Didn't'. *The Hindu Business Line*, Chennai, 17 April.

Philip, Saju. 2014. 'At Kochi Meeting of SC Group, Modi Says He is "Victim of Untouchability"'. *Financial Express*, 14 March. Available at https://www. financialexpress.com/archive/at-kochi-meeting-of-sc-group-narendra-modi-says-he-is-victim-of-untouchability/1224578/

Philipose, Pamela. 2019. *Media's Shifting Terrain: Five Years that Transformed the Way India Communicates*. Hyderabad: Orient BlackSwan.

Pillai, Ajith. 2019. 'Media Credibility Hit a New Low under Modi'. NewsClick, 3 May.

Polanyi, Karl. 1957. *The Great Transformation: The Political and Economic Origins of Our Time*. Boston: Beacon Press.

Potter, David C. 1996. *India's Political Administrators: From ICS to IAS*. New Delhi: Oxford University Press.

Poulantzas, Nicos. 1975. *Classes in Contemporary Capitalism*. London: New Left Books.

Prabhakar, Siddharth. 2016. '20 Years after Mandal: Less Than 12% OBCs in Central Jobs'. *The Times of India*, Bengaluru, 26 December.

Prabhu, Nagesh. 2003. 'VRS Scheme has had a Negative Impact: Study'. *The Hindu*, Bengaluru, 26 December. Available at https://www.thehindu.com/2003/12/26/stories/2003122606640400.htm

———. 2015. 'Indian Middle Class and Politics'. In *The Trajectory of India's Middle Class: Economy, Ethics and Etiquette*, edited by Lancy Lobo and Jayesh Shah, 115–135. Newcastle upon Tyne, UK: Cambridge Scholars Publishing.

———. 2017a. 'Private Players will Make Profit, While Govt. Takes All the Risk'. *The Hindu*, Bengaluru, 1 December. Available at https://www.thehindu.com/news/national/karnataka/pvt-players-will-make-profit-while-govt-takes-all-the-risk/article21236439.ece

———. 2017b. *Reflective Shadows: Political Economy of World Bank Lending to India*. New Delhi: Oxford University Press.

Prabhu, Nagesh. 2018a. 'Kumaraswamy Announces ₹34,000 Farm Loan Waiver'. *The Hindu*, Bengaluru, 6 July. Available at https://www.thehindu.com/news/cities/bangalore/kumaraswamy-announces-34000-cr-farm-loan-waiver/article24344526.ece

———. 2018b. Dasara is an Integral Part of Our Identity, Says Sudha Murthy. *The Hindu*, 7 October.

Pradhan, Kunal, and Jayant Sriram. 2013. 'Rise of the Cyber Hindu'. *India Today*. 1 November. Available at http://indiatoday.intoday.in/story/social-media-internet-cyber-hindu-twitter-narendra-modi/1/321267.html

Prasad, Krishna. 2019. 'Democracy can Die in Daylight Too'. *The Hindu*, Chennai, 14 June.

Prasannarajan, S. 2010. 'Newsmaker 2009: Rahul Gandhi'. *India Today*, 4 January.

———. 2013a. 'Inflation. Corruption. Ethnic Violence. Rape. An Indian Dillusioned with a Passive Establishment Erupted in Moral Rage in a Year of Multiple Injustices'. *India Today*, 7 January. Available at https://www.indiatoday.in/magazine/cover-story/story/20130107-s.-prasannarajan-on-recent-agitation-at-jantar-mantar-india-gate-over-delhi-gangrape-761241 –1999–11-30

Prasannarajan, S. 2013b. 'India Today–Nielsen Mood of the Nation Poll: How UPA-2 Lost India and Its Leadership Failed to Contain the Slide'. *India Today*, 24 January. Available at https://www.indiatoday.in/india/north/story/ india-today-mood-of-the-nation-survey-2013-152454-2013-01-24

Price, Lance. 2015. *The Modi Effect: Inside Narendra Modi's Campaign to Transform India*. London, UK: Hodder and Stoughton.

PricewaterhouseCoopers. 2010. 'The Gujarat Vision: Making MSMEs Globally Competitive'. Available at https://www.pwc.in/assets/pdfs/publications-2010/ msme_report.pdf

Purie, Aroon. 2019a. 'Ayodhya Time to Move On'. *India Today*, 25 November. Available at https://www.indiatoday.in/magazine/editor-s-note/ story/20191125-from-the-editor-in-chief-1618712-2019-11-15(accessed on 16 January 2020).

———. 2019b. 'Single & Happy'. *India Today*, 21 October. Available at https:// www.indiatoday.in/magazine/editor-s-note/story/20191021-from-the- editor-in-chief-1607812-2019-10-11 (accessed on 16 January 2020).

Quraishi, S. Y. 2019. 'The Election Commission Must Act Tough'. *The Hindu*, Chennai, 7 May.

Radhika Merwin. 2019. 'Sale of Assets of Nirav Modi's US Firms Fetches $10 m, but PNB Can't Rejoice'. *The Hindu Business Line*, New Delhi, 20 April.

Raghotham, S., Geetima Krishna Das, and Venkatesh Nayak. 2019. 'Modi's 5 Years: A Report Card'. *Deccan Herald*, 31 March.

Rajagopal, Arvind. 1999. 'Thinking about the New Indian Middle Class: Gender, Advertising and Politics in an Age of Globalization'. In *Signposts: Gender Issues in Post-Independence India*, edited by Rajeswari Sunder Rajan, 57–100. New Delhi: Kali for Women.

———. 2001. *Politics after Television: Religious Nationalism and the Reshaping of the Indian Public*. Cambridge: Cambridge University Press.

Rajagopal, Krishnadas. 2018. 'Make Lynching a Separate Offence, SC Tells Parliament'. *The Hindu*, New Delhi, 18 July.

———. 2019. 'Free Speech cannot be Choked by Arrest: SC'. *The Hindu*, New Delhi, 12 June.

Rajput, Rashmi. 2019. 'IL&FS Financial Services ex-CEO had Direct Role in Diverting Rs 17.5 k cr'. *The Economic Times*, New Delhi, 15 April.

Ram, N. 1999. 'What Wrong Did This Man Do?' *Frontline* 16 (10). 8–21 May. Available at https://frontline.thehindu.com/static/html/fl1610/16100220. htm (accessed on 5 January 2017).

———. 2017. *Why Scams Are Here to Stay: Understanding Political Corruption in India*. New Delhi: Aleph.

Ramakrishnan, Venkitesh. 2019. 'Right on Top'. *Frontline*, 7 June.

Ramnani, Vandana. 2019. 'Real Estate Sector Should Work towards Improving Credibility, Target New Middle Class: PM'. *Money Control*, 14 February. Available at https://www.moneycontrol.com/news/business/real-estate/

real-estate-sector-should-work-towards-improving-its-image-modi-3535651. html

Rampal, Nikhil. 2019. 'How PM Modi's Speeches Shifted Focus'. *India Today*, 29 April. Available at https://www.indiatoday.in/elections/lok-sabha-2019/ story/narendra-modi-speeches-lok-sabha-elections-1512995-2019-04-29

Rampal, Nitish. 2019. 'Rajnath Singh Says PM Modi Never Promised Rs 15 Lakh-But Did He?' *The Quint*, 11 April. Available at https://www.thequint. com/news/webqoof/rajnath-singh-ani-interview-pm-narendra-modi-never-promised-rs-15-lakh-fact-check

Ranjan, Rakesh, Vijay Kumar Singh, and Sanjeer Alam. 2019. 'Post-Poll Survey: Reposing Trust in the NDA and the Prime Minister in Bihar'. *The Hindu*, Chennai, 26 May. Available at https://www.thehindu.com/elections/lok-sabha-2019/post-poll-survey-reposing-trust-in-the-nda-and-the-prime-minister/article27249049.ece

Ranka, Ayush. 2015. 'The Middle-Class Supported the Emergency When it Was Declared: Interview with Inder Malhotra'. *The Wire*, 25 June. Available at https://thewire.in/culture/the-middle-class-supported-the-emergency-when-it-was-declared

Rao, Jarugumilli Rama Krishna. 2013. 'To Be or Not to Be a Civil Servant'. *The Hindu*, 2 February. Available at https://www.thehindu.com/opinion/open-page/to-be-or-not-to-be-a-civil-servant/article4372972.ece

Rao, Shakuntala. 2018. 'Making of Selfie Nationalism: Narendra Modi, the Paradigm Shift to Social Media Governance, and Crisis of Democracy'. *Journal of Communication Inquiry* 42 (2): 166–183.

Rapoza, Kenneth. 2014. 'In Social Media "NaMo" Becomes India's Obama'. *Forbes*, 12 May. Available at https://www.forbes.com/sites/kenrapoza/2014/05/12/ in-social-media-namo-becomes-indias-obama/

Ravallion, M. 2009. 'The Developing World's Bulging (But Vulnerable) "Middle Class"'. *World Development* 38 (2): 445–454.

Raveendran, G., and K. P. Kannan. 2011. 'India's Common People: The Regional Profile'. *Economic and Political Weekly* 46 (38): 60–73.

Ray, Shantanu Guha. 2014. 'Narendra Modi: Is India's PM Avoiding the Media?' *BBC*, 25 July. Available at https://www.bbc.com/news/ world-asia-india-28457775

Reddy, B. Muralidhar. 2013. 'It's Official. Modi is BJP's Choice'. *The Hindu*, 13 September. Available at https://www.thehindu.com/news/national/its-official-modi-is-bjps-choice/article5124375.ece

Roberts, K., F. G. Cook, S. C. Clark, and E. Semeonoff. 1977. *The Fragmentary Class Structure.* London: Heinemann Educational Publishers.

Rodrigues, Usha M. 2015. 'The Media, the Social Media and the Elections'. In *India Election 2014: First Reflections*, edited by E. Thorsen and C. Sreedharan, 114–124. London, UK: Bournemouth University.

Rodrigues, Usha M., and Michael Niemann. 2017. 'Social Media as a Platform for Incessant Political Communication: A Case Study of Modi's Clean India Campaign'. *International Journal of Communication* 11: 3431–3453.

Rosling, Alan. 2017. *Boom Country: The New Wave of Indian Enterprise*. Gurgaon: New Delhi: Hachette Books.

Roy, Aparna. 2019a. 'Will the Modi Government Be Able to Capitalize on the 'Success' of the Saubhagya Electrification Drive this Election?' *The Times of India*, New Delhi, 27 April.

Roy, Prasanto K. 2019b. 'The Decade of Data'. *India Today*, 23 December. Available at https://www.indiatoday.in/magazine/guest-column/story/20191223-the-decade-of-data-digital-technology-1627570-2019-12-13

Rudolph, L., and S. H. Rudolph. 1987. *In Pursuit of Lakshmi: The Political Economy of the Indian State*. Chicago, IL: University of Chicago Press.

Rukmini, S. 2018. 'Modi Got Most Prime-Time Coverage: Study'. *The Hindu*, 8 May.

———. 2019. 'The BJP's Electoral Arithmetic'. In *The BJP in Power: Indian Democracy and Religious Nationalism*, edited by Milan Vaishnav, 37–50. Washington: Carnegie Endowment for International Peace. Available at https://carnegieendowment.org/files/BJP_In_Power_final.pdf

Saavala, Minna. 2010. *Middle Class Moralities: Everyday Struggle over Belonging and Prestige in India*. New Delhi: Orient BlackSwan.

Sabnavis, Madan. 2019. NDA vs UPA: The Economic Scoreboard. *The Hindu Business Line*, Chennai, 29 April.

Saeed, Saima. 2015. 'Consent or Coercion: 2014 Election in India as a Media Conquest'. In *India Election 2014: First Reflections*, edited by Einar Thorsen and Chindu Sreedharan, 31–52. England: Bournemouth University.

Sainath, P. 2004. 'Mass Media vs Mass Reality'. *The Hindu*, Chennai, 14 May. Available at https://www.thehindu.com/2004/05/14/stories/2004051406111000.htm

Sainsbury, Diane. 1987. 'Class Voting and Left Voting in Scandinavia'. *European Journal of Political Research* 15: 507–526.

Salve, Prachi. 2015. 'India's Middle Class is 24 Million Not 264 Million: Report'. *Scroll.in*, 30 October. Available at https://scroll.in/article/765677/indias-middle-class-is-24-million-not-264-million-report

———. 2015. 'India's Middle Class is 24 Million, Not 264 Million: Report'. *Scroll.in*. 30 October. Available at https://scroll.in/article/765677/indias-middle-class-is-24-million-not-264-million-report

Sam, Cyril, and Paranjoy Guha Thakurta. 2019. *The Real Face of Facebook in India: How Social Media have Become a Propaganda Weapon and Disseminator of Disinformation and Falsehood*. New Delhi: Paranjoy Guha Thakurta.

Sangari, Kumkum. 2001. *Politics of the Possible. Essays on Gender, History, Narratives, Colonial English*. London: Anthem Press.

Santra, Sneha. 2018. 'How Pradhan Mantri Janaushadi Pariyojana is Affecting the Healthcare Industry'. *Franchise India Wellness*, 7 June. Available at https://www.franchiseindia.com/wellness/how-pradhan-mantri-janaushadhi-pariyojana-is-affecting-the-healthcare-industry.11193

Sanyal, Meera H. 2018. *The Big Reverse: How Demonetization Knocked India Out.* New Delhi: HarperCollins Publishers.

Saran, Rohit. 2005. 'Best and Worst States in India: Gujarat is India's Most Economically Free State'. *India Today*, 5 August. Available at https://www.indiatoday.in/magazine/cover-story/story/20050815-gujarat-is-most-economically-free-state-in-india-787229-2005-08-15

Sardesai, Rajdeep. 2014. *The Election that Changed India.* New Delhi: Penguin.

Sardesai, Shreyas, and Pranav Gupta. 2019. 'The Religious Fault Line in the 2014 Election'. In *How India Votes: A State by State Look*, edited by Ashutosh Kumar and Yatindra Singh Sisodia, 58–74. Hyderabad: Orient BlackSwan.

Sarkar, Sumit. 1983. *Modern India: 1885–1947.* Madras: MacMillan India Limited.

Sassen, Saskia. 2013. 'Why the Middle Class is Revolting'. *The Hindu*, 12 January. Available at https://www.thehindu.com/opinion/interview/why-the-middle-class-is-revolting/article4299097.ece

Saunders, Peter. 1980. *Social Classes and Stratification.* London: Routledge.

Sayal, Reetika, and Sandeep Shastri. 2014. 'Leadership in Context: Impact of Leadership in the 2014 Elections'. *Economic and Political Weekly* 49 (39): 77–81.

Schultz, Kai, Jaffrey Gettleman, and Hari Kumar. 2019. 'Indian Professor Who Compared Modi to Hitler is Waiting to be jailed'. *The New York Times*, 20 February. Available at https://www.nytimes.com/2019/02/20/world/asia/india-modi-intellectuals-dissent.html

Seal, Anil. 1968. *The Emergence of Indian Nationalism: Competition and Collaboration in the Later Nineteenth Century.* Cambridge: Cambridge University Press.

Sengupta, Aditi. 2018. 'Brand New Story'. *The Hindu Business Line*, Chennai, 10 November.

Shah, Ghanshyam. 2015. 'As Glitter of Vikas Fades, All BJP has Left to Woo Middle Class Voters is "Gujarati Pride"'. *The Print*, 30 November. Available at https://theprint.in/opinion/bjp-woos-voters-gujarat-pride-vikas-fades/19435/

Shani, Ornit. 2007. *Communalism, Caste, Hindu Nationalism: The Violence in Gujarat.* Cambridge: Cambridge University Press.

Shankar, B. L., and Valerian Rodrigues. 2014. *The Indian Parliament: A Democracy at Work.* New Delhi: Oxford University Press.

Sharma, Aman. 2019a. '"Modi Hai Toh Mumkin Hai", Says PM Stressing on Airstrikes & Development'. *The Economic Times*, 9 March. Available at https://economictimes.indiatimes.com/news/politics-and-nation/modi-hai-toh-mumkin-hai-says-pm-stressing-on-air-strikes-development/articleshow/68329424.cms

Sharma, Ashok. 2015. 'A Shift from Identity Politics in the 2014 India's Election: The BJP Towards Moderation'. In *India Election 2014: First Reflections*, edited by Einar Thorsen and Chindu Sreedharan, 15–30. England: Bournemouth University.

Sharma, L. P. 1988. *The Brown Rulers of India: Historical-cum-Sociological Study of Indian Affairs after Independence*. New Delhi: Konark.

Sharma, Mahesh Dutt. 2016. *Motivating Thoughts of Narendra Modi*. New Delhi: Prabhat Prakashan.

Sharma, Manoj. 2019. '50 Lakh People Lost Jobs Since Demonetization, Says Azim Premji University Report'. *Business Today*, 17 April. Available at https://www.businesstoday.in/sectors/jobs/50-lakh-people-lost-jobs-since-demonetisation-says-azim-premji-university-report/story/337980.html

Sharma, Rajendra. 2019. 'Modi Fires Back at Oppn, Forcefully Defends DeMon'. *The Times of India*, New Delhi, 27 April.

Sharma, Shubhangi. 2018. 'This is What Modi Government has Done for the Middle Class'. 23 December. Available at https://rightlog.in/2018/12/middle-class-modi-government-01/

Sheth, D. L. 1999. 'Secularisation of Caste and Making of New Middle Class'. *Economic and Political Weekly* 34 (34–35): 2502–2510.

———. 2005. 'The Chang of 2004'. *Seminar* 545, January. Available at http://www.india-seminar.com/2005/545/545%20d.l.%20sheth1.htm

Shukla, Rajesh. 2010. *How India Earns, Spends and Saves: Unmasking the Real India*. New Delhi: SAGE Publications.

Sidhartha, and Rajeev Deshpande. 2019. 'No Norms Violated, Cong's Interim Budget Gave Relief on SUVs of Rich, Ours will Help Middle Class'. *The Times of India*, Bengaluru, 3 February.

Singh, Charan, Deepanshu Pattanayak, Divyesh Satishkumar Dixit, Kiran Antony, Mohit Agarwala, Ravi Kant, Vipul Mathur. 2016. Frauds in the Indian Banking Industry. Working Paper No. 505, Indian Institute of Management, Bengaluru. Available at https://www.iimb.ac.in/sites/default/files/2018-07/WP_No._505.pdf

Singh, Rajesh. 2019. Budget 2019: The Moment Belonged to Narendra Modi Government and Middle-Class Taxpayers. *Wion News*, 4 February. Available at https://www.wionews.com/opinions/budget-2019-the-moment-belonged-to-narendra-modi-government-and-middle-class-taxpayers-194946

Singh, Siddharth. 2017. 'Modi's Winning Strategy: Credible and Consistent Positioning is the Key to Successful Marketing in Politics'. *The Times of India*, New Delhi, 20 December.

Singh, Tavleen. 2018. 'Fifth Column: Narendra Modi's Media Problem'. *The Indian Express*, 18 February. Available at https://indianexpress.com/article/opinion/columns/fifth-column-narendra-modis-media-problem-5068137/

Singh, Vijaita. 2018a. 'Chinese Intrusions Declined by 10% This Year, Says Official'. *The Hindu*, Chennai, 18 September.

———. 2018b. 'Lynching: Social Media Sites to be Held Responsible'. *The Hindu*, New Delhi, 30 August.

Sinha, Subir. 2017. 'Fragile Hegemony: Modi, Social Media, and Competitive Electoral Populism in India'. *International Journal of Communication* 11: 4158–4180.

Smith, Charlie. 2014. 'Arundhati Roy Explains How Corporations Run India and Why They Want Narendra Modi as Prime Minister'. *Straight*, 30 March. Available at https://www.straight.com/life/616401/arundhati-roy-explains-how-corporations-run-india-and-why-they-want-narendra-modi-prime-minister

Soundararajan, Thenmozhi. 2018. 'Twitter's Caste Problem'. *The New York Times*, 3 December. Available at https://www.nytimes.com/2018/12/03/opinion/twitter-india-caste-trolls.html

Speier, Hans. 1939. 'The Salaried Employee in Modern Society'. *Social Research* 1 (1): 111–134.

Sridharan, E. 2014. 'Class Voting in the 2014 Lok Sabha Elections: The Growing Size and Importance of the Middle Classes'. *Economic and Political Weekly* 49 (39): 72–76.

———. 2016. 'The Growth and Sectoral Composition of India's Middle Classes: Their Impact on the Politics of Economic Liberalization'. In *Elite and Everyman: The Cultural Politics of the Indian Middle Classes*, edited by Amita Baviskar and Raka Ray. New Delhi: Routledge.

Srivastava, Sanjay. 2007. *Passionate Modernity: Sexuality, Class and Consumption in India*. New Delhi: Routledge.

Staff Reporter. 2018. 'WHO Thumbs Up for Swachh Bharat's Rural Component'. *The Hindu*, Chennai, 4 August.

Stewart, F. 1995. *Adjustment and Poverty: Options and Choices*. London: Routledge.

Subrahmaniam, Vidya. 2015. 'From Emergency to Now: The Wide Arc of a Hack's Ideological Journey'. *The Hindu Centre for Politics and Public Policy*, 25 July. Available at https://www.thehinducentre.com/the-arena/current-issues/article7460647.ece

Subrahmaniam, Vidya. 2019. 'Narendra Modi: The Leader Who is Bigger than His Party'. *The Hindu*, Chennai, 25 May.

Subramanian, Arvind. 2018. *Of Counsel: The Challenges of the Modi–Jaitely Economy*. New Delhi: Penguin.

Sunderland, J. T. 1929. *India in Bondage: Her Right to Freedom and a Place Among the Great Nations*. New York: Lewis Copeland Company.

Suri, K. C., and Suhas Palshikar. 2014. 'India's 2014 Lok Sabha Elections: Critical Shifts in the Long Term, Caution in the Short Term'. *Economic and Political Weekly* 49 (39): 39–49.

Tang, Min. 2011. 'The Political Behavior of the Chinese Middle Class'. *Journal of Chinese Political Science* 16 (4): 373–387.

Tewari, Manish. 2014. 'Corporate India Defeated Congress'. *Deccan Chronicle*, Hyderabad, 14 June.

Thakurta, Paranjoy Guha. 2014. 'Mass Media and the Modi Wave'. *Himal South Asian*, 30 June. Available at https://himalmag.com/media-modi-elections/

Thapar, Karan. 2018. 'Why Modi Walked Out in 2007 and the BJP Now Shuns Me. An Excerpt from Karan Thapar's *Devil's Advocate: The Untold Story*'. *The Wire*, 22 July. Available at https://thewire.in/books/narendra-modi-karan-thapar-interview

Tharoor, Shashi. 2016. *An Era of Darkness: The British Empire in India*. New Delhi: Aleph.

———. 2018a. *Why I Am a Hindu*. New Delhi: Aleph.

———. 2018b. *The Paradoxical Prime Minister: Narendra Modi and His India*. New Delhi: Aleph.

*The Economist*. 2009a. 'Who's in the Middle? It's a Matter of Definition'. Special Report. 14 February. Available at https://www.economist.com/special-report/2009/02/12/whos-in-the-middle (accessed on 15 March 2015).

———. 2009b. 'Burgeoning Bourgeoisie'. Special Report. 14 February. Available at https://www.economist.com/special-report/2009/02/12/burgeoning-bourgeoisie (accessed on 15 March 2015).

———. 2011. 'The New Middle Classes Rise Up'. *The Economist*, 3 September. Available at https://www.economist.com/briefing/2011/09/03/the-new-middle-classes-rise-up (accessed on 16 January 2020).

———. 2018. 'India's Missing Middle Class'. *The Economist*, 11 January. Available at https://www.economist.com/briefing/2018/01/11/indias-missing-middle-class (accessed on 16 January 2020).

*The Hindu*. 1991. 'An Inevitable Collapse'. In Editorial in *The Hindu*, 7 March.

———. 2017. *The Second 100: A Selection of Editorials, 1978–2016, Volume 2*. Chennai: Kasturi & Sons Ltd.

Thorner, Daniel. 1964: *Agricultural Cooperatives in India: A Field Report*. London: Asia Publishing House.

Tiwari, Nimisha. 2018. 'Attracting Curious Tourists to Gujarat: The Statue of Unity is a Must-Visit'. *The Economic Times*, Ahmedabad, 27 December.

Tocqueville, Alexis de. 1835. *Democracy in America*. Translated by Henry Reeve. Pennsylvania State University, US.

Torri, Michelguglielmo. 2015. 'The 'Modi Wave: Behind the Results of the 2014 General Elections in India'. *The International Spectator* 50 (2): 56–74.

TRAI. 2019. *The Indian Telecom Services Performance Indicators, October–December, 2018*. New Delhi: TRAI.

Trivedi, Divya. 2016. 'The Pressure on Journalists to Toe the Government Line is Immense'. *Frontline*, 24 June. Available at https://frontline.thehindu.com/cover-story/managing-media/article8700833.ece

Udupa, Sahana. 2013. 'World Class Aspirations: The New Middle Class of India'. *Economic and Political Weekly* 48 (15): 29–31.

———. 2015. *Making News in Global India: Media, Publics, Politics*. London, UK: Cambridge University Press.

Unger, J. 2006. 'China's Conservative Middle Class'. *Far Eastern Economic Review* 169 (3): 17–31.

United Nations Development Programme (UNDP). 2013. *Human Development Report 2013. The Rise of the South: Human Progress in a Diverse World*. New York: UNDP.

Upadhya, Carol. 2007. 'Employment, Exclusion and "Merit" in the Indian IT Industry'. *Economic and Political Weekly* 42 (20): 1863–1868.

————. 2016. 'Software and the "New" Middle Class in the "New India"'. In *Elite and Everyman. The Cultural Politics of the Indian Middle Classes*, edited by Amita Baviskar and Raka Ray, 167–192. Routledge, New Delhi.

Urry, John. 1973. 'Towards a Structural Theory of the Middle Class'. *Acta Sociologica* 16 (3): 175–187.

Vaishnav, Milan. 2017. *When Crime Pays: Money and Muscle in Indian Politics*. Noida: HarperCollins.

————. 2019. 'Religious Nationalism and India's Future'. In *The BJP in Power: Indian Democracy and Religious Nationalism*, edited by Milan Vaishnav, 5–21. Washington: Carnegie Endowment for International Peace. Available at https://carnegieendowment.org/files/BJP_In_Power_final.pdf (accessed on 15 August 2019).

van de Walle, N. 2012. 'Barrington Moore in the Tropics: Democracy and the African Middle Class'. Paper prepared for presentation at the American Political Science Association Annual Meeting in New Orleans, LA 30 August–2 September.

Van der Veer, Peter. 1987. 'God Must be Liberated! A Hindu Liberation Movement in Ayodhya'. *Modern Asian Studies* 21 (2): 283–301.

Vanaik, Achin. 1992. 'Reflections on Communalism and Nationalism in India'. *New Left Review* 1 (196): 43–63.

————. 1997. *The Furies of Indian Communalism: Religion, Modernity and Secularization*. London: Verso.

————. 2002. 'Consumerism and New Classes in India'. In *Thinking Social Science in India: Essays in Honour of Alice Thorner*, edited by in Sujata Patel, J. Bagchi and K. N. Raj, 227–234. New Delhi: SAGE Publications.

Varma, Gyan. 2014. 'Narendra Modi Predicts a Coming "Decade of Dalits" and Other Weaker Sections'. *Live Mint*, 4 March. Available at https://www.livemint.com/Politics/5VX9f5MZjbiawak49bnMQK/Modi-criticizes-efforts-by-Left-regional-political-parties.html

Varma, Pavan K. 2007. *The Great Indian Middle Class*. Penguin: New Delhi.

Varshney, Ashutosh. 1999a. 'Mass Politics or Elite Politics? India's Economic Reforms in Comparative Perspective.' In *India in the Era of Economic Reforms*, edited by Jeffery D. Sachs, Ashutosh Varshney and Nirupam Bajapai. New Delhi: Oxford University Press.

Varshney, Ashutosh. 1999b. '1980s: Indira Gandhi Assassination Gave Rajiv Gandhi an Unparalleled Victory'. *India Today*, 30 November. Available at https://www.indiatoday.in/magazine/cover-story/story/20070702-congress-highs-and-lows-in-eighties-748413-1999-11-30

————. 2007. 'India's Democratic Challenge'. *Foreign Affairs* 86 (2): 93–106.

Venugopal, Vasudha. 2017. 'PM Modi has Referred Pakistan in Earlier Campaigns Too'. *The Economic Times*, 15 December. Available at https://economictimes.indiatimes.com/news/politics-and-nation/pm-modi-has-referred-to-pakistan-in-earlier-campaigns-too/articleshow/62079547.cms?from=mdr

Verma, Lalmani. 2013. 'Hindutva is Backdrop for Narendra Modi in UP'. *The Indian Express*, 21 December. Available at http://archive.indianexpress.com/news/hindutva-is-backdrop-for-narendra-modi-in-up/1210182/

Verma, Rahul, and Sanjay Kumar. 2019. 'The Implications of the 2014 Elections: Is BJP the New Congress?' In *How India Votes: A State by State Look*, edited by Ashutosh Kumar and Yatindra Singh Sisodia, 37–57. Hyderabad: Orient BlackSwan.

Verma, Rashmi, and Sushmita Sengupta. 2018. 'Swachh Bharat is not Just about Chasing Toilets'. *Down to Earth*, 12 April. Available at https://www.downtoearth.org.in/coverage/governance/ending-open-defecation-rather-than-building-toilets-should-be-the-aim-60150

Vij, Shivam. 2015. 'Sycophant Scribes: The Strange Ease of Modi and the Media: No to Questions Yes to Selfies'. *Quartz India*, 30 November. Available at https://qz.com/india/561306/the-strange-case-of-modi-and-the-media-no-to-questions-yes-to-selfies/

Vij-Aurora, Bhavna. 2019 (3 June). 'How Modi–Shah Arithmetic Proved Opposition Calculus Wrong'. *Outlook* 59 (21).

Visvesvaraya, M. 1936. *Planned Economy for India*. Bangalore: Bangalore Press.

Vyas, Mahesh, 2019. 'Jobs Are Human Capital'. *The Times of India*, New Delhi, 11 April.

———. 2019. '11 Million Jobs Lost in 2018'. *CMIE*, Mumbai.

Wade, John. 1966. *History of the Middle and Working Classes, Reprints of Economic Classes*. New York: Augustus M. Kelleys Publishers.

Watt, Carey A. 2005. *Serving the Nation: Cultures of Service, Association and Citizenship in Colonial India*. New Delhi: Oxford University Press.

Weber, Max. 1947. *Theory of Social and Economic Organization*. Translated by A. M. Henderson and Talcoot Parsons. Glencoe: Free Press.

———. 1958. *The Religion of India: The Sociology of Hinduism and Buddhism*. Glencoe, IL: The Free Press.

———. 1978. *Economy and Society: An Outline of Interpretive Sociology*. Edited by Günther Roth and Claus Wittich. Berkeley, CA: University of California.

Weiner, M. 1989. 'Rajiv Gandhi: A Mid-Term Assessment'. In *The Indian Paradox: Essays in Indian Politics*, edited by Myron Weiner and Ashutosh Varshney, 293–318. New Delhi: SAGE Publications.

Wessel, Margit van. 2004. 'Talking about Consumption: How an Indian Middle Class Dissociates from Middle Class Life'. *Cultural Dynamics* 16 (1): 93–116.

Westergaard, J., and H. Resler. 1975. *Class in Capitalist Society: A Study of Contemporary Britain*. Harmondsworth: Penguin.

Whitehead, Andrew. 2016. 'Modi's World: Beyond Selfies and Tweets'. In *Making Sense of Modi's India*, edited by Hasan Suroor, 168–176. New Delhi: HarperCollins Publishers India.

Wielenga, Bastiaan. 1976. *Marxist Views on India in Historical Perspective*. Madras: The Christian Literature Society.

Wiemann, Juergen. 2015. 'The New Middle Class: Advocates of Good Governance, Inclusive Growth and Sustainable Development?' *European Journal of Development Research* 27: 195–201.

Wietzke, Borge, and Andy Sumner. 2014. 'The Political and Social Implications of the "New Middle Classes" in Developing Countries: A Literature Review and Avenues for Future Research'. *EADI Policy Paper Series*, 13 May. Available at http://www.gc2014.org/wp-content/uploads/2014/01/GC2014_Background-Paper.pdf

Willis, Derek. 2014. 'Narendra Modi, The Social Media Politician'. *The New York Times*, 25 September. Available at https://www.nytimes.com/2014/09/26/upshot/narendra-modi-the-social-media-politician.html

World Bank. 2007. *Global Economic Prospects: Managing the Next Wave of Globalization*. Washington, DC: World Bank.

———. 2017. 'India Development Update: Unlocking Women's Potential'. Working Paper, India Country Management Unit. Available at http://documents.worldbank.org/curated/en/107761495798437741/pdf/115297-WP-P146674-PUBLIC.pdf (accessed on 7 May, 2018).

Wright, E. O. 1978. *Class, Crisis and the State*. London: New Left Books.

———. 1980. 'Class and Occupation'. *Theory and Society* 9 (1): 177–214.

———. 1989. *The Debate on Classes*. New York: Verso.

Yadav, Yogendra. 2000. 'Understanding the Second Democratic Upsurge: Trends of Bahujan Participation in Electoral Politics in the 1990s'. In *Transforming India: Social and Political Dynamics of Democracy*, edited by Francine R. Frankel, 120–145. New Delhi: Oxford University Press.

———. 2016. 'Time to Blow the Whistle'. *The Hindu*, Chennai, 12 December. Available at https://www.thehindu.com/opinion/lead/Time-to-blow-the-whistle/article16793830.ece

Yadav, Yogendra, Sanjay Kumar, and Oliver Heath. 1999. 'The BJP's New Social Block'. *Frontline* 16 (23): 6–19.

Yadu, C. R. 2019. 'Economic Reservation Bill: A Quota for Indian Middle Class?' *The Week*, 22 January.

Zuboff, Shoshana. 1988. *In the Age of the Smart Machine: The Future of Work and Power*. New York: Basic Books.

# About the Author

Nagesh Prabhu is a political analyst and currently Deputy Editor at *The Hindu*, Bengaluru, India. He is the author of the book *Reflective Shadows: Political Economy of World Bank Lending to India* (2017). He holds a PhD in Political Science from the Institute for Social and Economic Change, Bengaluru. Dr Prabhu did his master's in political science from Jawaharlal Nehru University, New Delhi, in 1990 and MPhil from Mangalore University in 1994.

He has been an active journalist for 25 years and writes regularly on issues related to political economy. Before taking up journalism, he taught for a brief period in Mangalore University. His articles have been published in academic journals as well.

# Index

52- 7